FIDEL

FIDEL

A Biography of Fidel Castro

Peter G. Bourne

Dodd, Mead & Company
New York

No part of this book may be reproduced in any form
without permission in writing from the publisher.
Published by Dodd, Mead & Company, Inc.
79 Madison Avenue, New York, N.Y. 10016
Distributed in Canada by
McClelland and Stewart Limited, Toronto
Manufactured in the United States of America
Designed by Erich Hobbing

First Edition

Library of Congress Cataloging-in-Publication Data

Bourne, Peter G., 1939–
Fidel : a biography of Fidel Castro.

Bibliography: p.
Includes index.
1. Castro, Fidel, 1927–   .   2. Heads of state—
Cuba—Biography.   I. Title.
F1788.22.C3B68   1986   972.91′064′0924 [B]   86-9039
ISBN 0-396-08518-0

1 2 3 4 5 6 7 8 9 10

For

Dai Williams of Brynteg
who taught me about the values
that really matter in life

Acknowledgments

I AM deeply indebted to the many individuals who gave their time and their support during the preparation of this book. I want to express particular gratitude to Wayne Smith, former Chief of the United States Interest Section in Havana, and to Sally Shelton, former United States Ambassador and Deputy Assistant Secretary of State for Latin America. I thank Dr. Bernardo Benes for facilitating the many contacts I made in Miami, and Andres Allamand Zavala for his help, especially in Chile. Particular appreciation is extended to the Council on Hemispheric Affairs, and to Laurence Birns. I am grateful for the translation skills and general interest of Jairo Arboleda and Shelley Dobyns. I thank Peggy Streit for her insights and for her moral support. I thank my editor Jerry Gross for guidance and for suggestions.

The facilities made available to me by the Library of Congress, Yale University Library, the Center for Cuban Studies, and the government of Cuba immeasurably facilitated my work.

Several people in the United States and Cuba provided me with invaluable assistance, but for their own reasons wish to remain unnamed. They have my special thanks.

Finally, I thank my wife, Mary E. King, for her help.

Preface

I RECALL vividly in 1953 as a thirteen-year-old boy, reading about a group of young men who had bravely but unsuccessfully attacked a military barracks in Cuba. They suffered severe casualties, and their leader, Fidel Castro, narrowly escaped. Having grown up in Britain during World War II, I understood only too well war between nations, but the idea of an armed band challenging its own military and government seemed to me not only fascinating—and romantic—but almost incomprehensible. What appalling conditions could drive young men to such an apparently suicidal act, and what kind of leader could evoke so much loyalty that his followers would be willing to face such almost insurmountable odds?

I did not forget Fidel Castro, but it wasn't until 1958, when I was in medical school in Atlanta, that I heard of him again. By then he was leading a full-blown guerrilla army in the mountains of Cuba against the tyrannical government of Fulgencio Batista. He was a romantic figure described by the U.S. press as an idealist seeking to correct a litany of evils that afflicted his country. As an active participant in the civil rights movement in Georgia, I felt like many of my generation a sense of commonality with the Cuban revolution's struggle for social justice. In June 1960, after Castro had come to power, I took a brief vacation from the wards of Atlanta's charity hospital, and drove to Key West, Florida, where I boarded a plane for the thirty-minute flight to Havana. I spent three days absorbing the ambience of revolution. There was a vibrant sense of excitement and frustrating disorganization, as jeeps filled with armed *barbudos* roared through the streets of the old city. What struck me most was that the entire country had been stood on its head by a man who was only thirty-three years old. Again I wondered what extraordinary sort of person he must be.

I watched America's brief honeymoon with Fidel Castro turn into bitter hatred, a hatred inflamed by his own intemperate statements. Why did we dislike him so much? There seemed to be something in our national character that evoked in us a far greater hostility toward Castro than we

ix

felt toward the leaders of the Soviet Union, even though Cuba posed no real military threat to us.

Still, Castro's buoyancy was remarkable. Not only did he survive, he was ready to stand up to the United States as though he was the leader of a major power. His turn to socialism and his alliance with the Soviet Union led tens of thousands of Cubans to leave the country, but the majority who remained appeared to adore him, even though the United States embargo, as well as Cuba's gross mismanagement of its economy, would mean years of austerity and deprivation. Cuba was too small to contain the ambitions of Fidel Castro as he gradually emerged in the vanguard of a new and influential force, the Third World Movement. As the years went by he became no less controversial. Indeed, his stature and influence continued to grow, and it became increasingly apparent that history would view him as one of the major figures of the century.

Having advanced in the meantime in my own career to become a psychiatrist with an involvement in politics and international affairs, I had been exposed to a number of major world leaders. I was intrigued by the personal and psychological factors that led some individuals to seek positions of immense power. None, however, fascinated me as much as Fidel Castro, a man of extreme physical daring, astonishing charisma, a larger-than-life personality, a rare talent for survival, and an audacity and self-confidence to project himself on the world scene in a way that no leader of a country of such modest size and population had ever done before. I wanted to know what produced a leader like this, what his life had been like, and what kind of man he was behind the often superficial accounts that appeared in the press.

As a presidential assistant in the Carter White House in the late 1970s, I was suddenly dealing with the government of Cuba in an official capacity. The health-care system Castro had created was the best in the developing world, and there were benefits to be derived on both sides by an exchange of ideas, experiences, and people. In setting up the programs to do this, I had occasion to invite the Cuban minister of health to my office in the West Wing of the White House—the first time since 1958 that a member of the Cuban cabinet had been inside the building.

Subsequently, on a visit to Cuba in 1979, I was received by Castro, and I began to get some answers to the questions I had asked as a thirteen-year-old boy. I found him to be a man of hypnotic charm and encyclopedic knowledge, but also a very complex and unusual individual who was both a product of his own difficult upbringing and a captive of Cuba's unique culture and troubled history.

Later, in the early 1980s, as an assistant secretary-general with the United Nations, I would make other trips to Cuba, and I would look at both the country and its leader through the less partisan eyes of an international civil servant. At the same time, over the years I had become progressively more involved in Caribbean and Central American affairs so that I viewed the region with an increasing degree of professional expertise. Eventually, stimulated by my continuing desire to understand fully this most uncommon man and my awareness that there had been no thorough biography of Fidel Castro in more than fifteen years, I decided to write this book. Most Americans hold strong views about Castro, but those views I found were generally based on scanty knowledge. This book will, I hope, help to satisfy what I sensed as a strong appetite for information about this enigmatic figure, making those opinions better informed whether or not it changes them. Apart from my personal fascination as a longstanding Castro-watcher, I hope to bring to the topic a unique perspective as someone trained as a psychiatrist, with a special experience and understanding of politics and international affairs, especially in the Third World.

I have talked to Fidel Castro's enemies and to his friends. I have also had the general support of the Cuban government, which provided access to its archives, and to the many Cubans inside and outside the regime, all of whom gave me their fullest cooperation. Although I had earlier spent time with Castro, this book was written without his direct involvement, a fact that some might feel, given his overbearing personality and seductive charm, allows for greater objectivity. Perhaps he elected not to subject himself to the probing questions that a psychiatrist would want to ask. Perhaps it was a legitimate problem of Castro trying to fit the time I needed into a heavy schedule. Perhaps he was just trying to be equitable, as he has similarly declined to meet with others writing books on the same subject. My personal judgments of Fidel Castro as a man are therefore dependent upon my earlier meeting with him in which our discussion covered a wide range of topics from health care in the Third World to U.S. domestic politics.

During the last several years I have remained intimately involved with Cuban affairs, making regular visits to the island. In the last year, as I was in the later stages of the preparation of this book, I made two extended trips to Cuba. Much of that time was spent with people who had worked with Castro throughout his career and continued to have regular, often daily, contact with him. As such a newsworthy personality, Castro receives extensive coverage in the international press, and his activities can be closely followed even when he is not in Cuba. Because Castro's role outside Cuba is so significant, I have also spent time in the last year in Grenada and Ethiopia, studying his influence in these Third World countries.

It has been my intent to tell the story of the life of Fidel Castro with as independent a political perspective as I could muster. Living in a democratic society, one cherishes such values as freedom of speech, freedom of the press, open and free elections, and the right to travel in and out of the country at will. When Castro came to power, the bulk of the Cuban population coveted access to education, health care, land reform, and a renewal of national spirit far more than they valued formal democracy. I have tried, therefore, to avoid a reflex condemnation of the society he has created merely because it was predicated on values different from my own. At the same time, Cubans today live under a regime that denies them certain human rights that are increasingly viewed as universally desirable by most of the world's population. Their standard of living falls short of what the revolution originally promised and of that achieved by several other developing countries with different political systems. In addition, I believe one can fairly judge Fidel Castro, his personal conduct, and his revolution by the standards he himself has set. He cannot be excused for perpetrating on the Cuban people those same violations of human freedoms that he decried during the Batista era. Yet at times even that is not easy. As the distinguished Cuban economist Felipe Pazos said, "Your logic and mine are not always applicable to Fidel and the Cuban revolution, which has a logic all its own. It is something like working in a fourth dimension."

There will be those who believe that merely selecting Fidel Castro as the subject of a biography is giving him unwarranted recognition and hence is tantamount to a sympathetic bias on the part of the author. There will also be those who feel that any North American's perspective will inevitably be critical of Castro's Cuba because it is not a mirror image of the United States. Finally there will be those hostile to Castro because, though the leader of a sovereign country, he elected to conduct a foreign policy independent of Washington, engaging in rhetoric that was perceived as inappropriately rash and aggressive for the head of a small, previously pliant client state. An independent view must be one that displeases those at both extremes of the ideological spectrum. If that is the case, then I have probably achieved a reasonable measure of the independent view I have sought.

FIDEL

Introduction

THE events of the last thirty years in Cuba cannot be properly understood without at least a modest appreciation of its tortured history.

Christopher Columbus, the first European to visit Cuba, described it as "the loveliest land ever beheld by human eyes." It was an island paradise with verdant valleys and soaring mountains blanketed by rich forests of mahogany, cedar, pomegranate, and mastic. Flocks of brightly colored birds flew through the trees. Food and water were plentiful, with tropical fruits in abundance, and the surrounding blue sea teemed with fish and turtles. The native population of Tainos and Siboney Indians lived a peaceful, idyllic existence.

The first European settlers who came in the mid-sixteenth century were interested primarily in gold and silver, and did little to disrupt the tranquil life of the island. But Spanish planters, spurred by the immense profits to be made by catering to Europe's growing sweet tooth, soon saw the impressive potential in Cuba for the large-scale cultivation of sugarcane. Virgin forests of the best timber were burned to the ground to make way for the lucrative new crop. The ambitious settlers tried to enslave the native population to work on the plantations, but they met stiff resistance. In some instances the population of entire villages committed mass suicide rather than be taken captive. The Spanish colonists then turned instead to the importation of African slaves, who were more pliable, and who, eventually, would be more numerous in Cuba than in any other country in the hemisphere.

During four hundred years of Spanish rule, Cuba generated immense wealth for its absentee European masters. Yet Spain's desire to extract the maximum profit from the land, while remaining blind to the needs of those, both white and black, who produced the wealth, led to a progressive distortion of the agriculture to benefit the merchants and bankers who lived in Spain, rather than the people who lived in Cuba. What began as a balanced rural economy, including cattle and other livestock, cereals, tobacco, fruit, wood, vegetables, and sugar, which allowed the country

1

to be economically self-sufficient and the people to be well nourished, gradually evolved into an economy dominated by cash crops, especially sugar and tobacco, at the expense of food cultivation. The remarkable gift of nature that made the soil and climate of Cuba so ideally suited to the growing of sugar, became an economic curse for her people.

Sugar—the money it generated, the slave trade it spawned, and the economic involvement in Cuba of other nations it lured—became central to Cuba's domestic woes and her economically entrapped role in the world. Encouraged no longer to plant food crops, but to use every last bit of arable land to grow sugar because it yielded cash, farmers frequently found that they barely earned enough money to buy the food necessary for their families' survival. It is true that there were some years when the international sugar price was high, and they did better, but overall these happy years were few. Besides, the growers could sell only to the government, and only through a small number of merchants in Havana. These brokers kept the prices they paid low, maintaining their own profits at the expense of the farmers, no matter what happened to the international sugar price.

The economic distortion and inequity created by the emergence of a monoculture economy were destined to bring Cuba into conflict with her Spanish overlords. It would be a recurrent and arduous battle, and in the first instance it was over tobacco rather than sugar.

Spain viewed Cuba as a money cow to be milked, imposing heavy excise taxes, and, through monopolies, a rigid quota system on the crops. The monopolies purchased the crops, extending credit to the growers until harvest time. But the price for the commodities rarely yielded enough to pay off the loan, and year by year the indebtedness grew—a familiar story in many underdeveloped areas of the world. In 1717, the tobacco growers *(vegueros)* rebelled, demanding an end to taxation and the right to grow and sell their product on the open market. Concessions were made to settle the revolt, but the promises were not kept and a strike ensued. This was viciously and bloodily suppressed, ending Cuba's first modest gesture of independence.

Native-born Cubans, or Creoles, became the landowners and cultivators with ties primarily to the countryside, while the Spaniards, immigrants, and sojourners remained in the cities as merchants and administrators. Growing local affluence and the influence of European enlightenment combined, by the end of the eighteenth century, to create a new class among the Creoles, a class educated in Europe or in the European tradition and stirred by the contemporary rising tide of intellectual ferment. During this same period, Spain sent to the island several progressive governors who, influenced at least in part by the momentous changes occurring throughout Europe as a result of the French Revolution, encouraged an open intellectual climate in Havana. Cultural societies were formed, newspapers and other publishing ventures were started, schools were built, and the scope of the University of Havana, established in 1728, was widely expanded.

It was out of this Creole enlightenment that the Cuban sense of national identity emerged. No longer content to see their homeland as an economic appendage of Spain, this new generation of educated, cultured, and intellectually sophisticated Cubans felt impelled to seek some form of independent identity for their island. Spurred on by the winds of change that had swept Europe and North America, they agitated for an attenuated relationship with the mother country. Some wanted merely an adjustment in the commercial relationship to create greater economic equity, others wanted complete independence, and still others favored separation from Spain and annexation to the United States. The more fervent disciples of the European egalitarian movement felt that the perpetuation of slavery was incompatible with the ideals of the independent Cuba they foresaw. The major landowners, however, more pragmatic in their outlook, not only believed that slavery was essential to the future of the country, but tended to favor annexation with the United States, another slaveholding nation. They felt that in the long run the United States was more likely than Spain to help them preserve their right to own slaves. There were several inspiring exceptions, plantation owners who in their idealistic zeal impoverished themselves by freeing their slaves and joining the abolitionist struggle.

In 1812, there was a slave revolt aided by sympathetic supporters from among the progressive movement in the country. It was suppressed with extraordinary ruthlessness, and intellectuals and landowners were executed along with the slaves for their complicity.

Spain clung to Cuba, the jewel among her New World possessions, with particular tenacity. Stung by the slow hemorrhage inflicted on her by the independence sentiment growing throughout her South American colonies, ultimately brought to a climax by the insurgent armies of Simón Bolívar, Spain made Cuba the cornerstone for maintaining her hold in the hemisphere. The crossroads for commerce in the Caribbean and much of Central and South America, Cuba was always a vital practical asset as well as an increasingly important symbol of Spanish presence in the region. Because it is an island, and because of its greater proximity to Spain, it was substantially more defensible against insurgency than was the vast continental empire.

Spain desperately opposed independence in any form, and reflexively crushed any spark of dissent lest it flare into a full-blown movement for self-determination. But as the spirit of independence swept across the

3

Americas, it unleashed forces that created a momentum of historic inevitability that could not be indefinitely denied. In 1868, a Cuban lawyer and plantation owner from a good family, Carlos Manuel de Céspedes, led an uprising that was to be the start of the war for independence. Joined by other plantation owners from Oriente and Camagüey provinces, he organized a rebel army that soon seized the town of Bayamo. There followed ten years of intermittent civil war, with great acts of heroism and bravery by individuals, many of whom gave their lives for this cause in which they passionately believed. In the Hispanic tradition, the memory of their acts became romantically enshrined in the minds of later generations of Cubans. Although ultimately this independence movement was quelled and the leaders were forced to accept a truce, that in no way diminished the reputation of these figures in Cuban history. Indeed, it may even have enhanced their stature.

The truce was signed in 1878, and an uneasy peace existed for a year. In 1879, fighting again broke out in what was to be called "The Little War." Led by the revered General Calixto García, this new rebellion lasted a year until it, too, was snuffed out.

Following this second war, as Spain continued to cling doggedly to Cuba, tenacious exiles started arriving in the United States to organize further support for the independence struggle. To the consternation of the government in Washington, these Cubans were not intent on annexation with the United States; they were deeply nationalistic patriots whose aim was to create an independent Cuba. The Cuban independence movement, unlike that of the United States, was not led by the landowning elite. It included intellectuals, small farmers, and former slaves who blended their concern for freedom from Spain with a degree of social idealism aimed at creating greater social and economic equity within Cuba.

Foremost among those exiles was José Martí. Born in Cuba in 1853 of Spanish parents, Martí was a man of prodigious talents who combined erudition as a scholar, poet, and lawyer with practical skills as a political organizer and orator. He was an admirer of the freedom and idealism he found in the United States, but also saw a more sinister "dark side" to the nation that was both aggressive and oppressive, seeking to restrict social justice domestically and to promote expansionism into the internal affairs of other nations in the hemisphere. He warned that this other face posed the ultimate threat to the survival of Cuban freedom.

Martí, whose life-long quest for Cuban sovereignty would win him lasting reverence as the nation's greatest patriot, returned to his homeland in 1895 to organize and launch a new war of independence, one that would ultimately prove successful. But three months after the first shot was fired, he was tragically killed in combat, a martyr to his cause. The war, launched in easternmost Oriente Province, lasted three years and swept the length of the island with some of the bitterest and hardest fighting in military history. The army of independence was led by a veteran of the ten-years war, a black, General Antonio Maceo. He was on the verge of capturing Havana when he was killed eighteen miles from the city. The rebel drive stalled as the Spanish threw two hundred thousand troops into the conflict.

In a last-ditch effort to hold their prized colony, Spain sent as governor, General Valeriano Wyler, a hardened veteran of Spain's African wars. Wyler instituted a program of "Reconcentration" in which Cuba's entire rural population was evacuated to the cities and towns to prevent the rebel army from receiving any support from the land, thereby hoping to break the will of the people to continue the struggle. The already malnourished and impoverished population, now cut off from sources of food or income, starved to death on city streets throughout Cuba. In a matter of months, over a million persons perished. Press accounts shocked the world, and governments, including that of the United States, protested to Spain. But the complaints were ignored.

Despite the starvation inflicted on them, the Cuban people refused to give in with the cherished hope of independence so nearly in their grasp. As a gesture of desperation, Spain finally offered autonomy rather than independence, which the rebel leaders rejected. The rebels also declined, with the hard-won victory imminent, an offer by the United States to intervene on their side. Arms they would welcome, but not American troops.

As a prize to be seized from the declining Spanish empire, Cuba had long been coveted by Washington. U.S. presidents, beginning with Thomas Jefferson, eagerly anticipated annexation. John Quincy Adams described Cuba as "an apple that had to fall by gravity into the hands of the United States." Under President Polk, the United States entered a period of expansionism during which Texas, New Mexico, California, and the northern part of Arizona were annexed to the Union. Cuban independence groups based in the U.S. were suppressed, and Polk sent a purchase offer of $100 million to Madrid. It was not accepted. Subsequently, in 1853, President Franklin Pierce increased the offer to $130 million. That offer, too, was rejected.

From the time of Jefferson, much of Cuba's lure had been its large slave population, an attraction that grew significantly after the slave trade from Africa was terminated. However, as the schism between North and South widened in the late 1850s, the North rejected annexation as being increasingly incompatible with the abolitionist sentiment. The Confederacy, on the other hand, continued to view the acquisition of Cuba as an even more important potential economic asset in anticipation that the

South would break away and become an independent nation. A significant segment of the landed and slaveholding oligarchy in Cuba continued to favor such a move.

After the Civil War, the United States enjoyed a period of unprecedented economic growth. In Cuba, the wars of 1868–78 and 1879 had left the country in ruin. Affluent investors from the United States took advantage of the situation in the last quarter of the century to buy up, at bargain prices, substantial portions of the Cuban economy. This process would continue in the early part of the twentieth century, so that by 1920 two-thirds of all of the arable land in Cuba would be in the hands of U.S. companies. Carnegie Steel Company, Pennsylvania Steel Company, and Bethlehem Iron Works bought control of Cuba's iron, chromium, and manganese mines. Later, U.S. companies would acquire a monopoly on the petroleum supply and public utilities. Most damaging to the young nation's economy, the United States placed high tariffs on any goods refined or manufactured in Cuba, ensuring that she remained solely a supplier of raw materials and could not develop industries that might compete with those in the United States.

Meanwhile, the United States was entering another phase of irresistible expansionism. As Samoa and Hawaii were seized, the press, increasingly under the influence of financial interests of unprecedented scope and size, again voiced the attractiveness of annexing Cuba. The only reservation expressed was the prospect of the United States burdening itself with "inferior races." Ignoring the inconsistency, one newspaper went on to commit the ultimate insult of suggesting that Cubans were effeminate because of the degree of culture, education, and other intellectual pursuits that existed in Havana. Another publication suggested, "The only hope we might have to qualify Cuba for the dignity of statehood would be to Americanize her completely, covering it with people of our own race."

Imbued by the public fervor for additional conquests, and none too concerned about the separation of church and state, President McKinley, in a message to Congress on December 6, 1897, declared, "God himself has favored me with a Divine Revelation to take over the Philippines." Although at the same time lending verbal support to the Cuban and Philippine rebels about to win their wars for independence, it was clear that he viewed the United States as the natural inheritor of any possessions from which Spain could be ousted.

Concerned by the imminence of a victory by the Cuban rebel army and by the rejection of his offer to send U.S. forces, McKinley dispatched a naval task force, including the battleship *Maine,* to Cuban waters despite contrary advice from the U.S. consul in Havana, Fitzhugh Lee. On the night of February 15, 1898, the U.S.S. *Maine* was blown up in Havana harbor, with the loss of 261 lives. Who was responsible remains unknown, but it provided the pretext the U.S. needed to enter the war.

Although Spain sent a message to McKinley on April 10 offering to end all hostilities, the following day he urgently delivered a war message to Congress in which he justified military intervention and emphasized that he did not deem it appropriate "to recognize at present the independence of the so-called Cuban Republic." The Joint Resolution had broad bipartisan support, but it was carefully worded to avoid any mention of or sanction for the Cuban army of independence that, unaided for three years, was now about to defeat Spain and take legitimate control of its own country. An amendment to the resolution was offered by enlightened Senator Henry M. Teller of Colorado, committing the United States to respect the right of Cuban self-determination. The Teller Amendment narrowly passed, but it infuriated segments of the press and the public at large. Former President Grover Cleveland condemned it as an outrage, describing the Cubans as "the most inhuman and barbarous cut throats in the world."

A document from the office of the assistant secretary of war to General Nelson A. Miles, Army chief of staff, containing the instructions for the conduct of the United States' intervention in Cuba, reveals the lurid intent of the administration in Cuba:

> The inhabitants are indolent and apathetic. . . . Immediate annexation to our federation of such elements would be folly. . . . We must clean the country, even though it be by applying the same means that were applied by the Divine Providence to Sodom and Gomorrah.
>
> We must destroy everything in range of our guns, we must concentrate our blockade so that hunger and disease, its constant companion, may sap the civilians and cut down their army.

And these were the allies the United States was supposedly entering the war to assist. The document goes on to suggest that the rebel army should always be forced into the most hazardous assignments, thereby simultaneously depleting the military strength of both the Spanish and the independence forces, while the United States minimized its casualties and maintained its ability to seize control.

The United States embarked on a blockade of the island and the systematic shelling of its coastal cities. The independence army, with little choice and still viewing Spain as the greater evil, joined forces with the United States troops. On August 12, 1898, after a disastrous naval defeat in the Philippines and the collapse of their garrison in Santiago de Cuba, the Spanish sued for peace. The United States immediately turned against its erstwhile ally, refusing the right of the rebel forces under General

7

Calixto García to enter Santiago de Cuba, and denying them any role in the surrender proceedings. Within a matter of weeks, the United States had seized complete military control of the country, and had forced the rebel army to disband. In a similar manner, in the Philippines the United States betrayed and crushed the independence movement it had earlier encouraged, making the Philippines instead a colony of the United States.

Under the subsequent Treaty of Paris, signed on December 10, 1898, Puerto Rico, Guam, and the Philippines were ceded to the United States. Thanks to the eloquent arguments of Calixto García and other Cuban leaders, their nation was promised its long-sought independence. However, the United States, unhappy with the agreement, continued to hold the country under military rule for four more years. And when war reparations were paid by Spain they went not to the Cubans, who had suffered so much and whose country had been destroyed, but to the United States.

Calixto García was a man of elegance and intellect who astonished official Washington by the surprising contrast he provided to the stereotype most Americans had come to hold of Cubans. He pleaded in Washington for the removal of U.S. forces and the right of his nation to the freedom it had been promised. The United States agreed to withdraw, but only on the condition that the Cuban leaders accept a constitution for their country prepared largely in the United States and including the so-called Platt Amendment, perhaps the single greatest cause of Cubans' hatred of the government of the United States. Under the Platt Amendment, Cuba agreed not to make any treaties or alliances with any foreign nation, or grant to any foreign country except the United States military bases or control over any part of the island. It also gave the United States the right to intervene militarily in the internal affairs of Cuba anytime it was dissatisfied with the manner in which the country was being governed. It further restricted the right of the Cuban government to obtain international loans essential for its independent economic development. In a clause that seemed aimed at demeaning Cuban self-respect, the government was required to take certain public health measures so that Cuba would not pose a health threat to the southern part of the United States. The Platt Amendment also required that the Cuban government allow the United States to establish naval bases on the island.

For Cuba's leaders, the proposition was simple: accept the Platt Amendment or forfeit the dream of an independent, sovereign Cuba.

A letter to President Theodore Roosevelt from General Leonard Wood, military governor of Cuba, left little doubt about the intent of this aspect of the new constitution.

There is little or no real independence left to Cuba under the Platt Amendment. . . . She is absolutely in our hands, and I believe no European government for a moment believes that she is otherwise than a practical dependency of the United States.

With the control we have over Cuba, a control that will soon undoubtedly become a possession, we shall soon practically control the world sugar market. . . . I believe Cuba to be a most desirable acquisition for the United States.

U.S. troops withdrew in 1902, elections were held, and Tomás Estrada Palma, the first president of "independent Cuba," was sworn in on May 20. But under the provisions of the Platt Amendment, U.S. troops returned for three years in 1906, following a disputed election. In 1912, U.S. marines landed to quell a revolt by former slaves in Pinar del Río, and they came back again in 1917 to ensure the uninterrupted flow of sugar during the final years of World War I. The threat of U.S. intervention cast a permanent shadow over Cuban politics. There could be no organized opposition to the provisions of the Platt Amendment because that itself could justify further intervention.

A venal symbiosis emerged in which no Cuban could be elected president of his own country without the backing of the United States. Weak, malleable individuals were chosen, men who would help the U.S. companies manipulate the international sugar market, condone the exploitation of Cuban workers and the violation of tariffs and regulations, and permit wholesale corruption. In return, U.S. business interests assured that during their term in office most Cuban presidents became wealthy men. There was never a truly free election, and the Cuban people came to view elections as a hypocritical pretense of democracy. There was no civil service, so every government job depended on political patronage. Public respect for government institutions suffered accordingly.

Cuba as a nation did become relatively wealthy. Despite appalling inequities in the distribution of wealth, by the 1920s Cuba was among the wealthiest of all nations we now label "developing." Also, because of its proximity to the United States, its more affluent citizens enjoyed access to a wide range of consumer goods and the latest in technology. For members of the small professional and upper class who could afford regular trips to the United States, their identification was often as much with America as with Cuba.

In 1925, Gerardo Machado was elected president of Cuba, ushering in one of the most savage administrations in Cuban history. Already a partner in several of the more lucrative U.S. business monopolies, he set new records in plundering the public coffers and laying open the ordinary Cuban for exploitation in order to benefit himself, his cronies, and his business associates. He was also a man of significant brutality who imprisoned opposition critics at the slightest provocation. He built on the

9

Isle of Pines south of Cuba a vast prison complex, where political prisoners were treated with great cruelty, many of them killed by sadistic guards for whom there was rarely any accountability.

To the further detriment of the United States' image in the eyes of the average Cuban, Machado maintained close ties with Washington, as well as with U.S. interests in Cuba, especially the banking industry. In 1929, he made a triumphant visit to Washington, where his dictatorship was warmly embraced by the Hoover administration. In 1933, at the depths of the Depression, Machado was finally overthrown by a coalition of students, young intellectuals, and striking workers organized by the Communist Party, an organization his oppression had done much to help build. His overthrow was hastened by the election of Franklin Delano Roosevelt, who withdrew his administration's support from the Machado regime, demonstrating what had always been true—no one could be president in Cuba without Washington's backing. It ushered in Roosevelt's "good neighbor" policy in Latin America, which two years later would lead to the rescinding of the hated Platt Amendment. Roosevelt was widely admired in Cuba, and during his terms in the White House, U.S.-Cuban relations were better than at any other time.

For several weeks after the overthrow of the Machado dictatorship, a power vacuum existed during which violent and bloody retribution was exacted against members of the Machado regime. The body of his hated chief of police was hung from a post in front of the University of Havana.

On September 4, 1933, a second coup occurred, this one led by an army sergeant who worked as a court stenographer, Fulgencio Batista. Batista would dominate the political scene in Cuba for the next twenty-five years. Following the coup of 1933, he remained the power behind several weak presidents, and then in 1940 assumed the presidency to head a wartime government of national unity. Although he could not succeed himself, and left office in 1944, the attraction of power remained irresistible, and after a brief sojourn in the United States he returned to Cuba to rebuild his power base in the military. On March 10, 1952, he seized power in a coup, ushering in a regime that eventually would be even more corrupt and brutal than that of Machado.

Rarely have the people of any nation been so thoroughly and chronically abused as the people of Cuba. Economically exploited by generations of Spanish overlords, and repeatedly frustrated and crushed with singular brutality in their aspirations for independence, Cubans nevertheless acquired an all-consuming yearning for nationhood. The most valiant exponents of those aspirations, like Martí, were accorded a mystical reverence approaching sainthood. When independence finally came after years of struggle and the sacrifice of hundreds of thousands of lives, it proved to be a sham. Cubans found that instead of true sovereignty they had merely exchanged one master for another. The relative benevolence of the new relationship, and the complexity of the economic dependence the United States imposed on Cuba, proved a more elusive target against which to focus Cuban nationalism than the Spanish. The material benefits many Cubans derived from the U.S. drew them into what amounted to a love/hate relationship with their giant neighbor. Cuban patriotism was further frustrated by collusion between a series of supposedly nationalistic Cuban leaders and the monied interests of the United States, which led to corrupt government with a commitment to preserving the privilege of a small oligarchy closely tied to the United States at the expense of the mass of the Cuban people. The wage of 5 cents per day remained commonplace for agricultural workers until World War II. Even as early as 1898, Senator Redfield Proctor, after a visit to Cuba, said of the Cuban people, "they are struggling for freedom and deliverance from the worst misgovernment of which I have ever had knowledge." For the bulk of the people, it was little different under "independence."

The mutilation of the Cuban national psyche over generations was substantial. Frustration of their nationalistic strivings generated deep anger that became incorporated into the culture. With few legitimate outlets, there was a tendency to turn the anger on themselves so that they depreciated their own value. Atrocities by Cubans on Cubans enhanced their feelings of worthlessness. Increasingly, Cubans looked at themselves as second-class citizens, perhaps unworthy of the independence they sought. A distinct sense of inferiority, especially with regard to the United States, gripped their minds. The lack of self-respect was compounded by the fact that a significant percentage of the population came from slavery, bringing with them similar psychological scars.

In addition, there was a cultural clash with the United States. Cuba remained an extension of Spanish and European cultures, sharing the history and values of the Old World. Cubans were educated as though they lived in Europe, so they were, for instance, far more familiar with the details of the French Revolution than the American War for Independence. The style and values of those who came from the United States were predicated on completely different cultural and historical underpinnings, quite alien to the Cuban culture. Americans had little time for Cuba's European heritage with its more elegant and leisurely pace, treating it with condescension. Cubans reacted defensively, both angry and doubtful whether their Spanish heritage did not in fact leave them at some disadvantage in the New World.

Buffeted by their history and their cultural disparity with the United States, Cubans viewed themselves with uncertain appreciation. With low

11

national self-esteem, and a series of national leaders who not only were weak but looked even weaker because they were surrogates for a foreign power, Cubans developed an overwhelming appetite to identify with a figure who was truly strong and nationalistic. They wanted someone who would restore their national pride, but in his absence they reverted to making greater and greater heroes of the independence leaders of the past. The first U.S. military governor of Cuba, Leonard Wood, observed, "Generations of misrule and duplicity have produced a type of man whose loyalty is always at the disposal of the man on top, whoever or whatever he may be." Himself an architect of this misrule and the denial to Cuba of her sovereign rights, Wood could hardly be expected to understand the sense of deep nationalism that led to the phenomenon he observed. Yet there is an underlying truth in what he said. Men such as Machado and Batista had immense popular appeal in the early years of their regimes because they captured the nationalistic feelings of the country and showed themselves to be strong leaders. But they both fell victim to the very evils they had opposed.

Cuba, at the midpoint of the twentieth century, waited expectantly for a man who could produce a sense of national pride, a man who would stand up to the United States and not be corrupted by money and the flattery of powerful interests. They sought a leader who could finally give them back their self-respect by creating a truly independent nation, who was ready to rid the country of the infestation of corruption at all levels of the government, and who could eliminate the plague of political violence that had been inflicted on Cubans for generations. If such a man appeared, most Cubans were ready to accept him as a messiah.

Chapter One

A PURPLE mist hangs in the early-morning air of Oriente Province, steaming off the humid land and clinging languidly to the soft tree-lined indentations in the landscape. Rugged mountains tower over the terrain, with dense tropical vegetation creeping up their sides. Cocks crow, and work-worn black women emerge from tumbledown shacks with untidy palm-thatched roofs to grind corn in the dawn light. Fishermen put out in flimsy vessels from the tiny bays along the tortuous coastline. To the casual observer, the scene suggests Africa as strongly as it does the Americas.

The harsh beauty of the land conceals poverty, hardship, and suffering that have changed little in the nearly three hundred years since Africans were first brought here as slaves to serve Spanish masters. Nearly half of the population of Oriente is neither black nor mulatto, yet the deprivations now touch all races without distinction as, over the years, the land, so reluctant to yield a profitable living, has made impoverished brothers of black and white alike. Vast tracts of property are owned by a privileged few. The many are landless peasants who scratch to survive. They are illiterate, plagued by disease, and without hope for themselves or their children. They have only makeshift housing with no clean water and poor sanitation. There is no health care, and unemployment ranges from 25 to 50 percent, depending on the season. Malnutrition is commonplace, and starvation a constant fear.

From all the benefit it received, Oriente Province, at the far eastern end of the island, might just as well be a million miles from Havana and its cosmopolitan lifestyle, a playground for wealthy Cubans and North Americans alike. The pleasures, rewards, and lifestyles of a modern society that the capital gained from being only a little over a hundred miles from Miami never spanned the five hundred miles and several centuries to reach the rural poor of Oriente. Cuban politicians, too, seemed to see little to be gained by expending national resources to improve the life of the average peasant. In part this was because they saw the peasants as politically inconsequential, and because few even bothered to visit the more impoverished rural areas. The real source of political power in Cuba was not the mandate of the Cuban people, but the sanction of the government of the United States.

This was Oriente Province up to the first half of the twentieth century. Yet from this improbable environment emerged one of the most consequential leaders of our time. Fidel Castro would become a household name around the globe, and the mention of him would stir violent controversy among even the most rational observers. Castro, perhaps as much as any major political figure of this century, could simultaneously raise to fever pitch feelings of love, hatred, loyalty, reverence, and contempt.

Fidel Alejandro Castro Ruz is one of those rare individuals history occasionally contrives who rise beyond any reasonable expectation of what their background might suggest, and stand so far above their contemporaries to defy any simple explanation of their success. They are the products of an exquisite combination of inherited and acquired physical and mental traits, cultural environments, and life experiences that mold the mind and teach the lessons to see and take advantage of events in ways that other men miss. Their homes and families generate ambition, overwhelming self-confidence, deep resilience to adversity, and audacious vision. Finally, historic happenstance thrusts that one special individual up to become a towering figure of his times. Perhaps most important of all, they are the products of luck. Fidel enjoyed the special combination of all of these factors, but that alone does not fully explain the nature of his success.

The formula for greatness involves not only the qualities of the individual, but also the circumstances of the times. Cuba was ready for Fidel Castro.

The need to believe that one's life is having at least a modest impact on the world lurks in the heart of most individuals, no matter how objectively inconsequential their existence. For a few, the urge to leave fingerprints on the pages of history becomes a consuming passion. For Fidel, it took on the quality of an awesome obsession. No other element in his character is as central to understanding his unique and unprecedented role as a world leader.

Fidel was born at 2:00 A.M. on August 13, 1927, on his father's farm, "Las Manacas," near the village of Birán not far from the town of Mayarí in Oriente Province. He weighed twelve pounds at birth. His father, Angel Castro Argiz, born near the city of Lugo in the Celtic Galicia region of northwest Spain, had come to Cuba at the end of the 1890s as a cavalry quartermaster in the Spanish army. Many of those named Castro from this region of Spain are of Jewish descent, although if this was true of Angel, the fact has been lost in the mists of history.

Angel Castro was a physically strong and determined man, used to hard work, and undeterred by the primitive conditions that existed in this wild and rugged part of Cuba at the turn of the century. Both his cultural background and his personality formed his belief that physical work, strength of character, and the tolerance of hardship were important reflections of manliness and the route to success. At the end of the war of independence, the Spanish authorities would not let him remain in Cuba, and he was deported to Spain. But he was determined to return to what he regarded as a land of opportunity, and in 1905 he came back as an immigrant. It was a time of severe economic depression. Without specific skills, but with an unlimited capacity for hard work, he was willing to take any job he could find. He worked initially in the nickel mines near Santiago de Cuba.

"My father was illiterate. He had never gone to school," says Fidel's brother Ramón. "In spite of being illiterate, he had a natural intelligence and learned to read and write without going to school."

He moved to the town of Guaro, where there were a number of other Spanish immigrants, Galicians, Astorians, and people from the Canary Islands. Railroads were being built at that time to service the growing sugar industry in the region, and Angel obtained contracts to prepare the railbed. He hired and organized his own gangs of workers for this purpose, and was able gradually to start putting money aside, with which he began buying land. During the same period, he bought teams of oxen and contracted to transport loads of sugarcane. With his growing profits, he opened a small restaurant and, with a Spanish friend who was an accountant, had a share in a clothing store.

Large-scale sugar cultivation was being developed in the province by American interests, and while beginning his own farming operation, Angel was also able to secure various jobs, including a contract for loading sugar into railroad cars, from the largest of the foreign corporations, the United Fruit Company. According to a vice president of the company, he was at one time charged with systematic theft from the corporation, although the charges were later dropped. This allegation is strongly denied by members of the family.

He established a mixed farm, although cultivating primarily sugarcane, by far the most profitable commodity, and raising cattle. A product of Spanish peasant society and its values, he continued to be driven by a burning desire to acquire ever more land, in his eyes the greatest measure of a man's success and something that would have been almost impossible for a man of his background to achieve in his homeland. He was always

15

willing to labor harder and longer than his neighbors, clearing large areas of virgin forest to create arable, productive land, including the lands of absentee landlords for whom he worked as a tenant sharing the profits. He made additional money selling the timber he felled. In 1920, he also made a significant profit by selling to the United Fruit Company, which surrounded much of his land, a strategic piece of property he owned.

By the 1950s, he was worth an estimated half-million dollars. There have been various reports of how much land he owned, but the most reliable estimate is that he actually owned almost two thousand acres, and rented an additional twenty-five thousand. This rented land was the property of two war veterans who lived in Havana.

Angel Castro was a mountain of a man, at times crude and belligerent. Even with his increasing wealth, he had little interest in comfort or luxury. He was not particularly religious, but he was a product of a deeply Catholic rural environment. Religion was an ingrained part of his culture. To the extent that he concerned himself with political philosophy, he was conservative in the traditional sense, being more concerned with how to accept and make the most of the status quo than with the possibility for revolutionary change. He retained great loyalty to Spain and a life-long resentment toward the United States, which he felt had stolen Cuba from the Spanish forces.

Although he ended his life a wealthy man, Fidel's father saw himself in terms of his peasant background. He felt, and conveyed to his children, a far closer identification with the struggling peasants of Oriente Province, whose hard lives were similar to those his own family had endured in Galicia, than with the wealthy landowners of Cuba with whom he has often been erroneously categorized. This was true even though by today's standards some might feel he was at times guilty of treating local peasants harshly. Such treatment was an inherent product of a system in which absentee landlords abused and cheated the tenants who farmed their land, and they in turn exploited the workers they hired to help with the manual work. "My father was a very human man," says Ramón. "No one [of their workers] went to bed there without eating. . . . On the United Fruit Company lands, workers died of hunger. But there were injustices."

Angel married twice. His first marriage was to a local woman, Maria Louisa Argote, who bore him two children, Lidia and Pedro Emilio. She had other children who died in infancy. During World War I, when there was a boom in international sugar prices, many people moved from the poorer parts of Cuba to Oriente in search of work. One of these, who came from the tobacco-growing area of Pinar del Río, was a young girl, Lina Ruz González, whose father, Francisco, owned oxen and, like Angel, worked as a contractor hauling sugarcane, timber, and anything else people would pay him to move. Angel and Francisco became friends, and Lina was hired as a maid in the Castro household. A forceful young woman in her own right, she caught Angel's eye and became pregnant by him. As a result, Maria Louisa left him, and they were subsequently divorced. She died in 1984. Over the next several years, Lina bore Angel three children, Angela, Ramón, and Fidel. Although born out of wedlock, Ramón says, "Remember, we were the children of love." Later, after they were married, Lina had four more children, Juana, Raúl, Emma, and Augustina.

In a deeply moralistic Catholic environment where the integrity of the family was sacrosanct, it was a harsh burden on Fidel as a child to be illegitimate and to come from a broken family. His father, financially successful, a powerful figure in the community, and immensely strong emotionally, could afford to shrug off any public opprobrium. But for a little boy seeking the acceptance and approval of his peers, especially in a Catholic school, it was a different matter. It is not surprising that from the earliest years Fidel was in constant fights with other children and viewed the world as an inherently hostile environment. Unable to change the facts or the stigma society imposed, he had only his fists with which to defend himself. Angel was a difficult man to get along with in his own right, but Fidel's deep conflict with his father must be attributed in significant part to his resentment toward Angel for inflicting him with what at times must have seemed like an insurmountable barrier to any sort of social acceptance or success in life.

Angel's word was law, and occasionally his style was tyrannical. Yet he did not crush the individuality and initiative of his children when they challenged him. If they were assertive enough and willing to withstand their father's wrath, they often got their way. Fidel's conflicts with his father were frequent and severe. But he identified with his father's strong personality and over the years would become increasingly like him. At age thirteen, Fidel reportedly organized a strike of the sugar workers on their plantation. Fidel was not unique in his battles with his father. All of Angel's sons had similar conflicts to varying degrees.

As with most sons, Fidel's judgment of his father has mellowed over the years, and today he plays down the degree of conflict, but there is little doubt that his relationship with Angel played an important part in shaping his relationship with authority figures throughout his career. As late as 1965, he told an interviewer that his father was a wealthy landowner who exploited the peasants, had paid no taxes on his land or income, and played politics for money. From Angel, Fidel inherited his physical stature, one attribute that he himself has acknowledged as an important reason for his success as a leader. He also inherited a prodigious capacity for hard work and an ability to pursue goals, which he set with unerring determination. No one could have had more machismo than Angel, a value Fidel embraced and which always enhanced his appeal in the Cuban culture. Like his father, Fidel also grew up strong-willed, decisive, and sure of his convictions. Angel tolerated little dissent from those around him, and Fidel easily adopted the same style. Fidel's sister Juanita, in a 1964 interview with *Life* magazine, described Fidel as spoiled and always demanding his own way. Although others later tried to make something different of him, Fidel accepted both his father's and his mother's peasant backgrounds and essentially identified with that heritage. Angel also had considerable contempt for the conventions of society, and Fidel shares this irreverence.

As a child, Fidel often had doubts about how much his parents loved him, particularly when at an early age he was sent away from home. Yet, according to the writer Luis Conte Agüero, Angel once told him, "You know, Fidel was always my favorite."

There was discipline in the home in the sense that Angel ruled with an iron hand, but he was not a particularly organized man, and thus was unable to teach the children neatness, self-discipline, or the ability to plan their activities in a structured way. Fidel would later become fascinated with discipline for himself and others. It was a vital ingredient in all of his activities, but it was something he learned later in school. Its attraction seems to be in part based on the importance he attached to it in helping him organize his own unchanneled energies.

Angel was not overtly demonstrative with his children, and although wealthy, he was relatively tightfisted. Periodically, Fidel obtained money from him, but it was usually after repeated pleas. As a student he engineered several schemes to get money from his father. In later years, however, it was mostly his mother who sent him cash, usually without his father's knowledge.

Although there were few churches in rural Cuba, Fidel's mother Lina was a highly religious woman. She had little education, but great determination and strength. Like the mothers of so many successful men, she combined warmth and affection with high expectations and determination that her children should succeed. Denied the benefits of education herself, it was she who constantly stressed the importance of learning, and inculcated, especially in Fidel, her tenacious belief that there was no level of success too lofty for her children to achieve. The innate ability of this determined woman was demonstrated in later years by her skillful management of the family estates after Angel's death. Ramón describes her as "afraid of nothing, she could kill a cow, she had veterinary knowledge and vaccinated the swine . . . she was the best horse rider. She was the main sponsor for her children's education. She had a different conception [from Angel] with respect to studies. He had little faith in schools because he had learned by himself, but my mother always worried about the education of her children. She wanted her children to have success, and that was her constant endeavor." Fidel's later preoccupation with providing education for Cuba's peasants derived in part from memories of what the denial of education had meant to a talented woman like his mother.

In most respects, it seems that Fidel's childhood was happy and carefree. The family lived in a large, rambling farmhouse, a two-story frame building on piles. It was partly Spanish in style, and the cattle were brought in underneath to a dairy barn. As with most children growing up on a farm, he spent much of his time outdoors, hunting and fishing, surrounded by dogs and other animals. As a little boy, Fidel was taken by his father on the tractor to the forests to haul lumber. And as he grew older he rode horses and swam with his friends in the Birán River. He is remembered as wild, athletic, and unruly. By all accounts he was a hyperactive child, indicating that he already possessed the prodigious energy level he would exhibit as an adult. He also grew up with an understanding of the struggle by which people eke out a living from the land, where the vagaries of the weather, outbreaks of plant or animal disease, or the impact of distant wars on commodity prices can bankrupt even the hardest working farmer overnight. Agriculture became ingrained in his bones at an early age and was a recurrent interest throughout his life.

"The *latifundia* [large plantations] was a school for Fidel," says Ramón. "From his early years he saw the injustices." He spent long periods with the Haitian cane cutters employed on the farm, and frequently he and his sister Angelita ate their meals with the workers. On one occasion, Fidel was present when a Haitian worker employed by the United Fruit Company died, and lacking family or possessions, was buried without even the dignity of a coffin. "To see children without food, [their parents] without jobs, that makes a man into a rebel. Even the most religious become rebels," comments Ramón.

Fidel also had a particular interest in the sea. "Las Manacas" was about fifteen miles from Nipe Bay, and he went there frequently. He spent time with the local fishermen and acquired a passion for the sea and the seashore. Skin diving would become a favorite recreation in later years.

At the turn of the century, Mayarí had been an arid, dusty little town of simple wooden shacks. Most of the land around it was already owned by the United Fruit Company, the primary employer of the townspeople. Between 1901 and 1904, they purchased an additional seventy-five thousand acres and built two large sugar mills, Boston and Preston. When the railroad that Angel helped to build came to the nearby sea town of Antilla, a dramatic period of population growth began. According to the 1953 census, only about half the population in the area over the age of six had attended even the first grade, and only 1 percent of the adult population had attended any university course. Set against this poverty was the affluence of the United Fruit Company, which operated for its expatriate managers hospitals, schools, swimming pools, stores filled with U.S. goods, and a polo club. Perhaps nowhere else in Cuba was the U.S. presence so strongly felt and brutally exercised. Though he grew up with considerable wealth by local standards, the sight of foreigners flaunting their affluence and protected by their own armed guards from the hungry eyes of the local population, whose labors had helped make them wealthy, left a lasting impression on Fidel. Yankee imperialism was not a rhetorical term; it was something of which he had first-hand experience, and it raised very strong emotions.

Fidel recalls first going to a public school in the little community of Marcane in 1931, when he was four years old. Later, in a letter from prison, he described with great sensitivity the plight of his fellow students: "My classmates, sons of humble parents, generally came to school barefoot and miserably clad. They were very poor. They learned their ABCs very badly and soon dropped out of school, though they were endowed with more than enough intelligence. They then foundered in a bottomless, hopeless sea of ignorance and penury without one of them ever escaping the shipwreck. Today, their children will follow in their footsteps, crushed under the burden of social fatalism."

From a very early age, Fidel was aware that he came from a family with money, putting him in a different category from his classmates. "Everyone lavished attention on me, flattered, and treated me differently from other boys we played with when we were children," he told Carlos Franqui. "All the circumstances surrounding my life and childhood, everything I saw, made it more logical to suppose I would develop the habits, the ideas, and the sentiments natural to a social class with certain privileges and selfish motives that make it indifferent to the problems of others." Yet, while acquiring an early sensitivity to suffering and injustice, he quickly understood that he was, in virtually every respect, ahead of these other children, giving him an early unshakable self-confidence. In that little school where he had learned to read faster than any other student, he was intellectually, socially, and physically superior to any other child. In that setting he was exceptional, he saw himself in that light, and it was this self-esteem that he carried forth with him into the larger world.

He reacted to the teacher, a Miss Felieu, as he did to his father, entering into constant arguments and repeatedly challenging the woman's authority. He says, "Whenever I disagreed with something the teacher said to me, or whenever I got mad, I would swear at her and immediately leave school, running as fast as I could. There was a kind of standing war between me and the teacher." On one occasion running from the teacher he tripped and fell, landing on a board from a guava-jelly box, a nail from which pierced his tongue. When he got home his mother told him, "God punished you for swearing at the teacher." He believed for a long time that this was true.

When Fidel was six years old, his parents decided to send him to Santiago de Cuba with Ramón and Angelita. The reasons for this decision remain somewhat obscure. They were sent to live with Belen Felieu, the sister of their village schoolteacher, and her husband Luis Hibbert, who was the Haitian consul. Ostensibly they were to be given special tutoring in their foster home. It appears, however, to have been at least in part a scheme by the Felieu sisters to get Angel, shrewd in most matters but naive when it came to his children's education, to pay out a significant sum each month for their care. It was apparently argued by Miss Felieu that because the Castro family was relatively wealthy the children deserved a better education than she could provide at the village school. That they were disruptive may also have been a consideration. That it was the three children born out of wedlock who were sent away may also explain the decision.

The children went by train to the city. Fidel had never been there before and it all seemed extraordinary to a child's mind—the high arched station, the crowds of people, and the hubbub of activity. The first night, Fidel recalls, he wet the bed.

Fidel remained in the foster home for more than two years, with the tutoring being mostly an effort to make him memorize multiplication tables. He was unhappy and homesick, with a deep sense of rejection by his parents.

After two years, Fidel's parents decided to enroll him and Ramón in the La Salle school in the city run by the French Marianist brothers. It was a school to which the sons of many wealthy families in Oriente were sent. In order to enter his sons, the registrar insisted that Angel go through a religious marriage to his new wife, and that Ramón and Fidel be baptized and confirmed. This Angel arranged through the Bishop of Camagüey, Enrique Perez Serantes, a friend and fellow immigrant from Galicia who, years later after the Moncada assault, would be involved in the efforts to save Fidel's life. Technically, Fidel was a year too young to enroll, but according to Ramón, in the course of the baptism the date of birth on his records was pushed back one year to make him eligible. This has created a constant source of confusion for biographers, as it remains the official position of the Cuban government that Fidel was born in 1926. In a recent interview with Brazilian priest Frei Betto, Fidel claimed that he was born in 1926, despite his brother's statement.

Fidel was enrolled as a day student, a distinct disadvantage. The boarders were regularly taken on outings to the beach and other places during their free time, while he was stuck at home with his guardians, who by all accounts were quite insensitive to a child's needs. He launched a campaign to become a boarder by behaving in a belligerent and disruptive way. His foster parents were reluctant to lose the income he brought them, but eventually—in exasperation and perhaps happy to be rid of the boisterous little troublemaker—they acceded to his demands and he was enrolled as a boarder.

How much impact the experience of being sent away to a foster home at a young age and then enrolled in boarding school had on the development of Fidel's character is a matter of conjecture. For any child, to be sent away from home is a traumatic event. The question of parental rejection, the perceived lack of parental love, and the possibility that it is an act of punishment immediately surface in a child's mind. For children secure in the knowledge that their parents really do care about them, however, there is an ability to grasp, at least cloudily, their parents' reasoning behind sending them away, and there need be under those circumstances no real emotional damage. Damage may be irreparable when a child is sent off because of the breakup of the family, or a real desire by the parents to be rid of the child. Boarding schools, even for the most well-adjusted and emotionally secure children, are lonely places, and they demand that children mature rapidly and make certain adaptations to cope with an alien, competitive, and sometimes hostile environment without the immediate emotional support of their family. The experience leads most children, especially boys, to become surprisingly emotionally self-sufficient at a young age, resilient to psychological trauma, but also later in life tending to avoid deep sentimental attachments to people. The experience also has a propensity to generate a high level of self-confidence.

For some children it can be a hardening experience, but for others the early unhappiness they may have experienced when first separated from their parents can put them in touch with their feelings in such a way that in later life they have an enhanced sensitivity and empathy with the suffering of others. As an adult, Fidel on several occasions has made reference to the lack of appreciation by many people for the suffering children go through, alluding to his own childhood experiences.

In assessing the overall impact of Fidel's early separation from his parents, it appears that he came out of it remarkably intact, having acquired an astonishing degree of emotional self-sufficiency. Fidel's early years in Santiago de Cuba also came at an age when chance events or initial exposure to certain aspects of life have a searing impact that influences one's attitudes and perceptions forever.

On one occasion Fidel, still only six or seven years old, was standing near the public high school when a group of students approached and passed by some sailors carrying guns. The students made a few joking, derogatory comments to the sailors, who followed them into the school and minutes later dragged them out, beating them with their gun butts, and took them off to jail. Fidel never forgot the sight of the terrified children.

On Thursdays and Sundays, the La Salle fathers would take the boys on a motor launch, *El Cateto*, to the island of Rente, owned by the wealthy Cedoya family of Santiago de Cuba. There they had a recreation center where the boys could play. Returning to Santiago in the evening, they would walk up the narrow streets from the Alameda to the La Salle school through an area lined by bars and brothels. They walked in two lines on each side of the street, and the prostitutes and their customers would come to the windows and doorways to make fun of the boys and the priests. Being held up to derision and unable to strike back angered Fidel, as did the humiliation of the priests, with whom he felt a strong identification. He later attributed to this trauma his revulsion for the red-light districts in every Cuban city, as well as his deep hatred for those who profited from their trade.

Fidel also had his first experience of prison at this time. He accompanied a country woman from near his home who had come to visit her husband, jailed for being a Communist. He told Franqui, "I went with her into the prison, and the sight of the jailers impressed me very deeply. I still remember Antonio in his cell."

One day, he was talking with a priest who was commenting on the wealth of each of his classmates. In the course of the conversation Fidel mentioned that his father often made three hundred pesos a day. He recalls that a dramatic change come over the priest, who subsequently treated him quite differently. It brought home to him in the most forceful manner what he had been aware of since his first day in school, that the way a boy was treated reflected to a substantial degree his family's wealth. It was the beginning of his disillusionment with the church as an institution.

Although often in conflict with the priests, Fidel was attracted by their tough discipline and the absoluteness of their power. Because they were resolute, he tended to identify with them. They set limits for him and he respected them for it. Unlike his father, they also provided structure, enabling him to channel his copious energies in an organized way.

On one occasion, he had a fistfight with a boy named Ivan Losada, who was a particular pet of the fathers, and gave him a black eye. After

23

benediction in the evening, a priest called him in and asked him about the fight. As Fidel started to explain, the priest caught him with a flying slap across the face. As he reeled from the blow, the backhand caught him on the other side of his face. He was dazed and shaken, but he particularly remembers how painfully humiliated he felt. He remained bitter about this and other instances of ill-treatment, and says that he later developed a determination to see that such people, with so little sensitivity to the psychology of children, should not be allowed to become teachers.

When Fidel went home for Christmas in the third grade, he was preceded by reports to his father that he, Ramón, and Raúl, who by then was also enrolled at La Salle, were intractable fighters and bullies. Raúl says of Fidel during this period, "Every day he fought. . . . He defied the most powerful and the strongest, and when he was beaten he began again the next day. He never gave up." Fidel's combativeness must be attributed in part to the confrontational style he had learned at home. However, despite his father's wealth he was still a first-generation son of peasant immigrants among, for the most part, the children of the established upper-class gentry of the province. As is often the cruel nature of children, he was constantly reminded that he and his brothers were different. Whether at this point his peers also knew about his father's marital background is unclear, but it would have provided further basis for the sort of vicious teasing that young boys inflict on one another. At home, Fidel's family was the richest in the area, but here he became aware of a different kind of class consciousness in which he was the one looked down on.

Their father decided to pull them out of school. Fidel, despite his battles in school, angrily protested, and when his father seemed unmoved he threatened to burn the house down. Finally, his mother interceded on his behalf, and he returned to La Salle.

Because he was bright, Fidel did well in class at La Salle, even though he did not apply himself as well as he might. He continued to be disruptive, partly because, as usual, he contravened authority, but also because he had begun to attract a gang of followers that in a boarding school setting was hard to manage and disturbing to the priests. They eventually decided that he might do better under the tighter control of the Jesuits, and he was transferred in the fifth grade to Colegio Dolores, also in Santiago. There he played the bugle in the school band, dressed in a navy blue uniform with a white Sam Browne belt. In 1940, Fidel wrote to President Roosevelt, congratulating him on his successful reelection victory. The State Department's letter of thanks was posted on the door of the school.

At about the same time, a poetry contest sponsored by a radio station was held among the students. All the students took part, and the parents voted for the best poems. Fidel's were by no means the best, but because of his persuasive influence with the other boys he was able to get them to convince their parents to vote for him. Fidel acknowledges that a boy named Elpidio Espada wrote the best poems, but the letters from the parents would say, "Elpidio's poems to mothers are very beautiful and touching, but our vote goes to Fidel. . . . "

Shortly after switching schools, Fidel developed appendicitis and was taken to the Colonia Española Hospital. The operation was successful, but the wound became infected and he was kept there for three months. It was a frustrating and emotionally trying experience for this energetic young boy with little to do to pass the time and, because of the distance, largely cut off from his parents. He read comic books and, being gregarious by nature, made friends with every other patient in the ward. He reflects that the latter was probably a clear indication, even at that age, of his constitutional propensity toward politics. Like many children who are forced to spend protracted periods of time in hospitals, he became enamored of the idea that he might become a physician. Subsequently, on several occasions he "operated" on lizards using a Gillette razor blade. It was no more than a fleeting ambition, although as an adult, health care has been one of his greatest interests and several of his close friends have been physicians.

When he transferred to Colegio Dolores, Fidel was again placed in the home of foster parents to be a day student rather than a boarder. These new guardians were by all accounts mean and disinterested in the boy, taking him into their home only for the small remuneration they received. To induce him to study, the couple would lock him in his room when he came home from school. Rather than studying, he passed the time acting out fantasies associated with events he had read about in history books. Usually these involved elaborate war games in which he was the battle commander leading his troops through one heroic conflict after another. History was already, and would remain, the one subject at which he would excel and to which he would be willing to devote unlimited study. He was also, however, a budding and extremely promising athlete. "I played soccer, basketball, jai alai, all kinds of sports. All my energy went into them," he says.

When he was thirteen, Fidel experienced what must have been a deeply traumatic event. A soap opera was broadcast on the radio about a fictional family in the village of Birán that bore sufficient resemblance to the Castro family that people who knew them identified it as such. In it a point was made of describing the children's illegitimacy. The public revelation, just as he was entering adolescence, of this fact, even if it was already known to many of his peers as well as the priests, must have been an excruciating and humiliating experience that must have left an emotional scar.

25

There are frequent examples in history of individuals, including T. E. Lawrence, Adolf Hitler, and Juan Perón, who appear to have been driven to achieve greatness by their belief that society was rejecting them, or that they bore a special stigma because of their illegitimacy. They are motivated, it is speculated, by a relentless inner need for public redemption to expunge what they feel to be the insufferable burden of their tarnished heritage. Fidel's intense drive to achieve recognition of historic proportions can reasonably be attributed in part to his psychological need to overcome this stigma.

In 1942, at the age of fifteen, Fidel went on to Belen, the famous Jesuit school in Havana. There his life took a completely new turn. The school, the most prestigious in Cuba, served the nation's upper crust. The Spanish Jesuit priests who ran the institution embodied the patrician values and traditions of their homeland, and represented a primary residue of Spanish cultural influence and thinking within Cuban society. They prided themselves on the notion that they not only offered the best education in Cuba, but that they groomed the future leaders of the country, and thus maintained a substantial influence over Cuban thinking, politics, and society. In some other Latin American countries, the priests were native born, and the Catholic Church was a champion of the poor against the rich. But in Cuba, the church hierarchy was made up almost entirely of Spaniards whose loyalty was to the upper classes, to the perpetuation of their power, and to the maintenance of close ties to Spain.

The Jesuit philosophy emphasized freedom of thought, but also rigid obedience to authority. Intellect was prized over emotion, eloquence over sensuality and materialism, and the universal over the particular. Historically, these values had often led to the perception of the Jesuits as ruthless, and to the emergence of the term jesuitical to connote craft and intrigue. At that time among the Spanish faculty at Belen there were strong feelings of allegiance to Generalissimo Franco, whose Fascist forces had recently overthrown the republican government of Spain, and who had posed himself as the protector of the Catholic Church against the Communists. Fascism, with its emphasis on bringing order out of chaos with discipline and authority, was highly compatible with Jesuit thinking and was presented to the students as such. "The Jesuits then," says Carlos Rafael Rodríguez, now Cuba's vice president, "were different from the present-day Jesuits. . . . They were the vanguard of conservatism."

From the moment Fidel arrived at the school, he was spotted by the fathers as a boy with exceptional talent and leadership potential. His innate ability, his immediate Spanish background, and his father's wealth transcended any reservations they may have had about his parents' social class or the circumstances of his birth, which by now was ancient history.

26

Shortly after he arrived, and perhaps still needing to achieve acceptance, he rode a bicycle full-speed into a brick wall to prove to onlookers that he had the willpower to do things they would never dare to do. Fidel, however, no longer fought physically with his classmates as he had done as a little boy. Now he sought to beat them in the classroom and on the athletic field. He developed a burning desire to be always in the winner's circle.

The embryonic sense of personal predestination that many individuals develop as a defense against social ostracism grew in Fidel, reinforced by his increasing success and the flattery of his teachers. He was a good student, finishing in the top third of his class. History remained his greatest love, but sociology, geography, and agriculture also became among his special interests. As his understanding of history grew, he developed a fascination with the great figures of history, an interest that under the Jesuits' analysis did not focus so much on ideology or personality, but rather on the exercise of power and their ability to shape events. While at Belen, he became aware of the lives and works of many of the great figures of history from Julius Caesar to Mussolini. In later life, his choice of actions and his public utterances reflected detailed scholarship in this area.

A figure to whom Fidel was automatically exposed was the Cuban national hero José Martí. Martí, like Fidel, was the son of a sergeant in the Spanish army, and it was against the independence struggle launched by Martí that Fidel's father had fought for Spain. Martí also had a bitter conflict throughout his youth and young adulthood with his father. Known as the "Apostle," Martí is in the consciousness of every Cuban, as George Washington is in every American's, but it was not until he was at Belen that Fidel became familiar with Martí's writings and the details of his life. Fidel, perhaps because of their family similarities, developed a powerful identification with Martí, and in a way he worshipped him. Martí was the truly towering figure of Cuban history, and his life offered a blueprint that Fidel, especially in his early years, would go back to time after time in making decisions about his own life. He even tried to speak, act, and write like Martí. Martí had, in addition, set the standard against which greatness would be judged in the history of Cuba. No matter what Fidel achieved the question would always be asked, was he greater or lesser than Martí?

Fidel was significantly influenced by Fathers Amondo Llorente and Alberto de Castro, under whose direction he read the works of Antonio Primo de Rivera, the founder and theoretician of the Spanish Falange party. De Castro admired Franco as someone who had freed Spain both from Marxism-Leninism and from Anglo-Saxon materialism. He also shared

27

with the students his belief in a more unified Latin America with close ties to the "New Spain." Fidel was attracted to Primo de Rivera as someone from a wealthy background who gave it up to fight for what he believed in. Like Martí, he was in Fidel's mind a powerful historical role model.

Fidel, in addition to having an insatiable intellectual curiosity and being a fine debater, was a superior athlete. He was awarded the prize as Cuba's best all-round school athlete for the period 1943–44. He excelled at basketball, baseball, track, and soccer. At that time, the Washington Senators' scout, Joe Cambria, lived at the American Club in Havana. He was on the constant lookout for talented young Cuban players and held regular "tryout camps," two of which were attended by Fidel. Fidel was a promising pitcher, but in the end he was not offered a contract. Even if he had been, his contemporaries consider it highly unlikely that he would have accepted. His academic and professional prospects, as well as his general financial situation, seemed so good that professional baseball would have been a step down. His reason for trying out was clearly more for the gratification of showing that he could have made it.

Fidel was very active in a Jesuit organization similar to the Boy Scouts, the "Explorers." On occasion, they went on rigorous camping trips into the rugged mountain areas, and Fidel acquired a reputation for stamina and endurance, eventually becoming the leader of the troop. In later years, he would only half jokingly attribute his skills as a guerrilla fighter to being in part due to this experience.

By the time he left Belen, Fidel had clearly established himself as a young man of whom great things were expected. His entry in the yearbook sums it up well:

> 1942–1945. Fidel distinguished himself always in all subjects related to letters. A top student and member of the congregation, he was also an outstanding athlete, always courageously and proudly defending the school's colors. He has won the admiration and affection of all. We are sure that, after his law studies, he will make a brilliant name for himself. Fidel has what it takes and will make something of his life.

The Jesuits did not single out Fidel. It was their pattern each year to try to influence all the top students with their ideas. However, they had every reason to believe that Fidel would be a celebrated advocate for their cause. With his talents, and their training and backing, he stood on the threshold of the Cuban upper class. Moving from immigrant peasant to the top echelons of society in one generation seemed an irresistible attraction for an ambitious young man. His espousal of their political philosophy seemed a foregone conclusion.

"Fidel was trained by the Jesuits to become their representative," says

Carlos Rafael Rodríguez. "The revolution does less propaganda [promoting] for Fidel than the propaganda by the Jesuits. The yearbook . . . is completely devoted to Fidel: Fidel the athlete, Fidel the scholar, Fidel the speaker. And I recall in a newspaper, *Diaria de la Marina* [the conservative Catholic newspaper]—Fidel does not like this said—in an article about Fidel, Fidel speaking about fascism in a favorable way, a boy, a teenager, of fifteen or sixteen."

At Belen there were the children of the very rich, the moderately rich, and the nouveau riche. Fidel fell into the last category, which was somewhat looked down on by those from the more established families. He came from the country rather than the city, and additionally was from Oriente, an area against which there was a regional snobbery in the rest of the country. As a result, despite his success he was never in the mainstream of the socially conscious student body.

Fidel spent eleven years in Catholic boarding schools, seven of them in Jesuit institutions, during those years which are the most formative in a child's intellectual development. The foundation of his thinking about the nature, structure, and governance of society derives from that period. Other ideologies would be veneers layered on the top. As one member of the Cuban government today observes, "Fidel is a Jesuit first, a revolutionary second, and a Marxist third."

During those years in boarding school, Fidel had also learned to stand alone and be emotionally self-reliant, truly needing no one but himself to survive. He knew he could handle what life had to throw at him without having to turn to others for help, because that is what he had been doing since he was five years old. He had also learned to be, like his father, tough and aggressively determined to pursue any goal he set for himself.

Above all, Fidel appreciated and admired the Jesuits for the superior education they had given him, particularly because they inspired him with an insatiable thirst for knowledge and they taught him how to think. He told Franqui, "I feel that creating habits of discipline and study was good. I am not against that kind of life, Spartan to some degree. And I think that, as a rule, the Jesuits formed people of character." He has criticized the separation of the sexes in Jesuit education, which he felt led to his classmates' constant preoccupation with thoughts of women.

The Jesuits ultimately tamed Fidel's rebelliousness. He came to accept and revere their strict discipline, which was probably the single greatest legacy from his years at Belen.

Fidel's earliest religious exposure came from his parents, especially his mother, whose beliefs were those of a primitive rural Christianity emphasizing Christ's compassion for the poor and the dispossessed. It helped to instill in him ethical values to which he would adhere throughout his life. While at Belen, he went through the formalistic rituals of the church, but he had already in his mind rejected the church in Cuba. To him it was an institution of hypocrisy that responded more to the secular world and the maintenance of its own power and privilege, than to the fundamental teachings of Christianity. After he left Belen, he would have no further dealings with the church or the Jesuits until after the revolution. However, Christian values as he interpreted them remained at the heart of the way Fidel perceived the world, and religious references would constantly surface in his oratory.

Chapter Two

AFTER graduating from Belen in June 1945, Fidel went home for the summer. It was the last extended period he would spend with his family. His mother was particularly proud of his accomplishments. In some respects, however, his education and his exposure to the more cosmopolitan and sophisticated life in Havana served to widen the gap between him and his father. Despite their continuing conflicts, Fidel valued his roots, and he cherished dearly the time that he was still able to spend back in Oriente Province.

During the summer, Fidel decided that he would need a car when he entered the University of Havana in September. He turned to his father, who initially resisted vigorously but finally gave in. Angel bought him a new 1946 Ford the day before he was to leave for Havana, notwithstanding the fact that Fidel did not know how to drive. With a certain blind determination, Fidel set off from "Las Manacas" at the end of the summer, arriving in Havana three days later, having taught himself to drive on the way. It was a skill he never enjoyed, and later, despite his meager income, he preferred to pay a driver.

Fidel moved into a boarding house with other students in the university district at #8 Calle 5, between Second and Fourth streets. He enrolled in the law school, a decision that was a foregone conclusion while he was still at Belen, but one that critic Theodore Draper, in his book *Castroism: Theory and Practice,* attributes to the fact that law was "a field of study in which the standards were notoriously low, the pressure to study minimal and his future profession already overcrowded." It is a questionable observation given Fidel's strong academic record and his apparent inclination for hard work. Fidel himself has said about the choice, "I asked myself why I studied law. I don't know. I attribute it partly to those who said, 'He talks a lot, he ought to be a lawyer.' Because I had the habit of debating and discussing, I was persuaded I was qualified to be a lawyer." On another occasion, he said, "How often have I not regretted that I was not made to study something else."

31

About one issue there can be no doubt. From his first day on campus Fidel was fascinated with politics. He spent a good deal of time at a café, Las Delicias de Medina, at Twenty-first and L streets. (Today it is a pizzeria.) There he talked for hours with fellow students. As one of them recalls, "We were young, carefree; it was a happy time." Of Fidel he says, "He talked politics all the time, *all* the time, with a very, very grandiose, and at the same time idealistic scheme of how to run the country, how to improve things. He did it with a great deal of passion, emotion, vehemence—convincing people. He had that capacity."

Fidel is remembered for two physiological characteristics that would amaze his friends throughout his life. He was apparently incapable of sitting still and had such an excess of energy that he was in constant motion, usually pacing. He also had an immense appetite. While he was quite capable of doing without food for long periods, at other times he would eat four or five times the amount of his companions. It was a matter of astonishment that people recalled years later.

Fidel has described himself as a political ingenue when he arrived on campus. Perhaps he was, in terms of not yet having formulated his own set of political beliefs. But he had been heavily exposed to the politically active minds of his Jesuit mentors, and however uncrystallized his ideology, his fascination with politics was visibly intense. From his first day on campus he plainly saw himself as a leader and had the clear intent to become president of the Federation of University Students (FEU).

Fidel wore a dark blue suit and tie most of the time. That plus his physical stature made him stand out immediately among his classmates. He made a dramatic, although inaccurate, initial impression on his fellow students. His patrician bearing and appearance, together with his height, his apparent wealth, his agile mind, his powerful personality, and his private elite education created the immediate image of a preordained aristocratic leader. Alfredo Guevara, a fellow freshman who would become a close friend of Fidel, and who had himself arrived on campus with burning political ambitions, describes his first impressions: "I was in a panic. Here was this Castro dressed up fit to kill in his black party suit, handsome, self-assured, aggressive and obviously a leader. He had come out of Belen parochial school, and I saw him as a political threat. Here was the specter of clericalism threatening the campus, and I believed that Castro would be its instrument."

What Guevara did not know was that Fidel's dress and style were in part a conscious effort to hide his less than patrician background. At this early stage, he was more eager to have his image reflect Belen than Oriente Province. Juan Bosch, a Dominican journalist in exile who would later briefly become president of the Dominican Republic, believes that Fidel was still sensitive about the circumstances of his birth, and as a reaction to it was determined to convey an exemplary impression. As one friend also recalls, "He never mentioned his family . . . or his background."

Fidel quickly set about methodically pursuing his political ambitions. A delegate was elected by the students taking each course. These delegates elected from among themselves a representative for their year. These five representatives then elected one of their number to be the president of the law school. The president of the law school, together with the presidents of the twelve other schools in the university, then chose the president and other officers of the Student Federation. Fidel chose the course legal anthropology in which to run as delegate. He arranged to be assigned the task of keeping the attendance role, and for this purpose he was given by the professor a set of cards on each of which was the name, photograph, and some background information on each student. He memorized this information so that he could quickly address all the students by name and impress them with his knowledge of their home towns and something about their families. With little difficulty he was elected delegate, and subsequently he was voted in as representative of the freshman year.

Fidel already demonstrated a charisma that enabled him to attract a loyal following. A fellow student who knew him well says, "Around noontime a group of us went to the campus, and I have this very, very vivid memory of Fidel, very well dressed in his navy blue suit in the midst of a big discussion with a group of students, making these many gestures with his hands. He had at that time the reputation of being a little bit crazy. It was sort of a joke among the students. They would say, 'Oh, he is crazy,' something like that. . . . Crazy in the way that he had great ambition and grandiose fantasies." Although Fidel's ideology could be considered at this point generally "leftist," it was hardly enough to distinguish his position from that of the bulk of the students. Ideology also was largely irrelevant in student politics. Fidel, like his fellow student leaders, was concerned with campus politics primarily as a way of establishing power and prestige in the university community that could later be translated into a political career in the outside world.

During the 1940s, organized violence had become so significant a factor in campus politics that many aspiring student leaders saw it as an essential ingredient for their success. For Fidel, who was, despite his intellectual ability, very physically oriented, this violence seemed to have a certain appeal. Whether he found the violence itself attractive or whether he viewed it as an unfortunate necessity in satisfying his ambition to become a prominent student leader is hard to say. From the context of the American or European university experience, the phenomenon was almost incomprehensible. For about ten years, as an extension of the national political decay, violence-prone gangs terrorized the students and the faculty. Murder was a frequent part of campus power struggles, and on several occasions the machine-gunning of students and faculty by rival factions occurred. Any student who wished to play even a modest leadership role had to contend with this state of affairs, and even students who had no interest in politics frequently had to get support from the right gangs to get a passing grade.

Fidel's experiences in this setting over the next five years were to have a profound effect in shaping his understanding of the politics of survival in Cuba. To the outsider unfamiliar with Fidel's campus involvements, his extreme and often ruthless reaction later in his career to those who posed a threat to him often seemed to have a paranoid quality to it. However, its origins lie at least in part in the harshness of his political baptism. He learned how easily the unwary could become the victims of duplicity and violence.

How had a center of higher learning become such a playground for gangsterism and violence? Violence has a long history in Cuba as a way of settling disputes. Following the overthrow of the dictator Machado in 1933, there was an absence of strong national leadership. Those who were responsible for the cruelty and savage abuses of the Machado regime were never systematically brought to justice by the weak subsequent administrations. Many people felt, therefore, that they were justified in avenging themselves outside the judicial system if the state was not prepared to do it legally. Initially there was an element of idealism as some angry citizens formed "action groups" and meted out their own form of justice against Machado's henchmen. Others, of both the right and the left, taking advantage of the political vacuum, justified the violence against their fellow Cubans on ideological grounds, claiming to be anti-Communist, anti-imperialist, or merely for social justice. In that atmosphere, there were young men for whom the idealism disappeared and who found that the use of violence, including murder, could by itself be a way of wielding political power and becoming rich through corruption.

Perhaps most important, since the war of independence there had been little consensus about what constituted a legitimate route to the access to power. In recent memory, the only national figures who had had real power were those who seized it. Thus, there was an increasing number of Cubans who believed that power was an end in itself; it was the acquisition of power, rather than the manner in which it was achieved, that mattered. The exercise of power was defined in people's minds as the potential for inflicting violence. Hence the military rather than the politicians was always seen as the ultimate power.

Playing into this belief was another strong theme in the Cuban psyche—

admiration for the "man of action" as opposed to the individual concerned with ideas. The romantic image of the man who takes events into his own hands and shapes his own destiny or that of the nation meshed with the traditional Hispanic concept of machismo and was greatly admired, so much so that it often obscured any objective assessment of the merits or dangers of the acts involved. The political theorist concerned exclusively with ideas and procedural matters was largely disparaged.

The situation with the "action groups," now little more than violence-prone gangs competing to control government graft and corruption, was made dramatically worse in 1944 when Professor Ramón Grau San Martín assumed the presidency. Although Grau was elected president as a reformer, the real power remained—as is the case in most developing countries—in the hands of the military. Although Batista spent the four years of the Grau administration (1944–48) in the United States, and Grau had purged the army of three hundred officers he thought loyal to Batista, the former sergeant, who had strong support in Washington, still exerted considerable influence.

Rather than trying to eliminate them, Grau sought to resuscitate and use the "action groups" to strengthen his hand against his opponents. In return for government jobs, including key positions in the Havana police, the gangs assassinated Grau's enemies in the labor unions and other institutions, allowing him to gain undisputed control without having to be beholden to Batista and the military. At the same time, unfettered by government constraint, the gangs enriched themselves through extortion and corruption.

Control of the university was crucial because it was the anteroom to power. There was a continuum between university politics and national politics, so that a position in the student leadership assured a subsequent position in the national leadership. In addition, the university enjoyed autonomy. The police were prohibited from setting foot on the campus.

By 1945, there were two major competing "gangs," each with an organization on the University of Havana campus. The Unión Insurrecional Revolucionaria (UIR) had as its leader Emilio Tro, who had fought in the Spanish Civil War and also for the U.S. Army in World War II. The second group was the Movimiento Socialista Revolucionaria (MSR). Their leader was Rolando Masferrer, a one-time Communist Party member who now was avowedly anti-Communist, anti-U.S., and an advocate of the overthrow of Rafael Trujillo, the dictatorial leader of the Dominican Republic.

At the time Fidel entered the university, the departing president of the Student Federation was Manolo Castro (no relative), a man in his thirties who was also the campus leader of the MSR. For six years he had dominated campus politics and ruled the student body with a dictatorial hand. He had been offered the position of National Sports Director by President Grau San Martín, but he had made it clear that he still intended to keep control of campus politics through the MSR. Fidel, already elected as the freshman class representative in the law school, was quickly recognized as a student with leadership ability and political potential. Representatives of both the UIR and the MSR sought to enlist Fidel in their organizations. Fidel, fully cognizant of their power and their ability to assist his political ambitions and, according to acquaintances from that time, not averse to their violent methods, tried initially to get support from both without making a full commitment to either. This led him into serious difficulty, especially with the MSR, which demanded his total loyalty. Later Fidel would greatly regret his involvement with gangs, especially as he developed his idealistic philosophy. However, at least during his first eighteen months at the university, he seemed convinced that he needed their help to succeed politically on campus.

According to law school classmate Rolando Amador, Fidel, to placate the MSR leadership, during his freshman year was convinced to go with some other individuals to the university stadium to shoot a student, Lionel Gómez, following a football game. Gómez was about to come to the university from the Instituto de Vedado (a high school) where he had already been involved in gang politics. When Gómez came out of the stadium, he was surrounded by several other people, so the attackers were too frightened to shoot. One tried, but his gun jammed. Only Fidel fired, and he inadvertently shot in the leg a fellow law student, Fernando Freyre de Andrade. Early the next day, Fidel was at his bedside in the hospital begging his forgiveness. Such were his powers of persuasion that Freyre not only forgave him but became a loyal supporter.

Fidel's attempt to use, but remain independent from, the UIR and the MSR, as well as criticisms he had made of the Grau administration, led him toward the end of his freshman year into direct conflict with Mario Salabarria Aguilar, the vicious and unscrupulous chief of the Department of Alien Activities. Salabarria controlled many of the more lucrative rackets in Havana through the Revolutionary Legion, an offshoot of the MSR. In collaboration with Manolo Castro, he exerted significant control over the campus of the university, which he regarded as his personal fiefdom. He gave Fidel an ultimatum: cease his criticism of the Grau administration and his ambiguous involvement with the gangs, or get off the campus for good. The implications of Fidel's failure to take this advice were clear. Fidel said of this period:

> The political atmosphere in the University of Havana had been con-
> taminated by the national disorder. My impetuosity, my desire to excel

fed and inspired the character of my struggle. My straightforward character made me enter rapidly into conflict with the milieu, the venal authorities, the corruption and the gang-ridden system that dominated the University atmosphere. The pressure groups of corrupt politicians made the gangs threaten me and led to a prohibition on my entering the University. This was a moment of great decision. The conflict struck my personality like a cyclone. Alone on the beach, facing the sea, I examined the situation. Personal danger, physical risk made my return to the University an act of unheard of temerity. But not to return would be to give in to threats, to give in before bullies, to abandon my own ideals and aspirations. I decided to go back and went back . . . with arms in my hands. Naturally I did not find myself fully prepared to understand exactly the roots of the profound crisis which disfigured the country. This resulted in my resistance being centered on the idea of personal valor.

He faced this crisis alone, turning neither to his family nor to friends. In many respects his decision was predictable. Risk offered challenge, and challenge was something he never backed away from. Machismo played a part, too, for on this and many other occasions he made it clear that he would rather die a hero than live with himself knowing that he had backed down out of fear.

At this point, whether in self-defense against the MSR, or merely because he felt that their help was now more beneficial to his political career, Fidel became closely associated with the UIR. Whether he technically joined the organization is a matter of contention, although José Diegues, a student leader of the UIR at the time, has said, "Fidel used us for his own political battles within the university without ever really identifying publicly with the UIR." The official position of the Cuban government today is that he did not become a member, and that he would never have allowed himself to be subjected to the sort of discipline the organization demanded. Others say categorically that he did become a member. They add that he was personally close to several of the top student and non-student UIR leaders, including a man named José Jinjaume, whom Fidel is said to have particularly admired.

One friend described an evening immediately prior to an exam in civic law when he and Fidel met to study together. Fidel said that he first had to go to the UIR headquarters to repay some money he had borrowed from Emilio Tro, the head of the UIR. When they arrived, they were told that Tro had been seized by an MSR group, and they were expecting an armed attack on the headquarters at any moment. Fidel explained to his friend that he felt an obligation to stay and help defend the headquarters. So they remained and studied there for several hours, waiting for the attack. It did not occur, and eventually Tro reappeared unharmed.

At the start of Fidel's second year at the university in September 1946, he was again elected class representative for his year. A friend of his from Oriente Province, Baudilio Castellanos, entered the freshman class, and under Fidel's tutelage became the class representative for that year. It was Fidel's hope that with Castellanos's vote, and that of one more class representative, he could get himself elected president of the law school. The representatives from the other three years would not, however, support Fidel, and instead elected one of their own number.

Several months later, Fidel organized an assembly of the entire law school student body at which he successfully called for the ouster of the student who had defeated him, claiming that he had failed to carry out properly his duties as president. Fidel was then elected by public vote of the assembly to replace him. For a period of time there were two law school presidents as the man ousted appealed to the University Council. Eventually his position was sustained, and Fidel's election was declared invalid because it had violated the established constitutional procedures for electing student officials.

Subsequently, Fidel's own class sought to remove him as their representative because of his close connections with the UIR. Their efforts were declared invalid by the Council as also being in violation of the constitution.

By early 1947, there was an independent group of students emerging at the university who were idealistic in their outlook and fervently opposed to the effects of political corruption on society in general, and its subversion of campus life in particular. The group, which at this point was not an organized political entity, included several of Fidel's friends: Rolando Amador, Leonel Soto, Antonio Núñez Jiménez, Flavio Bravo, and Alfredo Guevara, whose initial reaction to Fidel had been so negative when they first arrived on campus together. Some of the students in the group were members of the tiny Socialist Youth (Communists); others came from devoutly Catholic backgrounds. There was considerable overlap between the two groups. Communism, with its professed commitment to helping the oppressed, seemed to some students to have much in common with the teachings of Christianity, and several students saw it as a secular vehicle for achieving Christian ideals.

For Fidel, a gradual evolution in his thinking began to take place during his second year. Instead of a narrow preoccupation with his original goal to become president of the Student Federation, he began to take a greater interest in national politics. In January 1947, as a representative of the law school, Fidel lent his name to a toughly worded petition condemning the excesses of Grau San Martín: "We pledge to fight against the reelection of Grau 'though the price of struggle be our blood.' "

38

It might be argued that Fidel's awakening to more idealistic concerns was no more than his adaptation to the evolving political winds at the university in an attempt to maintain himself in a leadership position. His effort at this stage to disassociate himself from the UIR could also be seen as coming at a time when the influence of such organizations on the campus was waning, and the connection had become more of a liability than an asset for him.

It seems, however, that he had undergone a degree of political maturation, and was beginning to be aware of substantive issues rather than merely the blind pursuit of elective office for its own sake. During his first two years at the university, as his awareness of the corruption and misgovernment in Havana grew, these concerns began to become interlocked in his mind with his awareness of the problems of the rural poor in Oriente Province. What gradually emerged as a political target for him was an increasingly cohesive picture of the disease that afflicted the country as a whole.

The independent student group had become organized under several banners. One of them was the 30th of September Movement, with which many of Fidel's friends were involved. However, when he sought membership because one of its primary goals was to end the influence of the political gangs on campus, Fidel was rejected on the basis of his association with the UIR. One member recalls that "Fidel begged us to let him join."

At this point, he began a new and important phase of his political career. He associated himself with Eduardo Chibás, a leading politician who espoused at a national level the reformist political philosophy that Fidel and his friends had been promoting on campus. Chibás, a congressman and member of Grau's Auténticos (Authentic Revolutionary Movement), had taken a public stand against corruption and graft. Each week, on his widely followed radio program, he provided damning disclosures against his fellow politicians' involvements in kickbacks, embezzlement, payroll padding, gambling, and narcotics. Predictably, he became the target of venomous attacks from those he exposed. In September 1946, one such individual, Rubén de León, viciously attacked Chibás at an outdoor rally. Fidel had been among a group of students who heckled de León until he was forced to leave the stage.

As the population observed the continuing political murders, the public demand for peace, reform, and an end to corruption grew. On May 15, 1947, Eduardo Chibás announced that he was forming a new party, the Party of the Cuban People (Ortodoxos). Fidel attended the founding assembly and was to remain a staunch party member for eight years. The party's fundamental principles of "nationalism, anti-imperialism, socialism, economic independence, political liberty, and social justice" could equally well be said to summarize Fidel's own political thinking at the time.

Chibás's leadership and the public outcry for clean government had its effect on campus, boosting the stature and clout of the reformist movement with which Fidel was now becoming increasingly identified. In the weeks following the creation of the Ortodoxo Party, a student constitutional assembly was convened with the aim of reorganizing the student government along more progressive and democratic lines. One of its goals was to eliminate the complicated system of electing the members of the Student Federation through a series of class, year, and school delegates, and institute instead a popular vote. Fidel worked hard to organize the assembly and to make it a success. Part of his agenda, together with his friend Alfredo Guevara, was to institute a system through which Fidel, with his already highly successful populist appeal and skills as a political organizer, could still realize his dream of becoming president of the FEU. Despite their friendship, Fidel ran against Guevara for the position of secretary of the assembly. Guevara, with the backing of the Socialist Youth and their superior organization, won by a narrow margin.

The effort to get the constitution revised failed, and from then on Fidel largely abandoned his efforts to become the president of the FEU.

The assembly took place in mid-July after final exams. Although losing the election for secretary, Fidel addressed the body in his capacity as representative of the law school. It was the first political speech he had made before a formal audience. It was a classic exhortation in the style that would become his trademark. He invoked the names of dead heroes, and spoke of the importance of the assembly in the great flow of Cuban history. Then he attacked the Grau administration in vehement terms, describing it as "a tyranny that hovers over the country." He called for bold and audacious action to confront this evil, condemning apathy and resignation by his fellow students. It was a speech still well remembered by those present, which reflected a deep sense of conviction, but also the commanding authority of the speaker. Above all it was a speech of strong leadership, especially impressive from someone who was a month short of his twentieth birthday.

While the assembly was still going on, rumors were sweeping Havana that an invasion force was being assembled to topple the regime of dictator Rafael Trujillo of the Dominican Republic. Trujillo, who had held power since 1930, was a stereotype of the ruthless corrupt Latin dictator despised by progressive forces throughout the region. He savagely suppressed dissent, even sending death squads to assassinate his enemies in exile. Meanwhile, he enriched himself at the expense of the people of the Dominican Republic, most of whom continued to live in abject poverty. He had opened his country to exploitation by foreign interests, who provided him with arms and helped to keep him in power. An expedition to overthrow this tyrant had both powerful romantic and practical political appeal to democratic and reformist forces throughout the Caribbean. To Fidel it offered an opportunity for direct, morally righteous action, unlike the frustrating internecine struggles in Havana.

For several weeks, more than twelve hundred men had been assembling in Oriente Province. They were Cuban action groups, Dominican exiles, and assorted soldiers of fortune. Ultimately this group would form the nucleus of the Caribbean Legion that would help bring José Figueres to power in Costa Rica, and for several years would serve as an important force for progressive democratic leaders in the region. The Cuban leadership came, however, from the MSR. Manolo Castro, who had long despised Trujillo, saw in this venture an opportunity to wrap the tainted MSR in the cloak of idealism. Because of his now bitter relationship with the leadership of the MSR, it was necessary for Fidel to work out a private truce with the MSR leader in order to join the expedition. It was ironic that although a major part of the appeal of the expedition for the young and idealistic Fidel was its ideological purity and simplicity compared with the vicious and corrupt politics of Havana, the leadership and support for the invasion group came from these same forces he opposed at home and was seeking to escape.

Fidel joined the expedition in Oriente Province, even though his mother tried to talk him out of going. The force assembled at the Instituto Politecnico at Holguín, where they were organized into platoons. From there, on July 29, 1947, they loaded onto three ships in the harbor of Antilla, which that night sailed to Cayo Confites, a small, barren island off the coast of Camagüey Province, where they were to receive military training. There they sat in the baking sun, eaten by mosquitoes, for fifty-nine days, with no way of knowing why the order to proceed with the attack never came.

Grau's motivation for backing the invasion force may in part have been a scheme to get rid of some of the more disreputable gang members, but was also an effort to boost his sagging political fortunes. Chibás accused him of doing so in the expectation that he could use the invasion as a rationale for suspending the coming elections. The canceling of the operation seems to have been due primarily to pressure from the United States, as the operation was terminated immediately on the return of the chief of the military from a trip to Washington. Grau sent the Cuban navy to intercept the boat that had finally picked up the miserable and dispirited group of men marooned at Cayo Confites. This posed a serious problem for Fidel: not only was he disappointed by the abortion of the potentially

41

dramatic venture, but he feared that the truce he had worked out with the MSR was no longer valid, and his life was in serious jeopardy there in the clutches of his enemies. He and some others escaped on a small boat, but during the night it overturned, and he was forced to swim more than a mile across the shark-infested waters for the Bay of Nipe, carrying with him an Argentinian-made submachine gun and a pistol. He was accompanied on the swim by a Dominican, Horacio Ornez, and a Honduran.

On September 15, 1947, before Fidel returned to Havana, Salabarria's agents had gunned down Emilio Tro, the leader of the UIR, in a three-hour street battle. Salabarria was arrested and jailed by the army, but it triggered further rounds of violent retribution.

With Grau's term in office coming to an end, Education Minister José Alemán prepared to seek the nomination of the Auténticos, which would virtually assure his election to the presidency. He had, however, no political base among the general population, and was under attack as a master of corruption who had reputedly embezzled more than $100 million. To improve his image, he used his fortune to organize a public relations campaign, and a rally with a motorcade was planned. As it was about to start, a car stalled and jeering students began to throw stones. One of Alemán's followers shot and killed a high school student, Carlos Martínez.

At the funeral, held only a few hours later, Fidel joined thousands of students and citizens who poured into the streets and carried the coffin in a demonstration to the Presidential Palace. There, an angry but inspired Fidel addressed the mourners, lambasting the gangsterism and corruption of the administration, and holding the president personally responsible for Martínez's death. There were repeated shouts for Grau to resign. Alemán was seen as merely the most corrupt member of Grau's corrupt government, and the student's death was used as an excuse for attacking the entire administration.

In its drama, the event was not unlike the storming of the Bastille during the French Revolution, and it was the scenario that Fidel was consciously following. He understood the immense power created by mobilizing a mass of angry people. The experience of that day became a model that he would try to duplicate several times in the future.

Within a matter of days following the student's death, on October 9, 1947, a nationwide student strike was organized. Fidel was at the center of the action, organizing, speaking at rallies, and urging ever greater confrontation with the Grau administration. He was becoming an increasingly dramatic orator, who could extemporaneously speak fluidly and lucidly for long periods of time while simultaneously holding his audience with a dazzling emotional appeal. Some recall him as an agitator and demagogue, some as a galvanizing, inspirational leader. All remember his effectiveness.

Increasingly, Fidel denounced corrupt government officials by name, as his hero Eduardo Chibás was doing. This made him a particular target for Grau's agents and the MSR gangs. On several occasions, the latter planned attempts on his life, which he avoided mostly by sheer luck. Having by now severed his ties with the UIR, and indeed added them to the list of those he attacked for their corruption, he was particularly vulnerable. On one occasion a fellow student challenged him to a fight in the early hours of the morning at the university stadium. Only by chance did Fidel realize at the last minute that it was an ambush. "It was a miracle that I came out from that alive," he said. Indeed, he has on several occasions described that period of his life as having been far more dangerous than his entire time as a guerrilla leader in the Sierra Maestra. But the lessons he learned then about the need for constant vigilance and the depths to which his enemies would stoop to destroy him better enabled him to protect himself later on. In these university years he learned that those who dropped their guard for a minute or expended trust unnecessarily did not survive. He took risks, but only those which were the most prudent and carefully calculated.

It was at this time that the only disciplinary entry on his university record was made. He was brought before a faculty committee, accused of having been involved in a fistfight on the steps in front of the university. The charge was dropped.

That fall Fidel again placed himself in the vortex of a political storm. Convinced that Grau must be overthrown, and that he, despite his youth, could be instrumental in toppling the president, Fidel devoted himself unremittingly to that cause. Always in the forefront of the action, he constantly sought the dramatic, the confrontational, and the creation of events in which he would be the star. The flare for leadership that the Jesuits had noted and nurtured grew daily.

In a moment of inspiration, he devised the idea of bringing to Havana from Manzanillo in Oriente Province the historical bell of Demajagua, the ringing of which in 1868 signaled the start of Cuba's war of independence against Spain. In Havana, he envisioned that it would again become the symbol for justice and freedom around which thousands would rally in a massive march on the Presidential Palace, culminating in the demand that President Ramón Grau San Martín step down. It was his first attempt to repeat the "Bastille model."

In fact, Grau himself had earlier sought to obtain the bell to serve as the centerpiece for his administration's official celebration of the anniversary of Cuba's war of independence. On that occasion, he was turned down flat by the mayor, Angel Vázquez González, and the city council. Accompanied by his friend Leonel Soto, a member of the Socialist Youth, Fidel succeeded where the president had failed. Filled with ecstatic anticipation, they boarded a train for Havana with the three-hundred-pound bell and two chaperones from Manzanillo whose job was to protect it.

It was the afternoon of November 3, 1947, when the train pulled into the station in Havana. Fidel's friends and followers were waiting with a large convertible in which he, Soto, and the bell rode in a triumphal procession to the university campus.

The bell was deposited in the rector's office under the guard of the university police as a crescendo of controversy swirled around it. Grau's supporters condemned its proposed use for partisan political purposes, and several dozen armed henchmen of Masferrer and Salabarria showed up threatening violence if the anti-Grau scenario was pursued. Meanwhile Fidel became locked in an all-night negotiating session with other anti-government students about what sort of rally should be staged. Against the moderates he held out for "the most violently antigovernment position—that which wanted to call for Grau's resignation to the ringing of the bell."

But when the doors of the rector's office were finally opened on the morning of the rally, the bell had gone, a theft that could have occurred only with the connivance of the campus police. Fidel, hastily arriving on campus, addressed his followers in outrage, and led them to the local police station, where he reported the theft and accused by name to the police and the press, Manolo Castro, Rolando Masferrer, and Eufemio Fernández, chief of the secret police, as culpable in the crime.

The rally went ahead as planned that night without the bell. Fidel gave perhaps the finest speech yet of his young political career. In his characteristically powerful and emotional style, he castigated Grau for his failure to deliver on any of the idealistic promises he had made when he took office. He criticized the continuing orgy of graft and corruption, and warned of the growing power of the military. The speech was important not just for its stirring tones that enthralled the crowd, but because it was a skillful and sophisticated analysis of the political shortcomings of the Grau regime and of the broader problems then facing Cuban society. It reflected in particular the continuing maturation of Fidel's political thinking.

A few days after the rally, the bell was quietly turned over to President Grau by those who had absconded with it, and it was subsequently returned to Manzanillo.

During this same hectic period, there were almost weekly events in which Fidel was an outspoken and visible leader. Jesús Menéndez was a black Communist trade-union leader, secretary-general of the sugar workers union, and a congressman with a reputation for incorruptibility. When the government decided to remove the elected union leaders such as Menéndez and replace them with appointed officials who would be more compliant with the government's wishes, Fidel took strong exception and rallied behind him. When attempts were made to take Menéndez into military custody, he invoked his congressional immunity, but as he walked away from Captain Casillas Lumpuy, who had tried to arrest him, the latter shot Menéndez in the back with his .45 pistol. The body was brought to Havana to lie in state, and tens of thousands came to pay tribute. The funeral procession was one of the largest ever seen in Cuba. Fidel was enraged by the killing, yet again he saw how the event had mobilized an otherwise apathetic population to action.

Becoming increasingly skilled as a mobilizer of mass emotion, Fidel organized a demonstration on February 12, 1948, against police brutality, which turned into a pillaging rampage. The police drove the students back toward the sanctuary of the campus, but as they escaped up the Escalinata steps, the police chief, Major Carames, caught and beat a student. The next day, Fidel organized another demonstration to protest the violation of the university's autonomy, stressing nonviolence. Although ostensibly nonviolent, students armed with pistols and other weapons left over from the abortive Dominican invasion of the summer waited in the buildings flanking the Escalinata. The student column was led by Fidel and another student carrying a Cuban flag. Singing the national anthem and shouting "Out with Carames. Down with Grau," they approached a police barricade on San Lazaro Street several blocks from the campus. Suddenly the police charged with swinging clubs and broke up the demonstration. Fidel suffered a hairline fracture of the skull. It was the only time in his political career that he was injured.

It was perhaps inevitable that this escalating ferment should reach some sort of climax. It did so for Fidel on February 22 with the murder of Manolo Castro. Manolo Castro had gone from student leader to national sports director, and had become increasingly enmeshed in the violence and corruption of the Grau administration. At the same time, he had progressively alienated many of his old friends and allies, particularly those on the left. On that evening, as he came out of the Cinecito, a movie theater of which he was part owner, he was shot down on the street. A UIR member was captured a few blocks away with a recently discharged pistol. Next morning in the report of the assassination the newspapers described the captured man as a member of a university group "captained by Fidel Castro." Although Fidel had for all practical purposes terminated his connections with the UIR the previous summer, the reputation lingered, especially with those who sought to discredit him.

The word was out on the street that the police were looking for Fidel.

In addition, Rolando Masferrer charged Fidel with complicity in Manolo's death, a statement tantamount to putting out a contract on him. There is no evidence that Fidel was involved in the murder, but it clearly provided an opportunity for all of his enemies to eliminate him as a troublemaker and an irritant on the political scene. Confronting the crisis, Fidel and two other individuals also implicated by rumor presented themselves at the third precinct police station three days after the murder, even though no warrants had been issued for their arrests. Fidel made a statement in which he described how on the night in question he had gone to the El Dorado café with two friends, and had then spent the night at the Hotel Plaza. The police released all three of them on "provisional liberty."

Helped by his friends Alfredo Guevara and Mario Ichaustegui, who gave him a list of safe houses, and his sister Lidia, Fidel went into semi-hiding, fearing, doubtless correctly, that his very survival was at stake. An unexpected opportunity to leave the country may well have saved his life.

Argentinian President Juan Domingo Perón was in the process of forming various Latin American organizations that were nationalistic and anti-imperialist. In the past, several Latin American student associations had been formed and dissolved. Perón was willing to help sponsor a new student congress for which a preparatory meeting was to be held in Bogotá, Colombia, followed in the autumn by the congress itself. The planning session would precede, but overlap, the Ninth Inter-American Conference, which had as a primary objective the creation of the Organization of American States, originally intended as a vehicle to strengthen United States influence in the hemisphere in response to the growing anti-Communist hysteria. Perón sent Diego Luis Molinary, chairman of the foreign relations committee of the Argentine Senate, to Cuba. Together with a local representative, Cesar J. Tronconi, he sought support for the planned student congress. They lavishly entertained students at the Hotel Nacional, initially with only modest success because there was considerable ambivalence toward Perón as a result of his suppression of human rights, particularly aimed at leftist student groups. However, the opportunity of a trip abroad proved irresistible to several of the student leaders, including Fidel. Among themselves they rationalized that they could turn the congress into a podium for an attack on the United States and imperialism. More important for Fidel, it provided a face-saving way of extricating himself from his personal problems without it looking as though he was a coward and fleeing. His sister Lidia sold her refrigerator to help pay for the trip.

On March 19, when Fidel went to Rancho Boyeros airport to board a plane for Caracas, he was taken into custody and charged with attempting to violate the terms of his "provisional liberty." He was brought before a judge to whom he claimed that he was going on a special mission to strengthen the ties of friendship with other Latin American students. He also let it be known that there were people in Havana intending to kill him. The next day Fidel's passport and other documents were returned, enabling him to travel. However, when the plane made a brief stop in the Dominican Republic, an alert immigration official, after looking at his passport said, "Aren't you the Castro who is in trouble in Havana?" to which Fidel replied, "Yes, but I am not anymore." He was allowed to proceed.

Fidel was accompanied by a Cuban-American student, Rafael del Pino. They stopped first in Panama to meet with student leaders there in the hope of recruiting their support for the congress. Fidel was surprised by the political sophistication of these students, who were locked in the struggle over Panama's rights to the canal. He says, "I was amazed by the strong anti-imperialist sentiment expressed at the university center, politically so far ahead of our own. We got their support for the congress." This support was in large part due to a fighting anti-imperialist speech that he made to the students.

Fidel was also deeply affected by visiting the Canal Zone and seeing the endless succession of bars, brothels, and nightclubs catering to United States servicemen. He was offended, in part because of a deeply puritan- ical streak attributable in no small degree to his Jesuit background.

Their second stop was Caracas, where they tried to meet with Vene- zuela's recently installed Social Democratic president, Rómulo Gallegos. They went to his house and managed to talk to members of his family, who called the president in his office and arranged an appointment for the next day. Unfortunately, Fidel had to catch his plane and was forced to cancel the meeting.

On April 1, 1948, Fidel and del Pino arrived in the Colombian capital. They began right away to meet with student delegates, most of whom were followers of Jorge Eliécer Gaitán, the charismatic and immensely popular leader of the Liberal Party. The idea of the congress was received enthusiastically, and several planning meetings were held under Fidel's chairmanship. They prepared an agenda for the congress, including Puerto Rican independence, the future of the Panama Canal, the struggle against military dictatorships, and the organizational structure of the Latin Amer- ican student federation. Students continued to arrive, including Fidel's friend Alfredo Guevara, and Enrique Ovares, president of the Cuban FEU. Ovares, being senior to Fidel in the Cuban delegation, took his prerogative in taking over the chairmanship of the planning committee from Fidel. Fidel argued vehemently against this, contending that his knowledge and expertise on the topics under discussion far exceeded that of Ovares (almost certainly true). He added that it was important to his own political career to keep the chairmanship. By Fidel's own account, he won and continued to preside. Other accounts, probably more accurate, recall that Ovares prevailed.

The Ninth Inter-American Conference opened on April 3 at a formal ceremony in the Teatro Colon. As the foreign dignitaries, Colombian officials, members of Bogotá society, and the press listened to the dignified speakers, thousands of pamphlets attacking U.S. imperialism suddenly rained down from the balconies. Many of the pamphlets had been printed in Havana, and among the students flinging them onto the heads of the startled delegates were Fidel and del Pino. They were ordered to report to police headquarters three days later, on April 6, where they were told to cease their disruptive activities. While at the police station, their hotel room was searched and additional "Communist" pamphlets were seized.

The Colombian students had suggested at one point that they might be able to persuade Gaitán to be the opening speaker for their congress. They arranged a meeting with him for April 7 to deliver an official invitation.

There were striking parallels between Gaitán and Fidel's hero Eddy Chibás. Both were incorruptible populists who had galvanized a powerful opposition movement against reactionary conservative governments controlled by the oligarchy to serve its own interests. Both also had a large and loyal student following. At the meeting, Gaitán's sincere commitment to legal and social reform impressed Fidel. Gaitán asked the students to come back two days later on April 9 at 2:00 P.M.

On April 9 at 1:20 P.M., Gaitán was murdered by a deranged individual, Juan Roa Sierra, whose motives were not overtly political, but merely pique because Gaitán would not receive him. He was soon lynched by an infuriated mob.

At the time Fidel and del Pino were walking toward the Hotel Granada for their appointed meeting, they saw people running in their direction screaming hysterically, "Gaitán has been murdered!" The event threw the city into a convulsion of fury and violence, unleashing pent-up feelings of rage and fear that Gaitán in life had been able to channel and modulate, but that now, without leadership, were turned loose against any target the mob could find. There has been considerable speculation about exactly what role Fidel played in the subsequent riots, with considerable misinformation disseminated, much of it years later, in an attempt to discredit him. His own account, given to Carlos Franqui, is probably as accurate a chronicling of his actions during those three days as history will get, and while clearly self-serving, it is not substantially repudiated by any of the more objective accounts.

I walked down a street to the park in front of the capitol building where the foreign ministers' conference was in session. A cordon of police in blue uniforms with fixed bayonets had been guarding the building, but the crowd in the park was now converging on it, smashing the cordon and entering the building, which must have seemed to the people a symbol of the power they hated.

I was in the middle of the park, where I could see what was happening. People were wrecking street lights; rocks flew in all directions. Glass store fronts were shattering, and it was impossible to tell what would happen next, but a popular uprising was obviously underway.

I knew nothing about uprisings of this kind, except what had been engraved on my memory by accounts I had read about the taking of the Bastille and the alarm bells of the revolutionary committees in Paris, rallying the people in the first glorious days of the French Revolution. But no one was in command here.

Fidel joined a crowd heading for a police station in a search for arms. Originally all he could obtain was a tear gas gun and several cartridge belts of ammunition, a military cape, a cap, and some boots. Subsequently a police officer sympathetic to the rioters and amused at the sight of this earnest young man struggling with his inappropriate gear gave him a gun and sixteen rounds of ammunition. Then Fidel moved on with the surging crowd armed with guns, machetes, and iron bars toward the Presidential Palace. They encountered shooting and the crowd briefly drew back, but then surged again.

When I tried to find out what was going on, somebody told me that the crowd had been fired on from the Catholic university and there had been an exchange of gun fire. I must admit that I did not believe it then, having spent so many years in Catholic schools; I could not imagine priests shooting at the people. As I stood there looking on someone pulled me roughly toward a wall. Days later, after all I had seen, I decided that there were clergymen reactionary enough to fire at the people without qualm.

Students were haranguing the crowd and had placed the bodies of their dead comrades on the tops of cars for everyone to see. A rumor was spreading in the crowd that a dissident army unit had seized the radio station, and Fidel joined some students he recognized heading in that direction. But when they reached the Ministry of War building they encountered a tank and a column of soldiers. The students hid behind benches until they passed. At that point the army was uncertain with which side to align, and different units were with the government and the rioters. A few minutes later, a second group of soldiers started shooting at the

49

students, and they escaped only by jumping on an empty bus and driving away. They drove to the university campus, where agitated students were milling around without arms or leadership. Dodging sporadic machine gun fire as they went, they left for a rumored assault on a police post, only to find it already captured.

> That's where I first saw anyone making an attempt to get people organized and lead the action. A police chief had come into the station and was trying to see how the revolutionary forces—made up of ordinary civilians and policemen—that had taken over the police station could be utilized. I had a quick talk with him about how to start organizing and offered to help. He accepted readily, and we went in his jeep to the Liberal Party's headquarters in the center of Bogotá.

Fidel and his fellow students became separated and toward nightfall he ended up at Police Post #11, where again he hoped to find some semblance of central command. There were several hundred men there and they were being organized into what approximated a military force. Fidel, however, felt obliged to seek out the apparent leader, and explaining that he was from Cuba and knowledgeable about the revolutionary history there, he advised that trying to defend a fixed position against superior forces from the army was inviting defeat. One can imagine the reaction of the chief to this aggressive and opinionated young foreigner. According to Fidel, his suggestions were received courteously, but not acted on.

During the night, Fidel was attracted by screams from a police officer who had remained loyal to the regime but was now being tortured at the hands of his colleagues who had gone over to the rebels. Fidel was revolted by the unnecessary inhumanity and claims to have interceded on the man's behalf. It did nothing, however, to allay his fears about his own future as repeated rumors came in that the army was about to attack them in force. He asked himself what he owed to the Colombian people other than some shared ideas, and gave serious thought to making a run for it. He told Franqui that he said to himself, "Okay, the people here are just like those in Cuba or anywhere else; they are the victims of crimes, abuses, injustices; and these people are absolutely in the right, so I will stay." Actually, it was largely a rationalization because he had nowhere to run to that was not likely to be at least as dangerous.

In the morning, he did convince the commander to let him take out a patrol and establish a defensive perimeter. He looked down on the city and saw that much of it was in flames. Looting was occurring all around.

After another nervous and sleepless night, Fidel decided to take his chances and he headed back to his hotel. He found it filled with conservative supporters of the oligarchy. He slipped out and headed for a boarding house where some of the other students had been staying. The landlord, a government supporter, accused him of being involved with the instigators of the riot and would not let him stay there. It was now 5:45 P.M., fifteen minutes before a shoot-to-kill curfew was to go into effect. Fidel was in extreme danger. Suddenly he encountered an Argentine friend from the congress driving a car with diplomatic plates. He was petrified to see Fidel and told him the word was out that the entire insurrection was the work of "Cubans, Communists, and other foreign agents." He berated Fidel for getting into such a mess, but agreed to drive him to the Cuban Embassy.

Fidel says, "I remember quite well the president of the Cuban delegation [actually the consul in the Embassy] to the conference; he was a friendly man, very considerate about our plight. . . . Strangely enough, the last name of the Cuban consul, in whose home we slept, was Tabernilla. He and his wife were very kind to us." Tabernilla's brother was a ruthless military commander who was to become the Batista army's chief of staff, and one of Fidel's bitterest antagonists.

On April 13, arrangements were made to fly Fidel and the other Cuban students back to Havana in a plane that had come over to pick up some bulls for a unique exhibition bullfight in Cuba.

Fidel says of the experience in Bogotá, where more than thirty-six hundred died, as he has said about so many events in his life: "It's incredible, truly incredible, that we weren't all killed." He was still vulnerable to the arguments of the pragmatic liberals like Gaitán and Chibás who believed that through espousing programs of honesty, integrity, and social justice they could mobilize a tidal wave of public support and ride to power against the oligarchy through legitimate democratic means. The death of Gaitán (although seemingly nonpolitical), was one more step in convincing Fidel that such men, no matter how fine or popular, had little chance of prevailing against an entrenched corrupt oligarchy that cared little for democracy.

Once the rioting broke out, Fidel was constitutionally incapable of remaining uninvolved. The excitement alone was beyond his power to resist, and the opportunity to be at the center of the action and even play some leadership role that might be of historical consequence was one he could not pass up. Communists were widely blamed by the Colombian and United States governments for the riots, yet there is no evidence that they were the prime instigators. They were, however, happy to bask in the undeserved credit they were given. Certainly for Fidel it was the action, not the ideology, that impelled his participation.

Perhaps the most profound educational aspect of the whole experience in Bogotá for Fidel was new awareness of the raw high voltage the street

51

mobs represented. As a born leader, he was immediately struck both by the absence of leadership in directing the mass of people and by the magnitude of the force that had been unleashed. He realized that strong, decisive leadership at the start would have swept the revolutionary forces to power in a matter of hours. Again he had been reminded of the French Revolution and the storming of the Bastille. It was a lesson not lost on him.

Chapter Three

FIDEL'S experience with the Cayo Confites expedition, and especially the events in Bogotá, were decisive turning points in his political development. From the moment he returned to Havana in mid-April 1948, Fidel abandoned his earlier fascination with campus politics and turned his entire attention instead to the national scene.

Elections were scheduled for June 1, 1948, and the race for president was already heating up when Fidel arrived back in the city. Eddy Chibás, rotund and gregarious, was running as the Ortodoxo Party candidate against Carlos Prío Socarrás, the minister of labor and prime minister in the Grau administration, on the Auténtico ticket. Fidel, an increasingly active member of the Ortodoxos Youth, revered Chibás, and saw him as embodying all of his own ideals. He threw himself wholeheartedly into his friend's campaign. Had Chibás been elected, Fidel's life and career might have taken a very different course.

Fidel, like most of his fellow countrymen, had a fundamental distrust of the national electoral process, mainly because in his experience, elections in Cuba were invariably corrupt and rigged, and seemed inevitably to return to power individuals with little commitment to the Cuban people. As a child he had witnessed the payoffs with which his father was involved to fix elections. He was doubtful that a person of the integrity of Chibás would ever be allowed to win the presidency in a fair election. Besides, the ultimate power was not in the hands of the elected president and the government; it remained with the military. And above it all loomed the United States, which exerted considerable control, not by direct interference, but by creating in the minds of many Cubans the belief that the country could not afford to elect a leader who did not enjoy Washington's blessing.

In the view of many young Cubans, a fundamental change was required if the populace was ever to regain faith in its government. Fidel was part of a small group with this aim that organized within the Ortodoxos Youth a splinter faction, Acción Radical Ortodoxos (ARO), committed to the

53

overall objectives of the party but with a more extreme liberal utopian philosophy combining nationalism, socialism, and capitalism. They attracted a following of the younger, more idealistic, members of the party.

These differences, which after all were between a seasoned politician running for the highest office in the land and a group of young, mostly student, admirers, did not affect Fidel's willingness to help Chibás's campaign. As an increasingly recognized student leader, Fidel joined the campaign entourage, traveling the country with Chibás and occasionally preceding him as a speaker on the platform. During the early summer of 1948, he learned important skills from his mentor. Chibás had charisma, and he knew how to exploit it to mobilize a mass movement. He also knew how to use symbols to concentrate his message; he used a broom to signify the sweeping away of evil, and slogans that would be on everyone's lips, one of which was *"Vergüenza contra dinero"* ("Dignity against money"). He particularly understood the importance of radio and how to use it effectively. He had a program every Sunday on station CMQ and maintained that radio broadcasts were as powerful as military weapons. That fall, Fidel himself began appearing with a friend and student UIR member, Justo Fuentes, on a regular radio program in which students addressed the people. Fidel's later brilliant use of television as a medium can be traced directly to the lessons he learned from Chibás.

Chibás lost the election to Prío Socarrás, partly because he lacked United States backing, but more importantly because he had been unable to put together the grass-roots structure necessary for victory. It was a lesson not lost on Fidel.

Fidel's absence in Colombia had helped to cool tempers inflamed by Manolo Castro's death. He was, however, by no means out of trouble with his old enemies. The senseless killing that plagued the Havana University campus continued, and on June 6, 1948, Oscar Fernández Caral, a campus police sergeant, was slain. Before he died, he allegedly identified Fidel as the person who had shot him. A witness supported the accusation. Fidel, again forced into hiding, claimed that it was a plot by his enemies. Subsequently the witness recanted, saying that he had been coerced by the police, and Fidel's name was dropped from the list of the accused.

Shortly after the university's fall term began, the Council of Ministers of the Grau administration, as one of its last acts, authorized an increase in bus fares, touching off a violent citywide reaction. Fidel and Justo Fuentes led a mob of angry students who hijacked and burned several buses. For a while it appeared that they might trigger a Cuban version of the recent events in Bogotá, but the Council rescinded the order and tranquility was restored.

His Jesuit education had kept Fidel cloistered as far as women were concerned until he arrived at the university. But even then his political preoccupations left little time for a normal social life. He had had a brief relationship in his freshman year with a young woman at the Colegio Immaculada. In early 1948, he was dating two sisters who lived near the university, when he met Mirta Díaz Balart, the sister of fellow law student Rafael Díaz Balart, with whom he and Baudilio Castellanos had earlier edited a mimeographed publication, *Saeta* (Arrows). Fidel was intensely attracted to the petite dark-eyed philosophy student, and for once allowed something to interrupt his frenetic political activities. Mirta came from an established and moderately wealthy family in Oriente Province that strongly opposed the relationship.

Fidel married the twenty-two-year-old Mirta on October 12, 1948, two days after President Prío was sworn into office. The ceremony took place in a Roman Catholic Church in the town of Banes, from which her family came. Fidel's father was delighted with the marriage, and paid handsomely for a lavish wedding celebration.

The newlyweds left for a three-month honeymoon in the United States, also financed by Angel. But after a brief time in Miami they ran out of money, and Fidel had to pawn his watch and other valuables until his father cabled him additional funds. They went on to New York, where they stayed with Mirta's brother Rafael and his wife in an apartment at 155 West Eighty-second Street. Rafael was doing a brief stint as a lay worker for the Presbyterian Church among low-income Hispanic families. They stayed for two weeks, during which time Fidel rented a large white convertible in which he and his bride drove around the city. Fidel says that while in New York he gave serious thought to enrolling at Columbia University. According to the writer Lionel Martin, during this trip Fidel bought a copy of Marx's *Das Kapital*.

Fidel's marriage was by all accounts the result of an intense love relationship, unmotivated by any other considerations. It was, however, a step toward conventionality.

Back in Havana, they moved into an apartment at Third Street and Second Avenue in the Vedado district, across the street from the Riviera Hotel today. On September 14, 1949, their only child, Fidel, was born.

Despite his heavy involvement in politics, Fidel had studied hard from the first day he arrived on campus. He passed all his exams with little difficulty, and his university record is filled with *sobresaliente* (excellent), the equivalent of an "A," or a score of between 90 and 100 on his final exams. However, because he had missed so much time in Bogotá, during the Chibás campaign, and during his honeymoon he had fallen behind the rest of his class. To graduate with them he had to enroll as an "irregular student," taking the courses he had missed as well as those for the current year. This meant devoting significant extra time to studying. However, despite the extra course load his grades for his last two years include an even higher percentage of *sobresalientes*.

Enrolling as an irregular student meant also that he was no longer a member of a specific class. This precluded him, whether he wanted it or not, from seeking any student political office.

Studying was not easy. In January 1949, the conflict over the bus fares flared up again. When the company again proceeded to raise the fares, students began hijacking buses and driving them onto the campus, still off-limits to the city police. In this instance the students enjoyed the support of the usually cautious leaders of the Communist Party. Fidel, as usual at the center of the protest, joined in decorating eight captured buses with student government and Cuban national banners. They then threatened to take extreme action against the police if they violated the sanctity of the campus to retrieve them. When night came Fidel went home to study for an exam. In the morning a breathless worker from the Communist Party came to tell him that the buses were gone and that there was a rumor that the bus company had paid off some of the students to get their vehicles back. "Unless you want people to think you were in on the deal, you better get your ass over there," he said. Fidel angrily threw down the book he was reading, and raced to the campus. There, at an angry meeting, he accused even his friend Justo Fuentes of selling out. At least his own sense of integrity was saved. But the bus fares remained raised.

Fidel had frequent dealings with the Communists during this period. Several of his close friends were party members and he regularly talked with party officials. What kept Fidel from becoming a member, according to Carlos Rafael Rodríguez, at the time a party official and today Cuba's vice president, was "sectarianism," which he defines as "very narrow and dogmatic approaches or conceptions. . . . Fidel saw no flexibility in our positions." Later, Fidel, only half jokingly, would say, "I would have joined the party, if I could have been Stalin." The rigid party discipline and hierarchy were unattractive to him, but if he could have come in at the top—as ultimately he did—it would have been a different matter. The People's Socialist Party (Communist Party) had its greatest strength among the labor unions during this period, but had relatively few members and little influence at the university where the attitude, while radically reformist, was also predominantly anti-Communist. Several of Fidel's friends who were members of the Socialist Youth tried at this time to get him to join, but he declined on the grounds that he was too thoroughly committed to the Ortodoxos Youth.

Importantly, Fidel never publicly criticized the Communist Party, perhaps in part because of his close friends who were members, but also because one of the fundamental political strategies he was developing was alliance-building. He assiduously avoided antagonizing any group that shared his general objectives. Chibás, on the other hand, eager to take advantage of the anti-Communist sentiment to win votes, attacked them relentlessly.

In March, two months after the bus incident, a group of United States Marines, on leave and apparently drunk, climbed up on the statue of José Martí, and one of them urinated on it. To Cubans, this was an unspeakable insult to their country. The offenders were rescued from the angry crowd and taken to a local police station, but a jeering crowd yelling angry anti-U.S. slogans gathered outside. When news of the event reached the campus, Fidel organized an honor guard to flank the statue all night, and called for a protest demonstration at the U.S. Embassy in the morning. The demonstration was a boisterous affair in which rocks were thrown at the building, and a demand was made that the Marines be turned over to Cuban authorities. Eventually the demonstration was broken up by club-swinging police led by Fidel's nemesis Colonel Carames.

The incident was resolved after U.S. Ambassador Robert Butler met with the Cuban foreign minister and provided him with a statement of apology. Afterward he laid a wreath, bought by and provided to him by the Cuban Foreign Ministry, at the statue of Martí. In film withheld at the time but released after the revolution, it was discovered that when Butler first filmed his apology he could not remember Martí's name.

Fidel had been up all night and had been involved in intensive activity most of the time. That afternoon he went as scheduled to a meeting of the University Committee to Fight Racial Discrimination, of which he was an executive-board member. Although one participant in the meeting recalls that his eyes were bloodshot, it was an early public demonstration (to be frequently repeated) of his powers of physical endurance and capacity for sleep deprivation, abilities that were to become legendary.

In the summer of 1950, Fidel graduated with a Doctor of Laws. He submitted a thesis entitled, "The Letter of Exchange in Private International Law and its Comparative Legislation." He had all of the attributes necessary to become a wealthy and successful lawyer; he was brilliant, widely known, and socially well connected. Yet money and social acceptance were now inadequate rewards for him. Politics dominated his thinking, and had become his only real source of gratification.

With two of his classmates, Fidel founded a law firm, Azpiazu, Castro and Resende, with offices at Tejadillo 57 in the old section of Havana, near the docks. Most of his clients were poor or represented a political cause with which Fidel indentified. They included the vegetable vendors in the Havana market, an association of coal workers, students, and a carpenter who paid him by making furniture for the office. He saw the practice of law as a way of trying to make a living while he pursued his primary interests with Chibás and the Ortodoxos Youth. Money was always short despite the wealth of both his own family and his in-laws, who had shown their displeasure with the marriage by letting their daughter live in relative penury. They were constantly in debt to the grocer or the butcher, and periodically the power company cut off the lights. It was only the occasional remittance from Angel that enabled him, Mirta, and baby Fidelito to survive.

Rolando Amador recalls visiting the couple on one occasion when the baby kept crying. Mirta gave Fidelito a bottle, but Fidel angrily pulled it away and threw it to the floor, saying that his son needed to grow up tough, not gratified every time he demanded it.

With a desire to broaden his education beyond the law, Fidel enrolled in several courses at the university that might eventually lead him to three additional diplomas, including a doctorate in social sciences. Among the courses he signed up for were Greek and Roman history, economics, and French. Ultimately, however, politics consumed him and he never sat for the exams in any of these subjects.

He began an association with the paper *Alerta*. The editor, Ramón Vasconcelos, was a man of oscillating loyalties who at that point was an admirer of Fidel. He published Fidel's writings, usually in the form of reports on his statements before the courts, and gave prominent coverage to his activities when other papers ignored them.

Early in 1951, *Alerta* published Fidel's statement before a government tribunal exposing the abuses of the owner of a fruit canning factory who had fired dozens of employees in order to replace them with cheaper labor, and condemning the failure of the Labor Ministry to take any action on their behalf. He further attacked a major landowner for arbitrarily seizing the land of small farmers. On another occasion they reported a speech he made at the university championing the cause of Puerto Rican independence at the time an armed attack was made on Blair House and the House of Representatives by Puerto Rican nationalists. During this same period, when the Korean conflict was underway and Cold War sentiment was at its most intense, he lent his name to the Cuban Youth Committee for Peace, a local support effort on behalf of the Stockholm Peace Appeal organized by Lord Bertrand Russell and other intellectuals. In the United States, the organization and Russell's role were viewed as patently pro-Communist. The reaction was less dogmatic in Cuba.

Fidel's first political priority, however, remained his relationship with Eddy Chibás. Chibás was continuing his relentless attacks on corruption as he prepared a base for another run for the presidency·in 1952, a race in which he was emerging as the front-runner. The Auténticos had not yet chosen a candidate and it was uncertain whether Batista would run. Chibás had attracted considerable attention by not merely attacking corruption in general, but by singling out specific individuals and exposing to the public their wrongdoing. Late in July 1951, Chibás, apparently set up with misinformation that had been fed to him, accused Minister of Education Aureliano Sánchez Arango on the Senate floor and in his weekly radio broadcast of embezzling funds from the education budget to purchase real estate in Guatemala and elsewhere in Central America. Sánchez Arango challenged Chibás to provide proof. He was able to show evidence that funds had been misappropriated, but not that the purchases had been made in Guatemala. Seeing a political opening, the Auténtico leaders swung into an all-out attempt to discredit Chibás and undermine his lead in the presidential race. They accused him of lying to the Cuban people, a charge that devastated Chibás, who above all prided himself on his integrity. People laughed at him and made fun of his self-righteous morality that now seemed off base.

Depressed and shaken by the setback, he went with Fidel and others at his side to radio station CMQ on the afternoon of Sunday, August 5. On the air he stated that although he had no proof, the charges he had made were true. Then after reviewing his political career and exhorting the Cuban people to wake up to the corruption in their midst, he pulled a .38-caliber pistol from his belt and shot himself in the abdomen. Supporters believed that as a man of unimpeachable integrity he could not stand the humiliation of having his credibility called into question, and that in this last desperate act he sought at least to restore his public honor. Cynics pointed out that in 1946 he had shot himself and then gone on to win an election as a senator, and claimed that he was merely trying to resecure the allegiance of the electorate that would guarantee him the presidency.

Chibás was rushed to the hospital as Fidel remained at his side. The injury was not severe, but Chibás developed a massive infection and died. Fidel maintained a constant vigil.

Following his death on August 16, an argument ensued as to whether the body should lie in state at the capitol building, the Ortodoxo Party headquarters, or the university where Chibás had started his political career. Fidel vociferously argued for the university. The capitol too closely symbolized the very corruption against which Chibás had fought, and the party headquarters were too small to accommodate the large crowd expected. Besides, argued Fidel, in selecting the campus where the national police by tradition could not set foot, they would keep control over the way people were allowed to pay their respects. Fidel's point of view, forcefully argued and shared by most of Chibás's younger followers, prevailed. When the corrupt politicians whom Chibás had opposed came to fulfill the niceties of political protocol by filing past the coffin, they were hurried on their way and the flowers and wreaths they left were taken out and burned. In the funeral cortège, Fidel was a member of the guard of honor.

Harking back to his seminal experience with the funeral of the high school student Carlos Martínez, he made an unsuccessful plea to the leaders of the party that they march on the Presidential Palace and demand Prío's resignation. Subsequently, however, at the home of Chibás's successor, Roberto Agramonte, Fidel made a moving speech about the legacy of the man and the ideals he had left. He warned that those ideals, which were without question his guiding philosophy at that point, must not be betrayed.

The death of the ebullient and crusading Chibás significantly affected Fidel in two ways. First, he felt that the mantle of Chibás as the untiring exposer of corruption had now fallen on his own shoulders, and that the most significant way he could honor his hero's memory was to carry on that struggle. It was also inevitable that whoever was seen as the inheritor of Chibás's role would have a chance to capture a portion of his political following. Despite his youth and relative obscurity in the eyes of the general public, Fidel was eager to grab that chance. Second, and perhaps more important, the death of Chibás created a sympathetic backlash that gave tremendous momentum to the Ortodoxos cause and a belief among the Cuban people that perhaps the ballot box could be used to rid the country of corrupt politicians. Anticipating an Ortodoxos victory, Fidel decided to run as a candidate for the House of Representatives. It was not a position of great power or significance; nevertheless, he was desperately seeking at that point any opportunity to advance his political career.

In later years, he was to argue that his intent if elected was to use his position inside the government to promote his revolutionary agenda. However, from the overall pattern of his activities during 1950 and 1951, it appears that he was also pursuing the option of a more conventional career through the elective process. One has only his word as to what he would have done had he been elected. The immensity of his outrage when Batista's coup prevented the elections must be seen in part as a reflection of his anger at being thwarted, and of the degree of emotional investment he had in winning the congressional race. His outright advocacy of armed revolution as the sole course for Cuba occurred only after the elective route to political advancement had been closed to him.

Within a few months of Chibás's death, Fidel picked up on his legacy and launched a blistering attack on the Prío administration. He learned from Chibás's mistake that every accusation must be meticulously substantiated. His aim was to expose a scandal of such magnitude that it would shake the government to its foundations. He began a systematic investigation of Prío's finances that continued throughout the second half of 1951. He discovered that a dummy corporation set up by Prío had acquired a 166-acre farm near the tobacco center of Santiago de las Vegas, close to Havana. By various means, the property had been expanded to more than 2,000 acres during Prío's three years in office, and other farms in the area had been bought by the same corporation. Workers were employed on the farm in slavelike conditions, working ten hours a day for a pittance. In addition, directly violating the law, army personnel were observed working on the property, and were photographed by Fidel's friends.

Fidel further unearthed the fact that four years before he became president Prío represented, as a lawyer, a wealthy man who had been accused of raping a nine-year-old girl. Convicted, the man had been sentenced to six years' imprisonment and ordered to pay the girl's family $10,000. However, once he assumed the presidency, Prío had pardoned him on condition that he turn over a farm he owned, and then he appointed him presidential civil secretary.

Armed with this damning evidence, Fidel sought time on the Sunday radio program of the Ortodoxo Party, which had been Chibás's podium. But the party leaders, leery of his volatile style and eager not to do anything to promote his political popularity, refused him. They rightly viewed as a threat this charismatic young maverick who had so frequently showed contempt for their traditional liberal views. Undeterred, Fidel raised enough money from his supporters to buy time on Radio Alvarez and, during the first three months of 1952, told his story. Vasconcelos, eager to publish anything that might sell a few more papers, made the story a banner headline on the front page of *Alerta*. Fidel kept the issue alive after the initial publicity by filing suit against the president for violating the labor laws, using military personnel as farm laborers, and abusing the right of presidential pardon.

Fidel gained further public exposure by serving as the lawyer for the prosecution against Major Rafael Casals Fernández and Lieutenant Rafael Salas Cañizares, two policemen accused of murdering a worker involved in an antigovernment demonstration. There was considerable public interest in the case, and Fidel won high regard for the skillful and tenacious way in which he achieved a guilty verdict.

Despite his admiration for Chibás and his growing public visibility in

61

exposing the wrongdoing of the Prío administration, Fidel's decision to run for Congress was not received with much enthusiasm among the leaders of the Ortodoxo Party. Although reform-oriented and committed in the Chibás tradition to eliminating corruption, these men, mostly liberals from the upper and middle classes, were still cautious, traditional politicians. They looked on Fidel as a loose cannon. He was a firebrand filled with righteous indignation, but undisciplined and unschooled in the traditional courtesies of Cuban politics. He treated them with little respect, and did not hesitate when he felt justified to criticize them publicly, especially those who were wealthy. They viewed his advocacy of radical social and political change as a sign of immaturity, and considered his still well-remembered association with the UIR, as well as the accusation (even though never substantiated) of his involvement in at least two violent deaths, as justification for dismissing him as an irresponsible "gangster."

In February 1952, party leader Roberto Agramonte issued an approved list of candidates who would have his personal support in the June election. Fidel's name was not on the list. He went with a group of friends to the home of Manuel Bisbé, Ortodoxo Party president in Havana Province, and announced that he was nevertheless planning to contest one of the congressional seats in his jurisdiction.

Fidel launched an energetic, populist, grass-roots campaign. He had the addresses of eighty thousand party members in Havana Province, and to each of them he mailed his campaign material. His friends helped him stuff the envelopes, and he used the party's parliamentary franking stamp. "I had no right to do it," he says, "but there was no other way." He spoke at dozens of clubs and meetings around Havana, often at several in one night. His base was the Party club in the Cayo Hueso district, a run-down area of slums and warehouses. To his blue-collar audiences his speeches were immensely popular for their irreverent and fearless attacks on Prío, corruption, and even the leaders of his own party. Already a fine orator and performer, this campaign enabled him to hone those skills. The death of Chibás had left a palpable vacuum at the local level that the new Ortodoxo leaders, idealistic but uninspiring, aloof and removed from the concerns of the average citizens, could not fill. By contrast, Fidel reveled in the brash, sweaty, backslapping environment of the local party clubs in the poorest barrios. Easily identifying with these impoverished voters, Fidel built in a few short weeks a sizable and dedicated following.

Fidel's father was enthusiastic about the campaign, and gave his son some financial backing.

February 1952 was a busy month for Fidel. Not only had he launched his congressional campaign, but he brought to a climax his months-long investigation of the Prío administration with even more dramatic revelations than in his earlier exposé. On February 19, he went on the radio to announce that he would soon offer detailed proof of the connection between Prío and various gangster groups. It was a clever use of the media; he titillated public interest and created a degree of anticipation that guaranteed that the actual revelations would get maximum attention. They came in the form of charges he filed against Prío in the fiscal watchdog court. Again *Alerta* gave the story big play, running Fidel's picture and reprinting the brief he filed in its entirety.

Perhaps as a way of purging his conscience for his past association with the UIR, Fidel reviewed the history of the revolutionary action groups and their degeneration over the years into violent, corrupt gangs that were the antithesis of their original intent. He traced their mutual co-optation by corrupt politicians, including two successive presidents, Grau and Prío. He then detailed the number of phony government jobs allocated to each gang, the exact monthly payments to each gang leader, the ministries that made the payments, and the individuals who picked up the paychecks for the nonexistent jobs. Finally he accused the presidential secretary Orlando Puente of handing out each month to the gangs sixty envelopes each containing $300.

Although the circulation of *Alerta* was only thirty thousand, Fidel's exposé won him considerable public attention, and by serving as righteous accuser it also helped to blur in people's minds the gangster image many had of him.

By the beginning of March 1952, with his campaign progressing well, Fidel was justified in having little doubt that he would be swept to victory in the congressional race. The polls also indicated that Ortodoxo Party leader Roberto Agramonte, although a lackluster candidate, would likely become the next president. The graft and corruption of Grau and Prío had left the Auténtico Party with little credibility, and their candidate, Carlos Hevia, lacked stature and electoral appeal. The remaining candidate was Fulgencio Batista, the strongman of Cuban politics since his coup of 1933, who had served as president from 1940 to 1944. No longer content to remain a sinister figure behind other presidents, he now wanted the job again for himself. He ran as the candidate of the Partido Acción Unitaria (PAU), essentially a one-man party.

The Communist Party, Partido Socialista Popular (PSP), had no candidate of its own. It had been its pattern to form pragmatic alliances. In 1940, during World War II, they had joined Batista in an "anti-Fascist" coalition established at the instigation of the United States to show solidarity in the war against Hitler. Now they sought a formal alliance with the Ortodoxos. It had been Chibás's rule that the Ortodoxos would form no alliances with other parties, establishing the "principle of political independence." The anti-Communist hysteria that prevailed in the Americas in the fifties, and particularly fear of United States reaction, further led Agramonte to disavow any public unity with them. Nevertheless, the Communists issued a statement to their supporters encouraging them to vote for Agramonte as president and for their own candidates on the rest of the ticket. As a pragmatic politician concerned about getting the largest number of votes, Fidel maintained his arm's-length relationship with the Communist Party. He neither rejected nor acknowledged their support. Emotions were so strong and irrational during the McCarthy period that virtually every other candidate saw it as to his advantage to condemn the Communists.

His growing sympathy for the Communists doubtless played a part in his silence. More important was his innate political sense of long-range alliance building and his recognition that nothing would be gained by antagonizing such a powerful organization, with whose philosophy he had no particular disagreement.

If the elections had taken place, and if, as expected, Fidel had won, the course of his political career might have been very different. One can only speculate what election to the Congress at the age of twenty-four would have done to his revolutionary fervor. Despite his avowal that he intended to use his election to launch his revolutionary reforms from inside, one wonders whether, had he acquired power through this conventional route, he would have felt quite the same compulsion to remake Cuban society from top to bottom. Perhaps if Cuba had evolved as a more stable democracy Fidel would have eventually emerged as another moderate reformer in the mold of Betancourt or Figueres.

The elections did not take place, because on the morning of March 10, 1952, there was a coup in which Fulgencio Batista seized power. It was a moment of despair for those who thought that through the elections and the idealism of the Ortodoxo Party Cuba was finally going to end fifty years of turmoil and become a tranquil democratic country. No one was more angered than Fidel, who saw his hopes for a political career dashed. The months of effort spent exposing the corruption of the Prío presidency and the time devoted to his electoral campaign were completely wasted. To add insult to injury, one of the two police officers against whom he had worked so hard to get a successful murder conviction, Rafael Salas Cañizares, emerged as a key conspirator in helping Batista seize power, and was rewarded by being made chief of the National Police.

The groundwork for the coup had been laid by junior officers. Then, at 2:40 A.M., Batista had arrived at Campo Colombia, the central military headquarters, where officers loyal to him had seized control. A sizable percentage of the officer corps opposed the coup and were subsequently forced out of the military. From there he telephoned the army chiefs in the other provinces to secure their loyalty. Prío, alerted at dawn, rushed to the Presidential Palace where he met at 7:30 A.M. with a delegation from the Federation of University Students led by Alvaro Barba. Of all the groups outraged by the coup, none felt more strongly than the students. Prío finally escaped in disguise to Matanzas, and then after twenty-four hours took refuge in the Mexican Embassy.

Fidel had been up until 2:00 A.M., and was still asleep when his friend Rene Rodríguez came to his apartment with news of the coup. Fearing arrest Fidel went to the apartment of his sister Lidia, four blocks away, and that night moved to the Hotel Andino in the university district.

Meanwhile, thousands of people representing all of the political parties had gathered on the university campus because it was the only place that was safe from the forces of the coup that had forcibly closed all of the party headquarters. They waited vainly for the arms promised by Prío to arrive, amid an angry crescendo of antimilitary sentiment and vociferous demands that the provisions of the 1940 Constitution guaranteeing democracy be respected.

Fidel, Rene Rodríguez, and another young Ortodoxo Party member, Eva Jiménez, left Havana by bus and went to a farm owned by Eva. There, as a catharsis for his frustration and anger, he composed a manifesto denouncing Batista's actions. It was entitled *Revolucion no: Zarpazo!* (*Zarpazo* is the blow of a wild cat's paw.) No newspaper would publish it so they had it mimeographed and distributed by hand.

Zarpazo was Fidel's description of the coup, refuting Batista's claim that he had led a needed revolution to rid the country of the corruption and gangsterism associated with the Prío regime. The document, Fidel's first real political treatise, was a challenge to Batista in the strongest terms. It was also filled with romanticism, and ended by quoting from the Cuban national anthem, "To live in chains is to live in shame." The blend of tough political rhetoric and baroque turn of phrase was a definitive style tailored to the Cuban psyche and capable of moving people in a powerful and emotional way. It is a style that does not have the same appeal in other cultures, but was effectively used by Martí and increasingly adopted and refined by Fidel.

One sentence in the manifesto reads, "Once again there is a tyrant, but once again we shall have Mellas, Trejos, and Guitcrases." These were three heroes who fought against the Machado dictatorship, and all died under the age of thirty. It suggests not only that Fidel was thinking that it would be up to a new youthful generation to lead the struggle against Batista but, more important, that he was identifying with these individuals and already thinking in a very Cuban tradition that his own destiny might be to give his life in a heroic youthful struggle. Conscious awareness of the idea of historical destiny had been a characteristic of most of the great Cuban leaders of the past, and Fidel was adopting that tradition, knowing that it was acceptable to the populace. Melding the Spanish tradition of admiration for heroic feats, and the Christian tradition of martyrdom, Cubans readily accepted the idea that the passion of youth should make one want to die for his ideals.

Six days after the coup, the top leadership of the Ortodoxo Party gathered at the tomb of Eduardo Chibás in Colón cemetery to honor his memory in light of the new developments. It was memorable for the strikingly colorless and uninspiring speech given by sociology professor and thwarted presidential front-runner Roberto Agramonte, who made a point of saying that the Ortodoxos should oppose Batista with "civic resistance only."

Fidel, who had come directly from the farm, climbed on a tombstone, and in a loud voice disrupted the proceedings by pointing out that such a position was absurd. Against a military dictatorship only force would bring about change, he argued. It was a harsh reminder to the gathered leadership of the Ortodoxos Party that the presidency had been stolen from them and they were powerless to do anything about it. Batista had seized power because he clearly could not win the election, and because his cronies in the government, through whom he had continued to exert control, had increasingly been displaced by individuals loyal to Prío.

In certain quarters Batista's coup was not unpopular. He quickly won the support of the Chamber of Commerce, commercial and land interests, most of the major banks, and the government of the United States. He skillfully used the revolutionary rhetoric to identify himself with the struggle of the 1930s that had led to the writing of the 1940 Constitution. He justified his actions in terms of the need to rid the country of the terrible corruption of the Prío administration and the alarming influence of the gangster groups, objectives that most Cubans, who had little faith anyway in the elective process, applauded. Ironically, Fidel's superb exposés, although not widely read, had identified exactly the same rot in the fabric of Cuban political life that Batista now used to justify his coup. What many Cubans did not realize was that in welcoming Batista's coup they were merely exchanging a corrupt democracy for a corrupt dictatorship.

Cuba's political leadership was divided between those who were willing to make an accommodation with Batista and those who were determined to oppose him. Those who were committed against Batista included most of the top members of the Auténtico and Ortodoxo parties. But because of their weak leadership, their organizational structures were disintegrating, and Batista quickly compounded their problems by ordering the dissolution of all parties and the suspension of constitutional guarantees.

The Auténtico Party, because it had grown out of the struggle against Machado in the 1930s, had a revolutionary tradition and included individuals who in their youth were experienced in armed revolt and conspiracy. From their ranks would come some support, both people and money, for armed efforts to overthrow Batista. This was particularly true of Prío and those around him, although some of them had gone into exile with him, and already wealthy, they were no longer willing to risk their lives.

The Ortodoxo leaders, on the other hand, were mostly idealistic liberals, deeply loyal to the spirit of the 1940 Constitution, and committed, like their founder Chibás, to social justice through gradual change and the ballot box. They had no experience with and little stomach for insurrection. The coup only widened the split in the party ranks, especially along generational lines, and the validity of Fidel's call to arms served to fragment the party even more.

Batista's coup was the most consequential milestone in Fidel's life. Whatever possibility might have existed for a political career within the elective process had vanished overnight. Ambitious and impatient, he had tried the conforming route, and the door had been slammed in his face. He was most comfortable when he was acting in concert with the deep resentment toward the social structure that he had nurtured since his childhood, rather than when he was trying to suppress his feelings. His total and irrevocable commitment to revolution at this point fitted his fundamental psychological needs, and now had a degree of consistency with the prevailing political reality. Batista also represented the ideal symbol of the evil authoritarian father figure against whom Fidel could vent all of his unresolved frustrations. It is significant that it was at this point that Fidel seemed to develop a true sense that he was pursuing a special destiny, the result of acting consistently with his inner drives rather than trying to be someone he wasn't.

The leaders of the Auténtico and Ortodoxo parties filed a civil suit in the Court of Constitutional Guarantees charging Batista with violation of the provisions of the 1940 Constitution. With Batista having assumed total power, there was now, in practice, no separation of the executive and judicial branches of government. Fearing for their own futures, the judges not surprisingly rejected the suit. Fidel elected not to question whether Batista had broken the Constitution, but to take that as a given. He therefore filed a criminal suit in the Court of Urgencies demanding that Batista be sentenced to a hundred years in prison for crimes against the Constitution. This court, too, predictably dismissed the brief, but the suit served to stake out Fidel's legal justification for his later attack on the

Moncada barracks. He would argue that when the Constitution had been criminally violated the people had the right to seek their own redress.

During the remainder of 1952, there were rumors that armed groups connected with the Auténtico Party were being organized and that they had money and bases of operation outside the country. Prío, in exile, offered them willing leadership as he had a personal debt to settle with Batista for overthrowing him.

Through his acquaintances in the Ortodoxos Youth, Fidel began to build a network of contacts, primarily in the Havana area, who shared his commitment to armed insurrection. Fidel has described his thinking during this period as he began working with these different groups: "My idea then was not to organize a movement, but to try to unite all the different forces against Batista. I intended to participate in the struggle simply as one more soldier. . . . But when none of these leaders showed they had either the ability or the seriousness of purpose, or the way to overthrow Batista, it was then I finally worked out a strategy of my own."

One of the groups with which Fidel had contact was headed by Abel Santamaría, an accountant for a subsidiary of the Pontiac automobile company in Havana. He had moved to Havana from the countryside in search of an education and better working opportunities. He was subsequently joined by his sister, Haydée, with whom he shared a tiny two-room apartment on the seventh floor of a building at Twenty-fifth and O streets. The crowded apartment with its sparse furniture and glass-fronted bookcase filled with political tomes, including the works of Lenin, became a center for their friends to discuss politics and to socialize. Among their most frequent guests were two other accountants, Jesús Montané, who worked for General Motors and, after November, Boris Luis Santa Coloma, Haydée's fiancé, who worked for Frigidaire; a young woman attorney, Melba Hernández; and a man named Raúl Martínez Arará. Gradually a cohesive group developed with a similar political agenda. Although espousing a revolutionary solution to the Batista problem, they remained members of the Ortodoxo Party and loyal to the memory and ideals of Eddy Chibás. Although they may have seen one another earlier at the headquarters of the Ortodoxo Party, at Prado 109, Abel Santamaría first formally met Fidel on May 1, 1952 at Colón cemetery. There, at the grave of Carlos Martínez, the high school student who had died a year earlier, they were introduced by Jesús Montané.

Fidel became a frequent visitor to the Santamaría apartment. The group was already publishing a mimeographed underground newspaper, *Son Los Mismos* (They Are the Same). Fidel became the political editor and, reflecting his strident posture, he suggested that the name be changed to *El Acusador* (The Accuser). Fidel wrote several articles under the pseudonym "Alejandro." Alejandro was his middle name, and the name of his mother's brother. Throughout his later time in exile and the period in the Sierra Maestra it would be both his code name and the way people addressed him.

On August 16, 1952, the anniversary of Chibás's death, members of the group planned to attend a mass rally at Colón cemetery and distribute *El Acusador*. That morning, the police raided the house where the paper was being printed, and all the members of the group were arrested, except Fidel and Haydée who had already left.

Increasingly, more by force of personality than anything else, Fidel began to dominate the group. Haydée Santamaría has said, "Three days after Fidel started coming to our apartment it was no longer Abel that I followed, it was Fidel. And only someone of tremendous personality and tremendous character can do that."

In the summer of 1952, Abel and Fidel began to organize an insurrectional movement. They established a military committee to recruit and train an armed force, and a civil committee to maintain their political activities. Continuing to rely on their long-standing friends in the Ortodoxo Party, Fidel and Abel sought out other groups that shared their enthusiasm for revolution and were willing to become involved in a military training program. Fidel used his charm and charisma to great advantage, persuading a diverse array of individuals to come under the umbrella of his leadership to form a loose network of nascent insurrectionists. Those they recruited had been organized into cells of ten men in the towns where they lived. Within six months, they had groups of a dozen or more willing fighters in Pijirigua, in Capellania, in the traditionally rebellious Artemesa, and in the Havana suburb of Marianao. Most were only eighteen or nineteen years old, yet they were self-confident and defiant. Each group had a leader who was responsible for the training and discipline of his men, and he in turn was answerable to Fidel.

For the first few months, they received military training in out-of-the-way parts of the University of Havana campus provided by an older engineering student friend of Fidel's, Pedro Miret. They had few weapons, but they trained regularly, and met to discuss politics and revolutionary strategy. After November 22, 1952, they abandoned the university, partly because of difficulties with the authorities, but also because another revolutionary, apparently connected with the Auténticos, sought to recruit some of the men. From then on they trained in their home communities.

Martínez Arará and Fidel made a trip to Oriente Province to ask Angel Castro for $3,000 to finance their insurrection. They came away with only $140.

In the town of Colón, Fidel and Abel established relations with Dr.

69

Mario Muñoz, a physician in his forties who was also a radio expert. He agreed to build them two radio transmitters so that they could start clandestine political broadcasts.

Perhaps the most vital ingredient in Fidel's strategy was his obsession with secrecy. Throughout his career as a revolutionary it would be central to his success. In a society with a reputation for people with loose tongues, Fidel early recognized the value of restricting information only to those whose need to know was essential. He never told anyone the entirety of his plans. None of the groups training around Havana were aware of any of the others. That way if the members of one group were arrested they would not be able to jeopardize the rest of the movement. Most of the other revolutionary efforts of this era were destroyed because their plans became public knowledge. Haydée has said, "Fidel taught us the importance of secrecy." Critics have argued that this was Fidel's way of keeping control, and indeed it was, but it was also the way to succeed.

Some have argued that he deliberately stayed away from his old university friends because they were less likely to fall under the spell of his leadership and accept the discipline he demanded than young men from lower-middle-class and farming backgrounds. Others have felt that he rightly had little faith in the part-time revolutionaries around the university who might be willing to attack a police station in the afternoon, but in the evening wanted to return to the pleasures of Havana's night life. It may also have reflected an ideological perspective on Fidel's part that you were not going to make a revolution with a bunch of disenchanted college students. The position of the Communist Party at that point was against armed insurrection, and therefore he was also unlikely to have the support of his several friends who were members. Perhaps the simplest explanation is that Fidel had had relatively little to do with campus politics since his trip to Bogotá, and he just did not have many remaining close relationships within the university community. Besides, since childhood he had always been most comfortable around people from a working-class background.

At their headquarters at the Santamaría apartment it was a heady time. They had little money and very little else with which to make a revolution, yet as Haydée says in a romanticized description, "We were never happier than when we were planning. We gave up food, coffee, and smoking to buy bullets." When they complained to Fidel about how little they had, she recalled that he said, "We have nothing, there is nothing, and the problem now is not one of how much, but of beginning."

Fidel and Abel never missed a rally or demonstration where they could vent their hostility toward the hated Batista regime, and their efforts were reinforced as more antigovernment leaders were jailed and by the growing numbers and militancy of the opposition, particularly among the young.

Early in 1953 (Melba Hernández estimates February), Fidel and Abel began to discuss concrete plans for an attack on a specific target, the Moncada barracks in Santiago de Cuba, where Fidel had gone to school. A simultaneous attack would be launched on the military post in nearby Bayamo to prevent reinforcements from reaching Moncada. If they could seize the barracks and particularly the arms stores, they would then distribute the weapons to their growing number of sympathizers in the province which they hoped would stimulate a general revolt. The province farthest from the capital, with ideal geographic features including three mountain ranges, Oriente was a region in which it was hard for the military to concentrate its forces. Fidel and Abel dreamed that it could become the base for a nationwide movement to overthrow the dictator.

They enlisted the support of a sympathizer, Ernesto Tizol Aguílera, who worked for Sears Roebuck and also operated a poultry business. Tizol had earlier led his own revolutionary-minded group. They convinced him to move to Santiago de Cuba. There, in April, he rented from José Vázquez a two-acre farm in the nearby seaside town of Siboncy. He told people he planned to raise chickens. The first shipment of arms he received was labeled "chicken feed." The farmhouse was spartan but spacious, and was located about fifteen minutes from the center of Santiago de Cuba.

What was particularly important about this period was that for more than a year after the March 10 coup, a steady process of disillusionment and alienation had set in, especially among young people, as the Batista regime showed itself to be increasingly autocratic and oppressive. There was a gradual evolution during those months toward armed insurrection in which Fidel's movement was one manifestation of a larger groundswell in the country.

The Auténticos had finally put together an organization, the Asociación de Amigos de Aureliano (AAA). They were importing arms and supporting preparing armed units.

A more visible revolutionary group during the same period was the Movimiento Nacional Revolucionaria (MNR), headed by a philosophy professor, Rafael García Bárcena. The movement had less of a philosophy than a clear and public intent to oust Batista. García Bárcena was a somewhat anomalous figure. He had been close to Eddy Chibás and had joined him in forming the Ortodoxo Party. He also had close connections with the military after teaching for six years at the Escuela Superior de Guerra, a school for military officers. As a respected journalist, politician, and intellectual, he was well known among university-educated young people in Havana, and as the strongest apparent opposition leader they gravitated toward his cause. His followers came largely from the Ortodoxos Youth to which Fidel also appealed, but they were mainly the educated and more wealthy young people whom Fidel had deliberately decided not to use in his own venture.

García Bárcena intended to use his connections in the military to orchestrate a bloodless coup that would climax with his walking with his supporters into Campo Columbia and taking over the military reins of power. From there he would dismiss Batista. His apparently naive strategy was widely known, and on April 5, as he and his supporters were preparing to march on the camp, they were rounded up and imprisoned. He and several others were brutally tortured. Eventually he received a two-year prison term. Thirteen of his followers were also incarcerated for varying periods. According to one source, García Bárcena had invited Fidel to participate in his revolt, but Fidel declined, saying he considered it suicidal. He and his followers left the city on the day of the planned coup so that the police could not try to implicate any of them.

The decimated MNR was held together over the next two years by a small group that would later fuse itself with Fidel's organization.

Another significant opposition group, Acción Libertadora, was formed by Dr. Justo Carrillo, the former head of the Agricultural and Industrial Development Bank. Although not at that point openly committed to insurrection, Carrillo would remain an ally and financial supporter of Fidel for several years to come, ultimately serving in the first revolutionary government.

At the beginning of June, a meeting was held in Montreal between all the major established opposition leaders except the Communists. The meeting, although it did issue a general statement of principles, achieved little consensus and was mainly characterized by squabbling among the various participants in attempts to promote their own personal agendas. Fidel was not invited to the meeting, but he went to the airport when the leaders returned. His friend, Max Lesnick, secretary-general of the Ortodoxo Youth, told him they were anticipating Batista's overthrow, and implied that they were considering supporting some other revolutionary groups, an option that had been discussed. It is Lesnick's impression that Fidel was immediately concerned that his movement could be usurped, and was thus determined to push ahead as quickly as possible. In the event that someone else should seize power, he could still be holding the Moncada barracks and Oriente Province, putting him in a powerful bargaining position with any new regime.

Fidel had handpicked 150 individuals from among the different cells that gave him allegiance and ordered them to begin traveling by car and train to Santiago de Cuba in the third week of July 1953. Most were agricultural workers, factory workers, and shop assistants. Not more than six, including Fidel, had a higher education. The group from each locale had its own leader. Abel and Haydée traveled together, posing as husband and wife. Melba Hernández went to a florist on Neptuno Street in Havana to buy a long flower box in which to place shotguns for the long train trip to Santiago.

Fifteen days earlier, Fidel began shipping weapons and ammunition to the farm. From the Thion Laboratory, he obtained sample bags in which the arms could be sent without raising suspicion. Renato Guitart, a conspirator from Santiago, obtained a copy of the plans of the fort for them.

Fidel's younger brother, Raúl, who had returned in early July from several months in Eastern Europe, including attending the World Youth Conference in Vienna in February, joined the operation at the last minute. His involvement, however, was clearly more out of brotherly interest than ideological commitment. Only a month before, he had applied for membership in the Communist Party of Cuba.

Throughout the period since Chibás's death, Fidel had maintained a relationship with the Communist Party. It was, according to Carlos Rafael Rodríguez, a relationship of mutual respect even though they disagreed on strategy. Two weeks before the Moncada attack, he went to the Communist Party headquarters and bought some books and Marxist literature. On the way out he ran into his friend Flavio Bravo and mentioned that he would like to talk with a party official. Bravo took him to meet Carlos Rafael Rodríguez. Rodríguez, then in charge of ideological issues for the party, says that they had a long discussion in which Fidel impressed him with the depth of his knowledge about political philosophy, but he did not mention his plans for Moncada. Fidel's reasons for making this visit were almost certainly less ideological than strategic. He wanted to establish a line of communication so that should the attack be successful he would have a better chance of attracting the party's backing.

His wife Mirta knew nothing about the planned attack. In fact, it was a difficult time in their marriage. In November 1952, Fidel had met an attractive young woman, Naty Revuelta, then married to a doctor. She had helped to raise money for the movement. Fidel became romantically involved with her during this period, and the affair would survive throughout his time in prison and his divorce.

Two days before they departed from Havana, Fidel and Martínez Arará went to visit Fidel's brother-in-law and former university friend, Rafael Díaz Balart, now deputy secretary of interior. As a pretext, they said that they wanted to find out the status of one of their group who had been imprisoned by the government without trial. In fact, they wanted to determine whether their security was watertight or whether any suspicion of their plans had leaked to government intelligence. Díaz Balart, suffering from a severe cold and eager to keep the meeting short, took them for a brief discussion with the chief of national security. There was nothing to suggest that they were under suspicion, and they left. Because their political paths were about to take dramatically opposite directions, Fidel would never again see his brother-in-law, who now lives in Miami.

Chapter Four

SHORTLY after midnight in the seaside community of Siboney near Santiago de Cuba, a rented blue 1952 Buick with a white roof drove up the dusty road to the little stucco farmhouse with its distinctive red trim. The headlights illuminated palm trees around the darkened building. The car stopped, and Fidel, tall and powerful, climbed out. He was accompanied by the slight, wiry Abel Santamaría and Renato Guitart. The quiet outside was deceptive. Inside, more than a hundred men and two women had gathered in the crowded living room. They spoke in whispers. Fidel warmly greeted the men from the different contingents from around the country. His arrival had caused an expectant hush to fall over the group, but a palpable air of excitement prevailed.

The men had come in small groups by bus, car, and train. Only the leader of each group knew that Santiago de Cuba was the destination. Each had been given the address of a house or a hotel in the city, where they had waited until late that evening. Then they had been brought to the farm, still not knowing the exact purpose of the trip.

Fidel had left Havana twenty-four hours earlier, stopping on the way in Bayamo. In Santiago, he had rendezvoused with Abel and Renato, and together they had driven the few miles to the farm. Fidel and Abel had huddled with Haydée Santamaría and Melba Hernández to review the preparations they had made earlier that day. Assured that all the work had been satisfactorily completed, the two men left again in separate cars to drive back into Santiago.

On his way from Havana, Fidel had also stopped in Colón to tell the physician-radioman, Dr. Mario Muñoz, to drive to Oriente Province. Fidel instructed him to go to the little town of El Cobre near Santiago and wait there until he came for him. Muñoz had been waiting since midafternoon, and it was Abel who finally came to take him to the farm. Fidel went to the Santiago home of his friend Luis Conte Agüero, to whom he intended to divulge his plan, and ask him, should they be successful, to be their spokesperson on the radio. Several days earlier Fidel had told him to be sure to be there that night as it was important, but he found only Conte Agüero's mother at home. She said that Luis was in Havana. Fidel arrived back at the farm around 3 A.M.

A document had been prepared, "The Moncada Manifesto," of which Fidel was the primary author. It was first and foremost an exhortation to revolution for the people of Cuba. In it he had also attempted to explain the need for the attack, and had outlined a program of political and social reforms. More important in a way, he had a tape of Chibás's last speech, which he intended to play. The eleven-point revolutionary program was a smorgasbord of liberal reformist ideology and fervent nationalism. It drew heavily on the inspiration of Martí, and bore close similarities to the program published by Joven Cuba (Young Cuba) and its leader Antonio Guiteras in 1934, a program of democratic socialism laced with vehement anti-imperialism. Guiteras, like Fidel, had led a revolutionary movement in Oriente Province. He had captured and briefly held the military barracks at San Luis, then fought off Machado's troops for several weeks in the Sierra Maestra before finally being captured. After Machado's overthrow in 1933, Guiteras, still in his twenties, was made minister of interior, war, and navy in the new government. After he had forced through a number of radical reforms, the government was overthrown, and he was driven into hiding. He led an underground guerrilla movement, but was wounded. He planned to go into exile in Mexico and organize a new invasion force, but was shot and killed as he was waiting for the boat to take him out of the country.

When Guiteras had launched his successful attack on the barracks at San Luis, he had intended to mount a simultaneous assault on Moncada, but it had not taken place.

Fidel was driven at this moment not by ideology, but by the romantic perception of himself as the reincarnation of three men, José Martí, Antonio Guiteras, and Eddy Chibás, and it was their actions as national heroes as much as their political theory with which he primarily identified. He had no quarrel with their political philosophies, and was therefore content at this stage to present as the position of his own movement a distillation of the views of all of them. Fidel knew that to give credibility to the actions he and his men were about to take, some sort of ideological document was essential. But it is obvious that the military and historic aspects of the insurrection were vastly more important to him at this moment than the promotion of a particular program.

When Fidel arrived back at the farm, he was greeted by Melba Hernández, who told him that all of the preparations were complete. Melba had arrived on the train from Havana the previous day. She had joined Haydée and a young man who would later die in battle, Elpidio Sosa, and they had spent the subsequent twenty-four hours cleaning the place up and preparing for the arrival of the rest of the force. Renato Guitart had rented a quantity of mattresses that they had scattered around the house. He had told the store owner that they intended to lease the farm out to revelers coming to the city for the carnival that weekend. They also bought three large buckets of milk from a neighboring dairy farmer, and gathered a quantity of caney mangoes, Cuba's tastiest variety, which were ripe on trees around the farm at that time of year.

In keeping with Fidel's policy of strict secrecy, still only five people—Fidel, Abel, Renato Guitart, Pedro Miret, and Jesús Montané—knew the purpose of their trip to Santiago, and of those besides Fidel only Abel and Miret knew the entire plan. Even the two women, who knew that some sort of attack was planned, were unaware of the actual target. The primary consideration was security, but Fidel must have also felt that the shorter the time between announcing the plan and actually embarking on the venture, the less chance there would be for the men to back out.

On his return trip from Santiago, Fidel gathered the men together, and as Melba and Haydée walked among them passing out glasses of milk, he unveiled his plan.

"When I asked you to come to Santiago de Cuba and then to this farm," he said, "I could not tell you, for security reasons, what our mission would be. Now I can tell you that our target is the Moncada barracks." There was a muffled gasp at the audaciousness of the objective. "We will attack at dawn, when the guards are only half awake and the officers are still sleeping off their drunkenness from last night's carnival parties." He paused to let his dramatic words sink in and to judge their reaction. "It will be a surprise attack, and should not last more than ten minutes."

He then reviewed the plan. "We will go by car. The squad in the first car will take advantage of the confusion caused by our uniforms to take the guards at Post 3 prisoner. We will remove the chain between the two stanchions at the entrance. We will drive in, leave the cars, and enter the buildings to our left, taking prisoner those in the dormitory there who surrender. A second force of twenty will seize the hospital whose back windows open on the fort. They will then provide harassing fire through the windows against the rear of the barracks. A third group of six will take the Palace of Justice and from the roof neutralize the machine guns on top of the barracks inside the fort." Fidel paused, then stated, "You joined the movement voluntarily, and the same is true of this attack." There was silence followed by whispers. Most, he knew, would follow him anywhere, even to their deaths, but a few, he could tell, were truly stunned and shaken by the plan.

With the help of the two women, Abel dragged out the boxes of uniforms from a back room where they had been stored. Fidel had saved the largest uniform for himself, but still it did not fit and hurried alterations were required. Abel Santamaría looked as little like a military man with a uniform as without, and Fidel worried that their planned deception to pass themselves off as legitimate soldiers would not work. To add to the problem, they had only a limited number of hats, and none of the high leather boots Cuban soldiers wore.

"Look, Abel," he said half jokingly, "you have to act like a military man."

Melba Hernández says Fidel insisted that Muñoz take off his uniform and accompany them dressed in civilian clothes, making clear his role as their physician and as a noncombatant.

As the laughter at their paradoxical appearance subsided, and the final adjustments to their ill-fitting garb were made, Fidel was everywhere among the men, constantly talking, exhorting, cajoling, joking. Originally all the uniforms were to bear the rank of sergeant, but they had run out of insignia. Apart from the tasks assigned to specific individuals, there was no formal military structure.

Finally the weapons, extracted from a well in the front yard and from between the floors in the house, were passed out. There were three U.S. Army rifles, six old Winchester rifles, one ancient machine gun, some revolvers, and a large number of hunting rifles. With these they were to launch an attack in which they would be outnumbered ten to one by fully armed and trained soldiers. For many in the group, this was the moment of frightening truth, when naive romanticism came face to face with hard reality. Years later, Juan Almeida, who originally thought they might be going to the carnival in Santiago as a reward for their performance in earlier weapons training, said, "I waited for my rifle as if it had been a Messiah. When I saw it was a 0.22, I froze."

Suddenly it was glaringly apparent to many of them that they could well die, but at that point it was difficult to back out.

Sensing the new concern, Fidel spoke to the group again. "You know the objectives of our plan; it is a dangerous plan, and anyone who leaves with me tonight will have to do so willingly. There is still time to decide."

Ten men, representing two cells, quietly made known to Fidel their desire not to participate. Of these, four were students, five were worker-activists from Havana, and one was a radio technician. Fidel had them isolated in the kitchen, away from the rest of the men. "It was an act of cowardice," says Melba. There was also concern about the adverse reaction toward them from the others. The group of students was told to leave in a large Chrysler that belonged to the father of one of them, the workers were given another car, but all were told to remain at the farm until the attack force had left.

Capturing Post 3 of the barracks was the key to the entire attack, because once secured, the force could pass through the gate it guarded into the fort.

Perhaps chastened by the earlier defections, Fidel said, "We should take the sentry post by surprise. This is a suicide action and for it we want volunteers." In fact, Fidel had long since decided whom he wanted for that mission.

When Abel stepped forward to join the group, Fidel said, "Abel, you cannot go in that action, you are the second in command of the organization, and what would happen if we both got killed? No one would know what happened here, and we would be left without direction. You must command the group going to the hospital."

After a brief exchange, Fidel convinced Abel, saying, "I am going to the fort, and you are going to the hospital because you are the soul of the movement, and if I die you will replace me."

Abel was in part asserting his right as one of the leaders to be in a position of heroism and high danger. "On the other hand," says Melba Hernández, "we had the conviction that the one person who must not fall was Fidel. We all knew that by preserving Fidel's life we were assuring the continuity of the struggle until final victory. We were all convinced our own lives were of no importance, but not Fidel's. It was in that spirit that Abel engaged in the discussion with Fidel."

Fidel would lead the attack on the main fort, Lester Rodríguez would lead the group taking the Palace of Justice, and Abel Santamaría would command the group to seize the hospital.

As the final minutes approached before they left the farm, Fidel began an oration aimed at inspiring the fighting force. It focused, however, more on the historic nature of their venture than on the ideals for which they might die or the immediate political consequences it might achieve. Fidel may have thought this was the emphasis that would most inspire his men, but it also suggests that he had come to grips with the possibility of his own death. It was how they would be remembered, rather than what he would do after the event, that was uppermost in his mind.

In his comments, later reconstructed from memory by several of those present, he said in part:

> In a few hours you will be victorious or defeated, but regardless of the outcome—listen well, companeros!—this movement will triumph. If you win today, the aspirations of Martí will be fulfilled sooner. If the contrary occurs, our action will set an example for the Cuban people, and from the people will arise young men willing to die for Cuba. They will pick up our banner and move forward. The people of Oriente Province will support us, the entire island will do so. Young men of the

centennial [referring to 1953 as the centennial of Martí's birth], as in 1868 and 1895, here in Oriente we make our first cry of "Liberty or Death!"

After Abel had left the house, Melba and Haydée approached Fidel and told him it had always been their intention to participate in any combat action. According to Melba, Fidel felt it would be ungentlemanly for him to let them do so, especially without Abel's concurrence. Fidel clearly did not want the women involved. He was insisting that they were putting him in a difficult position, when Dr. Muñoz, who had overheard the conversation, interceded. "Fidel, the girls are right," he said. "I will take them in my car, and I will be responsible for both of them. Besides, they can be very useful to me as nurses during the fighting."

They went over the final plans, and as the men got into the different cars they quietly sang the Cuban national anthem. Haydée Santamaría subsequently recalled looking at the bright stars and the palm tress near the house and thinking about her little niece, wondering if she would ever see her again.

At 5:00 A.M, a convoy of twenty-six cars pulled away from the farm. Fidel had brought to a climax six months of careful planning that would immortalize him in the pages of Cuba's history. He had had almost no sleep for three days except during the ride from Havana. In keeping with his dislike of driving, his car was driven by a member of the movement from Santiago.

Meanwhile, eighty miles away in Bayamo a similar train of events had taken place.

It was a much smaller group, numbering only twenty-seven men, and led by Raúl Martínez Arará, who together with Abel Santamaría, Fidel, and the other leaders of the movement had hatched the plot for this two-pronged attack over the previous several months. This team was to assault the barracks in Bayamo so that should the attack at Moncada prove successful, reinforcements could not be sent from here to aid the garrison. The town of Bayamo also carried important historical and symbolic significance for the Cuban people, for it was the first city freed in the abortive war of independence in 1868 and was the only city completely destroyed in the war of independence against Spain in 1895. The whole town was viewed as a monument to liberty, so to start a new strike for freedom there carried great symbolism.

The conspirators had assembled at a motel in the town. It had been rented a week earlier by Gerardo Pérez Puelles and Renato Guitart, who met the trains from Havana carrying the key organizers and their carefully hidden weapons and uniforms. As at the farm in Siboney, they had told

80

the owner that they were in town to start a new chicken farming business. But he was an old man with nothing to do and posed a constant threat to the revolutionaries—he wanted to pass time by getting involved in their activities.

Fidel had arrived around seven in the evening on the night of the attack, and after reviewing the plan with Martínez Arará he made a brief speech to the men. It was essentially the same inspirational message that he would later deliver at the farm at Siboney, but at least two of the men present remembered it as being somewhat pessimistic in tone as far as their chances of success were concerned. As at the farm, his stress was on the historic significance of the event, and that win or lose, live or die, they would be enshrined in history.

Martínez Arará, the leader of the Bayamo contingent, says the entire idea of this secondary attack had posed a serious dilemma for Fidel. Although the strategic military arguments and the symbolic reasons for striking there were persuasive, Fidel could not be in two places at one time. He would be forced to relinquish the leadership at Bayamo to someone else. Should the attack there succeed while the force he led at Moncada failed, he would be potentially jeopardizing his leadership of the movement, and certainly his immediate as well as long-term historical recognition as a consequential revolutionary leader. As a result, according to Martínez Arará, he had agonized over the decision and avoided, until the very last week, sharing, even with Abel Santamaría and Martínez Arará, his two closest coconspirators, his decision whether the Bayamo strike would be included. Part of this may merely have been a product of Fidel's customary secretiveness.

At any other time, this long convoy of cars in the middle of the night would have attracted immediate attention, but during carnival time, when lines of cars were on the streets at all hours, it was not an unusual sight. The lead cars quickly covered the short distance into the sleeping city, passed San Juan Hill, and swung onto the four-lane avenue, Victoriano Garzon. Ten blocks from the barracks they passed an army patrol jeep. The driver, seeing cars full of men in uniform, saluted them. The three cars in the lead turned down Avenue Liberator, and then two blocks from their destination onto Calle Moncada, where the gate guarded by Post 3 was in sight.

The driver of the lead car, Renato Guitart, pulled to the curb, jumped out, and ran to the gate, followed by Jesús Montané and Ramiro Valdés. He yelled at the sleepy soldiers, "Attention, the general is coming," and unhooked the chain from across the driveway. The guards, momentarily fooled by the uniforms which they mistook for those of a military band that had been brought in from Havana to perform in the carnival, presented arms. They were quickly relieved of their weapons. Guitart ran inside the fort, expecting Fidel to drive the second car through the now secured gateway followed by the rest of the column. But there was a crucial pause. Some say that at that moment Fidel inadvertently drove his car violently against the curb, attracting the attention of a patrol jeep that appeared suddenly on the scene, moving to block his access to the gate. The jeep was part of the so-called "Cossack Patrol," a series of roving vehicles constantly circling the fort. They had been instituted only during the carnival period, and so in his lengthy observations and study of the fort's defenses, Renato Guitart had seen only the fixed sentry positions.

Fidel leapt from the car, shotgun in hand, at the same time a lieutenant with a pistol stood up in the jeep.

"Get the lieutenant," Fidel yelled back at Gustavo Arcos, who was emerging from the rear seat of the car. But the lieutenant fired first, hitting Arcos, who clung desperately to the car door. Then a machine gun opened up on the vehicle. A sergeant ran from the jeep to the guardhouse and was hit by a shot, but he was able to grab the alarm bell as he fell. Confusion reigned. The cars emptied and bullets flew in all directions. Some of Fidel's men ran inside the gate; others took cover between the parked vehicles on the street. It had been anticipated that most of the defenders would be asleep at this early hour, but the majority of the soldiers had been given passes the night before to attend the carnival, and were now drifting back in small groups to the fort, hung over but awake. In addition, their numbers were larger than normal due to a routine influx of reinforcements because of the carnival.

To compound the problem, the students who had declined to participate in the attack had not waited as instructed at the farm until the attackers left. They had pulled out simultaneously, inserting themselves in the motorcade. They turned off on a side street entering Santiago, and the drivers in the following cars, who had not previously driven the route, followed them and became lost. At the moment Fidel most desperately needed them, his reserves were wandering the back streets of Santiago trying to find their way to the barracks.

Meanwhile, Lester Rodríguez and his number two, Raúl Castro, had successfully captured the gleaming white Palace of Justice. From the roof, they had a commanding position from which to support the attack across the street. They did their best to provide covering fire, particularly by shooting at soldiers trying to climb a steel ladder to a .50-caliber machine gun on the roof of the fort, which could have devastatingly raked the entire interior courtyard.

At the Saturnino Lora Civil Hospital, Abel Santamaría, gun in hand, walked up to the astonished policeman at the door and said, "This is not the army. We are the people who are going to occupy the hospital. We are not going to harm you. We are only going to disarm you." Abel, Haydée, Melba, Mario Muñoz, and twenty-one men then took over the hospital.

About fifty men had made it through the gate into the fort. They shot several soldiers, and the officer of the day, Lieutenant Morales. They surprised a dormitory of bewildered, half-dressed soldiers. In their confusion searching for the armory they went to the wrong building, which turned out to be a barber shop. (The armory actually had been cleared of weapons to provide a sleeping area for the visiting band and the other reinforcements.) Renato Guitart, who led the men into the fort, was gunned down and killed on the steps of what he thought was the communications center. In fact, the radio equipment, like several other facilities in the fort, had been moved to a different location from that shown on the plan Guitart had obtained. The intent was to storm the building and cut off the military's radio connections with the outside world. Had the attack been successful, the center would have been vital for learning the outcome of the assault at Bayamo. It was also to be used to get several smaller military installations in the province to surrender peacefully, knowing Moncada had fallen, and for making their demands to the military headquarters in Havana.

Now fully alerted, the garrison was awake and the attackers were in danger of being cut off. Fidel gave the order to retreat. Two men—Pedro Miret, who was wounded, and Fidel Labrador, who lost an eye—fought a valiant and heroic rearguard action to allow the others to escape. Seeing the disarray and the hopelessness of the military situation now that the element of surprise was gone, Raúl decided to abandon the Palace of Justice. Lester Rodríguez, a resident of Santiago, left his rifle leaning against a wall, stepped out the front door, and walked home.

At the hospital, they had not heard the order to retreat and Abel kept firing out of the window in the hope that it would distract the soldiers. Haydée has quoted her brother as saying, "The longer we keep on fighting here the more the others will be able to save. There is always one fighter who must die without a bullet in his rifle—if a bullet has not gotten him first." Then they heard the shooting stop and saw the soldiers in the street. It was too late for them to escape. With the help of an intern, Dr. Mauricio León, they put on hospital gowns and bandages and got into beds, pretending to be patients. The two women went into the children's ward and acted as though they were nurses. When the soldiers came searching through the hospital the ruse almost worked, but as they were about to leave a man wearing a checkered shirt, dark trousers, and glasses, who had taken shelter in the hospital from the shooting outside, called the sergeant in charge and whispered the secret to him.

The revolutionaries were dragged from their beds and hurled to the floor. As the prisoners were being herded into the street at gunpoint, the soldiers separated Dr. Mario Muñoz from the rest and while he argued for respect as a physician, they shot him in the back at point-blank range. Later they would argue that he had tried to escape. He died where he lay. It was his forty-first birthday.

Excluding Dr. Muñoz, Fidel lost three men in the battle. The army lost nineteen men, including three officers. Both sides had a substantial number wounded. The battle lasted a little over an hour.

At Bayamo, following Fidel's departure there had been much of the same questioning about the wisdom of the mission as there had been at the Siboney farm. The men slept, or at least passed the night at the motel, three or four to a room. When they assembled around 4:30 A.M. to prepare for the attack, one of the rooms that had a door to the street was empty.

At the same hour that Fidel was driving with the motorcade away from the farm, Martínez Arará led his group toward the Bayamo barracks. They walked stealthily along the road to the fort. There was a roped-off area near the main gate in which horses were corralled. A man tending the horses saw this strange group of armed men in their ill-fitting, almost comical soldier's uniforms, and some who had refused to wear any uniform at all.

"Who are you?" he yelled at them.

"We are revolutionaries here to take over the fort," responded Orlando Castro.

Then, with a complete breakdown of discipline, one of the revolutionaries fired a shot at the horse-tender, missing him but stampeding the horses. The uproar alerted the guards inside the fort and they started firing from the walls down on the would-be attackers. Pinned down and unable to advance to the front gate of the fort, Martínez Arará and his men exchanged gunfire with the soldiers for about fifteen minutes, and then they fled. Accounts vary, but Martínez Arará believes that not more than two men were killed in the actual fighting.

Fidel had not told the men to go to any specific regrouping point in the event of a failure of the attack. Win or lose, he had seen it as a point of no return, and his intention from the beginning, if he survived, was to make this the starting point for a continuing armed struggle. He planned to take the survivors with him to the Sierra Maestra mountains and continue the fight from there. In April, over Easter, he had visited a manganese mine in the area at Charco Redondo. There, miners toiled in slavelike conditions, and Fidel was affected by their suffering. He instructed a member of the movement who lived in the area, Oscar Ortega, to begin recruiting support among these men. An option that he had clearly kept in mind was to go to the mine and convince some of the miners to join him in the mountains.

Now as they made their escape from Santiago, Fidel suggested that they attack the police station in the small town of Caney. However, as they left Santiago the driver either inadvertently or deliberately missed the northeast cutoff on Garzon Avenue, ending up on the road back to Siboney.

Sixty exhausted and frightened men returned to the farm. Several of them, dispirited, argued that they should turn themselves in. Fidel, resolute and unbowed by defeat or lack of sleep, announced firmly that he was going to the mountains, and anyone who wished to follow him could do so. Eighteen, mostly those from Artemisa, set out on foot with Fidel for the Sierra Maestra. One became separated from the group and was later found dead, apparently from natural causes brought on by exposure and exhaustion. They stopped briefly at a farm close to Siboney owned by a man named Nuñez, who was sympathetic to their cause. A short time later, when the Army arrived, he deliberately directed them in the opposite direction to that taken by Fidel and his men.

They reached the house of an old black woman who dressed their wounds and instructed her grandson to act as a guide. However, when he had taken them several miles, Fidel made him turn back so that he would not know exactly which route they had taken, lest the military force him to talk. In an area inhabited almost entirely by blacks and mulattoes, many of whom had by then heard about the Moncada attack, they were relatively safe. They were led to the community of Sevilla Arriba, where a man killed a pig and they all feasted. The man told of his struggles with the landowners, and Fidel gave him his treasured nickel-plated .45 pistol. Fidel advised him, "When they come to bother you, open fire with this pistol. Don't believe in anyone. Defend what is yours."

Later, at the home of Feliciano Heredia, they were given a change of clothes and they listened on a portable radio to Batista decrying their exploits. He blamed the attack on "millionaires, resting on a cushion of money, proclaiming revolution . . . buying arms overseas." It was clear that he believed the insurrection had been planned and financed by former President Prío. In a contradiction he did not attempt to explain he also claimed that at "Siboney" they had found "Communist documents, Soviet propaganda, and books of Lenin."

It was now July 29, and the wounded were in great pain and unable to go on. At the same time, the presence of military spotter planes overhead made it clear that they were being tracked by the army. Although reluctant to split up the group, Fidel decided that Rosendo Menendez and Antonio Rosell should take the wounded men, Jesús Montané, Reinaldo Benítez, and Mario Lazo, back to Santiago. The decision was made in part out of humanitarian concern, but also pragmatically to free the others and increase their chance of escape.

Meanwhile, those who had been captured were being viciously tortured and murdered.

In Havana, Mirta had contacted Fidel's friend Rolando Amador, and together they went to the palace of the archbishop to seek the church's intervention on behalf of the men. Monsignor Enrique Pérez Serantes, archbishop of Santiago de Cuba, and a close friend of Fidel's father—he had presided at Fidel's confirmation and married his parents—demanded an end to the massacre of the prisoners. Together with the rector of the university, Judge Subirat Quesada, and Enrique Canto, the owner of a large department store, he met with Morales del Castillo, Batista's principal secretary. They offered to act as intermediaries to secure the surrender of Fidel and his men, on condition that their lives be spared and they be brought to trial. The offer was accepted by del Castillo and Colonel Alberto del Río Chaviano, the army commander in Santiago. However, not trusting the army, Bishop Pérez Serantes gave a press conference announcing the agreement, and then drove with his colleagues to La Gran Piedra, a mountain where he had accurately guessed that Fidel and his men were hiding. They climbed for many hours over the mountainside, calling through a megaphone the offer of safe conduct to those who would surrender. But to no avail.

On the morning of August 1, a sixteen-man rural guard patrol stumbled on Fidel and his men. The group had broken up and several of the men were captured following a brief fire fight. Some distance away, three men, one of whom was Fidel, were found asleep in a shack. In one of the many extraordinary strokes of luck in Fidel's life, the commander of the patrol turned out to be a Lieutenant Pedro Manuel Sarriá, a tall black man who had known Fidel at the University of Havana. Although twenty years older than Fidel, he had taken a course in administrative law through the "Open University" program while still a career military officer. His normal job at Moncada was as an administrator, and only by sheerest chance was he asked to take out this patrol. Entering into the hut where the three men were sleeping, he alone recognized Fidel and, because the order had clearly been given not to bring him back alive, he leaned over Fidel and whispered in his ear, "Don't say who you are or they will kill you." He gave orders to his patrol that he wanted these prisoners taken back alive. Sarriá's men were confused. They were angry because of injuries some of their number had sustained in the fire fight with the other revolutionaries in Fidel's group, and wanted to kill the prisoners. But Fidel argued with them that the revolutionaries, not Batista's soldiers, were the true patriotic

86

descendants of the liberation armies of the War of Independence. Had they known who Fidel was, it is unlikely that Sarriá could have prevented them from killing him.

Receiving the news of the rebels' capture, Colonel del Río Chaviano, ignoring his agreement with Bishop Serantes, dispatched a twenty-man detail commanded by Lieutenant Colonel Pérez Chaumont to take custody of the rebels, and to shoot them. Sarriá, in the meantime, had commandeered from a farmer a closed truck to transport the prisoners. With the farmer driving, Sarriá sat with his broad shoulders deliberately blocking the window on the passenger side so that people could not see who was inside. When they encountered the contingent commanded by Pérez Chaumont, Sarriá refused to relinquish the prisoners, saying that since he had captured them it was his responsibility to deliver them into safe custody. Sarriá, energetic and overbearing, was able to make the younger man, who substantially outranked him, back down by arguing that as he was from an administrative unit he was not subject to the command of someone from a combat unit. Uncertain of himself in the face of an expert on military administration, Pérez Chaumont allowed Sarriá to proceed.

When they arrived in Santiago, instead of going to the fort, Sarriá had the farmer drive the truck to the municipal prison, where he turned Fidel and the other men over to the civilian authorities. The rumor had reached the city that more prisoners had been taken, so there was a small crowd waiting outside the jail. The delivery of Fidel and the others, uninjured, was witnessed by this little throng, making it impossible for the authorities to torture or kill them, particularly in light of the public outcry over the atrocities that had been committed against the other prisoners in the week since the attack.

Del Río Chaviano was infuriated with Sarriá, but there was very little that he could do. The savagery of the reprisals against the captured attackers during the few days that Fidel and his band were still at large in the mountains had been so extreme that even a population used to excesses of violence was shocked. Eighty of the men captured were killed in cold blood, many of them after brutal torture. Some were driven into the countryside by soldiers and shot. At Bayamo, three men were dragged behind a speeding jeep. Miraculously, one survived.

Melba and Haydée were not harmed, but initially after their capture they were held in the garrison where they could hear and see the atrocities going on all around them. "It was a real bloodbath," says Melba. "They [the soldiers] would come to Ye-Ye [Haydée] and myself to tell us the things they had done. . . . We saw how Raúl García Gómez was murdered. He was thrown beside us totally physically destroyed—his face was a shambles . . . and they finished him off by throwing him against a wall

87

repeatedly. . . . One had a wound in the abdomen, not fatal, and they stomped on his abdomen until he simply burst." Abel Santamaría was tortured to death within earshot of the two women, and his eyes were brought to his sister, ostensibly an attempt to make her confess that the group had connections to former President Prío, but more likely an act of pure sadism.

The soldiers tortured and killed young men they thought suspicious who had nothing to do with the attack. One youth with his arm in a cast from an accident was picked up on the street and badly beaten. In another incident, they entered the operating room in the hospital and dragged out an innocent patient undergoing surgery for wounds unrelated to the attack on the garrison. And one of the students who had been at Siboney and had withdrawn from the attack at the last moment was also caught and killed.

Those involved in the atrocities during the first few hours after the attack were, for the most part, ill-educated soldiers, still drunk or hung over from the carnival the night before. However, the commanders of Moncada, Colonel del Río Chaviano, Captain Pérez Chaumont, and the head of military intelligence, Captain Manuel Lavastida, made no attempt to discourage the brutalities—if anything they encouraged the men. Later, in the effort to track down Fidel and the other survivors, it was clear that del Río Chaviano had ordered them killed.

The extent of the torture and killing became widely known by word of mouth, and subsequently, despite censorship, through the press. The effect on public opinion, particularly among the educated liberal class, was to swing sympathy overwhelmingly to the side of the attackers. What otherwise might have been dismissed as just another wild if not insane escapade of dubious morality and utility by a young political maverick and his friends became an event of great heroism in which any shortcomings in their political wisdom were obscured by sympathy for their suffering.

In leading the Moncada attack, Fidel had been willing to sacrifice his own life. Indeed, it was due only to a series of astonishingly lucky events that he did survive. Although his willingness to die can be interpreted on several different levels, there can be no doubt that his urge to carry out this highly dangerous act far outweighed his instinct for self-preservation. It has been argued that he minimized his own exposure, putting others in the more hazardous positions. If there is any truth to this, it was, as Melba Hernández points out, more the product of a conscious effort by the others to protect him than any initiative on his part. Besides, the distinctions between dangerous and less dangerous roles in this venture were so meager as to be almost meaningless. One can also argue that a strong element of denial was operating in his thinking, and that perhaps he had not faced the true dangers involved in the operation. It is clear that he thought, because of the element of surprise, that the fort might be taken without a shot being fired. This may be true to some degree. But his speeches in the months leading up to the assault, especially his references to Mella, Trejo, and Guiteras in *Zarpazo*, the manifesto he had issued in response to Batista's coup, suggest that he had come to grips with the strong possibility that he might die. The Cuban notion that nothing was more honorable than dying in defense of liberty had a powerful effect on him. Such thinking filled Cuban history, and Fidel would have been following a long and venerated tradition. From his illegitimate birth to his later regretted involvement with the gangs while at the university, Fidel was greatly concerned that his public honor had been besmirched. The idea of redeeming it by one heroic act must have had great appeal.

Fidel's political advancement had been stymied by the coup, his marriage was in some difficulty, and he was having an extramarital affair with a married woman. The previous year had been the low point in his career. So much had been expected of him, but fate and society seemed to be conspiring against him. It was a time when the worth of his life was truly devalued in his own eyes. The Moncada attack offered the chance to follow in the footsteps of his heroes, forcing, through the parallels he himself had constructed, an association of his exploits with theirs. This one act would demand of society that it accord him the acceptance and recognition as someone truly exceptional that it had denied him since childhood. Even if it meant paying for this honor with his life, it was a price he had clearly decided he was willing to pay. Indeed, to complete the public identification with Martí, Guiteras, and Chibás it was almost necessary that he die in the attack. Whether interpreted as an extraordinary act of patriotism or a drastic effort to deal with personal emotional needs, Fidel's decision to launch the Moncada attack was a true gamble with life and death and history.

Chapter Five

BY the time Fidel and his companions reached the city jail on August 1, the other surviving prisoners, including the two women, had been transferred there from the military prison at Moncada. Knowing that Abel was dead, they had clung dearly to the hope that the rampant rumor that Fidel has survived was true. Melba and Haydée, in a cell on the upper floor, could barely see down to the entrance. More than thirty years later Melba says, "I am still moved by the memory. That day we felt something very extraordinary, very unusual [was happening], and we ran to the bars with the hope that it was Fidel. From behind the bars we were able to see part of his body, but not all [of him]. But it was his stride, his gait. We immediately identified Fidel."

In a few days, the prisoners were moved to the Puerto Boniato prison. All were taken by bus, except Fidel and the women, who were transported by car. Fidel was in the front between the driver and a Captain Morales. The women were in the back, but they were able to converse with him. He asked guardedly how they were, what had happened to Abel, and of the fate of others. When they arrived at Boniato, the three were left to spend several more minutes standing alone together, and the women were able hurriedly to fill him in on other more sensitive events since their capture.

Boniato was made up of several large white prison blocks, and all of the Moncada captives except Fidel were put together in one half of a single block. Fidel was put in a cell in the opposite half, which was used as a hospital ward, where there were only common criminals. The two adjacent cells were left empty, isolating him from the other prisoners as well as the Moncadistas. To reach the women's toilet, Melba and Haydée had to pass in front of Fidel's cell, and they gradually worked out a complicated system, often using other prisoners walking in the hallway, of passing notes back and forth.

It was inconceivable to Batista that Fidel and his men had acted alone. He believed that they had to be part of a larger conspiracy involving the older generation of Cuban politicians. He particularly suspected supporters of former President Prío, whom he blamed for most of the problems his administration was encountering. The Moncada attack also provided the opportunity for Batista to take a slap at all of the formal opposition, and wholesale arrests were made of Ortodoxo Party leaders and Communists. By sheer coincidence, several senior members of the Communist Party were in Santiago de Cuba over this same period to celebrate the birthday of their secretary-general, Blas Roca. The authorities were convinced that there must be a connection between their presence and the Moncada attack, even though the party's leaders had criticized the attack as "adventurist." Accordingly, they were rounded up and forced to stand trial wih Fidel's group. Eventually there were more than a hundred named defendants, including former President Prío. Of those who had actually taken part in the attack, only thirty-two stood trial; forty-eight had escaped entirely.

The trial began on September 21, 1953, before the Urgency Court of Santiago de Cuba in the ornate Palace of Justice that Lester Rodríguez, Raúl and their men had so successfully captured. During his two hours of testimony on the opening day, Fidel, assertive and gesticulating, seized the initiative from the prosecutor, and while freely admitting his role in the attack, used the forum of the crowded courtroom to give his version of it. He persuasively articulated his motives, and before an audience that included journalists, lawyers, and opposition politicians, he ridiculed the government's contention that he was part of a conspiracy involving Prío or any other political figure. "The only intellectual author of the attack on the Moncada is José Martí, the apostle of our independence," he declared. Before the end of the first day's testimony, Fidel requested and received permission to act as the lawyer in his own defense.

One person in the audience that day was an attractive twenty-three-year-old journalist from the magazine *Bohemia*, Marta Rojas (today the editor of *Granma*, the Cuban government's official daily newspaper). Unlike the other journalists present who had come from Havana, her home was Santiago. The Havana newspapers in 1953 were not willing to pay reporters per diem to stay at the trial throughout its duration, especially since the government had imposed tight censorship on the stories coming out of the trial. Marta Rojas, on the other hand, who was already deeply sympathetic to the defendants, was able to stay for the duration of the trial, meticulously taking down everything that transpired. She did this surreptitiously on strips of paper that she folded concertina-fashion and hid under her skirt or in her clenched fist. Each night she spent several hours at the typewriter, transcribing the day's notes. The result was a unique record of the proceedings that otherwise would have been unobtainable. She recalls that, even though she lived near the court, it often took her hours to get home because so many people cut off from any other news source would stop her to get a report of the day's developments.

There was a buzz of excitement in the packed courtroom when the defendants arrived for the second day of the trial. Fidel made good use of the license the judge had given him. Both as a lawyer and an orator he was in a different class from the other participants, and he continued to use his skills with withering effect. He elicited from the prosecution witnesses the most damning testimony about their torture and murder of the prisoners. The audience was visibly on his side, and the sympathy he generated for his cause reached far beyond the courtroom.

When the third session began on the morning of September 26, Fidel was not in the courtroom. A military officer handed the judge a letter that stated: "The main defendant has not been brought to court according to the report from the assistant chief to Colonel Chaviano because he is presently ill in jail as shown in the enclosed medical certificate."

The court broke into an uproar as Fidel's brother Raúl leapt up and yelled, "Fidel is not sick!" Melba Hernández then produced, hidden in her hair, a letter from Fidel that he had slipped to her in prison the previous evening. It stated that he was in perfect health, but warned that his assassination was being planned. Captain Jesús Yañes Pelletier subsequently revealed that he had been ordered to poison Fidel, but had refused to do so. In order to prevent others from carrying out the act he made the plan widely known in the city. As a result, he was court-martialed, imprisoned, and expelled from the army. Later he went into exile in the United States and began working for the revolutionary movement.

That evening, the three judges of the court visited Fidel in his cell and determined that he was in good health. However, the director of the prison, under pressure from the military, refused to let him attend any further sessions of the trial.

It proceeded in his absence with the other revolutionaries defiantly sticking to their stand, acknowledging their role in the attack, and arguing for its validity as a political act. At the tenth session on October 5, 1953, all those who had actually participated in the Moncada and Bayamo attacks were found guilty, while charges against all of the various other defendants were dropped. Raúl and two others received thirteen-year sentences, twenty received ten-year sentences, and three received three-year sentences. Melba Hernández and Haydée Santamaría each received sentences of seven months, to be served at the women's reformatory at Guanajay.

Eleven days later, Fidel, vigorous and unbowed by his confinement, was brought to trial again, together with Fidel Labrador, who had been badly wounded in the attack and was unable to attend the first trial. The hearing was held in the nurses' lounge of the Santiago Civil Hospital, where the authorities thought they could carry out the proceedings in relative secrecy. Marta Rojas was again present, however. In his own defense, Fidel made a two-hour speech, largely unrelated to the charges against him, in which he analyzed the human suffering and social ills that afflicted Cuba, and argued that revolutionary change was necessary. But it was not just the content, but his manner of delivery that stunned the court. Later known by the closing phrase, "History will absolve me," the speech represents the simplest and probably the most accurate statement of Fidel's political beliefs. Fidel had worked on the speech for several days and had tried it out the night before on a fellow prisoner, Gerardo Poll Cabrera, a railway worker, who had been put in Fidel's cell now that the other conspirators had gone.

Marta Rojas recalls the startling impact of his speech on the court. "There was something very unusual in 'History Will Absolve Me.' I was simply carried by his words. . . . It was the first time I was listening to such things. I had heard nothing similar to that before. The same was true with the guards. I was watching the guards standing with their weapons loose . . . listening, carried away by Fidel. . . . They were simply absorbed and engrossed by his words. When Fidel was through with his speech, there was silence, and he had to slap on the table and say something like, 'Well, I finished. This is all.' "

At that point, the stunned and flustered judge rang his bell and called, "Order! Order!" even though there was silence. Fidel walked around the table to his lawyer and old friend, Baudilio Castellanos, handed him a book he had borrowed, and asked what he thought of his speech. The court was in disarray, taken aback by the unprecedented oratory and commanding behavior of the defendant. Finally, however, reasserting control, the judge declared Fidel guilty and sentenced him to thirteen years. As he was leaving the room, Fidel asked Marta Rojas, "Did you take notes?" "Yes," she replied, and he smiled.

In sentencing the original twenty-six men and two women, the court had ordered that the men serve their time in la Cabaña Fortress in Havana. On October 13, they took off from Santiago de Cuba in two DC-3s, handcuffed in pairs and sitting on benches with their backs to the windows. As the planes approached Havana they turned left and flew south over the Gulf of Batabanó to the Isle of Pines. A last-minute decision had been made by the minister of interior, Ramón Hermida, to incarcerate them instead at the Presidio Modelo (Model Prison) on this island sixty miles off the southwest coast of Cuba. From there, both in prison and exile, they could not so easily continue to foment discord and revolution among young sympathizers as they could had they been imprisoned in Havana.

At the dusty landing strip, they were met by Lieutenant Pedro Rodríguez Coto, director of internal order at the prison. He was a tall, thin man with stooped shoulders and a large hooked nose. His eyes were masked by large dark glasses, and out of his back pocket protruded a coiled whip. He and a group of guards took delivery of the male prisoners, and the planes took off again to fly the two women to the National Women's Prison in Guanajay, in Pinar del Río Province.

The men were isolated from the other prisoners in a wing of the prison hospital. They slept in a long gallery, 120 feet by 24 feet. Whitewashed walls reflected the light of three bare 500-watt bulbs that burned twenty-four hours a day. Their iron beds lined the walls on either side. In the day they had access to a large courtyard. Discipline was strict and they were roused from bed every morning at 5 A.M. for a head count. Their only contact with the rest of the prison population was with two prisoners who brought in a sack of bread and a large can of milk for breakfast at 7:30 A.M. and returned at 11:00 with lunch and again at 5:00 P.M. with dinner. In the first few days, the leaderless group suffered from despondency adjusting to the new surroundings, reconciling themselves to their long sentences, and worrying about the plight of their families. They also anticipated that Fidel would be held apart from them as he had been at Boniato.

There was therefore great joy when, on Sunday, October 17, 1953, Fidel walked into Building 1 of the prison hospital and embraced his comrades, trying to hug them all at once. Immediately he started to reassert his authority and began organizing their activities. Their role in prison, he told them, was to be combative; they were not there merely to serve their sentences, but rather to use the time to prepare themselves for the continuing struggle after their release. They agreed to pool their few pesos and scanty supplies from relatives to meet the group's needs. They set up procedures for holding meetings, and established, under Fidel's direction, the Abel Santamaría Academy. Each morning, sitting at wooden tables at the edge of the courtyard in the shade of the overhanging roof, they gave instruction to one another in history, political theory, literature, geography, and mathematics. Fidel, however, did much of the teaching. In the afternoons they played chess, Ping-Pong, and volleyball. If any of the men had had the idea that once their sentence was over they would end their revolutionary career, Fidel had quickly dissuaded them.

By most accounts, the school was only a modest success because most of the men did not have the same academic interest or intellectual curiosity as did Fidel. He sought to galvanize their commitment to education by admonishing them with a quote from Martí: "A fortress of ideas is worth more than a fortress of stone." The idea was that they would be creating a fortress of ideas for themselves while in prison. But most of their efforts came out of loyalty to Fidel rather than any deep commitment to knowledge.

The opportunity for intellectual maturation that prison offered had a profoundly greater effect on Fidel than on the others. The setting was really not very different from the life he had lived in the Jesuit schools, and he found it relatively easy to commit himself to intensive study. As was the case in school, the external discipline of the prison system helped him to focus his own motivation and self-discipline on the task he had set himself. It was a crucial period in the development of his political philosophy and the crystallization of his dedication to revolution. After months of reading and contemplation, he would write in a letter, "I have rounded out my view of the world and determined the meaning of my life."

The prisoners were able to receive books, and they established the "Raúl García Gómez Library," named for their comrade who had been murdered in front of Melba and Haydée. By the time they were released twenty months later, thanks to the generosity of friends, relatives, sympathizers, and several university professors, the library contained more than a thousand volumes. Fidel read voraciously. During the first six months in prison his letters, mainly to Luis Conte Agüero and Naty Revuelta, contained lists of the titles he had read; added together they revealed his wide range of intellectual interests.

In a letter written in November, he mentions the works of Shakespeare, A. J. Cronin's *The Keys of the Kingdom*, André Maurois's *Memoirs*, García Llorente's *First Lessons in Philosophy*, Romain Rolland's *Jean-Christophe*, Victor Hugo's *Les Misérables*, Karl Marx's *The Eighteenth Brumaire of Louis Bonaparte*, and Axel Munthe's *The Story of San Michele*, the recounting of a physician's lifelong commitment to the struggle against social injustice and human suffering, a book that made a significant impression on Fidel.

"When I read the work of a famous author," Fidel wrote, "the history of a people, the doctrine of a thinker, the theories of an economist or the theses of a social reformer, I am filled with the desire to know everything that all authors have written, the doctrines of all philosophers, the treatises of all economists, and the theses of all apostles. I want to know everything, and I even go through the bibliographies in the books treasuring the hope of reading those books someday. Outside I chafed because I did not have enough time; here, where there seems to be too much time I am still chafing." The Jesuits had done a good job inculcating in him a fascination with ideas.

In a letter dated December 18, 1953, he mentioned William Thackeray's

Vanity Fair, Ivan Turgenev's *A Nest of the Gentry*, Jorge Amado's *Luis Carlos Prestes, Champion of Hope*, A. J. Cronin's *The Citadel*, Eric Knight's *Fugitives from Love*, the Dean of Canterbury's *Secret of Soviet Strength*, and Karl Marx's *Das Kapital*. A later letter referred to the works of Martí as his constant companion, which he was alternating with Victor Hugo's *William Shakespeare*, Honoré de Balzac's *The Magic Skin*, Stefan Zweig's *Biography of Little Napoleon*, Rómulo Gallegos's *On Equal Footing*, A. J. Cronin's *The Stars Look Down*, Somerset Maugham's *The Razor's Edge*, four of the eighteen volumes of *The Complete Works of Sigmund Freud*, and Dostoevski's *The Brothers Karamazov*, *The Insulted and the Humiliated*, *Crime and Punishment*, *The Idiot*, and *The House of the Dead*. These books represented only a sample of the literature he devoured during those first six months.

By March 1954, the scope of Fidel's self-tutoring program aimed at creating a thoroughly educated intellect was increasingly narrowing to the field of political theory. In a letter that month he wrote, "I have rolled up my sleeves and taken on a study of world history and political doctrines." He read a great deal of Marx and Lenin, but also a range of other political theorists, and on April 15 was desperately asking friends on the outside to get him information about Franklin Roosevelt.

> Roosevelt. I mainly want information on him: in agriculture, his price-raising policies for crops, the protection and conservation of soil fertility, credit facilities, the moratorium on debts and the extension of markets at home and abroad; in the social field, how he provided more jobs, shortened the workday, raised wages and pushed through social assistance to the unemployed, the old and the crippled; and in the field of the general economy, his reorganization of industry, new tax systems, regulation of the trusts, and banking and monetary reforms.

It is the custom today, both among the Cuban leadership and, ironically, right-wing politicians in the United States, to suggest that Fidel's Marxism long antedated the Moncada attack. That he early had strong ideas about social justice based on his Christian understanding of right and wrong is evident, but there is little to suggest that he had an ironclad commitment to any particular political theory. He continued to identify strongly with historic figures, but it was the conception of revolution, especially the French model, and the mastery of power that dominated his thinking. It was during this period in prison that he expanded his awareness of political ideology and began to formulate an independent set of political beliefs. Yet he found it very difficult. He saw the protean nature of political theory, and felt it had to be adapted to the times to achieve concrete goals. In a

96

letter of January 27, 1954, Fidel expresses lucidly his sense of the expediency of political ideology:

> Human thought is unfailingly conditioned by the circumstances of the era. In the case of a political genius, I venture to affirm that his genius depends exclusively on his era. Lenin in the time of Catherine, when the aristocracy was the ruling class, would necessarily have been a champion of the bourgeoisie, which was the revolutionary class at the time, or could have simply been ignored by history. If Martí had lived when Havana was seized by the English, he would have defended the standard of Spain alongside his father. What would Napoleon, Mirabeau, Danton, and Robespierre have been in the times of Charlemagne? . . . Julius Caesar would never have crossed the Rubicon in the early years of the Republic before the intense class struggle that shook Rome was sharpened and the great plebian party developed.

Fidel saw political ideology as a pragmatic tool to be adapted by "political geniuses" in the service of historic achievement. He made the further point in this letter that creative geniuses were not dependent for their recognition on the circumstances of their times. A great work of art was a great work of art in any era. Making that distinction, he said, "A literary, philosophical or artistic genius has a considerably broader field in terms of time and history than that offered by the world of reality and action, which is the only arena for the political geniuses." These views explain a great deal about what would later seem such enigmatic ideological positions. Pragmatism in the pursuit of power was clearly the underlying concept that he embraced.

In addition to his reading and letter writing, Fidel was permitted visits by family members twice a month. Mirta came regularly, as did his sister Lidia. Together they formed Fidel's vital conduit to the outside world, and with the help of Luis Conte Agüero they were able to keep his political life alive.

This free communication, as well as the strikingly tolerant treatment they had received from the guards, came to an end on February 12, 1954. On that day, President Batista made a visit to the prison to dedicate a new power plant. By standing on chairs in the corner of their ward, the prisoners were able to peer out of a high window and see the presidential entourage. Fidel, determined to take advantage of the unique opportunity, paced up and down as the men yelled taunts and insults through the window. They should sing the "26 of July hymn," composed earlier by one of the revolutionaries, he decided. This they did at the top of their lungs as Batista and his group were hustled away from the area. In reprisal, Fidel and several of the other men were placed in solitary confinement.

They were miserable little cells in a building for the mentally ill, without light, and into which the rain poured during the frequent thunderstorms.

A week after Fidel was put in solitary confinement, on February 20, 1954, Melba and Haydée were released from the women's prison. One of their first acts that day was to lay a wreath at the tomb of Eduardo Chibás, a striking reminder of the close allegiance they still considered the movement and Fidel owed to his memory. Within days they started reestablishing Fidel's network of political contacts and prepared to become his representatives in Havana. Their primary activity, together with Luis Conte Agüero, would be to organize groups around the country committed to amnesty for the Moncadistas.

Fidel was best known in Cuba as a student leader. Even after he graduated and was practicing law, the public still identified him in his student role and had an indulgent attitude toward his political activities. After Moncada, he was suddenly a hero to a much broader cross-section of young people, but was also seen as a serious political threat by the older politicians, particularly those who had opted for some compromise with Batista. Haydée and Melba found themselves confronted with considerable hostility and ostracism; many doors were closed to them, even by some former supporters. It required considerable dedication on their part to continue to work for the cause under these circumstances.

Shortly after his arrival on the Isle of Pines, Fidel started to reconstruct the speech he had given in his defense at the trial. "History Will Absolve Me" has been quoted in a variety of different forms, but the final version that appeared as a pamphlet in 1954, although a substantial elaboration of the original speech, contained almost verbatim what he had said at the trial. Writing with lemon juice between the lines of legitimate correspondence, or smuggling tracts between the double bottoms of matchboxes, Fidel was able, bit by bit, to get out the entire text.

Melba and Haydée had a list of people to whom Fidel was corresponding. They would retrieve the letters and after ironing them to make the words written in lemon juice legible, they would transcribe the material, which Melba's father, an excellent typist, would then type up. Marta Rojas was at Melba's house almost every day, and says that she was amazed, comparing the material with the notes she had taken in Santiago, at the accuracy with which Fidel had been able to repeat his speech.

Edited into this basic text was additional material contained in a long letter to Luis Conte Agüero, which Fidel had been able to send earlier in his confinement.

Fidel told Haydée and Melba to get 100,000 copies printed and distributed. The cost was prohibitive for an organization virtually without resources. "What is the difference between twenty-five and one hundred thousand, only paper and ink," Fidel responded when they argued the impossibility of the task. In the end they produced ten thousand and Fidel was very satisfied. "That is why I asked you to get out one hundred thousand," he said. "If I had told you to print five hundred you would have aimed for five hundred and never printed ten thousand." It was quintessential Fidel, believing that accomplishment was limited only by the inadequacy of one's own vision. He characteristically set goals that most would never have the audacity to suggest, and then expected heaven and earth to be moved to achieve them.

The pamphlets were distributed all over Cuba by several loyal friends, including Gustavo Ameijeiras, who traveled in an old jalopy begging money for gas wherever he could.

"History Will Absolve Me" is the classic document of the Cuban revolution. Fidel began by reviewing the difficulties he had encountered in preparing his defense, and the ways in which the government and the prosecutors had violated the judicial system. He then gave a detailed account of the entire Moncada event. It was in effect a full admission of everything with which he was charged, but it served, at a time when only the government version could get into the newspaper, as a way to tell his side of the story both for immediate political benefit and for history, the latter being particularly on his mind.

The strategy, he said, had been based on the belief that if they were successful in capturing Moncada the people would rise in their support. "When we speak of the people we are not talking about those who live in comfort, the conservative elements of the nation, who welcome any oppressive regime, any dictatorship, any despotism . . . we mean the vast unredeemed masses, those to whom everyone makes promises and who are deceived by all." There then followed a detailed documentation of the extreme poverty, deprivation, and suffering in which most Cubans lived: six hundred thousand Cubans without work (in a population of about six million), five hundred thousand farm laborers living in miserable shacks, two hundred thousand peasant families without a single acre of land on which to grow food, while half of the productive land in the country is owned by foreigners. He then detailed the levels of illiteracy, parasite infestation, malnutrition, and what amounted to indentured servitude under which most rural workers lived. He decried the lack of health care, education, and social services, and those which did exist, usually staffed by dedicated professionals, were weighed down by corruption at the top. All of this he contrasted with the lavish lifestyle of the millionaires and others in power, most of whom had acquired their wealth not by honest work, but by graft and corruption.

He offered as a remedy five "revolutionary laws":

99

- Return the power to the people and proclaim the 1940 Constitution the Supreme Law of the State, until such time as the people should decide to modify or change it. [This last phrase would later have particular significance.]
- Give nonmortgageable and nontransferable ownership of the land to all tenant and sub-tenant farmers, lessees, sharecroppers, and squatters who hold parcels of five *caballerías* of land or less. [One *caballería* is approximately 33 acres.]
- Grant workers and employees the right to share 30 percent of the profits of all large industrial, mercantile, and mining enterprises, including sugar mills.
- Grant all sugar planters the right to share 55 percent of all sugar production and a minimum quota of forty thousand *arrobas* for all small tenant farmers who have been established for three years or more. [One *arroba* is about 25 pounds.]
- Order the confiscation of all holdings, all ill-gotten gains of those who had committed frauds during previous regimes, as well as the holdings and ill-gotten gains of all their legates and heirs.

He went on to describe the terrible abuse and torture to which his men had been subjected after their capture, and he detailed the cold-blooded murder of several dozen of them. He tied responsibility for this directly to Batista, accusing him of being one of the most despicable tyrants in the history of the world.

Finally, citing extensively from Montesquieu, Thomas Aquinas, Martin Luther, John Locke, Rousseau, Thomas Paine, the United States Constitution, and other sources, he carefully laid out a legal and historical rationale to justify his right to try to overthrow an unjust dictator who held power illegitimately. Under such circumstances, he argued, he could not possibly be guilty of any crime.

Woven throughout the document is the thread of Cuban history and the story of the great Cuban heroes who had struggled against great odds for justice and national independence. Quoting, among others, Martí and General José Miró Argenter, chief of Antonio Maceo's general staff, Fidel lavishly wraps himself in the folds of Cuban patriotism, elevating himself to the stature of these revered national heroes.

"History Will Absolve Me" has been attacked by critics as unoriginal and a distillation or hodgepodge of existing ideas. It has even been suggested that it was lifted almost entirely from the work of another Cuban writer. In later years, Fidel was accused of betraying many of the ideals it contained as he made Cuba a Marxist state. There is some validity to these arguments. However, such criticism misses the fact that whatever its inspiration, the document, in describing the social ills that afflicted Cuba and a program of reform, represented exactly what Fidel believed at the time. In addition, having survived Moncada, even if unexpectedly, Fidel needed to begin orchestrating the future of the movement. "History Will Absolve Me" was a political document promulgated for very specific and carefully thought-out strategic purposes. It was intended to enshrine the Moncada attack in a cloak of idealism to counter any perception that it was an impulsive act of political frustration, albeit by brave men. In this respect it was an important answer to the Communists, who had denounced the attack in exactly these terms, describing it as a "putsch." It was vital to Fidel and his ambitions to have Moncada understood as one event within the context of a long-term struggle to achieve revolution in Cuba around a set of clear ideals. It must be remembered that in 1953 most Cubans saw Moncada as a failure, and Fidel, facing thirteen years in prison, as finished politically. Thus, it was essential to create an image of himself as the leader of a viable movement.

"History Will Absolve Me" was to serve as a core around which such a movement could be created. It was a way of giving potential supporters access to Fidel while he remained physically confined. He had an intuitive understanding of the importance of propaganda, describing it as "the soul of every struggle." While "History Will Absolve Me" caused apoplexy among the Cuban wealthy elite and United States investors, it was a document carefully crafted to mobilize the broadest possible support while at the same time offending the smallest number of potential backers. It was acceptable to the Communists (indeed, some of the statistical material seems to have come from a book by Blas Roca), but avoided mentioning communism, Marxism, or even socialism. It identified what most educated Cubans knew in their hearts were the great injustices in their country, without threatening them with either the time frame or the methods for redress. There was no attack on the United States and there was no call to revolution. It was intended to draw to his cause the idealistic youth of the country, whether they were currently affiliated with the Communists, the Ortodoxos, or, as in most instances, were independent. It never reached the mass of the population, and even within the educated community its impact fell far short of Fidel's grandiose fantasies. But it was stunningly successful in the quality of commitment it elicited from a relatively small group of new followers who were enough to form the basis of "The Movement." Vilma Espín, who later became a central figure of the organization, and who married Raúl, has said, "The tremendous impact of 'History Will Absolve Me' must be stressed. . . . I was in the laboratory when someone gave me a copy. . . . We were all fascinated. It spoke a new language and it set out a clear program around which we could all center our struggle, an advanced program that was attractive to young people."

In solitary confinement, with the labor of drafting "History Will Absolve Me" complete and its impact relatively modest, facing perhaps years more of isolation, Fidel became increasingly depressed. For an intensely energetic and ambitious young man who had used his boundless enthusiasm to try to make every moment in his life count, nothing was more discouraging than the prospect of the years slipping away as he languished in lonely seclusion. Others he knew were nurturing their political careers while he was in danger of being forgotten.

The situation was suddenly made profoundly worse by a development in his private life. He had always been too busy to devote the necessary time and effort to his marriage to Mirta, and too often she and Fidelito had been abandoned while he pursued his political ambitions. His romantic involvement with Naty Revuelta during the months prior to Moncada had compounded the problem. Despite these problems, his affection for Mirta was deep and sincere. Thirty years later, a member of her family would say, "I think she was the only woman he ever truly loved," a view shared by several people who knew them then. During the early part of his incarceration, she traveled regularly to the Isle of Pines to see him and served together with his sister Lidia as an essential intermediary in keeping alive his political network. Max Lesnick, president of the Ortodoxos Youth, recalls meeting her at the airport as she returned from one of these trips. Seeing her at the other side of the crowded arrival area, he called out, "Mirta Díaz Balart!" to which she responded, "Not Díaz Balart, Díaz Balart de Castro." To Lesnick it signaled the deep sense of loyalty she felt toward her husband.

Fidel, then, was stunned on July 17, 1954, when he heard about an announcement by the minister of interior stating that Mirta was to be dismissed from a sinecure in the ministry, an arrangement set up by her brother, the sub-secretary, whereby she received regular paychecks. Not believing that she had accepted money from his sworn enemies, he wrote to her the same day, saying that someone was obviously trying to slander him and it should be fought in the courts. He also wrote to his friend Luis Conte Agüero, attacking the minister of interior as effeminate, in Fidel's eyes the worst insult he could hurl at him. Describing himself as blinded by rage, he branded the announcement an attempt to discredit him in the eyes of the Cuban people. He again reaffirmed his complete faith in Mirta.

Four days later, on July 21, Lidia came to see him. She not only confirmed that the announcement was true, but told him that Mirta was planning to divorce him. Fidel's expectations of Mirta were probably unreasonable under the circumstances. He had gone to prison leaving her without income and of necessity dependent on her conservative and politically powerful family who had always opposed the marriage. Knowing that he might have to serve his entire thirteen-year term, experiencing constant pressure from her family, and even possibly knowing about his liaison with another woman, it was probably inevitable that Mirta should have taken the action she did.

The following week, on July 26, 1954, exactly a year after the Moncada attack, Fidel received a visit from the minister of interior, Hermida, and two other members of the Batista government. Hermida, perhaps hoping that Fidel would be more vulnerable at this moment of personal crisis, adopted a conciliatory manner and excused himself for his role in Mirta's sinecure by laying the blame squarely on her brother Rafael. He also tentatively held out the possibility of amnesty should Fidel be willing to change his ways. Fidel refused any clemency if it meant compromising his principles, but was willing to accept Hermida's contention that any differences between them should be kept at a political level and not be allowed to degenerate into personal attacks.

In rejecting the amnesty offer, Fidel issued a statement in which he said, "One thousand years of prison before I renounce any of my principles." This definitive Cuban style sounds excessively elaborate to Americans, but it struck an appropriate romantic chord for the average Cuban.

The following weeks were perhaps the lowest in Fidel's life. The loneliness of solitary confinement, the anguish of the divorce compounded by the fear that he might lose his son who was now living with the Díaz Balarts, and the increasing atmosphere of political moderation in the country all conspired to make the future look bleak. The personal hurt over the breakup with Mirta was compounded by what he saw as the damage to his political integrity of having his wife on the Batista payroll. During the same period, the family home in Oriente Province for which he felt great nostalgia burned down.

Fidel's resentment toward society and especially the ruling elite that existed before Moncada had hardened into a deep bitterness, as a result of both the torture and murder of his men and the months of suffering in solitary confinement.

There were occasional moments of elation. On October 24, 1954, he heard a radio broadcast from a political rally in Santiago de Cuba. In an effort to legitimize his presidency, Batista had called elections for November 1. Running against him was former President Grau San Martín, who was to address the rally that night. As he started to speak, Fidel, in his isolation, heard the crowd chanting, "Fidel Castro . . . Fidel Castro." Grau quickly responded, "Friends, the first act of my government will be to free all the political prisoners, including the boys of Moncada."

103

Fidel believed it was naive to think that a dictator who had seized power in a coup d'état would be willing to relinquish it if he lost an election. Fidel therefore directed his supporters on the outside to encourage people to boycott the election. By voting they would be lending legitimacy to Batista's seizure of the presidency. It became increasingly clear that the election was rigged, and as a result, on October 30, Grau withdrew, leaving Batista the winner by default.

Fidel has often been lucky in his career by finding himself allied with or counterposed against individuals whose personal characteristics and idiosyncracies offered a perfect foil off which he could play. This was never truer than with Batista. The onetime army sergeant of mixed ethnic background including both black and Chinese blood was, despite his great political acumen, a relatively simple man of limited intellect. Above all he wanted to be loved and respected as a national hero by the Cuban people. He never was and knew he never would be accepted as an equal by the old oligarchy, and he had to seize power because he could never win it at the ballot box. Once in the presidency, he was constantly looking for ways to improve his popularity with the average citizen and to undo his image as a ruthless dictator. Yet at the same time he suffered from a constant underlying fear of losing power, perhaps guilty about his illegitimate acquisition of it. When threatened, he reacted like a cornered animal, lashing out with uncontrolled viciousness. These two seemingly antithetical facets of his character created a pattern of leadership that appeared inconsistent and often contradictory. Fidel, however, understood Batista well, and over the next four years adroitly exploited these dual features of his personality to bring about his downfall.

After his inauguration on February 24, 1955, Batista was riding high, even though there was a deep sense of disillusionment in the country about the way he had rigged the election. Vice President Richard Nixon made an official visit to give the blessings of the Eisenhower administration, and a newly signed agreement to sell sugar to the Soviet Union promised an important boost to the economy. Batista launched a number of limited and long-promised public works programs aimed at improving the standard of living of the average citizen. The political opposition was in complete disarray. From such a position of strength Batista was lulled into believing that he could safely acquiesce to the demands of those who claimed that his government could have legitimacy only if he freed all of the political prisoners. Even his advisers concurred that it was an effective way of squelching the smoldering discontent. Fidel, appreciating Batista's psychological vulnerability in his quest for legitimacy, urged Luis Conte Agüero to intensify the efforts of the amnesty groups. Grau had promised in his campaign to free the Moncadistas, and under pressure Batista had then been forced to do the same. The question now was whether he would honor the promise. It is a reflection of his poor judgment and the minimal threat that he must have considered Fidel and his men that on May 7, 1955, he signed a law granting blanket amnesty. On May 15, the Moncadistas were set free.

The men were greeted by their families in a joyous reunion at the gates of the prison. Lidia, Juana, and Emma were there to welcome Fidel to freedom. However, even on this intensely personal occasion Fidel did not miss the opportunity to get some political mileage out of the situation. As he departed, he embraced the commanding officer of the prison guard, and to the members of the press present he said, "This is a spontaneous and sincere expression . . . because this officer is a gentleman in the full sense of the word." It was a continuation of the calculated effort begun at the trial to imply that the military was not the enemy but merely the tool of the enemy. It was an attempt to create a split in their ranks.

Fidel's return to Havana was triumphant. He held a press conference on the Isle of Pines, and reporters, photographers, and well-wishers followed him from the ferryboat to the mainland and onto the train to the capital, where he was greeted by a large crowd of supporters including throngs of students. They lifted him through the window of the train, and carried him shoulder high to Lidia's apartment on Twenty-third Street, where he would live for the next two months. There, more reporters were waiting. During his first few days of freedom he gave many interviews.

"Do you plan to stay in Cuba?" he was asked.

"Yes, I plan to stay in Cuba and fight the government in the open, pointing out its mistakes, denouncing its faults, exposing gangsters, profiteers and thieves," he replied.

"Will you remain in the Ortodoxo Party?"

"We will struggle to unite the whole country under the flag of Chibás's revolutionary movement. . . . I am an Ortodoxo."

Actually Fidel was carefully testing the waters during his first few days back in Havana. In his final months in prison he had methodically thought through a long-range strategy for seizing power, and was irrevocably committed to it. He envisaged a highly disciplined movement, with the veterans of Moncada at its "indestructible core." On the ferryboat from the Isle of Pines, gathering the men around him on the deck, he outlined his plans and obtained a pledge of loyalty and unity in the continuing struggle. It was to be a secret movement, but from the tightly organized nucleus they would build a broader organization. Their unequivocal goal was revolution.

But Fidel was returning to a much mellower political climate than the one he had left. Although he was personally acclaimed, and various groups were regularly exploding bombs around the country, the majority of the people were eager for tranquility, and a mood of compromise pervaded the political scene. Batista was increasingly seen as someone who could be negotiated with, someone who was reasonable, as evidenced by his freeing of the political prisoners. At the University of Havana, a new generation of leaders had emerged who felt no immediate loyalty to this former student. Fidel was grasping to see where he could fit in.

Even among the ranks of his own followers he had problems. Most of those involved in the July 26 attacks who had escaped had gone into exile in Mexico and Central America. They, too, were covered by Batista's amnesty, and many of them returned to Havana at this time. While they were in exile, Melba Hernández, after coming out of prison, visited them in Mexico City. She told them that Fidel wanted to organize a new movement to be called "The Survivors of Moncada." As many of the exiles had been involved at Bayamo, not Moncada, this news caused great consternation. They interpreted it as another effort by Fidel to write only Moncada into the history books. They suggested as an alternative "the 26 of July Movement." They had already used the name in Mexico on the invitations when they had invited the entire Cuban exile community to a celebration on the first anniversary of the attacks. Although Fidel subsequently accepted their advice on this issue, there were other sources of tension. When the exiles returned there was a joyous sense of reunion and camaraderie, but there were also varying degrees of persisting personal loyalty to Fidel and a range of ideological views. Some were not convinced that revolution was now the answer, or, if it was, only as a last resort, not a first choice. Some had remained unswervingly loyal to Fidel in Mexico, especially Nico López; the rest believed that these individuals kept careful note of what they did, where they went, and with whom they met, and then reported it back to Fidel through Melba. Because of this there was resentment that Fidel was trying to control them. For his part, Fidel was upset that Raúl Martínez Arará, while in Mexico, had had dealings with former President Prío, Fidel's old nemesis.

A memo to Fidel was drafted by several dissident members of the group. They suggested how they thought the new organization should operate. One of the authors, Orlando Castro, recalled that it contained three points: "First, we should be democratically organized like a political party. Second, we should tell the people of Cuba what our program was and what our goals were. Third, we did not want only a chief; we wanted a board of directors." Eleven signed the memo, including three who had been with Fidel on the Isle of Pines. Those whose names would go on the memo were carefully selected. "We did not want to have many signatures because we did not want to oppress him. We wanted only to show him there were people who didn't think it was okay the way he was doing things. We only took eleven signatures, but we chose people who were in prison with him, and we chose signatures of people who were [in Mexico] with us."

Fidel obtained a draft copy of the memo and sent first Raúl and later Pedro Miret to try to talk Orlando Castro out of formally presenting it to him. When this failed, a meeting was held in mid-June at the home of Jesús Montané, one of Fidel's most loyal supporters. It was a small group, including both Orlando Castro and Raúl Martínez Arará. Fidel was angry about the memo and flatly rejected it. "When have you seen a revolution led by a committee—never in history," he said. As for the need to present a program of action to the Cuban people, he reminded them that he already had written "History Will Absolve Me." On a more conciliatory note, he said that he had recently read *La Rebellion de la Massas* by the Spanish philosopher Ortega y Gasset and was convinced that the course of action he was planning was the only way to seize power. The meeting ended without ill feelings, but it was the parting of the ways for some of the Moncada/Bayamo group with Fidel. One of those who broke with him at that time recalls how he felt: "If we were fighting for democracy we had to tell the people what we were going to do when we inherited the power. If we are fighting for democracy we have to act as a democracy in our own group. If Fidel takes all decisions there is no democracy. He is a *caudillo* [dictator], another *caudillo*, and that's no good for Cuba. We are not fighting for that."

Only a handful abandoned Fidel, and several of those who had signed the memo backed down. As Orlando Castro says, "The personality of Fidel is very strong. And most of the people who did not agree with the way he was doing things went back with him afterward anyway. But I am sure Fidel never forgets that some of the people with him now once signed a document he did not like."

In order to regain his political momentum, Fidel had not only to re-organize the movement and solidify his relationship with his diehard loy-alists, he also had to carve out a niche for himself in the public mind and create a political atmosphere favorable to his cause. He set about the latter in an aggressive way. The recent relatively benign behavior of Batista had created an atmosphere in Cuba that was quite unfavorable to Fidel and his extremist views. There was what Marta Rojas describes as a "conspiracy of silence" against him in which both Batista and the political opposition tried to prevent his access to the radio or the print media. Fidel contended that despite the superficial political tranquility Batista was still holding power illegitimately and that the recent election had been a sham. If the Cuban people could be convinced of this, the apathy, he was sure, would disappear. Tactically he also knew that the quickest way to get the public on his side was by provoking the regime into overreacting against him. He therefore immediately launched into a series of vehement attacks against Batista.

Within ten days of his release, on May 19, 1955, Fidel went on the radio in Havana to launch his campaign of denunciation against Batista. Later, the station manager was arrested and warned against allowing Fidel to speak again. The following day, Fidel was scheduled to address a mass rally at the university. The government initially banned the broadcast of his speech, and then ordered the entire event canceled. The homes of several of the Moncadistas, including Raúl and Pedro Miret, were raided. On May 21, the Ortodoxo Party issued a manifesto, of which Fidel had been one of the coauthors, calling for new elections and the restoration of the 1940 Constitution. It was largely a ploy with the anticipation that Batista would refuse their call. Within three days Batista responded by banning any further radio and television programs by the Ortodoxos. On May 29, after Fidel published a condemnation of Batista in the magazine *Bohemia*, he was prohibited from making any more public speeches.

Fidel's strategy was already working. Provoked by Fidel's personal attacks, Batista responded impulsively by trying to use intimidation and the control of free speech to shut him up. Yet he was at the same time constrained by his desperate desire to maintain an atmosphere of tranquility and not, by excessive brutality, lose the good will of the people. He became a victim of his own ambivalence. His actions to suppress dissent earned him public enmity, but his caution in banning Fidel's speeches, but not his writing, left Fidel free to go on provoking him.

Batista made another political error. He took Fidel's attacks personally, and then responded personally. The result was that in his defensiveness he elevated Fidel to his own stature; he gave Fidel credibility by showing that he took him seriously as a threat. Had he stayed out of the conflict and had others in his administration appeal to the Cuban people to reject Fidel as a disruptive element, while he tried to create an environment conducive to political peace and economic prosperity, the results might have been very different.

Fidel forged ahead. He was now writing a daily column for *La Calle* and used it to make the average Cuban aware for the first time of the atrocities that had been committed after Moncada. Colonel del Río Chaviano responded by accusing Fidel of trying to malign the army and rejected the contention that he had any personal responsibility for the deaths of the prisoners. In return, Fidel published in *Bohemia* a scathing rejoinder entitled, "Chaviano, You Lie!" Again Batista took it upon himself to denounce the article, only drawing more attention to it and demonstrating the potency of Fidel's attacks on him.

In June, Jorge Agostini, a chief of the presidential guard under Prío, was arrested and then shot. While the official position was that he had been killed while trying to escape, Fidel in his column accused the government of being responsible for his murder. Also during this period, apparently random bombings were continuing to occur throughout the island. Fidel took the position that bombing and other forms of senseless terrorism did nothing but strengthen the government's hand by encouraging public support for oppression. He went further, however, accusing the government of using paid provocateurs to plant many of the bombs to justify their clampdown against any form of dissent. This was the final straw as far as Batista was concerned. He had *La Calle* closed down and the editor, Luis Orlando Rodríguez, arrested. The newspaper was accused not only of stirring up dissent and making wrongful accusations against the government, but also of being under the direction and control of Communist elements. Ironically, the individual responsible for carrying out Batista's orders in closing the paper was Ramón Vasconcelos, its former editor and Fidel's sponsor, who had since become minister of information.

At the same time, Raúl and twenty-six other people were accused in a blanket indictment of being involved in a conspiracy against the government with former President Prío. Raúl was specifically charged with planting a bomb in La Tosca, a movie theater. Skillfully avoiding arrest, he went to the Mexican Embassy where he was granted political asylum and given safe passage out of the country.

Raúl's departure was probably the final event in Fidel's own decision to go into exile. Life had become very dangerous for him, and the real possibility existed of again being imprisoned, or even killed. His strategy of provocation against Batista had run its course with modest success, but it had not mobilized the hoped-for massive public outcry against the dictator.

During the busy six weeks that he had been out of prison, Fidel had publicly taken the position that he favored peace and had asserted that a revolution could occur wihout armed struggle. "Sometimes a mass movement can accomplish what an insurrection can not," he said during this period. But he did not believe it. He was unwaveringly committed to a course of armed revolution and his only concern was how to bring it about. His growing support among young people and the progressive elements in the Ortodoxo Party led to his being offered several important positions in the party, including a member of the executive council and the party's candidate for president of the Havana city council. He turned down all offers because his ambition now was to gamble everything on leading his own national revolutionary movement, for which the activities of the Ortodoxo Party were becoming increasingly irrelevant.

The decision to leave Cuba was preeminently a pragmatic one. However, it had particular romantic appeal. Fidel was following in the footsteps of his hero, Martí, who had similarly gone into exile at a crucial stage in the independence struggle. It was also the course Guiteras had been planning at the time he was killed. Fidel's major concern was to insure that he leave behind a viable organization that would carry on the struggle in his absence. To this end he devoted himself intensively during the weeks immediately prior to his departure.

During this period he met with the remnants of the Movimiento Nacional Revolucionaria (MNR) and its former leader Rafael García Bárcena, who had led the attempted coup shortly before the Moncada attack. Fidel convinced the leaders of the organization, Faustino Pérez, a medical student, and Armando Hart, a lawyer, to fuse the MNR with the 26 of July Movement, as it now offered the best hope of overthrowing Batista. Through this fusion he acquired prestige, as the MNR was well regarded in activist circles. In addition, he obtained the services of several experienced and skilled organizers. Apart from Pérez and Hart, the most important was Frank País. Frank was a young Baptist schoolteacher from Santiago de Cuba who had organized his own revolutionary group in the province. He was brilliant and passionately committed to the revolutionary cause, and his own skeleton organization extended across Oriente. Fidel appointed him to head all of the "action groups" for the 26 of July Movement in Cuba.

There is conflicting evidence as to when the M-26-7 (26th of July Movement) was formally launched. The term had been used earlier by the exiles in Mexico, but it was probably at a meeting held within ten days of Fidel's release from prison that he officially adopted the label.

Although divorced from Mirta, Fidel had seen a good deal of Fidelito during this period. If he had any regrets about leaving the country it was that he and his son would be separated. He also had another personal matter to deal with. While in prison he had maintained his relationship with Naty Revuelta, and she was now pregnant by him. Prior to leaving, he told her that if she accompanied him to Mexico he would marry her. She declined. Later, when criticized for his conduct toward her, he said, "She had her chance but she missed the train."

It is interesting that after suffering as a child because of his illegitimacy, and feeling such resentment toward his father as a result, he should repeat the situation himself. This appears to be yet another example of his strong identification with his father and the extent to which he was becoming like him.

Money, as always, was a problem. Fidel received a small stipend from his parents, which enabled him to get by during this period and covered his airfare out of the country.

110

Fidel left Cuba on July 7, 1955. As he departed he sent a letter to all of the major political leaders in the country, simultaneously releasing a copy to the press. His time in prison had allowed him to decide irrevocably how he would use his life. From his extensive reading, he had acquired a sense of his place in history. His perception of himself as a man of destiny was becoming unshakable.

> I am leaving Cuba because all the doors of peaceful struggle have been closed to me.
>
> Six weeks after being released from prison I am convinced more than ever of the dictatorship's intention, masked in many ways, to remain in power for twenty years, ruling as now by the use of terror and crime and ignoring the patience of the Cuban people, which has its limits.
>
> As a follower of Martí, I believe the hour has come to take our rights and not beg for them, to fight instead of pleading for them.
>
> I will reside somewhere in the Caribbean.
>
> From trips such as this one does not return, or else one returns with tyranny beheaded at one's feet.

Chapter Six

MEXICO City had long been a place of refuge for Cuban exiles. Each oppressive regime in Havana forced a new group of dissidents to escape to the city. Some eventually returned home, others took up a permanent life in exile. What they had in common was the shared experience of being forced to flee their homeland because of their political beliefs. Thus they had great sympathy for one another's plight as well as an intense interest in the most recent political developments in Cuba. Together they formed a sometimes tightly knit and politically attuned community that was supportive and nurturing of new arrivals, especially those who still had aspirations to power back in Cuba. At the same time, they were also often split by the same disagreements that had divided them in Havana.

For the Mexican government, it was an uneasy relationship. Eager on the one hand to retain an image as a refuge for the oppressed, yet at the same time desirous of maintaining good relations with whatever regime was in power in Cuba, the government acted as an irritable host. Most of the time the refugees were quietly tolerated, but when their revolutionary activities became too overt, or when the government was pressured by Cuban officials, the laws would be used, often arbitrarily, to clamp down on the exiles. At times the government officials would be bribed into collaborating with Cuban agents spying on politically active exiles.

This was the milieu into which Fidel entered in early July. Raúl had arrived two weeks earlier, and Fidel joined him in a seedy hotel in the Insurgentes Norte district of the city. Because it was cheap, Fidel took a small garret at the top of the building. They ate a majority of their meals at the apartment of a Cuban woman, Maria Antonia González de Paloma, at 49 Calle Amparan. Maria Antonia's brother Isidoro was a revolutionary exile who earlier had befriended some of the Moncadistas and arranged for them to stay at the apartment. The connection and accommodations had then been passed on to Raúl. Subsequently, Raúl would move into the apartment.

Using introductions provided by an Ortodoxo leader, Juan Orta Cardona, and by the Moncada and Bayamo veterans who had been in exile there, Fidel began to establish relationships with potential sponsors. Through Maria Antonia González he met the sisters Odilia and Oneida Pino Izquierdo, who in turn introduced him to their brother Onelio, a former navy officer who had fled from Cuba at the time of the Batista coup. He also became acquainted with a third sister, Orquídea Pino, a beautiful former nightclub singer, and her husband, a Mexican engineer, Alfonso "Fofo" Gutiérrez. This couple, wealthy and well connected socially, lived in a house with a swimming pool surrounded by a high stone wall in the affluent suburb of Pedregal de San Angel.

This group provided the base on which Fidel was able to build the initial organizational structure for his revolutionary expedition. They lent their homes for meetings, they rented cars for him in their names, they made connections with potential supporters, and they provided accommodations for the M-26-7 members who periodically visited from Cuba. Fofo Gutiérrez, convinced by his wife of the justice of the cause, became Fidel's most generous patron in Mexico.

Despite the interest and support of these people, Fidel felt lonely and isolated in Mexcio. He missed the sustenance that the furious political activity in Cuba had provided, he missed the camaraderie of his political cronies, and he missed his family, especially his sisters and his son. In the first few weeks, he heard nothing from Havana. To deal with his discouragement, he buried himself in his writing. He studiously penned two important documents, "A Message to the Congress of Ortodoxos Militants" and "Manifesto Number One of the 26 of July Movement to the People of Cuba." The former was prepared for the party's national congress scheduled for August 16. He pawned his overcoat to pay the printing costs.

On August 1, he received the first progress report from Melba Hernández on the movement's activities since his departure, and was considerably cheered. Immediately he sat down and prepared a long response. In it he warned his followers against submitting to the seductive pressures to make accommodations with Batista, and especially not to be seduced by the call for legislative or presidential elections while Batista remained in office.

At the Ortodoxos National Congress in Havana on August 16, 1955, the forces of the M-26-7 were eager lobbyists, armed with mimeographed sheets and well prepared to recruit support for their cause among the younger party members. Most youthful Ortodoxos already identified with Fidel as their leader, and for the session at which it was rumored his message would be read, more than five hundred jammed the auditorium.

113

Faustino Pérez, Armando Hart, and a young woman, Maria Laborte, marched to the platform in the middle of the session and took over the microphone. The party leaders sat in stunned silence. Maria Laborte read Fidel's message, which ended by urging the party to pass a resolution supporting "a strategy of armed insurrection." To the consternation of the leadership, the standing, cheering delegates did so by what amounted to acclamation, amid shouts of, "*Revolución. Revolución.*"

The event was significant in several respects. For the first time a major party had, at least theoretically, adopted armed revolution as an official position, even though the party leaders subsequently paid no attention to the resolution and continued to work toward accommodation with Batista. It was also the beginning of the M-26-7 as a mass movement with a broad base of support. From this point on an irrevocable schism was clearly apparent in the country between the younger generation, which would accept no accommodation with Batista, and the older, jaded generation, which had been disappointed so many times that it was now convinced that some modus vivendi was the only realistic option. Increasingly, it was as though Batista was at war with the young people of Cuba, and it was against them that his anger and oppression were specifically directed. Being young became in itself sufficient cause for the police to believe an individual was against the regime, and the arbitrary brutality often meted out over the next several months to innocent young people antagonized even cautious moderates, convincing them that revolution was the only viable solution.

In August 1955, Fidel met Colonel Alberto Bayo, a part-time instructor at the School of Military Aviation in Mexico. The sixty-three-year-old Bayo had been born in Cuba in 1892, but as a child was taken to Spain. There he had joined the army and fought for the Spanish monarchy for eleven years, including an extensive stint in Morocco. Later he had fought as a guerrilla for the Republican Army in the Spanish Civil War. After the Republican defeat he had fled to Mexico, where apart from his teaching he ran a small furniture factory. He was a stout man with a well-trimmed vandyke beard and a missing right eye as a result of a combat injury. A romantic adventurer, he was also an exceptional authority on both the practical and the theoretical aspects of guerrilla warfare. Fidel asked Bayo if he would be willing to help train a small invasion force. Attracted by Fidel's evangelical zeal and his spirited determination, but doubtful whether the venture would ever get off the ground, Bayo asked Fidel if he had the men or the money for the enterprise. Fidel assured him he would have both in a few months. Bayo agreed, if the funds and men arrived, to carry out the training for 1,000 pesos ($80) a month.

When the Moncadistas exiled in Mexico City had returned to Havana after the amnesty the previous May, they told Fidel about a young Argentinian physician, Ernesto Guevara Lynch, whose revolutionary interests and fervor closely paralleled his own. Guevara, they reported, had expressed a strong interest in meeting Fidel. Shortly after Fidel's arrival in Mexico, Guevara was contacted at the General Hospital, where he was working. A few days later, a meeting was arranged with Raúl, who in turn invited the doctor to meet his brother at Maria Antonia's apartment. It was the beginning of perhaps the most important adult relationship in both their lives.

Fidel and "Che," as Guevara was to become universally known, talked through the night, until at dawn they watched the sun rising. They talked about international politics, economics, ideology, and above all about revolution in the Americas. By the time they parted, Fidel had invited Che to join the revolutionary force as the group's physician, and Che had accepted. Recalling the meeting, Che said later, "It did not take much to incite me to join any revolution against tyranny, but Fidel impressed me as an extraordinary man."

Che Guevara was born in Rosario, Argentina, on June 14, 1928, making him close to a year younger than Fidel. His family was of an aristocratic background but in reduced circumstances, and his father, trained in upper-class traditions, could never adjust to the bourgeois lifestyle that their lack of finances demanded. He drifted from one failing venture to another, keeping the family constantly on the verge of financial disaster. In contrast to his weak father, Che's mother, Celia, was a strong and determined woman who kept the family together through thick and thin by the strength of her personality. She, too, came from an upper-class background, but she had always been a flaming rebel who never hesitated to stand up against injustice and against her own social class on behalf of the poor, no matter whom she offended. She had a clear view of the inequities in the world and what needed to be done about them, and she instilled these convictions in her children, especially Che. Throughout his revolutionary career, Che seemed to be driven by his mother's radical expectations of him. Celia was also a warm, loving woman, and by all reports a devoted and affectionate mother. Che received her special attention and care, partly because he was her favorite, but also because from an early age he suffered from severe asthma attacks.

Che was a studious, introverted boy, remembered by one friend as a bookworm. However, perhaps as an overreaction to his infirmity, he engaged in sports, especially football, and was a tenacious competitor even though his small stature put him at a distinct disadvantage. Later, in medical school, he and a friend took off for several months on a motorcycle and hitchhiking trip around South America, during which he spent a period of time working in a leper colony in Peru, and briefly visited Miami. He returned to Argentina to finish medical school, but after graduation he immediately set off again, drawn more by a growing interest in radical politics than a desire to practice medicine. He was well read in revolutionary and Marxist literature, but he was not a joiner, and had never become a member of any political organization. His beliefs were personal, moral, even romantic, but not doctrinaire. He longed to find a situation to meet his need to play a role in bringing about social justice, even revolutionary change. He found this in part in Guatemala in 1954, where progressive Colonel Jacobo Arbenz Guzman had recently been elected president in surprisingly free elections.

Arbenz began instituting radical reforms and openly invited Communists to participate in his government. Che was strongly attracted by the opportunity to be associated with the Arbenz regime, which seemed to him to be trying bravely to address the fundamental changes necessary to bring Guatemala out of feudalism. Che's intent was to contribute his services as a revolutionary physician. But because he could not get the right papers, he did not accomplish even that. However, during the time he lived in Guatemala he met a Peruvian woman, Hilda Gadea, whom he would later marry in Mexico. She introduced him to Cuban Moncadista exile Nico López. From López, Che learned about Fidel and, based on what he heard, felt an immediate attraction to him.

The Eisenhower administration was alarmed by the social changes and the threat to American financial interests, especially Arbenz's intent to launch a land reform program that would involve the expropriation (with compensation) of a quarter million acres of land owned by the United Fruit Company. The administration backed, through the CIA, a Honduras-based invasion force led by Lieutenant Colonel Carlos Castillo Armas. In instituting the land reform program, Arbenz had failed to take into account certain vital factors: Allen Dulles, director of the CIA, and his brother John, secretary of state, were major stockholders in the United Fruit Company; the Dulleses' New York law firm, Sullivan and Cromwell, was United Fruit's counsel; General Robert Cutler, chairman of the National Security Council, which had to approve such covert operations, sat on the United Fruit board of directors. In an era when conflicts of interest barely raised an eyebrow, Arbenz found he had made a fatal tactical error. Eventually his government was overthrown and Che was forced to flee to Mexico.

The success of the CIA's overthrow of Arbenz would later be repeatedly cited by the agency as a model and as an argument for mounting the Bay of Pigs invasion.

Che arrived in Mexico City penniless, emotionally shaken, and per-

116

manently embittered against the United States. As he saw it, not only had the United States been willing to overthrow a democratically elected government, it had also taken a stand against social change. It had acted solely in support of vested U.S. financial interests and the old ruling oligarchy that had traditionally prevented, by brutal oppression, any effort to improve the lives of the impoverished majority. A friend, Dolores Moyano Martin, was to say later of him, "His strongest political emotion was a deep-seated hostility toward the United States."

Until he met Che, Fidel's sentiments toward the United States were couched in the traditional rhetoric of conventional Cuban nationalism. He had condemned imperialism in the hemisphere, as he did in Bogotá and Panama in 1948, but compared with the injustices he railed against in Cuba, this was still a relatively minor part of his agenda, and he was not passionate on the subject. Che eventually infused him with his own emotion and bitterness toward the United States, adding an element of passion to Fidel's intellectual views on the subject.

After five months in Mexico, Fidel did not have much in the way of concrete accomplishments to show for the time. To make good on his revolutionary plans, he had to raise substantially more money than he had been getting while in Mexico. In October, he left for the United States. He borrowed money for the plane ride to Miami and the train ride to New York, but could afford only a one-way ticket. Over a seven-week period, he visited New York, Philadelphia, Tampa, and Miami. Again he was knowingly following in the footsteps of José Martí, who eighty years earlier had made a similar fund-raising trip. Fidel's plan was to organize "Patriotic Clubs of the 26th of July" among the 26,000 Cubans living in exile communities throughout the United States. Many of the Cubans with whom he talked had left Cuba because of economic hardship, and his pitch to them was that once in power he would create a free Cuba to which they could return with a guarantee of jobs and prosperity. Stressing the considerable austerity in which he and his men lived, he proposed that each employed individual contribute to his cause one day's earnings, and all others a dollar a week. There were constant conflicts among the various exile groups, and Fidel after his return to Mexico had to be in constant correspondence with them to keep the money flowing. But the trip was a distinct success, both for the funds it raised and the organizational base that was created. The real payoff, however, came later when Fidel was fighting in the Sierra Maestra. At that time, when victory seemed imminent, the support network blossomed into a lucrative fund-raising machine.

Before leaving Miami for Mexico City on December 10, he issued "Manifesto No. 2 to the People of Cuba," thanking those in the United

States who were helping him. The manifesto was also designed to boost the morale of his supporters in Cuba by demonstrating that he was accomplishing something concrete in the United States (when not too much seemed to be happening in Mexico), and that he enjoyed wide support in the exile community.

Fidel left Juan Manuel Marquéz, a former city councilman from the Havana suburb of Marianao, in Miami. Marquéz had accompanied him on the trip, and was to serve as his main representative to the exile community. Fidel took back Miguel Sánchez, nicknamed El Coreano, to Mexico because he had fought with the U.S. Army in Korea. Sánchez agreed to assist Fidel as a military instructor.

Fidel's trip to the United States was the pivotal event of his time in exile, and when he returned to Mexico City he launched an entirely new phase of the revolutionary plan. In a speech in New York he said, "In 1956, we will be free or we will be martyrs." In his mind he had set a deadline of the following year for landing with his invasion force, so he now felt a new sense of urgency. In addition to the money raised on the trip, Pedro Miret had brought $1,000 in December, and in February 1956, $8,250 was delivered by Faustino Pérez from supporters in Cuba. Several of the Moncadistas and other loyal supporters had come to Mexico to join Fidel and the military training program he planned. Fidel had money and men. Now he needed to buy weapons.

Before he left Cuba, Fidel had been given the name of another potential supporter, Orlando de Cárdenas. De Cárdenas was of Cuban birth and married to an American woman from Kansas, but was not an exile. He had lived in Mexico for many years as a permanent resident, and therefore was not under the same scrutiny as the political refugees. Following the Batista coup, he had been helping former President Prío and his followers by buying weapons for them. Fidel had been made aware of this function. De Cárdenas recalls a night in December 1955: "Someone knocks at my door, and it was Fidel Castro. . . . It was very cold and he was wearing a very old overcoat that was too small. It looked very funny on him, but it was the only one he had." Fidel asked de Cárdenas if he would buy weapons for him, but de Cárdenas was reluctant. He had heard negative stories about Fidel from Prío's people, and also from Raúl Roa, the distinguished professor and activist from the 1930s who earlier had lived for a while in exile in Mexico City. Roa had been a professor at the University of Havana when Fidel was a student, and he remembered his UIR connection. For him Fidel's image as a "gangster" still lingered. Prío's people claimed that at Moncada he had unnecessarily lost the lives of his followers by leading them inadequately armed into a hopeless situation. He had also heard that Fidel refused to coordinate with other revolutionary groups or share power with anyone because he wanted to be the "maximum leader." But after an hour of discussion, impressed by Fidel's relentless determination in the face of the setbacks he had suffered, de Cárdenas began to change his mind. "He has such a convincing power. . . . When he puts his hand on your shoulder . . . ten minutes later you are saying yes to everything," he recalls.

Five days later, Fidel returned with Miguel Sánchez and Jesús Reyes, known as Chu Chu, who at that time were serving as his ever-present bodyguards. Taking de Cárdenas alone into a bedroom, Fidel quickly finished his artful job of persuasion. De Cárdenas says, "He convinced me: one hundred percent. The result was that the next day I was trying to get the contacts I had before to buy weapons, small arms, munitions." Not only did Fidel convince him to act as his arms buyer, he also persuaded de Cárdenas to let some of his men stay in his home. At one time as many as eleven men were living there, and every week three or four more arrived from Cuba. Money was always short, and whatever they had Fidel wanted to spend on arms rather than food, so that the family was often feeding them as well. At one point, de Cárdenas's elderly mother complained to her son that he should not be wasting his time and money on such an adventurer, who clearly had no real future. Fidel asked to talk with her, and after a private discussion she gave him an enthusiastic endorsement.

With de Cárdenas's help, and that of a Mexican businessman, Manuel Machado, ten lodging places were soon rented around the city for the eighty men who had now arrived. Bayo was commissioned to begin his training. Initially he did this where the men were living, going from place to place pretending to be an English language teacher. At that stage, the only practical training they had had was at a firing range, Las Guamitas, in Santa Fe, a suburb of Mexico City.

The cardinal principles of discipline and secrecy that had shaped Fidel's planning for Moncada were again rigidly implemented. Some might again argue that this was part of his need for absolute control, but these are also indispensable features of any military operation. His personality was so overpowering that his followers had little inclination to object. The men in each house were under the direction of a group leader who set the example for the others. Their time was entirely regimented—they performed household chores, underwent military instruction, and, in the evenings, studied revolutionary literature and engaged in political discussion. They were not paid, were not allowed to drink, and could not leave the house alone. One of the houses was set up as a prison for disciplinary purposes. In addition, as with Moncada, the residents of one house knew nothing about the location of the others. Only Fidel knew the entire plan.

The discipline, despite its harshness, had a positive impact on those around them and would stand them in good stead later in Cuba. As one observer remembers them in Mexico, "They were so nice, so young, so pure . . . and so well behaved." De Cárdenas's wife remembers men who had been without food all day sitting in a room with a well-stocked refrigerator and never touching the food until she came home to serve them. Their deep loyalty to Fidel also made an impression on observers. "How blindly they followed him, how much faith they had in him." Another associate viewed the relationship more negatively, "They were not like the revolutionaries I had known, but much humbler and cruder. Their language was coarse. . . . Fidel, calm, noble of bearing, stood out among them like a tower among hovels. . . . I came to understand that this was the basis of his absolute authority over them; it was why he was able to impose an extremely rigid discipline upon them, from which he and his three or four closest associates were exempt."

Fidel never drank. On one occasion he came to visit de Cárdenas and found him drinking Scotch. Fidel chastised him, and told him to stop. De Cárdenas pointed out that he was not a member of the movement but merely someone generously trying to help them, and therefore in no way subject to their rules. Fidel conceded that he was, of course, right, but asked him please not to drink in front of the men.

The high value placed on discipline has been a recurrent issue throughout Fidel's life. On the surface, its validity in a successful revolutionary movement is self-evident. However, its roots as a virtue unquestionably derive from Fidel's Jesuit training, and from a recognition, perhaps unconscious, that discipline as structure provided a productive complement to his own fertile energetic mind constantly bubbling up an uncontrolled barrage of ideas, plans, strategies, and visions. He assumed that his own needs enhanced the efficiency of others.

Fidel's dedication was unwavering. Of that time de Cárdenas recalls:

> What struck me was the way he concentrated one hundred percent absolutely on his goals. There were no women, no play. Many times I told my wife, "Fidel is not a Cuban at all, he doesn't like music, he doesn't drink." His only vice was smoking Cuban cigars. From time to time a box would arrive from Cuba. He would distribute the cigars among the others and keep one or two for himself.
>
> No hot or cold weather would affect him. He would work eighteen, twenty hours a day. Many times I ask myself, "When does he sleep?" He was always interviewing people so they would help him.

Occasionally he did go out with Mike Calzadilla, a Cuban who was the head of the Mexican Professional Baseball League, to watch a game at the Social Security Stadium. Later at the Calzadilla home they would eat oxtail with capers and olives, one of Fidel's favorites. He was "like a preacher," Calzadilla recalls. "The magnetic appeal of his eyes communicated his restlessness."

Fidel's appetite for serious reading had not diminished. On two occasions he bought books at the Librería Zaplana (charging the purchases to de Cárdenas). The eclectic nature of his political interests was reflected by the purchase he made on August 17, 1956. It included two volumes by Hitler, a book by Lenin, a biography of Disraeli, the memoirs of Rommel, a book about Hannibal, an introduction to Keynes, a book of poetry by the Nobel prize-winning Chilean Communist Pablo Neruda, and a book on political economics.

Drill practices and gunnery lessons in tiny rooms had strict limitations. In early April, Bayo, posing as the representative of a Salvadoran military officer, contacted a man called Rivera who owned a ranch, "Las Rosas," in the Chalco district, about twenty-five miles outside the city. He convinced the man that he would buy the ranch after six months for $24,000 if in the meantime he could have his men come in to clear the land for cattle grazing. During that interim period he would pay only $8 per month. Out of this remarkable con job, they obtained an ideal training site, ten miles long and six miles wide. Over the next three months, Bayo conducted an intensive and effective training program, including mountain climbing, map reading, survival, guerrilla tactics, and long night marches.

A majority of the men, including Che, participated in the course. Fidel was not formally enrolled, although he did sporadically join in some of the exercises. His absence was justifiable in terms of his many other responsibilities in connection with the venture. Perhaps, though, he decided that he could not put himself on an equal footing as a trainee with his own men. Nor would making himself subservient to Bayo have appealed to him. Bayo graded his students, and in the final rankings Che achieved the highest score. When Fidel expressed some surprise at Che's success, the old military man affirmed that he was unquestionably the best. Few people have ever been closer to Fidel than Che, but, as his careful questioning of Bayo may imply, at that moment Fidel felt a twinge of competitive jealousy that this man he enlisted as a physician, already very popular with the other men, should be excelling in the fields he regarded as his own, military leadership and guerrilla warfare.

Apart from preparing the invasion force, Fidel was keeping a close eye on political developments in Cuba. A great deal was happening there. Senior political and civic leaders, fearful of revolution and convinced that some compromise had to be worked out with Batista, had come together under the umbrella of a newly formed organization, Sociedad de Amigos de la República (SAR). For Fidel, such an initiative, if successful, would significantly undercut his revolutionary plans, and he lashed out at the SAR throughout his trip to the United States. At the same time, M-26-7 supporters in Cuba used every opportunity to disrupt the unity rallies. They called for revolution as the only solution and painted "26," "Revolution Now," and other slogans on buildings around the country.

The young who advocated revolution pointed to the impotency of the SAR and the intransigence of Batista. Those who sought compromise became more and more frustrated and angry—on the one hand with Batista, and on the other with the revolutionaries who they felt were undercutting any chance of a peaceful solution.

At the University of Havana, the era of the gangs had passed. A whole new generation of idealistic students dedicated to the ouster of Batista was making its views felt. José Antonio Echevarría, an exceptional and much admired leader, was then serving as president of the FEU. Students were increasingly being arrested, tortured, and even killed by Batista's police. In response, early in December 1955 they formed the Directorio Revolucionario, later referred to simply as the Directorio or DR. According to Echevarría, DR was to be the armed insurrectional wing of the FEU. However, it embraced both students and workers, and was aimed at creating a unified front of youthful opposition to Batista. In the following days, violent student riots flared up all across the country, with frequent gunfire between the police and demonstrators.

From Fidel's perspective, although this turmoil served the useful purpose of preventing conciliation, too great a success for leaders like Echevarría, who owed no particular allegiance to him, posed a threat to his revolutionary ambitions. Except for the hard core of the movement, his hold on his broader following in Cuba was tenuous at best, and the emergence of any major new revolutionary movement or figure could easily usurp his grip on his supporters. It underscored the urgent need to reestablish his presence in Cuba.

Fidel's trip to the United States had provoked an angry reaction from the Batista administration. Several derogatory references were made to it in the press. An article in *Bohemia* on December 18 entitled "The Homeland Is Not Fidel's" accused him of stirring up unjustified hostility against the administration among the exiles. The piece also implied that he could not be trusted to handle with integrity the funds he had raised. Fidel responded with a long piece in *Bohemia* on Christmas Day entitled "In Front of Everyone." He went to some length to itemize both the evidence of his financial integrity and the relative poverty in which he had lived thoughout his political career.

It was a curious anomaly of those times, and a direct reflection of Batista's character, that while student and union protesters and M-26-7 members were being treated with great ruthlessness, Fidel, who was organizing an armed invasion of the country with the publicly avowed purpose of overthrowing the government, could still get his writings published in *Bohemia*. The magazine rejected some of his writings, but a certain amount of credit must still be given to Fidel's friend Miguel Angel Quevedo, editor of *Bohemia*, who ran considerable personal risk running the material. The fact that he got away with it further reflects Batista's agonized ambivalence toward his critics.

By the end of December, as student and labor unrest swept the country, Batista, out of fear that the mass movement would get out of hand, sought to defuse the growing resentment against his rule by finally agreeing to meet with members of the SAR. Some compromise again seemed possible, as both sides agreed that a peaceful settlement must be found, and Batista implied a willingness to accept new presidential elections. Cosme De la Torriente, chairman of SAR, called on the leadership of the Ortodoxo Party to join in subsequent conciliation discussions with Batista, and at meetings on February 20 and 23 the possibility was discussed. Such a decision flew directly in the face of the resolution passed by the membership at the national conference the previous August, and was also contrary to the party's basic principle of not entering into any coalitions. On the night of the second meeting, an angry crowd led by Fidel's supporters gathered outside the house where the leaders had convened. A violent demonstration followed, which broke up the meeting. Later the leaders publicly condemned the absent Fidel for what happened.

The decision by the Ortodoxos to enter the discussions with Batista was the final straw for Fidel. On March 19, he issued a statement formally severing ties between the 26 of July Movement and the party. He did, however, claim for himself the spiritual legacy of Chibás by saying that the 26 of July Movement "is the revolutionary apparatus of Chibaism." Fidel conveniently mixed ideology and strategy. Chibás's ideas had been revolutionary, but he had never supported armed revolution. Nevertheless, Fidel's continuing loyalty to the memory of Chibás, the vehement anti-Communist, was important, in that it suggests even at that stage his political philosophy was still far from Marxist.

On April 4, a planned coup led by young progressive military officers who had opposed the original Batista coup and who would later be known as the *puros* (pure ones) was uncovered. The group was led by Colonel Ramón Barquín, Cuba's representative to the Inter-American Defense Board, who had connections with some of the senior Ortodoxos leadership including Roberto Agramonte and Raúl Chibás (Eddy's brother). The *puros*'s primary backer was Justo Carrillo and his Montecristo movement. He was to have become president of Cuba if the coup had succeeded.

Because of a three-day delay in launching the plot, and very poor security, word leaked out and they were betrayed. Barquín was imprisoned. On April 29, Fidel met with Carrillo at Tapachula on the Guatemala–Mexico border. There, Carrillo, now bereft of his own revolutionary initiative, gave Fidel $5,000.

On the same day that Fidel and Carrillo met, a group of young men, some of whom had connections to ex-President Prío, attacked Goicura barracks in Matanzas in a manner reminiscent of the Moncada assault. They were mowed down by machine gun fire.

Fidel understood that his ultimate success depended on building as broad a base of support as possible, and he pointedly praised the bravery of those involved in these ventures so that their disappointed followers might look to him to avenge their comrades. Of Barquín's *puros* officers he said, "One of the first measures of the successful revolution will be the reinstatement of these honest military men to their posts."

As Fidel's own military force grew, not only was he taken more seriously in Cuba, he also became a source of growing concern to the Mexican authorities. In addition, Batista sent agents to Mexico to assassinate him. Because he was constantly accompanied by bodyguards and always used a good deal of caution, they eventually abandoned the attempt, and Batista asked the Mexican authorities to arrest him instead. As was to become his pattern, Fidel rotated the places where he slept between the little third-class hotel in the Insurgentes Norte, the home of Alfonso Gutiérrez, a house on Calle Pachuca where Melba Hernández and Jesús Montané were staying, and several of the houses where his men lived.

On the evening of June 21, Fidel and Ramiro Valdés, one of the original Moncadistas, were riding in a car when they became aware that several vehicles were following them. The road ahead was suddenly blocked. Thinking it was an assassination squad, they attempted to escape on foot, but were soon surrounded. Fidel, reaching for his automatic and preparing for a shootout, suddenly found that a policeman had sneaked up behind him and was pressing a .45 pistol to his head. Five men were arrested at a nearby house, where information concerning the ranch was also found. It was raided five days later, and forty-five other revolutionaries were arrested and confined in the Miguel Schultz Immigration Prison. A story prepared by the Cuban Embassy immediately appeared in the local newspapers, announcing, "Seven Cuban Communists imprisoned for conspiring against Batista." They were charged with violating the immigration laws by conspiring to make revolution against a foreign government and of illegally possessing weapons. Several of the men were beaten and tortured, especially by being bound naked and dunked in cold water. One of the torturers remained masked; he was apparently a Cuban intelligence agent.

On the day after his arrest, Fidel issued a brief statement angrily denying that he had any connection with the Communists or with ex-President Prío. A couple of weeks passed, and a long article appeared in *Bohemia* written by a Mexican journalist sympathetic to and paid by the Batista regime. The article, under the headline "Group of the 26th of July in Jail," sought to discredit Fidel and his men in the eyes of the Cuban readers, again linking them to communism. Amazingly, Fidel's lengthy response was published by *Bohemia* the following week. With the help of a sympathetic Mexican lawyer, Fidel and his men were finally released on July 25. Later, through the intercession of former Mexican president Lázaro Cárdenas, they were able to avoid deportation. Che, because of his Argentinian citizenship and his past involvement in Guatemala, was held for an additional month.

Before they left prison, the men were visited by Teresa Casuso, a Cuban exile, actress, novelist, and employee of the cultural section of the Cuban Embassy. Tete, as she was called by her friends, was a well-known member of "the generation of the thirties." Her talented, idealistic husband, Pablo de la Torriente Brau, had gone in his twenties to fight for the Republican cause in Spain, where he had given his life. She had read about the imprisonment of Fidel and his men in a local newspaper, and decided to visit them. She describes Fidel at that first encounter.

> More than fifty Cubans were gathered in the large central courtyard of the Immigration Prison. In the middle, tall and clean-shaven and with close-cropped chestnut hair, and correctly dressed in a brown suit standing out from the rest by his look and bearing, was their chief Fidel Castro. He gave one the impression of being noble, sure, deliberate—like a big Newfoundland dog. . . . He looked eminently serene, and inspired confidence and a sense of security. . . . His voice was quiet, his expression grave, his manner calm, gentle. I noticed he had a habit of shaking his head, like a fine thoroughbred horse.

Fidel was flattered that this woman whom he knew so well by reputation should come to see him, and he eagerly accepted her offers of help. Accompanying Teresa Casuso to the prison that July afternoon was a strikingly beautiful eighteen-year-old girl with long golden hair, Isabelle Custodio. Isabelle's mother was Cuban, her father a Spanish Republican; both were writers. They had left Isabelle in Teresa's care while they went on a tour of the interior of Mexico. Isabelle had received a sophisticated liberal education, and despite her youth had a polish that combined with her beauty to make her a striking young woman. Fidel was visibly smitten by her charms.

Two days later, Teresa Casuso opened the door of her house to find Fidel sitting on a sofa waiting for her. They talked until late in the night.

125

Fidel wanted to talk about the various figures involved in the struggles of the 1930s. Every detail was important to him, and he absorbed the information like a sponge. Teresa Casuso makes a comment about him, which in one form or another has been echoed by dozens of people since: "He struck me as being a man who would never underestimate the value of anyone; everybody was important to him."

With his usual evangelical fervor, Fidel presented his plan for the overthrow of Batista, and by the time he left that night Teresa was convinced he could succeed. He asked if she would keep in her house "a few things" for him. She agreed, and he arranged to return the following evening.

When he came back at 1 A.M. the following night with his bodyguards, Cándido González and Rafael del Pino, the "few things" turned out to be three carloads of machine guns, pistols, bayonets, rifles, and ammunition. Fidel explained that the police knew about and were closing in on de Cárdenas's house, where the arms had been stored. They filled every closet, which were then locked or nailed shut. While his men carried in the arsenal, Fidel managed to spend time alone with Isabelle. Eventually she was exhausted and went to bed. But Fidel, in his usual indefatigable style, lit a new cigar and began pacing the floor, dictating an article for *Bohemia* while Cándido Gonzáles typed. They worked the rest of the night so that a courier could take the article to Cuba in the morning.

Over the next several weeks, Fidel came regularly to the house at 712 Sierra Nevada in the Lomas Chapultepec district. He came only with his bodyguards, never with any of the other men. Although he came ostensibly to maintain the weapons, it was clear that the real reason for his visits was to see Isabelle. At times they went out to eat together—Fidel, Isabelle, Teresa, and the bodyguards. When he was sure his security was not in jeopardy, Fidel and Isabelle would wander off alone.

On August 13, Fidel's thirtieth birthday by his reckoning (in actuality his twenty-ninth), Teresa Casuso gave him as a birthday present a German straight razor he had been admiring. He was visibly moved. He said it was the only gift he had received, and he promised he would keep it for the rest of his life. Ironically, in a matter of months he would cease forever to use a razor.

Fidel's personal life was further complicated at this stage by the arrival of Fidelito. He had worked out an agreement with Mirta to allow their young son to come to visit him for two weeks, but when the time was up, Fidel refused to send him back to Cuba. Mirta was in the midst of a romance and was about to get married again. She did not push that hard initially for the boy to come back. Fidelito lived at the home of Alfonso Gutiérrez and Orquídea Pino. He is remembered as having great affection for both of his parents, but as often asking, "Why can't my mother and father live together?" He played regularly with a son of de Cárdenas who was about the same age. Even at age eight, he organized a game with other children that was a war of the revolutionaries against Batista. Fidel wanted his son to have as normal a childhood as possible, and asked de Cárdenas to arrange for him to join the Boy Scouts, which he did. Within the constraints of his other commitments, Fidel tried hard to be a good father to his son, for whom he felt very deeply, yet it is impossible not to see parallels with his relationship to his own father. Fidel, like his father, sought to dominate and impose his will on those around him, and therefore had little sensitivity for his son's needs when they got in the way of his own.

After he was released from prison, Fidel went to see the man who had arrested him, Captain Gutiérrez Barios of the National Security Police. Making a friendly relationship, Fidel convinced him of the legitimacy of his cause, and Gutiérrez agreed to keep Fidel apprised of any developments in the police department that might threaten the expedition. Early in September, he warned Fidel of pressures from the Cuban government to move against him.

The pressure on Fidel to launch the expedition to Cuba was growing. He had on several occasions made a public commitment to be back there by the end of the year, and the growing strength of other revolutionary groups aiming to overthrow Batista held the potential for shutting him out of the picture. He desperately needed more money, and decided to follow the advice he had received from Justo Carrillo that the only person who could provide the kind of financing he needed was his old nemesis, ex-President Prío, now in exile in Miami. It was a very difficult decision for Fidel to bring himself to ask Prío for help. Similarly, Prío initially had no interest in seeing Fidel. Lengthy negotiations were conducted through Prío's former minister of communications, Juan Capistani. Teresa Casuso was an old friend of the former president, and at the end of August she agreed to fly to Miami to encourage Prío to agree to a meeting. Prío was in legal difficulties with the United States authorities and could not leave the country, so it was agreed that the meeting would take place at the Casa de Palmas Hotel, in McAllen, Texas.

Fidel drove with Juan Manuel Marquéz, now his second in command, Faustino Pérez, Jesús Montané, and Melba Hernández, to Reynosa on the Mexican side of the border. Faustino Pérez had a U.S. visa and was able to enter legally, but Fidel was forced to cross the border clandestinely. He joined oil refinery workers taking a midday swim in the Río Grande. Unnoticed, he swam across the river to the American side, where Faustino Pérez was waiting with dry clothes and a car to take him to the hotel. Prío, embittered against Batista, felt that Fidel might be the instrument for his revenge. There were two long meetings, one in the morning and the other in the afternoon. Contrary to some reports, both Melba and Faustino Pérez say that no money changed hands at that meeting, although Prío apparently pledged his commitment to provide $50,000. For Prío it was a cheap investment. Should Fidel succeed, he would be too young to take over the reins of government and he, Prío, would be in a powerful position to return as president. As it was not originally Fidel's intention to take over the government once Batista was overthrown, he probably fed Prío's hopes.

Under cover of darkness, Fidel was led across the bridge back to Reynosa. Juan Manuel Marquéz went back to Miami with Prío to pick up the first $25,000. It was then brought to Mexico by Antonio "El Cuate" Conde, a Mexican who had been buying arms for Fidel in the United States.

After he returned to Mexico City, Fidel proposed to Isabelle with the intention that she would accompany him on the expedition to Cuba. In the traditional manner, he also obtained her parents' consent. Isabelle left her job in a record store and prepared for the wedding. In a rare extravagance, because he now had some money, Fidel bought her new clothes and shoes, French perfume, and a new one-piece bathing suit to replace her bikini, which offended his Puritan sensibilities. Because of Fidel's illegal status, the marriage would have to take place in a small village away from the capital, where they could bribe a judge to perform the ceremony.

These developments in Fidel's personal life coincided with a crescendo of activity in connection with the invasion plans. To give his return the maximum impact, Fidel wanted to orchestrate a nationwide strike and a series of uprisings. During September most of the top M-26-7 leaders, except those from Oriente Province, came to Mexico to coordinate the master plan. Whatever their misgivings, none voiced them except Frank País, the coordinator in Oriente where Fidel planned to land. Frank came to Mexico in August, meeting Fidel for the first time, and returned in October. He argued that his organization in the province was incapable of staging the scale of uprising that Fidel proposed, particularly the objective that he and his men would seize the city of Santiago. According to Faustino Pérez, Fidel convinced País that it was politically more important that he honor the public commitment he had made to return by the end of the year than to delay until the preparations were complete. Because the Cuban people were so used to politicians who did not honor their promises, Fidel thought it vital to his credibility that he be different. Fidel ordered that the resources from all of the other provinces be channeled to Frank and authorized him to begin buying guns. He turned down

Frank's suggestion that they raise money by assaulting banks as potentially damaging to the movement's image.

País returned to Cuba, whether convinced or not, at least reconciled to the fact that Fidel would not, or could not, delay his return.

Both to enhance the impact of his arrival, and perhaps to co-opt the competing revolutionary groups, Fidel reached out to other leaders, arguing that a coalition of all such groups was mandatory to overthrow Batista. Even though Fidel had taken genuine affront when he had been accused of being a Communist, he remained favorably disposed toward the party and he knew that only they had the ability to produce the kind of nationwide strike he envisaged. He met with a party member who had come to Mexico, Oswaldo Sánchez. Sánchez, like Frank País, urged Fidel to delay his return until they were better prepared. Even though he declined to delay, the party leadership, although still doubtful about Fidel's prospects, decided to mobilize for such a strike. They like Prío felt that should Fidel succeed he would be unable to manage the revolution and they could then exploit the situation for their own ends. In November he met several times with Flavio Bravo, his old friend from his university days, whose dual loyalty put him in a position to look out for Fidel's interest within the party.

Not only did Frank País and the Communists encourage Fidel to delay his invasion, but Melba Hernández returned from a trip to Cuba to report that the M-26-7 forces were in disarray and were incapable of organizing a nationwide uprising. According to de Cárdenas, in a very heated meeting in which Fidel said he was planning to go ahead anyway, Melba accused him of being willing to sacrifice recklessly the lives of all of the loyal young men he had trained merely to satisfy his own vanity. It would, she said, be like Moncada all over again, and do nothing in the long run to bring about Batista's downfall. Fidel became extremely angry and made it clear that he would not tolerate that sort of insubordination even from his closest and most loyal collaborators. Melba was placed under what amounted to house arrest until the invasion force left Mexico to prevent her from sowing dissent among any of the others. Today Melba strongly denies that such a split took place.

José Antonio Echevarría, president of the FEU, came to Mexico on August 29, 1956, at Fidel's request. The two men agreed on one issue only—that Batista must be overthrown. It was the view of the FEU and the Directorio that the revolution should be brought about by striking at the top, assassinating leaders of the administration and, if possible, Batista himself. Fidel believed that such a strategy would leave the system intact, yet create a power vacuum into which another reactionary force, most likely the military, would move. He believed that a successful revolution could be achieved only by building overwhelming public support from the bottom up so that the traditional corrupted institutions, especially the military as a base of power, could be destroyed forever. In the final analysis, it boiled down to a clash of two strong personalities sharing many of the same leadership qualities and objectives, with neither willing to concede his own strategy or even to aid the political ambitions of the other at his own expense. When Fidel suggested that the Directorio Revolucionario be put under the overall command of the M-26-7, Echevarría dryly responded that it made more sense to merge the M-26-7 into the Directorio.

Both men were political realists. They recognized that it served neither of their interests to disagree publicly. On September 2, 1956, they jointly signed the "Mexico Pact," which spoke of ideological unity and the shared goal of overthrowing Batista, but it was, as far as tactics were concerned, an agreement to disagree. Echevarría then left for a student conference in Asia, stopping in Mexico on his way back to Cuba at the end of October. At this second meeting, he and Fidel talked in more detail about how to implement the pact. When Echevarría finally returned to Cuba, he found that some Directorio members refused to endorse the pact because of Fidel's gang connections when he was a student.

Throughout the summer of 1956, there were charges and countercharges between Batista and Trujillo. Batista with some accuracy accused Trujillo of aiding his enemies in planning an invasion of Cuba, and sought to link Fidel to that effort. Fidel hotly denied the accusation although he knew this was a venture that Prío was also backing. Although it lacked strong leadership, it was far better armed and financed than his own effort and posed a threat to Fidel because it siphoned off interest and potential fighters.

It caused some discussion among his men. One of them decided that if he was going to be involved in an invasion, the Trujillo venture now looked as though it had a better chance of success. He made plans to abandon Fidel and go to the Dominican Republic. Desertion at this stage was something Fidel could not tolerate. He asked de Cárdenas to deliver a message to the man at his house asking him to meet Fidel and others in an isolated location, but the man had already vanished. De Cárdenas discovered later that the intention had been to kill him.

"Would Fidel have done it himself?" he was asked.

"No. But Raúl would. Fidel would have done it only if there had been absolutely no other alternative," de Cárdenas replied.

The frenetic activity of September and October proved too much for Fidel's marriage plans. Isabelle felt abandoned and suggested that Fidel give up the revolution and stay with her in Mexico. At the same time, he became irked when his wealthy Mexican backers referred to her in front of them both as "the future First Lady of Cuba." Fidel felt that the idea had gone to her head. Finally it was she who left, returning to an old fiancé who had recently come back to town. Although initially shaken, Fidel seemed to accept that it was for the best, and he was able to put it behind him rapidly with no regrets. It was perhaps the only time in his career that he had allowed some self-indulgence to intrude on his single-minded commitment to the revolution. Teresa Casuso recalled that Fidel returned to his scruffy style of dress and was no longer interested in music, gaiety, eating in restaurants, and trips to the countryside. Sitting on a bed in her house with parts of a machine gun in his lap, he said that he had only one real fiancée—the revolution.

The involvement with Isabelle can best be understood within the context of Fidel's continuing feelings for Mirta. Shortly before he met Isabelle, he heard that Mirta was about to marry wealthy businessman Emilio Núñez Blanco, son of Dr. Emilio Núñez Portuondo, chief of the Cuban Mission to the United Nations. Although he spoke to no one about it, he was clearly upset. As someone who knew him then says, "I am convinced that one hundred percent of the time that he was in Mexico he was still in love with Mirta." The involvement with Isabelle was probably as much as anything a reaction to Mirta's final abandonment of him. This was true despite his interim involvement with Naty Revuelta, a relationship that did not seem to have particularly deep emotional ties.

An additional personal blow occurred on October 21. De Cárdenas received a telegram from Ramón Castro in Santiago: "Please tell Alejandro [Fidel] that papa died today." Fidel was pulled out of a meeting, and the news was broken to him. Without a trace of emotion, he put the telegram in his pocket and said only, "Please do not tell the others." He returned to the meeting and never mentioned his father's death again. On October 12, Fidel's sisters Emma, Augustina, and Lidia came to Mexico City and were staying at the house of Alfonso Gutiérrez. They had come partly to help Fidel, but also because life was becoming increasingly difficult for them in Havana. They were, of course, told of their father's death, but they were the only others who knew.

Fidel had earlier sent agents to the United States to look into the possibility of buying a Catalina flying boat. When that did not work out, they went to Baltimore to negotiate the purchase of a ship that they intended to register under the Panamanian flag as a trading vessel in the Caribbean. However, until it was entirely paid for, and also to sail it out of U.S. waters, it had to be registered in the United States. To do so required that it be owned by a United States citizen. In addition, it became evident that the sellers had contacted the Cuban Embassy, and it was subsequently revealed that the FBI and CIA were investigating the sale. Fidel ordered his agents to abandon the negotiations, sacrificing their $5,000 down payment.

Meanwhile, on a visit to the coastal town of Tuxpan, Fidel found a fifty-eight-foot motor boat, the *Granma*, belonging to an American physician named Erickson. Antonio Conde negotiated the purchase of the boat for Fidel for $15,000, using some of the money that had come from Prío. He also purchased a house owned by Erickson for $10,000, all in the form of a mortgage. The *Granma* was in sad shape and required a good deal of work. Its two Gray marine engines needed extensive overhauling, and even then the clutch continued to slip so badly that it could produce only 1,500 r.p.m. rather than the intended 1,800. The 1,000-gallon fuel tank was exchanged for one twice the size.

The repair work went on throughout October and November, with only five men knowing the location of the boat. At the same time, final military training was being completed at such locations around the countryside as Tamulipas, Jalapa, Boca del Río, and Ciudad Victoria.

In mid-November, as events were reaching their climax, Fidel was betrayed by his old comrade and bodyguard Rafael del Pino. As the day of embarcation approached, it became clear that del Pino really did not want to go on the expedition, and was attempting to make money by acting as an agent for the Mexican government. When he realized that he was under suspicion by the revolutionary group, he made good his escape and divulged to the authorities everything he knew. However, because of Fidel's system of compartmentalizing information, he could not sabotage the entire operation. On November 20, Teresa Casuso's house was raided, as was the house next door, where Pedro Miret had been living. All the arms stored there were seized, and they were dragged off to prison. Fidel received word from his friend in the police that a raid was pending. He ordered all his men to begin moving by car and bus to the house in Tuxpan. For security reasons, Fidel stayed in Cuernavaca for the final several weeks.

More and more often, it became Fidel's style to mark what he regarded as major points in his career by issuing written proclamations such as the one published when he departed Havana. He saw the launching of his invasion of Cuba as a historic milestone and wanted it enshrined in the public record.

He had prepared and sent to Cuba a document to be published as he left Mexico, but *Bohemia* refused to publish it. On the way to Tuxpan he wrote a will in which he left Fidelito to the care of Orquídea Pino, with whom the boy had been living since he arrived in Mexico.

Tuxpan was an ideal site, despite its distance from Mexico City. Although the Mexican Navy had an observation post there, there was no customs house or immigration service, making a clandestine departure much easier. However, as the men assembled there on the night of November 24, it was raining and there were storm warnings. As a result of Fidel's secrecy, many of the men did not know they were leaving that night. Others thought that the *Granma* was merely to ferry them to a larger vessel that would actually take them to Cuba. Several men suggested to Fidel that he delay the departure, but as usual he declined. The bad weather, he said, would convince the authorities that they would not be leaving, and thus decrease the chance of interception.

As they began to board the boat in the darkness, they saw the lights of an approaching car. The men took up positions with their weapons. Fidel ordered them to shoot to kill if it was the police, but it turned out to be one of their own group bringing a last-minute consignment of medical supplies.

The ship could sleep eight comfortably; Fidel intended it to carry eighty-two, plus all of their weapons and ammunition. They were crammed in so tightly that half sat while half stood and then periodically they exchanged places. Of the eighty-two, nineteen were veterans of Moncada. In the hushed blackness they sang the Cuban national anthem.

At 12:20 A.M. Fidel went ashore one last time to say an emotional farewell to those who could not fit on the boat, those like the de Cárdenases who had risked their lives for months to make this moment possible. He told them all to go into hiding until they knew either that the invasion force had arrived safely or that they had been killed or captured. Then the *Granma* chugged away into driving rain and the black of the night, using only one engine and no lights to reduce the chance of being spotted.

Chapter Seven

The sea was rough, and the cramped revolutionaries suffered severely from seasickness. The boat was making only a little over seven knots an hour, and the water pumps were not working properly. Waves broke over the vessel, and cold rain poured down on the men. They bailed frantically just to stay afloat. Che was suffering a severe asthma attack. Fidel, hyperactive as always, was frustrated by his inability to pace or move around. As they slowly crept out beyond the Yucatán Peninsula he worried that the boat would not be able to make it all the way to Oriente Province, and they might be forced to land on the first part of Cuba they reached. On the third day, the weather finally improved, and they continued to head toward their objective, a point southwest of Niquero on the southern coast of Oriente Province.

They were drastically behind Fidel's original timetable. By November 30, the day initially projected for the landing, they were just past the Cayman Islands, nearly 180 miles from their destination. They were further delayed when ex-Lieutenant Roberto Roque, the second in command of the ship who had climbed the mast to look for the lights of land, fell overboard in the dark. They had to circle for a long time to rescue him. Filled with frustration, Fidel heard over the radio news reports of the uprising in Santiago led by Frank País. It had been agreed that Frank would wait until he received word that the rebel forces had landed before launching the insurrection. However, using the same figures as Fidel he had come up with the same projected arrival date. He decided to proceed with the attacks on that day. País, despite his reservations expressed to Fidel in Mexico, managed to pull off a dramatic series of events. Still only twenty-one years of age, he was an exceptional leader and organizer. At dawn on the morning of November 30, he led close to three hundred young people wearing green uniforms with arm bands of red and black, the colors of the 26 of July Movement, in coordinated attacks on the Customs House, the police headquarters, and the harbor building. All were captured or set on fire. A group of M-26-7 prisoners held at the

134

Boniato prison made a successful escape timed to coincide with the uprising.

The intent of the uprising was to draw military units to the city and away from the small towns near the landing site. The invaders would then be able to seize the military outposts in Niquero and other neighboring communities, capturing more weapons to distribute to their local supporters, and then move on to the Sierra Maestra with a substantially augmented force.

Elsewhere the activities of the M-26-7 were, as Melba Hernández and others had predicted, ineffectual and disorganized, lacking weapons and leadership. In Havana they did not even seem to know for certain which day Fidel was to arrive. The Directorio did nothing, and the Communists waited to see if any other action developed before calling for a strike. In the end they, too, did nothing.

On December 2, the *Granma* finally went aground more than two miles south of Niquero, at Playa de los Colorados, near Belic. Using their radio to monitor transmissions between two of Batista's frigates that were searching for them, they sneaked in toward the shore. At the sandy beach where they had intended to land, there was a small pier alongside which the *Granma* was to have been moored while they unloaded their heavy equipment. Waiting there, and in nearby Belic, were members of the local M-26-7 with jeeps, trucks, weapons and other supplies, and fifty men. The reception party had been organized by Celia Sánchez, a key assistant to Frank País. That morning she was arrested in nearby Campechuela and never made it to the beach.

The landing was in fact a shipwreck in which all of their heavy weapons, food, and a large radio transmitter were lost. Led by Fidel, and holding their rifles over their heads, the men waded though a mile of tangled mangrove swamp to shore, completely lost to those waiting to receive them.

Finally reaching dry land, they encountered a charcoal maker, Angel Pérez, who offered to feed them. But at that moment a government patrol boat (a World War II PT boat) appeared offshore and started firing shells in their direction. Shortly afterward an airplane strafed the area. A quick head count revealed that eight men were missing, including Juan Manuel Marquéz, the second in command. Now that they had been discovered by the military and any element of surprise was gone, Fidel decided to push on inland without any more delay. A thousand soldiers and low-flying aircraft were now looking for them. Finally reunited, the group of eighty-two men struggled for three days through low brush growing amid jagged volcanic rock. Without food or water until the night of the second day, they at last came to an area of sugar cane, which they chewed for some sustenance. Exhausted, and with their feet badly blistered from ill-fitting boots, they marched at night and tried to sleep hidden among the trees during the day.

On the morning of December 5, 1956, they set up camp at Alegría de Pío at the edge of the woods near a sugarcane field. They were unaware that the army had cordoned off the region in which they had been walking, and supplied with information provided by a local guide who had abandoned them, had found their trail and was slowly closing in. It was, by Fidel's admission, a poor choice of location for the camp, and they placed their sentries too close to the sleeping men to provide adequate warning. At 4 p.m. they were suddenly caught in a deadly crossfire. The effect on the force was devastating. Three were killed outright, eighteen were captured then or later and summarily executed, twenty-one were captured and imprisoned, and another twenty-one managed to escape entirely, making it to the towns and abandoning the venture. This left twenty-one, many of whom were injured, to struggle on in scattered groups toward the mountains.

The army was able to capture even more men because on December 10 the air force bombarded the path to the mountains with leaflets proclaiming a two-day truce and an offer to spare the lives of those who surrendered. Several men, not knowing what fate had befallen Fidel, took advantage of the offer.

During the battle at Alegría de Pío, the army set fire to the fields where several of the men had taken refuge, and Faustino Pérez, who had been tending to the wounded, was forced to flee. He hid under a small bush in a state of total desolation. After an hour he suddenly heard his name being called, "Hey, Faustino. Hey, Doctor." He saw Fidel and Universo Sánchez hiding some distance away. Fidel, despite the devastating setback, evidenced no feeling that they should abandon their efforts. Indeed, he seemed confident that enough men had survived for them to go on. For several days the men crept through the sugar cane, often having to speak in whispers. Fidel, however, talked confidently of the support that would come from the local people once they knew they were alive, of the philosophy of armed struggle and his plans for the future, including his theories on land reform. Faustino says of those perilous days, "He was so confident we did not dare tell him we were not." Finally, on December 16, they reached the prearranged rendezvous point at the farm of Ramón Pérez, a supporter of the 26 of July Movement. Crescencio Pérez, Ramón's brother, was an influential peasant leader in the area.

During the next eight days, survivors dribbled in. A search was organized primarily by Guillermo García, a farmer, along with Celia Sánchez, Crescencio Pérez, his brothers, and his sons. They combed the scrub- and cactus-covered terrain for any stragglers. A group that included Raúl arrived, and Che, with a flesh wound in his neck, appeared in a group led by Juan Almeida.

On Christmas Day, after nine days of food and rest, fifteen men were ready to move on. Before they departed, Fidel addressed them. As was his style, he spoke to the little group in the same oratorical manner that he would have used to address a hundred thousand. The theme of his speech was that now that they had managed to survive, Batista's days were numbered. From now on the army of 26 of July Movement would not be defeated. He proclaimed, "Now we are going to win."

Under the circumstances, Fidel's optimism might have suggested that he had taken leave of reality, and indeed, some of those present did have a negative reaction to his speech in light of how many of their comrades had so recently and gruesomely died. Perhaps no better example exists of how Fidel could use his charisma. When all of the men were ready to abandon the venture, he evidenced not a shred of pessimism, and spoke in inspirational terms, appealing both to their courage and their patriotism. That plus his own example exerted such a powerful effect that even the men with the gravest doubts were ready to go on with him.

The romanticized versions of the trek into the mountains have spoken of twelve men, suggesting Christ-like parallels. Fidel himself has mentioned that number, but more often he has spoken of a "handful of men." Faustino Pérez had left directly from the farm for Havana, and Rafael Chao stayed behind to look for abandoned weapons with Guillermo García. Those who actually made the march with Fidel were Raúl, Universo Sánchez, Che Guevara, Ciro Redondo, Efigenio Ameijeiras, Rene Rodríguez, Armando Rodríguez, Juan Almeida, Camilo Cienfuegos, Ramiro Valdés, Reinaldo Benítez, Francisco González, and Calixto Morales.

Over the next few days, Rafael Chao and four other late-arriving survivors joined the group in the mountains. They were Calixto García, Luis Crespo, Julio Díaz, and José Moran, bringing the total number forming the nucleus of the revolution to eighteen plus Fidel. They could also include in their group Guillermo García and a half-dozen other peasant supporters.

Despite the extensive training they had received from Colonel Bayo, the men found the first few weeks a time of great physical hardship. Che noted, "Hunger, what is truly known as hunger, none of us had ever known before, and then we began to know it." Most of the first weeks were spent learning how to survive in the mountain environment. Importantly, Fidel also used this early time to acquire an intimate knowledge of the physical terrain of the region so that it could be used to their military advantage in the future. They also built a network of contacts and became aware of the local culture and social system. As the official government line was that the force had been wiped out and Fidel killed, the army did not mount any major campaign against them. However, Senator Rolando Masferrer, the former head of the MSR and one of Fidel's long-standing adversaries, had thrown in his lot with Batista. He now operated a private army in Oriente Province known as "Masferrer's Tigers," and his men were constantly hunting the rebels.

The harshness of their surroundings made daily shaving difficult, and it was soon abandoned. Instead, the men made beards a part of their rebel uniform, an emblem that Fidel has retained ever since. Sporting a beard would ultimately become a badge of honor identifying the wearer as one of the *barbudos* who had fought in the mountains.

At the end of December, Celia Sánchez established contact with the group through intermediaries. Celia was the daughter of an unusually humanitarian physician in Oriente Province who was known for his willingness to travel long distances into the mountains to treat peasants, often without charge. Celia had inherited his deep sense of social responsibility. She became the "quartermaster" for the rebels in Manzanillo, handling all their logistical needs and ordering and arranging delivery of all of their supplies. Celia would first meet Fidel face to face on February 17, 1957, the same day that Herbert Matthews, a reporter for *The New York Times*, arrived in the mountains. On that occasion she remained with the rebel force for only two days, but she returned at the end of April and stayed until June 1. She made a three-day visit again in September, and then in October she moved to the mountains for good. She became Fidel's most trusted aide, remaining at his side not only throughout the rest of the war, but for the rest of her life.

Media reports in Havana of Fidel's demise evoked a mixed reaction. It was a time of deep despair for the leadership of the M-26-7. The conciliationists, on the other hand, were not unhappy to believe that Fidel, the constant thorn in their side, was dead. Their cause, however, had been significantly set back by the death of Cosme De la Torriente on December 8. Gradually rumors of Fidel's survival began to filter back into the cities. It was like a miracle for the forces of the M-26-7. Perhaps more important, Fidel's survival from yet another horrendous escapade further developed the notion of his invincibility and the belief in the minds of Cubans, readily susceptible to romanticism, that maybe he was indeed a man of destiny. By so doing he had immediately raised himself, and the M-26-7 forces in the cities, to a position of unassailable credibility and preeminence among the revolutionary groups. It was a reflection of the seriousness with which Batista viewed the situation that on January 15 he suspended civil rights.

On January 17, Fidel and his men launched their first military attack against an isolated army post at La Plata. After thirty to forty minutes of intense fighting, the dozen or so defenders surrendered. It was a great morale booster for the rebels and, more important, it yielded them a Thompson machine gun, twelve rifles, food, and medicine. Five days later, the group successfully ambushed the vanguard of a government patrol, inflicting a dozen casualties. From the start, Fidel insisted that all soldiers captured be treated with respect and given the same medical care for their wounds as his own men received. There was never to be any abuse or torture of prisoners, thereby setting themselves in sharp contrast with Batista and the army. Similarly, he insisted that any food obtained from peasants be paid for, again consciously creating an unprecedented distinction for military forces in Cuba.

While the modest military successes were important for morale and to demonstrate to the Cuban people that they remained a viable and potent fighting force, the most important accomplishment for their ultimate survival during the first two months was the establishment of a base of acceptance and support among the local population.

The Sierra Maestra were significantly populated by people who had at different times fled oppression elsewhere in the country. They were tough people, and it was a hard life. That the rebels survived by itself commanded considerable respect; that they shared the peasants' resentment of the government, and were increasingly able to inflict meaningful blows against the government forces, caused a growing trickle of peasants to enlist in their cause.

Crescencio Pérez was considered by many to be more a bandit than a political revolutionary before his association with Fidel. But this white-haired, bearded patriarch with a .45 pistol always on his hip controlled a network of influence and allegiances throughout the Sierra Maestra, extending over an area of twenty-five hundred square kilometers in which fifty thousand *guajiros,* or peasants, lived. He reputedly had more than eighty illegitimate children across the region. Together with men such as Manuel Fajardo, cattleman Guillermo García, and others, he could deliver to Fidel and his men a finely tuned intelligence system, guides, a pipeline for food and other supplies, and a continuous stream of eager if untrained recruits. Unconvinced either of the validity of their cause or that they could win, some peasants in the early days, when confronted with bribes or intimidation, betrayed the rebels. But it proved a small price to pay for the indispensable support they received from the mountain community as a whole. Fidel had quickly achieved the primary objective of any guerrilla force—they were able to live off the land or, as described by Mao Zedong, live among the people like a fish swimming in water.

It was toward the end of January that Fidel faced his most serious threat from a traitor. A peasant leader, Eutimio Guerra, who had earlier served Fidel as a guide, was captured by Batista's soldiers. He agreed for $10,000 to rejoin the rebels and kill Fidel. Prior to his return, however, he flew over the area in a light plane and directed the pilot to the rebels' location. The pinpoint accuracy and ferocity of the attack by the fighter planes and B-26 bombers damaged the morale of the newer recruits, several of whom had previously insisted on being allowed to return to the towns because they found life in the mountains too tough. Fidel saw it as such a dangerous threat that he announced he would impose the death penalty on anyone who deserted, was insubordinate, or was merely "defeatist."

Guerra returned to the group on January 28, 1957, and that first night tried to get close to Fidel by convincing him that he was cold and needed to share his blanket. But, as always, Fidel's bodyguards hovered nearby, and remained awake all night. Guerra, holding his .45 pistol under the blanket, could not bring himself to shoot Fidel knowing that it would mean certain death for him, too. Two days later he left the rebels before the bombing started. Then, for the next several days the men were dispersed. However, a report on February 9 from a young boy that he had seen Guerra at the military headquarters raised suspicions. Finally, Guerra returned to the camp, was confronted with his treachery, and confessed. He was executed on February 17.

At the end of January, Fidel made an important but risky decision. Cut off from any press outlet through which he could communicate with the Cuban people, and with a continuing serious morale problem among his troops, he needed a master move to maintain the momentum of the movement. His knowledge of the press and of the United States led him to send Rene Rodríguez to the leaders of the M-26-7 in Havana with the message that he would be willing to meet with a member of the foreign press, preferably an American.

As has happened so often in Fidel's charmed career, the personal needs of another individual played into his own scenario. Herbert L. Matthews was a fifty-seven-year-old senior editor with *The New York Times*. He had had a distinguished career as an expert on Latin America and, in the 1930s, had covered the Spanish Civil War. He apparently felt, however, that he had not received the recognition he deserved for his contribution to journalism, and he lived in constant hope of the major scoop that had somehow eluded him all of his career. When Mrs. Ruby Hart Phillips, the *Times*'s correspondent in Havana, informed him of Fidel's offer, he eagerly took on the assignment himself.

Arriving in Havana with his wife to create the impression that he was there on vacation, the slight, balding journalist met with Faustino Pérez and Javier Pazos. The four of them traveled to Manzanillo, where Matthews's wife remained. Then, after six hours by Jeep and another two hours of walking, they arrived at the rendezvous point. Matthews and Fidel met on the morning of February 17. Fidel had taken a substantial risk coming down from the high mountains for the meeting. They talked for many hours, during which Fidel used his imposing and vibrant personality to persuade the journalist that the magnitude and influence of his revolutionary effort were far greater than was the case. The story is frequently repeated in Cuba that during the interview the same small group of men were marched in and out of the camp several times, on each occasion having changed their clothes and appearance, thereby making Matthews think the strength of the force was several times greater than it really was. Fidel talked vaguely during the interview of "the other camps," suggesting that he had many more men under arms in other locations. In reality that was the only camp and at that moment Fidel had with him only eighteen men.

Matthews's story appeared in *The New York Times* on February 24, 1957. He described Fidel in glowing and idealistic terms, making him an instant romantic hero to thousands of Americans. What he also did, in all innocence, was to inflate the currrent military and political significance of the rebel movement. To do so served both his needs and those of Fidel. Matthews was determined to make the story the scoop for which he had always longed, and until other journalists went to the Sierra Maestra the story was his alone. With his years of journalistic experience he knew well how to gain the biggest play.

When the air-mail edition of the paper arrived in Cuba, Batista had the story on Fidel cut out of every copy. The minister of defense, Santiago Verdeja, called the story "fantasy" and denied that Fidel was alive. Matthews had played his cards well, adroitly eliciting from Batista the implication that *The New York Times* had fabricated the story, thus fueling interest far beyond what the piece might otherwise have generated. In a dramatic rebuttal, *The New York Times* was then able to publish a photograph of Matthews and Fidel together during the interview. Batista, under pressure from the Inter-American Press Association that was about to hold its annual meeting in Havana, and eager to create an impression of normalcy, was then forced to relent, lifting the press ban so that the people of Cuba were able to read the interview in its entirety. The impact was profound. Not only did the article prove beyond any doubt that Fidel was alive and well but it suggested that he also had consequential military resources at his disposal. That such a prestigious American newspaper as *The New York Times* would interview him lent both prestige and stature to Fidel and his cause. Matthews had made Fidel an international celebrity overnight, placing him in the most favorable light. Whatever their political views, the nationalism that is so strong in most Cubans responded to this recognition for their fellow countryman. There was a great pride in a Cuban being given worldwide recognition, so that Fidel became a hero even to many whose current loyalties were to Batista.

In Cuba, the story came at a politically propitious time. The conciliation movement had collapsed entirely, and there was a growing conviction among the political opposition and intellectual leadership that Batista had to be ousted. A turning point for many moderate politicians had been a series of brutal killings of suspected agitators by the army during December, following which several of the bodies were left hanging from roadside trees. Raúl Chibás, brother of Eddy and now the leader of the Ortodoxo Party, Felipe Pazos, former governor of the National Bank, whose son Javier had accompanied Matthews to the mountains, and Ignacio Mendoza, a broker, and scion of a prestigious Havana family came together to form the "Civic Resistance" with the encouragement of Faustino Pérez and Armando Hart. It was a semisecret group of influential upper- and middle-class leaders committed to Batista's downfall. At this stage they avoided overt support for Fidel, but they were in close communication with the M-26-7 leadership, which had helped to organize the group. Much of the money they raised found its way into Fidel's hands. There were also those, like Justo Carrillo, former head of the Agricultural and Industrial Development Bank under Prío, who out of a combination of idealism and the hope for a political future for themselves after Batista were willing to support Fidel financially and politically as the single best hope for change. Business leaders eager to have access to whoever was in power covered their bets by surreptitiously increasing their financial support to Fidel after the Matthews interview.

Fidel's military situation at the beginning of March was precarious, as was the physical condition of his men. But the significant realignment of political power behind his cause that had occurred during the two months that he had been in the mountains vindicated his decision to return from Mexico in such a desperate rush. His mere survival against Batista for this period of time had been enough to move those who had been resigned in their conviction that Batista could not be toppled. Even those who personally disliked Fidel and had vehemently criticized him in the past were willing to support him now that it seemed he might be capable of achieving Batista's overthrow.

Perhaps spurred in part by a degree of competition as the drift of events moved in Fidel's direction, José Antonio Echevarría and the Directorio Revolucionario, pursuing their own distinct strategy, planned a dramatic event to regain the initiative for their movement. At 3:24 P.M. on March

13, 1957, fifty men attacked the Presidential Palace. True to his philosophy of striking at the top, which Echevarría had espoused to Fidel in Mexico, he believed that if Batista could be assassinated the rest of the government would crumble. Although sponsored by the Directorio, the attackers included not only students but also veterans of the Spanish Civil War, the Cayo Confites expedition, the Caribbean Legion, and assorted unaffiliated revolutionaries. Profiting by surprise, the attackers quickly secured the outside of the building, and with submachine guns blazing, a contingent entered the palace in search of Batista. They shot their way into the presidential offices, but Batista was not there. They realized he had retreated to the residential quarters on the floor above, but despite having plans drawn for them by one of the attackers familiar with the layout of the palace, they could not find the stairway. Meanwhile, Batista had concentrated his forces on the roof of the building, and they were raking the courtyard with gunfire as he waited for urgently summoned reinforcements to arrive. Very soon the building was surrounded by military units, including tanks, and the attackers were mowed down as they tried to escape. Echevarría and a handful of his men seized the Radio Reloj, announcing to the listeners that Batista was dead and urging them to rise against the government. Then as they headed toward the University of Havana campus, they encountered the security forces. In the ensuing gun battle, Echevarría was shot dead.

The attack on the palace could well have succeeded, leaving Fidel in temporary oblivion in the mountains. His position had always been, probably correctly, that killing Batista would not really change the society. The power vacuum created would only be filled, he argued, by another equally corrupt individual. Had the attack succeeded, it would have put Fidel in a difficult position in the short run.

In the aftermath of that attack, Batista launched another wave of extreme and often indiscriminate brutality against anyone even remotely suspected of association with the assault. The only beneficiary was Fidel. The more random and vicious the oppression, the more the average citizen was radicalized against Batista. Fidel remained the single viable expression of those feelings with which people could identify.

Fidel was quick to make the most of the situation by condemning the attack to two CBS reporters, Wendell Hoffman and Robert Taber, who, following Matthews, were the first of a long stream of journalists to reach the mountains. It was, he said, strategically ill founded, a view he sincerely believed. "Here in the Sierra Maestra is where they should come to fight," he told them.

The interview at the beginning of April 1957 was held on Turquino Peak, at 6,600 feet the highest point in Cuba. Fidel chose that location for several reasons. With a well-known statue of José Martí in the background there could be no argument that he was actually in the Sierra Maestra, and it was a symbolic way of linking his struggle with that of Martí. Also, being the highest point in Cuba, it was an important morale booster for his troops to climb it for the first time.

March 1957 was a military turning point for Fidel. Early in the month, the Batista forces had sought to establish an isolation zone around the rebels. They forcibly relocated peasants living in the area and set up token health and housing programs where they resettled them in an attempt to counter the appeal of the better life promised by the revolutionaries. The strategy had a polarizing effect. While it did wean away some support from Fidel, no one could remain neutral, and some of the peasants who might not otherwise have helped the rebels decided, as a result of being forcibly relocated, that their only choice was to support the insurgent cause. The fundamental objective of the strategy was to prevent anyone going in or out of the rebel zone, and in that it failed.

On March 25, 1957, fifty-two new men recruited in Santiago by Frank País and under the command of Jorge Sotús arrived to join the rebel force. Among them were three young Americans whose fathers worked at the Guantánamo base, Charles Ryan, Victor Buehlman, and Michael L. Garvey. They were untrained and poorly armed, but they represented the beginning of what would become a steady stream of recruits to swell the ranks of the rebel force. Fidel addressed them, making the observation, "Now we are again back to the number that came in the *Granma*," and he repeated his statement made on several occasions, "Well, now we will win the war." Others, mainly peasants, arrived to join the rebels, but being very short of arms, Fidel would not let them stay unless they brought a weapon with them. Often a man would leave and return a couple of weeks later, having bushwacked a government soldier and relieved him of his rifle.

The next two months were a period of consolidation during which the new recruits were trained and the skeleton of a more conventional army structure was developed. It was also known as "the period of the long walks," as Fidel was constantly on the move expanding, by marathon treks, his area of geographical knowledge and his links with the peasant population. Everywhere he went he kept with him his rifle with a telescopic site to which he was deeply attached and of which he was immensely proud. Many of the recruits complained, "I came for fighting, not for walking," but Fidel's intention was in part to use the walks to strengthen them and build their endurance. At times he would become irritable and stay by himself, unapproachable. His behavior during these periods supports the contention of Conte Agüero that he has always suffered bouts of depression.

Three companies were set up under Sotús, Juan Almeida, and Raúl. Vanguard and rearguard units were created, led by Camilo Cienfuegos and Efigenio Ameijeiras. The headquarters unit was made up of Fidel; Ciro Redondo, Manuel Fajardo, and Luis Crespo, serving mainly as bodyguards; Che Guevara as the doctor; and Universo Sánchez as chief of staff. With Celia's help, lines of supply and communication were firmly established. Careful sorting out of which peasants could be trusted and which could not occurred, and an assessment was made of the quality of intelligence they received from their various informants. Safe areas and locations where food and munitions could be stockpiled were identified.

It was also during this period that Celia Sánchez took over the role as Fidel's "personal manager." Physically tough, unswervingly loyal, and meticulously organized, she stayed with Fidel like his shadow. On patrol, she had endurance as great as any of the men, always walking immediately behind Fidel. She served not only as a secretary and personal assistant, keeping for posterity meticulous records of everything they did, she also worked hard to complement Fidel in his areas of weakness. While Fidel dealt with the grand schemes, she became the executor of the details. She managed the money and kept the records. When they ate in the home of a peasant, she quietly passed the family a few pesos as they left. When Batista's soldiers whom they had taken prisoner wrote home to their families, she arranged that a few pesos were slipped in with the letters. In general she served as the liaison between on the one hand Fidel and the rebel army, and on the other the local peasant population. She was the one who made Fidel rest when he was reaching physical exhaustion, and led an effort with the other officers to try to prevent him from risking his life by personally leading the attack on military outposts. He was, she argued, too valuable to the revolution to take that kind of risk anymore.

There has been considerable speculation about the exact nature of their more than twenty-year relationship. Most believe, as do members of her family, that the relationship was a romantic one during this period, and continued as such for a while after they left the mountains. Celia's love for and loyalty to Fidel were total. And there is every evidence that these feelings were fully reciprocated.

May 28, 1957, represented the coming of age of the fledgling rebel army. Armed with a consignment of machine guns and carbines that had arrived ten days before, eighty of the rebels attacked and overran a military outpost at El Uvero, defended by fifty-three soldiers. Fidel commanded the action from a hill overlooking the fort and launched the action with a shot from his precious rifle with its telescopic site. Although ultimately successful the assault was fraught with confusion and errors. There was confusion among the various units as to how they were to be deployed, and the attack, intended to begin before dawn, did not get underway until

145

the sun was rising. Although outnumbering the defenders, it took nearly three hours for the battle to be won. In part this was because of the tenacity of the defenders, and because the attack was mounted across open ground without the cover of darkness. Whatever the shortcomings in terms of military strategy, its impact on morale was electric. In a captured truck they carted away supplies of arms, food, and medicine. Fourteen prisoners were held for a period of two days and then released unharmed. Although seven rebels died as a result of the engagement, it was a cause for joyous celebration. The event also received wide press coverage, further damaging the reputation of Batista's forces.

Batista's response was to intensify the program of forced relocation, placing two thousand families into well-guarded strategic hamlets that were little more than concentration camps. The public outcry at this inhumane behavior and Batista's continuing pathological need to make himself popular with the general public led him to reverse the policy. He did, however, remove all the remaining isolated army outposts in the Sierra Maestra to deny Fidel any similar dramatic victories.

In June 1957, a young Catholic priest, Father Guillermo Sardiñas, joined the rebels. Later, other Catholic priests and ministers from other denominations would join the force. Through the rest of the campaign, with Fidel's encouragement, they conducted services for the rebel army. At this time there were no chaplains in Batista's army.

Fidel's guerrilla force would have had a hard time surviving in the Sierra Maestra without the sustenance of the M-26-7 forces in the cities. Yet as the overall success of the movement increased, a growing tension emerged between these two complementary elements of the struggle. In Fidel's mind he was the leader of the entire movement; the guerrilla force was its primary strategic focus, and the lowland organization was there to provide the necessary support to those fighting the "real" war. He made the policy decisions and gave the orders for everyone to follow, expecting that they would be carried out even in distant Havana. Increasingly, however, those in the cities felt they should be accepted at least as equals in the struggle, and many felt that ultimately they, not the forces in the mountains, would bring about, through massive strikes, the collapse of the Batista government. While the guerrillas got all the glory, dozens of city dwellers risked their lives anonymously every day, planting bombs to keep the administration off balance.

On July 7, 1957, Frank País wrote a letter to Fidel in which he made the case for the lowlanders. He expressed the view that a revolutionary general strike would be the climax of the struggle, and recommended that a national directorate be set up to oversee the policies, strategies, and programs of the entire 26 of July Movement. The directorate would, he suggested, have thirteen members, but he allocated only one seat to a representative of the guerrillas. País further suggested that it would be a good idea if the M-26-7 had a specific program of action, and added that he was working on such a document for which Fidel's input would be very welcome!

The episode is reminiscent of the events that occurred after Fidel came out of prison on the Isle of Pines, when Orlando Castro and other Moncadistas had made similar suggestions.

It is argued in Cuba today that Fidel accepted the letter as a routine communication concerning the future organization of the movement and had no adverse reaction to it. His matter-of-fact response to Frank is cited as evidence of this. However, Fidel's style was in general so totally dominating, reserving for himself all major organizational decisions, that it begs credibility to believe that he would have accepted such a communication with equanimity. Frank País was a superb organizer, and immensely brave. His fundamentalist Baptist background was the basis for his deep moral convictions, but they were unaccompanied by either a sophisticated appreciation of political theory or much sense of political maneuvering. In Mexico, he had strongly argued that Fidel's return to Cuba be delayed, and he had apparently acted independently in launching the premature insurrection in Santiago. However, events would soon make this issue academic.

País was correct that Fidel had a problem in being far better known for his opposition to Batista than for what he planned to offer as an alternative. One of the few weaknesses, which was to become a cause for constant criticism from now on, was his failure to lay out detailed program plans that derived from his policy decisions. The reasons were several: as a brilliant political strategist he focused always on the maneuvering for power, disdaining detailed follow-through that he felt would take care of itself; he had had no experience running any sort of organization that required disciplined managerial skills, much less any understanding of how government worked on a day-to-day basis; and he instinctively understood that once you started laying out detailed program plans you began to limit your options. "History Will Absolve Me" was as close as he had come up to that point to producing a political manifesto or a statement of his position on issues, and it was certainly no blueprint for governance. Carlos Franqui had sent Frank País a letter in January, after they had discussed the subject, suggesting that it was a widely recognized problem. He said, "The conversations I had with Fidel last year in Mexico . . . have convinced me—other comrades feel the same—that Fidel does not want any kind of written program. It may have something to do with his personality and his short-range planning methods, and I know there is not

147

much chance of changing him." Although fascinated by political ideology and widely read on the subject, Fidel seemed to have great difficulty formulating either his own philosophy or program beyond the feelings expressed in "History Will Absolve Me." He generally found it easier to adopt already existing ideologies, but was leery of the political implications that entailed. He therefore found it safer not to go beyond that original document.

The only thing important to Fidel in mid-1957 was winning the war. Despite a fine mind he was always more oriented to physical action. While in the mountains he had no expectation that after the victory he personally would be running the government. His concern with ideology at this stage was only as a tool for achieving his immediate goal.

During the time in the mountains, Fidel had talked about political theory extensively with Che and to a lesser extent with his brother Raúl, the only two men besides himself with a higher education. Neither of them had any more experience with government than he had, and both were consciously oriented toward Marxist theory.

Fidel knew that any intimation of sympathy for communism at this stage could lose the revolution for him. His public statements at this time were an attempt to rally the broadest range of support, and thus they were the most restrained and moderate of his career. He would later claim that this was a deliberate strategy, and that he was, in truth, thoroughly committed to Marxist-Leninist theory by this point, but there is no evidence to substantiate that contention, even from reports of his private discussions. In the final analysis, he remained preoccupied with the struggle to achieve power; what he would do with it once he had it continued to be of secondary importance in his mind.

Later, in February 1958, Fidel wrote an article in the first person transmitted through journalist Andrew St. George for *Coronet* magazine aimed at a United States audience. In it he said he was "fighting to do away with dictatorship in Cuba and establish the foundations of genuine representative government." He disavowed, apparently honestly, any personal interest in becoming president, pointing out that under the Constitution he was ten years too young to assume the position. Among the objectives of his revolution, he cited immediate freedom for all political prisoners, full and untrammeled freedom of public information, and the wiping out of corruption. He also said, "We have no plans for the expropriation or nationalization of foreign investments here." He stressed land reform and a campaign against illiteracy as two key elements in the program the revolution promised.

The piece is interesting, in part because it was so obviously aimed at neutralizing his critics in the United States and buying time against those he knew would advocate United States intervention. It also reflects, in the repetition of the issues of illiteracy and land reform that were central to "History Will Absolve Me," that these concerns were still foremost in his thinking.

In early July 1957, Raúl Chibás, the Ortodoxos leader, and Felipe Pazos, Cuba's senior economist and a distinguished leader, went to the Sierra Maestra to meet with Fidel. Pazos was also in league with Prío, and it is clear that the motivation of these two men in coming to the mountains was to put themselves in a pivotal position among all the anti-Batista forces. Che, seeing through the strategy and imbued with his sense of ideological purity, was contemptuous of the two men. He later referred to Pazos as having "a small Machiavellian brain." Fidel, on the other hand, second to none in the art of political maneuver, was convinced he could turn the relationship to his advantage. Although this meeting occurred before the death of Frank País, Fidel did not involve him or any of the other M-26-7 members from the lowlands in the discussions or the signing of the document that would come out of the meetings. By so doing, he reiterated his absolute authority over all elements of the movements. Like Frank País, however, Chibás and Pazos stressed to Fidel the desperate need for a program of action or a manifesto so that people would know what he stood for. What was different now was that they were willing to lend their stature to such a document by signing it with him, thereby enabling him to gain credibility with a broad segment of the middle class.

The Sierra Maestra manifesto was issued on July 12. In the end it was a relatively benign document, although Fidel had argued for a more radical statement. It stressed the need for a revolutionary front that included all opposition parties, by implication excluded the United States from any involvement in the ultimate settlement, and spoke of the need for free elections and a democratic government, an absolute guarantee of press freedom, and free elections in all trade unions. Fidel wanted a strong commitment to radical land reform, but Chibás and Pazos would agree to only a modest program for redistributing unused land.

Fidel clearly saw the manifesto purely in terms of his struggle for hegemony over the anti-Batista forces. While he wanted it to reflect his views where that was possible, he had not reached definitive decisions on many topics. He was therefore willing then to accept positions for pragmatic reasons that he would later completely reverse. From early in his career, Fidel was guided by a statement of Martí that he could quote by heart; "There are things that in order to be achieved must be hidden. . . . By proclaiming what they are would only raise difficulties that would make it harder to attain the desired end." It was a rationalization for dissembling that had moral acceptability because it came from Martí. He knew that Chibás and Pazos were there to use him, and he had no compunctions about returning the favor. They enabled him to get respectability and stature among the old-line political and professional leadership. Virtually every significant opposition figure was now behind his cause. Whether the document had any bearing on what he would ultimately do mattered very little to him at that point.

On July 30, 1957, in Santiago de Cuba, Frank País was captured and killed. On a tip from an informer, the police were searching for a cache of weapons on a street where Frank was hiding. He tried to escape and was captured. Initially he was not identified, but subsequently he was recognized by Colonel José Maria Salas Cañizares, the brother of Batista's chief of police, and one of Fidel's bitterest enemies from the past. He shot Frank in cold blood.

Frank's funeral the next day triggered citywide unrest, and when on August 1 the newly appointed U.S. ambassador, Earl T. Smith, visited the city, he was greeted by an immense throng of demonstrating women dressed in black. They begged him to use his influence to end Batista's reign of terror, and then they were set upon by the police, who beat many of them brutally. Smith, clearly shaken, deplored the "excessive use of force."

The loss of Frank País was a devastating blow to the M-26-7. His death was sincerely mourned. It is said that Che, who described him as "one of the purest and most glorious" of the revolutionaries, cried when he heard the news. His loss was a profound setback.

Earlier in July, Fidel had spontaneously elevated Che to the rank of *commandante* (major), giving him command over a second column, ultimately Column 4. Celia Sánchez gave him a little silver star as a symbol of his promotion. Thus, Che became not only a full-fledged military commander as opposed to the group's physician (Dr. René Vallejo took over that role), but also assumed a position almost on a par with Fidel. On July 31, 1957, Che led his men in the capture of a military post at Bueycito. And on August 29 they ambushed a detachment of soldiers at El Hombrito. It was not of great military consequence; each side lost one man. Che later described this as the end of the "nomadic phase," as he set up a permanent base. It was a manifestation of their different personalities; Fidel preferred to stay on the move, establishing only temporary camps.

By mid-1957, growing sympathy for the M-26-7 had developed among some noncommissioned officers in the military. They plotted a military uprising, which they envisioned would be coordinated with a civilian strike organized by the M-26-7, leading to the toppling of Batista. Fidel was aware of the plan and gave it at least tacit encouragement, although it was not his idea and was clearly inconsistent with his overall strategy to insure that Batista's fall be based on a popular uprising. The original plan called for the military men on September 5 to seize their barracks in Havana, Cienfuegos, Mariel, and Santiago. However, due to confusion about the planned date for the uprising, or a deliberate decision to call it off that did not reach everyone involved, only the men in Cienfuegos acted on schedule. Led by former navy lieutenant Dionisio San Roman, who had been a part of the Barquín mutiny in 1956, they rapidly seized the military base and the city, only to find they had acted alone. Within hours, Batista brought to bear on them the full force of the loyal military with tanks and air power. The revolt was crushed, and predictably it was followed by excessive carnage, torture, and brutality. Again the biggest winner was Fidel. Another potentially competing revolutionary movement, which likely would only have replaced one military leader with another, had been annihilated. At the same time, moderate military men previously unsympathetic to his cause but appalled by the viciousness of Batista's reaction against their colleagues were converted to the belief that Batista had to go.

Accusations were subsequently made that the M-26-7, under Fidel's direction, had cynically encouraged the planning of the military uprising, and then at the last minute had pulled out their support with the deliberate intention of sabotaging the competing revolutionary faction. There was great bitterness that the M-26-7 had been willing to sacrifice the lives of several hundred idealistic young men to enhance its own position of domination. There is no hard evidence to support this view, and it is vehemently denied by the M-26-7 leaders who were involved with the action, especially Faustino Pérez.

The Batista regime was looking increasingly shaky, and it was widely believed among opposition leaders that it was only a matter of time before it would fall. On October 15, 1957, representatives from seven opposition groups met in Miami at the home of Lincoln Rodón, former president of the Cuban House of Representatives. They formed the Junta de Liberación (JL), supposedly to follow up on the Sierra Maestra manifesto, and called for a united struggle until democratic rule was restored and elections were held. It was in fact another rather blatant attempt by Prío, who had financially backed most of the groups present, to position himself for a return to power and to create a counterbalance to Fidel.

Prior to the meeting, Felipe Pazos and Lester Rodríguez (the representative of the M-26-7 in exile) wrote to the National Directorate of the movement in Havana, asking to be authorized as the official representatives at the meeting. They received an ambiguous reply that was sent to them without clearance from Fidel, which they chose to interpret as

151

approval. A document was later produced by the committee that was in large part a restatement of the Sierra Maestra manifesto. It contained, however, several important differences. It failed to warn categorically against United States intervention, it allowed for the establishment of an interim military junta after Batista's overthrow, and it called for the ultimate incorporation of the rebel forces into the regular army. Fidel received the document and first heard of the Junta de Liberación on November 20, 1957. He was furious about the new elements in the document, and sent a letter to the JL saying that the 26 of July Movement did not designate or authorize any delegation to discuss such negotiations.

He was particularly angry that Pazos, whom he saw as opportunistic, should seek to speak for the M-26-7 and make commitments on his behalf. His reaction was also a sharp rebuke to the M-26-7 leaders in Havana, reminding them that he was in charge and they had no authority to commit the organization to something this consequential without his clearance. Although he did not say so, the poor political judgment involved also rankled considerably. Apart from the unacceptable passages in the document, which anyone who really understood Fidel's position could never have accepted, there was no advantage at that stage for the M-26-7 to participate as an equal among a group of relatively impotent opposition organizations. Fidel recognized that they wanted to use the M-26-7 to enhance their own stature and enable them to create a new power base away from the Sierra Maestra. They sought to achieve it by playing to the vanity of his underlings and getting their knowing or unknowing cooperation. After Fidel's blistering repudiation, the Junta de Liberación eventually fell apart.

The later months of 1957 through the first half of 1958 saw a transition from a war of "movement" to a war of "positions." Che had already established a fixed base with a field hospital, a forge, "factories" for making boots, uniforms, and explosives, and eventually schools, a lecture hall, and a prison for disciplinary problems. In May 1958, Fidel moved down from the high mountains to establish a similar base at La Plata. There he also took over the operation of Radio Rebelde from Che. Field telephones connected Fidel's headquarters with distant outposts. Except for a battle at Veguitas on December 14, in which a Batista force of 300 sustained 170 casualties, military activity dropped into a phase of relative quiescence. This was mainly because Batista withdrew the army to protect the harvest.

On February 16, 1958, the lull was broken. Fidel attacked and captured an outpost at Pino del Agua, killing ten men. It proved to be the turning point in the campaign, with the initiative from then on being with the rebel force as it increasingly took on the structure of a formal army. In many respects, it was the start of the final phase of the war.

The lowland leadership of the M-26-7 had always believed that Batista could ultimately be overthrown by a massive general strike that brought the country to a standstill. This had been Frank País's view, and it was now being vigorously espoused by Faustino Pérez, who had long ago taken over the lowland leadership of the movement. In the first few days of March, he went to the Sierra for lengthy discussions with Fidel. He argued that with the growing momentum of bombings and other disruptive activities they were carrying out in the cities, and the impact of Radio Rebelde that had started broadcasting from the free zone on February 24, the time was now right for such a strike. Fidel had always seen a strike as part of the overall strategy, but he had doubts about its timing. He finally agreed to a target date of early April. On March 12, 1958, he issued with Faustino Pérez a joint declaration calling for the strike backed by escalated military action. It also announced publicly for the first time that the president of the new provisional government would be Manuel Urrutia Lleó, a name Fidel had first raised in his letter in December responding to the Miami manifesto.

Urrutia, a judge who had served on the bench for thirty-one years, was a political moderate unconnected with any political faction. He had distinguished himself in Fidel's eyes by ruling that the Moncada rebels had acted constitutionally in trying to overthrow Batista. What was more important was that Fidel knew him to be a relatively weak and politically unsophisticated man whom he could use to block the ambitions of seasoned political veterans like Prío or Carrillo, who were waiting in the wings to take advantage of the rebel victory to assume power for themselves. It was a shrewd move. Fidel, whether he wanted the presidency or not, was too young for the job under the Constitution, and to have suggested that was his intention would have created a fire storm of controversy. Urrutia, on the other hand, was a man almost impossible for the other aspirants to criticize. He had been approached on Fidel's behalf by Armando Hart and Luis Buch on November 26, 1958. Urrutia, flattered by the offer, accepted. He wound up his affairs and went to Miami at the end of December to await the rebel victory.

The general revolutionary strike was an unmitigated disaster. A combination of poor planning, inadequate communications, failure to involve adequately other sympathetic forces, overconfidence in their own abilities, and a misreading of Batista's ability to mobilize the police to quash their efforts all led to the single greatest failure of the campaign. Although the Communists had called for their members to support the strike, the M-26-7 leaders in Havana, many of whom had a strong antipathy toward the party, failed to coordinate their planning with them at the grass-roots level.

A meeting was held on May 3, 1958, at Alto de Mompie between leaders

153

of the guerrillas and the city-based forces of the M-26-7 to analyze the failure of the strike and assess the damage. Presided over by Fidel, the bitter and acrimonious meeting exposed not just the reasons for the failure of the strike, but the more fundamental power struggle between the two wings of the movement and their substantially different ideological views. Fidel and the guerrillas were irrevocably committed to a revolution that would transform the society, especially the conditions in the rural areas of the country. In the lowland movement, there were elements narrowly focused on the sole objective of overthrowing Batista and then returning the country to some semblance of democratic government, free of its accustomed vices, but with power remaining in the hands of the bourgeois elite. Both groups were speaking on behalf of their constituencies, from which their day-to-day strength derived. However, the failure of the strike left the lowlanders in a position of weakness, and Fidel seized the opportunity to consolidate absolute control. Faustino Pérez and other lowland leaders were removed from their positions, and Fidel was formally made commander in chief of all the revolutionary forces of the M-26-7 and secretary-general of the National Directorate of the movement. From this point on, Fidel began to dismantle the power of the M-26-7 in the lowlands. This split he caused would have implications for several years after the victory of the revolution.

The failure of the April 9 strike was read by Batista as a sign of Fidel's weakness. At the beginning of May, he moved ten thousand troops into Oriente Province, placing a cordon around the Sierra Maestra that he gradually tightened. On March 10, 1958, Fidel had launched two independent fronts led by Raúl and Juan Almeida. They were not as immediately threatened by the government offensive as the unit remaining under Fidel.

Heavy bombing by United States–supplied planes had little effect on the rebels, but inflicted heavy casualties on the civilians in the area. The United States, earlier concerned by Batista's use of the arms for other than defense against external threats, had imposed an embargo. However, in a risky move, Raúl and his men captured ten Americans and two Canadians working at Moa Bay. Raúl demanded of the U.S. consul in Santiago who came to see him that the United States government stop supplying parts and fuel for the planes, and that they make Batista promise not to use any U.S.-supplied weapons against the rebels. The demands caused considerable consternation in Washington, with John Foster Dulles telling a news conference that the U.S. could not be blackmailed into helping the rebels, while hotter heads in the Defense Department as well as the U.S. ambassador, Earl Smith, urged that a division of marines be sent in. Fidel responded negatively to Raúl's actions, feeling that he had needlessly run the risk of provoking United States intervention. The matter was finally resolved with an implied agreement between Raúl and the U.S. consul, with which Batista apparently concurred, that the planes not be used against the rebels for three weeks.

The experience of seeing the peasant population decimated, and especially witnessing the death of a child of a close friend with arms supplied by the United States to someone as venal and corrupt as Batista, had a deep effect on Fidel. In a brief, handwritten letter dated June 5, 1958 to Celia Sánchez, who was then in another part of the combat zone, he wrote:

> When I saw the rockets firing . . . at Mario's house, I swore to myself that the Americans were going to pay dearly for what they are doing. When this war is over, a much wider and bigger war will commence for me: the war that I am going to wage against them. *I am aware this is my true destiny.* [author's italics]
>
> Fidel

This was a most important and revealing letter, one written to the person he probably trusted above all others, and with no expectation that it would become a part of the public record. From this moment on, Fidel was probably irrevocably committed to a course of conflict with the United States. There is reason to believe that Che had increasingly influenced Fidel's thinking on this subject, and the bombing only served to add an intense emotional element to his intellectual concerns about the United States.

The Batista offensive lasted seventy-six days, during which there were thirty clashes ranging from skirmishes to major battles. The growing confidence and skill of the rebels were reflected in their repeated victories. The morale of the government forces was in a tailspin, and soldiers began deserting and coming over to the guerrilla side.

By August 7, 1958, as heavy rains were beginning, the government offensive fizzled. Beaten and demoralized, the army pulled out of the Sierra Maestra for the last time. Batista's back was broken.

With the ignominious end of Batista's summer offensive, the way was open for Fidel to make his final push. The plan Fidel followed was exactly the one that had been used successfully by Cuba's leaders in the independence war of 1895. Fidel had studied it in great detail, beginning during his imprisonment on the Isle of Pines, and he had been waiting four years for the moment when he could put it into practice. Again it was his sense of historic destiny and drama that impelled him to duplicate this particular strategy. In the three-part plan, Fidel was to remain in Oriente Province and attempt an encirclement of Santiago, Cienfuegos was to lead a column

155

to Pinar del Río at the far end of the island, and Che was to take a detachment of 148 men to Las Villas, where he would attempt to cut the country in two by severing all transportation and communication links. Ultimately all the countryside would be in rebel hands, and the cities would be surrounded and isolated. Che also had a more delicate mission to perform. Fidel appointed him to be commander of all opposition units in Las Villas, making him, in effect, the head of the rebel government in the province.

The Directorio, devastated after the abortive palace attack, had resuscitated itself, and under the leadership of Faure Chomon was operating a guerrilla force in the Escambray mountains. Another group originally collaborating with Chomon broke off, seeking its own route to power and became known as the Second Front of Escambray. Che's job was to bring both groups under Fidel's control.

With the military situation moving strongly in his favor, Fidel focused much of his attention on the issue of how to maintain his hegemony over the various groups eagerly scrambling for power. In July all the opposition groups except the Communists met in Caracas, Venezuela, where a new unity declaration was prepared. This time, unlike the earlier meeting in Miami, Fidel was in contact with the meeting by radio, and was coming from a position of strength. A follow-up meeting was called, which Fidel tried hard to insist should be held in the Sierra Maestra so that his overall leadership of factionalized anti-Batista forces could be most forcefully demonstrated.

Che and Cienfuegos left in August for their respective destinations. They met relatively light government resistance, in part because the army was now without effective leadership and the troops had lost any fighting spirit. But their progress was slowed by bad weather and logistical problems. Trucks in which Che had planned to move his men were hit by air strikes and those which survived subsequently became mired in deep mud. Che and his men suffered considerably under the conditions.

The Communists were the one opposition group excluded from the Caracas meeting. Fidel, however, had long recognized their importance to any revolutionary movement that was to be organized from the bottom up. And although he had never been willing to enter their rigid organizational structure, and his own nationalism made him uncomfortable with their Soviet ties, he felt a degree of compatability with their commitment to the poor. He also recognized that they were the one political group in Cuba that could not seek exile in the United States, and therefore he understood that if he did come to power they would have to deal with him on his own terms. He was, at the same time, very careful never to alienate them by engaging in the extravagant anti-Communist rhetoric of some of the other opposition groups. But most important, he knew that his own cause would be doomed if he was seen as linked with or sympathetic to the Communists. Fidel knew that intervention by the United States, as history had shown and as Che had constantly warned from his own experience in Guatemala, posed the greatest long-range threat to the revolution. Batista constantly sought to show links between Fidel and the Communists because he knew that it was the one sure way to keep United States backing for his new regime. Similarly, the dominant concern in the State Department in Washington and in the United States Embassy in Havana was not what shortcomings of Batista or social conditions in Cuba made the country ripe for revolution, but whether or not Fidel was a Communist.

Fidel had such faith in his own political skills that he seems to have been convinced that he could ultimately bend the Communists to his will. While in Mexico, in a discussion with Justo Carrillo, Fidel said, "The Communists will never be in a majority though their strength will grow in this struggle . . . you also like I, will prevent them from dominating." Even in the Sierra Maestra, his reservations about the party persisted, as reflected in an anecdote reported by Spanish journalist Enrique Meneses. It was a custom for Che and Raúl to exchange letters between their two bases, in which they would expound on various political topics, including Marxist theory. One such letter was intercepted by the Batista forces and was then used as propaganda against Fidel to show he was a Communist. Fidel was enraged at his brother's stupidity, and is quoted as saying, "When he gets here I'll shoot him. I don't care a fuck if he is my brother! I'll shoot him." Celia Sánchez tried to calm Fidel down, and when Raúl arrived it turned out that the letter did not contain what the Batista propagandists had claimed. However, in chiding Raúl, Fidel said, "I hate Soviet imperialism as much as I hate Yankee imperialism. I am not breaking my neck fighting one dictatorship to fall into another."

In early 1958, when Fidel extended an invitation to all opposition groups to send representatives to meet with him in the Sierra Maestra, only the FEU and the Communists took him up on his offer. It was not the Communists' ideology that was of much concern to Fidel at this point. What he perceived was that if he had the quiet support of the Communist Party, and especially its incomparable grass-roots organization throughout Cuba, it would help him to prevent one of the other opposition leaders, especially Prío, from seizing power and subverting the revolution. At the same time, by remaining part of the opposition coalition group that was visibly anti-Communist, he would not scare away moderate support, and especially the United States government. He further believed that by a skillful balancing act he could use the coalition to help keep the Communists in check.

During 1958, several members of the Communist Party came to the mountains to talk with Fidel. The party's official position continued to be one of skepticism toward his revolution, but as it became clear that Fidel might succeed, their overtures to him became more substantial. In June, Carlos Rafael Rodríguez, the party official who had always been the most admiring of Fidel, and with whom Fidel had met shortly before Moncada, came to the Sierra Maestra as the party's official representative. He would remain with Fidel from then on. Sixteen years Fidel's senior, his maturity, competence, and experience as a political organizer later made him a valued adviser whose influence would grow steadily.

The columns of Che and Cienfuegos arrived in Las Villas during early October. After considerable negotiations, Che was able to sign the Pedrero Pact, an agreement with the leadership of the Directorio establishing a united guerrilla front in the province. Neither group, however, was able to get any cooperation from the second front, which remained vehemently independent and hostile. In the end, the group was too small and weak to be of any consequence. Fidel, now increasingly concerned lest the internal struggle among the opposition groups compromise the final military push, ordered Cienfuegos to remain in Las Villas to help consolidate the Fidelista control rather than moving on to Pinar del Río.

By the end of October 1958, the bearded rebel forces were mounting an intense offensive throughout the country, with military outposts and small towns falling almost daily. In Las Villas, they succeeded in the planned strategy of cutting the country in two by closing the major roads and rail lines. Batista mounted a last futile offensive at the end of November to try to reopen communication lines in the province, but his dispirited troops were now no match for the rebel juggernaut swelled with the support of local military units who had defected, and the overwhelming encouragement of the local population. Toward the end of December, Che began to close in on Santa Clara, a city of 150,000 that lies at the geographic center of the country, as he described it, "the axis of the central plain."

After a two-week battle, Fidel's forces on November 30 captured the town of Guisa, the first town of some size outside the Sierra Maestra that they had seized. Fidel entered into negotiations with General Eulogio Cantillo, commander of all military forces in Oriente Province. They agreed that on December 31, Cantillo would lead the army in revolt. However, he immediately informed Batista of the discussions and together they conspired as to how they could deceive Fidel and keep power for the military.

Early in December, the United States government had reluctantly come to the conclusion that Batista could no longer be saved. John Foster Dulles sent businessman and former ambassador William Pawley to convince him to leave the country so that a strategy could be implemented to enable someone other than Fidel to come to power. Batista would not listen. As the month wore on and the military was in a state of total internal collapse, he came under the same pressure from church and civic leaders, businessmen, and even some members of the military itself. Seemingly oblivious to the house that was burning around him, he clung on, enabling Fidel day by day to strengthen his control over the country at the expense of all the other opposition groups. Finally, on New Year's Eve, with the fall of Santa Clara only hours away, he met with his closest friends and advisers and made the decision to flee. At 2 A.M. the next morning, he flew out of the country to refuge in the Dominican Republic.

Chapter Eight

BEFORE Batista fled, he handed over the reins of power to General Eulogio Cantillo, commander of the military forces in Oriente and chief of the Joint General Staff. Only days before, Cantillo had been duplicitously negotiating with Fidel to have the army join the revolt. Simultaneously, Fidel had arranged for the prison director on the Isle of Pines to release Colonel Ramón Barquín. Barquín had been the leader of the 1956 liberal officer's coup attempt that had been backed by Carrillo and his Montecristo movement. Cantillo, realizing that he could not mobilize the support necessary to maintain power, turned over command to Barquín, who enjoyed support among the younger and more progressive military officers. Barquín, after taking over as chief of the armed forces, arrested Cantillo and then surprised many people by telephoning Fidel in Santiago and asking when Judge Urrutia would take over as president. Barquín had earlier committed himself to the M-26-7, but the motive for his actions was more likely the reasoned judgment of a military man who knew that no one could hold power against a rebel army that controlled 90 percent of the country. His long-term prospects clearly seemed brighter by pledging his fealty to Fidel. These were only the opening events in the jockeying for power that would not be resolved for almost four years.

Fidel's overwhelming concern was to prevent a seizure of power by the military. On hearing of Batista's flight, he issued a proclamation condemning Cantillo and his residual military junta, and demanded their surrender. He warned that the civil war would continue unless the armed forces completely stepped aside. On January 1, he called for a general strike, which effectively immobilized the country. Some observers have questioned the rationale for bringing the country to a standstill, adding to the confusion created by Batista's departure. But it was a very carefully calculated move to frustrate, with a state of national immobility, any other would-be plotters, especially the military, while his own forces moved to consolidate control. To thwart any such move, Fidel had ordered Che and Cienfuegos to move with their forces on Havana, where they arrived in the early hours of January 2.

On New Year's Day, Colonel Rego Rubido, the commanding officer in Santiago, flew by helicopter to Fidel's headquarters to surrender the city. The following evening, while Che and Cienfuegos were arriving at the outskirts of Havana, Fidel addressed a huge crowd in Santiago, which he proclaimed as the interim capital of Cuba. In an event filled with high emotion and historic symbolism, he spoke at the Moncada barracks with Judge Urrutia on one side of him, and Monsignor Enrique Pérez Serantes, the archbishop of Santiago who had presided at his confirmation and had saved his life after the 1953 attack, on the other. In his soiled green fatigues and luxuriant beard he announced the "popular election" of Urrutia as provisional president. He spoke of the watershed nature of the revolution and the new future for Cuba. He extended a conciliatory hand to members of the military who had not been involved in "war crimes."

On the morning of January 1, the residents of Havana, expecting the riots and civil disorder that usually accompany the overthrow of governments in Latin America, boarded and shuttered their homes and businesses. Unlike the wave of violence that followed Machado's ouster in 1933, there was an eery silence in the city. By 2:30 P.M., people started venturing out of their homes. Suddenly they broke out into effervescent enthusiasm. Minute by minute, a carnival atmosphere spread though the city like a wind-fanned forest fire. Convoys of cars draped with Cuban flags wound through the city and Cubans swarmed into the streets in their gayest clothes. Music blared, horns honked, and everyone was yelling *"libertad"* at the top of his lungs. For a few short hours, the people celebrated their freedom with unrestrained joy and happiness.

Late in the day, armed hoodlums began to seep through the crowds and take over the city. The celebration stopped as quickly as it had begun, as people fearfully returned to their shuttered homes. Some of the young men with guns were legitimate members of the revolutionary movement; others were opportunists from the Havana underworld. Many had crudely made arm bands declaring themselves adherents of the Directorio or the M-26-7. Between them they carved up the city and took control, assuming authority at gunpoint over the traffic and the pedestrians on the street. No uniformed policeman dared show his face. Then the looting and shooting began. Parking meters were the first target, then slot machines. Guns went off accidentally or in celebration, but each shot generated a pointless salvo in response. Occasionally, rumors of the whereabouts of a hated Batista henchman would lead to the spraying of a building with bullets.

The anarchy continued until midnight on the second day, when the advance units of the rebel army from Las Villas arrived in the city. British journalist Edwin Tetlow, who several times had come close to being killed during the previous forty-eight hours, said that bearded rebels who quickly restored order were "one of the best behaved armies you could imagine.

They were too good to be real. . . . To a man they behaved impeccably." Fidel's fierce discipline had paid off, as they quickly brought the city back to a state approaching normalcy.

Elsewhere in the country, revolutionary groups were taking control of public buildings, barracks, and radio stations. For the most part these were the forces of the M-26-7, because they were by far the most numerous. The forces of the Directorio seized the university and the Presidential Palace, which had so nearly been theirs twenty months earlier. These they refused to relinquish to the rebel army. Members of the Second Front of Escambray held some police stations and other minor government facilities. Che and Camilo Cienfuegos held Campamento Columbia and La Cabaña, the major military installations in the city.

In Mexico City, Fidel's friend Teresa Casuso put on her best dress and walked under an umbrella in the pouring rain to the Cuban Embassy where, without objection, she took over from the chargé d'affaires and installed herself as de facto ambassador "in the name of the Revolutionary Government headed by Dr. Manuel Urrutia Lleó." Mexico gave immediate diplomatic recognition to the new government and provided police protection for the Embassy, as much against Cuban exiles seeking vengeance against a hated symbol of the Batista regime as against anyone else. For three days, Teresa went without rest as hundreds of exiles descended on the Embassy, desperate to get back to Cuba.

In Washington, the M-26-7 representative Ernesto Betancourt went to the Cuban Embassy on Sixteenth Street. In the previous months, he had successfully infiltrated the Mission so that several members of the staff, including the number-two man under the ambassador, had switched their loyalty to Fidel. Together they took over the building and asked the ambassador, who was in the residence on the fourth floor, to leave.

Fidel left Santiago and began a long meandering journey by Jeep, car, and helicopter in the general direction of Havana. He tried to insure that as many Cubans as possible saw him. Partly it was a way of mobilizing support and demonstrating to all Cubans that he had led a truly popular revolution that enjoyed the overwhelming support of the mass of the people. He wanted also to savor and extend the pleasure of his triumph with the people to whom he felt closest. For many, it was the celebration of a victory for generations deferred. The emotional impact of the journey was extraordinary, even for seasoned journalists. Tetlow, a reporter for the conservative *Daily Telegraph* of London, wrote, "He was almost christlike during this first simple pilgrimage in his love and concern for the people." He added, "He was drunk with triumph, but glowingly so." In light of subsequent events, it seems an excessive and naive observation, but as similar themes were sounded by many others who watched his progress, it clearly reflects the sense people had at that moment. At the same time, while politically beneficial, the slow journey also reflected the relative reluctance with which Fidel approached the responsibilities awaiting him in Havana, and its meandering course was symbolic of the vagueness and uncertainty that would characterize the early months of the new government.

Although he had repeatedly urged restraint among those who sought immediate vengeance against the Batistanos, all along his route he heard the clamor for revolutionary justice from grieving relatives of those who had been tortured and slain. On January 5, in Camagüey, Fidel issued an order to his provisional commanders in each province to begin summary courts-martial to try "war criminals," officers and lower-ranking military personnel, policemen, and civilians accused of killing unarmed civilians or torturing and killing members of the revolutionary movement. It was in accordance with the rebel directive he had issued on February 11, 1958. He ordered those convicted to be executed by firing squad.

The journey was taking longer than planned because Fidel could not or would not say no to anyone who wanted to meet with him. To make up some time, he leapfrogged part of the way by helicopter. In Matanzas, he stopped to film an interview with Ed Sullivan, who had flown in from New York. He also stopped for an emotional meeting with the mother of the slain leader of the Directorio Revolucionario, José Antonio Echevarría. She expressed to him her sense of vindication for her son's sacrifice in Fidel's victory. In Matanzas, he also met with British journalist Jeffrey Blyth, who had come from Havana with Buck Cannell, a baseball commentator known all over Latin America. When Cannell arrived, Fidel immediately recognized him and, jumping up from his chair in the mayor's office, his temporary headquarters, he launched into a fifteen-minute heated discussion about what he felt was a bad ruling by an umpire in a Chicago Cubs–Boston Red Sox game broadcast by Cannell several months earlier. When the matter was finally resolved to his satisfaction, Fidel asked what was happening in Havana.

The next day, he was scheduled to have lunch with the directors of the Bacardi rum company at their distillery near El Catorro. But he received word that Fidelito had been flown in from his school on Long Island, New York, where he had been sent for fear of kidnapping during the last year of the war, and was waiting for him at a service station on the outskirts of the town. He canceled the lunch and rushed to meet Fidelito. He embraced him and lifted him into the Jeep for the rest of the ride to Havana. The final triumphant entry into the city was aboard a tank, through a crowd of hundreds of thousands of wildly cheering men, women, and children.

President Urrutia had finally negotiated an agreement with the Directorio to vacate the Presidential Palace. He met Fidel at the Avenida de Las Missiones and escorted him to the Palace on foot through a screaming crowd of well-wishers. There, standing on the north terrace, he made a brief speech. His major address of the day was scheduled at the military headquarters, Campo Colombia, but the press of the cheering crowd was so great that it took four hours for him to cover the distance by tank. Thousands of citizens and all the top political leaders, including former President Prío, had waited hours for this climactic moment. His speech was emotional and it touched deep chords of nationalistic feeling in the audience. The speech was made even more memorable by one unusual event. As he started to talk, several hundred white doves were released from cages. One of them settled on Fidel's shoulder and sat there throughout his oration. It was a startling spectacle that the crowd took as a magnificent omen.

Fidel moved into a suite on the twenty-second floor of the recently built Havana Hilton, quickly renamed the Habana Libre. He chose that location to be with other members of the rebel army who had been billeted there. It is interesting, however, that he should choose to make his headquarters in this glaring symbol of United States power rather than in an older building that might have better symbolized solidarity with traditional Cuban nationalism. He shared the floor with Celia, his sisters Lidia and Emma, who had flown in from Mexico, and a few other close aides. A tight security cordon was set up, which included Captain Jesús Yañes Pelletier, who had saved Fidel's life after the Moncada attack by refusing to poison him. The only political figures who could walk in on Fidel unannounced were Che and Raúl.

Fidel was only thirty-two years old, far below the minimum age of forty stipulated for the presidency in the 1940 Constitution. However, at that point had he wanted the job, there would have been little public complaint if a special provision had been made. He had given himself the implausibly modest title of Representative of the Rebel Armed Forces to the Presidency. He was not, as critics have claimed, adroitly biding his time to execute a Machiavellian plan to acquire total power. January 1959 was, in fact, a month of confusion and personal crisis for Fidel, in which he desperately sought to work out what his new role would be. Tetlow says, "He had made no plans to meet the responsibility of victory." For six years, he had applied himself with a rigid singlemindedness to being a revolutionary military commander, and that was his sense of himself. Overnight the role had ended. Dr. Antonio Núñez Jiménez, archivist of the revolution, says, "Fidel has said on several occasions that when the war was finished he noticed the only thing he had learned to do well, in which he had become a specialist, was in how to win a war. . . . He was not prepared, nobody was prepared for the government. . . . Fidel felt laid off, jobless." Fidel himself has said, "We were very ignorant of government problems. That is, we were ignorant about the government apparatus and how it functioned." At the same time, Fidel's perspective had always been that of an internationalist, and he strongly identified with the great liberator, Simón Bolivár, who had carried his revolutionary struggle against Spain from one country to another. Fidel harbored the fantasy of himself in a similar role as the knight on the white horse who, having defeated one malevolent dictator in Cuba, would move on to rid the region of other evil men. His first planned target was Trujillo. At this moment, he seemed enraptured with glory, not power.

Fidel's uncertainty at this time is further reflected in an anecdote told by Carlos Rafael Rodríguez concerning an evening late in the war when, following a battle, they were preparing to bury four of their men at nightfall. As they waited for it to become dark, he had a discusson with Fidel, who told him that once the war was successfully concluded he planned to devote himself to organizing an expedition against Trujillo and then subsequently against the dictatorship in Guatemala. Rodríguez pointed out to Fidel that he did not fully appreciate the significance of the revolution he was on the verge of bringing about in Cuba, and that he must abandon any plans to lead new revolutions overseas in person. His place had to be in Cuba because he could not avoid having to deal with the extraordinary forces his victory would unleash. The implication is that even at that late stage Fidel did not understand that he was going to have to take on the responsibility for running the government and could not just walk away to lead other revolutions.

That Fidel had not been able to accept that reality fully was evident during those first weeks in Havana. Of that period he says, "I must admit that we really believed for a time that it would be possible to leave the power to others; we were a little . . . utopian. In the first days after victory, we kept away from the government altogether and took no part in the decisions of the council of ministers." Of course, he had all the power because he controlled the rebel army. He did nothing to consolidate the strength of the M-26-7. Its usefulness was over.

He spent much of his time roaming around the city by Jeep or car. He was mobbed wherever he went and the adulation he received from the people seemed to counter the anxiety he had about governing the country or his own future role. By one account, he carried with him a checkbook tucked into the breast pocket of his green fatigues, and whenever he encountered a project that he thought particularly worthy he would write a check against the national treasury for funds to support it. Despite his efforts to distance himself from the day-to-day running of the government, foreign dignitaries, journalists, and even the ministers he had appointed to run the government constantly scrambled to get meetings with him, as he was the only person whose decisions really mattered. Often he would ignore the appointments completely or arrive hours late. Most nights he was up until dawn, as he had been as a guerrilla, and then after eating breakfast in the coffee shop at the hotel, he would go to bed, but rarely for more than three hours. When asked by a reporter why he slept so little, adding that sleep was good medicine, Fidel replied, very accurately, "My medicine is the people. I thrive on seeing and talking to the people." By the end of the month, despite daily doses of multivitamins from Celia Sánchez, he was so exhausted and sick that he was forced to spend three days in bed.

Whatever the subconscious motivations for Fidel's reluctance to become involved directly in the governing of the country, he spent hours with the people in the streets, in their homes, and at their jobs. The overwhelming sincerity of his interest in their problems had the effect of creating a level of popular support and faith in his personal leadership that made it increasingly difficult for those charged with running the country to establish any credibility for themselves. The astonishing and unrealistic expectations the people had of Fidel is reflected in a statement by a Presbyterian minister who said, "Fidel Castro is an instrument in the hand of God for the establishment of his reign among men." Writer Lloyd Free quotes a man who said, "Fidel has the same ideas as Jesus Christ our protector and guide." Even among exiles later fleeing to Miami, a survey revealed that 22 percent thought Fidel was "the savior of Cuba" when he came to power. Few men have ever experienced such adulation, and it is perhaps not surprising that he, too, increasingly began to feel he could do no wrong.

But he did begin to make some mistakes. He held his first public news conference in the "Sugar bar" at the Habana Libre on January 15. At it he was asked what he knew about the Popular Socialist Party of Cuba (the Communist Party). Trying to continue buying time, as he had done in the mountains, by downplaying any association with the Communists, his answer implied that he knew nothing about the party. His statement seemed not only untrue, as he had been in close dialogue with key members of the party during the preceding six months (and they had had representatives in the mountains with him), but, much worse, several of the reporters who were previously well disposed toward him felt he was being deliberately deceptive. Suddenly, his image as the revolutionary hero who always told the truth was gratuitously tarnished. A few days later, as he returned to the hotel, he was mobbed as usual in the lobby

166

by a crowd of admirers including bearded revolutionaries, several fawning young women, and a couple of reporters whose presence he had apparently not noticed. He was in a relaxed and jovial mood, putting his arms around those nearest to him. Someone asked about the possibility of the United States invading. He brashly responded, "Yes, I tell you, two hundred thousand gringos will die if the United States sends marines to Cuba." It was an unguarded comment intended for the ears of his adoring fans, but when it hit the international wire services it caused paroxysms of indignation and concern. The flattery of the crowd and his own bravado had momentarily overcome his usual shrewd political judgment and allowed him to make exactly the provocative jibe toward the United States that he had gone to such lengths to avoid while in the Sierra Maestra.

For domestic consumption alone, the comment had considerable appeal. The day after Batista fled, *Bohemia* had run a story below the headline "Disgrace for North America. Ambassador Smith: Servant of the Despot." It went on to criticize the way Smith to the very last had gone out of his way to associate himself, and therefore the United States, with the dictator, saying, "Smith laughed and partied while all of Cuba was drowned in blood and horror." Although Smith's hastily submitted resignation was immediately accepted by President Eisenhower, it was hard for the families whose sons and husbands had been slaughtered by Batista to forget whose side the United States had been on.

Despite Fidel's generally cautious tack with regard to the United States, he was heading into unexpected difficulties over the issue of executions. Again he was caught in a dilemma between the expectations and demands of the Cuban people and the radically different perspectives of the international community, especially the United States. He knew that the failure to bring to justice those responsible for the atrocities during the Machado era had allowed people to justify for years afterward private acts of vengeance. These acts had been the genesis for much of the violence and anarchy that had plagued the society during Fidel's university years. He wanted to prevent the same thing happening again. He also knew, from what the people were telling him every day, that the pent-up emotion against Batista and his followers for the murders and other brutal acts that had been committed was very great. To maintain its own credibility, the new government had to move decisively to satisfy the public demand for retribution. Despite his legal training, Fidel, like other Cubans, viewed the issue as one of moral justice rather than one of legal justice. Fidel was eager not to execute more people than necessary. He insisted that Batistanos who had taken refuge in foreign embassies be given safe passage out of the country, something all the other top members of the government opposed. At the same time, he shared their consuming anger toward and

167

hatred of those who had killed and tortured so many of their friends and supporters. At that moment, he clearly represented the embodiment of the will of the Cuban people. In retrospect, one can argue that perhaps Fidel should have distanced himself from the executions and allowed others to take the responsibility and criticism, or that his popularity at that point was so great that he could have insisted that there be no retribution, and should have taken greater steps to restrain Che and Raúl, who were clearly bent on vengeance. Both arguments fail to recognize the overwhelming demand for retribution that existed in Cuba at the time and the extraordinary faith the people had in Fidel to be their instrument in seeing that justice was done. Had he not ordered the executions, the average Cuban would have felt he had betrayed the trust placed in him. At the same time, the executions, viewed quite differently outside Cuba, ended the honeymoon he had enjoyed with the people of the United States.

Following Fidel's order on January 5, Raúl instigated the trial in Santiago de Cuba of seventy individuals in the very same courtroom where the Moncadistas had been tried. They were condemned to death and executed, with the last execution being put on film, which was then given to CBS television. Public reaction in the United States was extremely negative and in many ways irrational. It was as though Americans saw Fidel as a kind of romantic Hollywood hero, an idealist with whom they did not want to associate the necessary sordid realities of revolutionary politics. That he should be involved in executions ran completely contrary to the image people wanted to have of him, no matter how inaccurate or unrealistic that image might be.

Fidel found the criticism incomprehensible. He was, in fact, the force for moderation, restraining the more extreme elements in the government who wanted a bloodbath. Yet he had to bear the brunt of the criticism. As he said, "These men are murderers, assassins. We are not executing innocent people or political opponents. We are executing murderers and they deserve it." He felt that North Americans, because they had never lived under tyranny, could not comprehend what had to be done in Cuba. The case against the Batistanos was, he argued, at least as strong as the case the United States had at Nuremberg. What upset him most was that he had not only held back a wave of indiscriminate killing, but he was insisting that every case be brought before some sort of tribunal, even if the deck was stacked against the defendants. (Some defendants were, however, acquitted.) Batista's men had killed an estimated twenty thousand people, many of whom had simply disappeared. How could the press, which for years had ignored such brutal outrages, now criticize him for bringing the perpetrators to justice, he asked.

On January 22, Fidel addressed a mass rally of several hundred thousand people in front of the Presidential Palace. It had been carefully organized, with women and children in the front rows. Fidel had expressed the desire that they be obviously from poor backgrounds. A young woman from a wealthy family, who, as a teenager, was present while Fidel was giving the instructions, says he pointed at her and said, "I don't want ones who look like her." Many held banners in Spanish and English demanding the executions. It was an attempt to show the world the unanimity of opinion that existed in Cuba concerning the "war crimes" trials. Fidel then invited journalists from around the world to come to Cuba for what he labeled "Operation Truth." Three hundred and eighty reporters from twenty countries accepted. They were shown evidence of Batista's atrocities and invited to attend a public trial.

In an ill-conceived effort to counter criticism that the trials were not sufficiently open to the public, Fidel ordered that a major trial be held in the sports palace, where seventeen thousand people could watch. It was grotesque theater as the primary defendant, Major Jesús Sosa Blanco, a fifty-one-year-old commander of a military district near Havana, with a notorius record for murder and torture, was brought manacled into the stadium. He handled himself with dignity as dozens of photographers jostled to shoot his picture and the crowd yelled abuse and taunts, and while ice cream and peanut vendors ran up and down the aisles. The proceedings continued all night under the direction of the presiding judge, Dr. Humberto Sorí Morín. Under the circumstances, Judge Sorí Morín did a relatively competent job, although he did not do much for the sense of judicial decorum when, during an intermission, he stood in the middle of the arena eating an ice cream cone. Eventually the trial came to its inevitable conclusion. Sosa Blanco was found guilty and sentenced to death.

The effect of the trial outside Cuba was the opposite of what Fidel had hoped. Instead of appreciation for the openness of the trial, there was disgust at the garish spectacle. When international opinion became too negative, Fidel reversed himself and set aside the verdict, ordering that Sosa Blanco be forced to go through the ordeal of another trial, this time in a small room at Campo Colombia. Only a small group of selected spectators was invited. Of course, the outcome was the same, and ultimately Sosa Blanco was executed.

Immediately following the trial, Fidel departed for Venezuela to attend the first anniversary celebrations of the overthrow of the dictator Pérez Jiménez. He was treated as a national hero. His host, President-elect Betancourt, observed that if Fidel were to run for elective office in Venezuela, he would be elected overwhelmingly.

Fidel's rise to power coincided with a shift in the political climate in Latin America that was distinctly in his favor. The preceding few years had been among the worst economically in decades. As a result, there had been a strong trend toward supporting socially conscious leadership that was responsive to the impoverishment and human hardship in the region. In Brazil, Jânio Quadros, and in Argentina, Arturo Frondizi, both left of center, had been elected president. In both Venezuela and Colombia, military dictatorships had been overthrown. In Mexico, López Mateos was proving the most progressive president in years, and in Chile, the Communist Party, again legalized, was getting representatives elected to the national legislature. No one better embodied the new spirit of nationalism and anti-imperialism that was sweeping the continent than this young, outspoken, charismatic leader from Cuba who had rid his own country of a hated dictatorship as so many others in Latin America only wished they could do. The immense cheering crowds that greeted Fidel at each of his speeches must have convinced him not only of the continentwide appeal of his message, but also that the timing was right to extend his reach to help bring about revolution in the rest of Latin America. At that moment, it must have seemed as if a tidal wave of indigenous revolutions was about to sweep the Americas, and that he would be its inspiration and leader.

In his speeches, Fidel reiterated that he was not interested in becoming president of Cuba and that the revolution was not Communist. He talked about the potential for a common market in Latin America, the Organization of American States being filled with democrats rather than dictators, and his desire for a special relationship between Cuba and Venezuela in which visas would be abolished. There would perhaps be a shared passport and the notion that the Venezuelans would send a military team to instruct the rebel army. His stimulated, creative mind produced a rich outpouring of ideas, which characteristically had not been thought through in any depth.

At the heart of his thinking was his concern about United States domination throughout the region, to which he increasingly alluded in his speeches. He was clearly interested in developing a broad, continentwide coalition to begin fighting what he referred to as "the calumnies of some monopolistic sectors." Nationalism in Latin America was synonymous with anti-imperialism, essentially anti-Americanism, and Fidel realized that appealing to this sentiment was the easiest vehicle for achieving unity. More immediately, he was looking for financial backing for Cuba that would allow him to begin breaking the bonds of her dependence on the United States. This led him, in a private conversation with Betancourt, to propose that Venezuela make him a loan of $300 million and supply him with oil so that he could "have a game with the gringos." Somewhat taken aback, Betancourt declined and pointed out that he himself was committed to evolution, not to revolution. The matter of oil would, as much as any other issue, haunt Fidel throughout the rest of his career. It would be the noose around his neck by which the Soviets controlled him, and the unsuccessful search for some other source of supply must have been a factor in the development of his close relationships with the leadership of Algeria and Angola, two oil-rich countries.

Fidel returned to Cuba to find himself facing a rapidly worsening political crisis. There were in effect two governments in Cuba, one that was officially designated, and a second that was wherever Fidel happened to be. Whether he wanted it or not, he was a one-man administration. No one would make a major decision without being sure that it met with his approval, and the entire country turned to him for direction and leadership, paying no attention to anyone else. The Cabinet, meeting in marathon sessions, often late into the night, struggled to cope with a plethora of problems in an environment that approached chaos. Urrutia agreed early on with Fidel that there would be no elections for at least eighteen months and that in the meantime there would be rule by decree. The Congress elected under Batista was dissolved, the old political parties were abolished, and all those who had participated in the Batista-rigged elections of 1954 and 1958 were banned from political life. The bank accounts of all civil servants who were thought to have corruptly benefited under Batista were frozen. The Cabinet passed these decrees because they were what Fidel wanted, but also because there was no significant opposition. The Cuban people wanted a break with the past; they were fed up with the old corrupt institutions, and did not want to see them rebuilt. The sacrifices that so many Cubans had been making for years were aimed at getting rid of the traditionally squabbling and morally bankrupt political parties, the gangsterism in politics, and the elections that were inevitably bought or stolen. Now they had a leader who was so popular that any election would be redundant, who promised to build a new Cuba free from all of the evils of the past, and who radiated a spirit of idealism, nationalism, and vigor. There was such a sense of euphoria and excitement about what the future held for Cuba that the people were willing to dispense with what in other countries were viewed as the fundamental institutions of democracy. Elections were not viewed that way in Cuba. Rather, they were seen as the symbolic vestiges of a rotten past they wanted to forget. Sociologist Maurice Zeitlin and journalist Robert Scheer quote a woman referring to elections: "We need them like the plague, they served only to rob us." There were those who wanted and expected elections because that was what they had fought for, but in general Fidel understood that he was dealing with a society where the bulk of the population coveted access to education, health care, land reform, and a renewal of the national spirit far more than they valued formal democracy.

There was opposition. Those who had become wealthy and powerful under Batista and who initially thought they would be able to reach an accommodation with the new regime were increasingly seeing that there would be no place for them. There was also a group, some of them former members of the 26 of July Movement, who had always conceived of a truly democratic society and were already alarmed by what they saw as a totalitarian trend in the country. Comments made by Che Guevara publicly and privately about the abolition of private property and what he envisioned to be the role of government fueled these fears. Opposition cells began to organize against Fidel, but they were so few and so much at odds with the prevailing public sentiment as to be of little real consequence.

At this point there were essentially three power groups of consequence. First, Fidel and the bearded members of the rebel army. At the nucleus were Che and Raúl, around them a group made up mostly of the veterans of the *Granma*, bound together more by personal loyalty to Fidel than by ideology. Second, there were the liberal reformers. Most had been members of the M-26-7 in the cities. They supported Fidel and shared much of his vision, but their loyalty was not so much to him personally as to their own desire to create a politically pluralistic Cuba. Their alliance with Fidel had been a pragmatic one that had grown out of their shared desire to overthrow Batista. Although dominating in the government, their political base was narrow. They represented the progressive, educated bourgeoisie, but not the mass of the people to whom Fidel appealed. Third, there were the Communists. Although critical of Fidel in the past because his revolutionary strategy flew in the face of Marxist teachings, convincing them that he could never succeed, they had thrown their full support behind him during the last six months in the mountains. While Fidel continued, in speech after speech, to repudiate any connection between himself and the revolution and the Communists, he was also scrupulously not anti-Communist. There were no members of the Partido Socialista Popular (PSP), the Cuban Communist Party, in the government, but their great strength, which no other group had, lay in their grass-roots organization of approximately seventeen thousand individuals. With the freedom that Fidel had accorded them, they spent the early months after the revolution building that organization and carefully expanding their influence into key targeted areas of Cuban society. Several of their leaders still believed that Fidel represented only a transitional phase in the revolutionary process and that ultimately, through their organized mobilization of the masses, they would come to power. Fidel's great political skill during this period was playing off each of these three forces against the others, so that none had the upper hand and all depended on him.

The inevitable problems created by Fidel promulgating policy from his power base outside the government came to a head in mid-February. Lacking any real power and yet with the responsibility for running the government, Prime Minister Miró Cardona resigned, recommending that Fidel take over the job. Fidel accepted the position reluctantly, primarily with the encouragement of Celia Sánchez. It meant further responsibilities that would restrict his personal freedom. He told a reporter at this time, "I miss my mountains." He accepted the job on the condition that its powers be broadened, including that he preside at Cabinet meetings and Urrutia no longer be present. Subsequently, Urrutia tried to resign, but was persuaded to stay. Much of Fidel's problem was that he wanted power without responsibility. A simple, naive quality in his personality coexisted with a naturally brilliant and astute Machiavellian bent. In contrast to the constant interpersonal pressures of running the government, the war in the mountains, despite the danger, had been comparatively simple and straightforward.

Under Fidel's leadership, Cabinet meetings became less frequent, and although his participation was erratic, his undisputed authority to make decisions and provide direction insured that they were no longer mired in endless and inconclusive hours of deliberation.

Because Fidelito was now back with his mother in Havana, Fidel also occasionally saw Mirta. Fidelito enjoyed riding around the city in military vehicles, and on one occasion was involved in a serious accident when a Jeep overturned. He was rushed to a hospital with internal injuries requiring an abdominal operation. However, the physicians would not operate until the patient's father arrived to give his permission. Fidel was in the midst of a long television address in which he was very much wound up. Although notified of his son's condition, Fidel felt his first obligation was to finish his speech. He continued for a long time, until people aware of Fidelito's condition started calling in to the station begging him to forget the speech and go to his son's side. Raúl, who was in the studio, eventually convinced him to stop. When he finally arrived at the hospital, Mirta was furious and reportedly yelled at him, "You haven't changed—you are irresponsible as usual."

In mid-February, a German cruise ship, *The Berlin*, visited Havana. Fidel and some of the other *barbudos* went on board at the invitation of the captain. Fidel met and was strongly attracted to the captain's nineteen-year-old daughter Marie (Marita) Lorenz. He tried to convince her to stay in Havana, and even offered her a job as his secretary. She declined, but two weeks later, when the ship docked in New York, Cuban officials went aboard with a message from Fidel imploring her to reconsider, saying that he desperately needed an interpreter. This time she acceded and was flown in a government plane to Havana, where she moved into Fidel's suite at the Habana Libre.

Toward the end of February, Fidel received an invitation from the Society of Newspaper Editors to visit the United States. At about the same time, the new United States ambassador, Philip Bonsal, arrived. In contrast to his predecessors, Bonsal was a competent, experienced career diplomat with an extensive background in Latin American affairs. Over the next year, he was to make a herculean effort to hold together the relentlessly fraying relationship between the two countries. Unfortunately, he inherited, undeservedly, the animosity of the average Cuban that earlier ambassadors, through their ineptitude and insensitivity, had generated toward the post. At the same time, he was welcomed by surviving Batista supporters and other privileged Cubans who had traditionally looked to the United States to protect their special interests. This made it particularly difficult for Fidel and his followers to associate with Bonsal, despite his qualities, and still maintain that they were embarking on a new era in relations with the United States. Bonsal continued to urge patience and responsible restraint in his reports to Washington, but he was increasingly seen at home as an apologist for the new regime.

Fidel accepted the invitation of the newspaper editors. He arrived in the United States on April 15 with an entourage of around seventy people. From a public relations standpoint, the trip was an overwhelming success. Everywhere Fidel went he was greeted by large and enthusiastic crowds. In New York, on his way from the airport to the Statler Hotel, he stopped his motorcade so that he could get out and shake hands with the crowd. In Washington, where he was greeted on his arrival by Deputy Secretary of State Roy Rubottom, he again broke away from the official entourage to plunge into the crowd, grabbing hands in every direction. Thousands attended his speeches in Boston, Princeton, and Central Park in New York City. When he spoke to the newspaper editors at the National Press Club, they had the largest turnout in their history.

The arrangements for Fidel's trip had been handled by public relations man Bernard Relling of New York, who deserved much of the credit for its success. Fidel accepted most of Relling's recommendations, but not that he require his men to cut their hair or that he include in his entourage only those rebel soldiers who had a college degree and could speak English. One recommendation he apparently did follow was to avoid including any individual who could be identified as a known Communist. Despite this and the generally positive public response he received, Fidel spent

Fidel (marked with an "X") at about age ten, in school picture at Colegio Dolores.

Fidel (center) was the champion high school athlete in Cuba during his final year at Belen (1944–45).

"El Castro-Forward" from a poster advertising a high school basketball game (1944–45).

Fidel with other members of the Ortodoxos Youth surround his hero Eduardo Chibas during one of his weekly radio broadcasts in 1948.

Fidel addressing a group of fellow students at the University of Havana in 1948 or 1949.

Fidel as an Ortodoxo Party candidate in early January 1952.

Fidel arguing with a police official during a political demonstration in early 1952.

Fidel and the other Moncadistas upon their release from prison on the Isle of Pines in 1954.

Fidel walks in Central Park, New York, during fund-raising trip in November 1955.

Fidel the young guerrilla talks with an interviewer in the Sierra Maestra in 1958.

Celia Sanchez dressing an injury on Fidel's hand, Sierra Maestra, 1958.

Fidel the guerrilla fighter holding his treasured rifle with the telescopic sight.

Celia Sanchez relaxing at her father's house in 1958.

Fidel at the monastery of El Cobre in December 1958, surrounded by young women who, aided by the priests, have helped to smuggle arms and food to his men in the mountains.

Fidel and Che triumphant, Havana, January 1959.

Fidel contemplates another historic figure. U.S. Capitol, Washington, D.C., April 1959.

Fidel meets with Vice President Nixon, April 1959.

Raul, Ramon, and Fidel at the wedding of their sister Emma, Havana, April 30, 1960.

Fidel with Hemingway at the Ernest Hemingway Annual Fishing Contest, May 15, 1960.

(Korda, Black Star)

Khrushchev warmly embraces Fidel at the United Nations in September 1964.

Fidel at the front during the Bay of Pigs invasion in 1961.

Baseball has always been one of Fidel's passions.

Fidel has always had a profound interest in health care. During a 1964 visit to a clinic, he listens to a staff nurse's heartbeat.

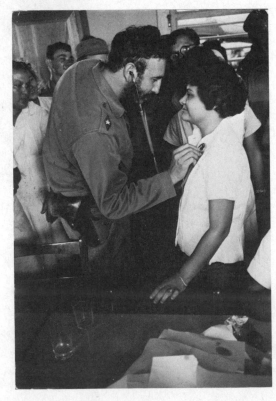

Fidel has never been hesitant to join farmers cutting sugar-cane.

(Bohemia)

(Dennis Brack, Black Star)

Fidel hosts Senator George McGovern in 1975.

Fidel greets Agostinho Neto, who visited Havana in 1976.

(Bohemia)

Fidel on his way home from the United Nations in October 1979.

(Karen Ranucci, Black Star)

much of the trip fending off accusations that he was surrounded by or under the influence of Communists. While consistent with the anti-Communist hysteria of the time that was the legacy of McCarthyism, he felt obliged to prove his innocence in this regard. The theme was repeated on "Meet the Press," in his meeting with the Senate Foreign Relations Committee, and in a session with a man from the Central Intelligence Agency. By contrast, there was little or no interest in what he hoped to do to improve the quality of life of the Cuban people, to eliminate the corruption and the Batista era, or the implications of brutality of his revolution for the future relationship between the United States and the rest of Latin America.

President Eisenhower conspicuously and conveniently left town on a golfing trip, leaving Vice President Richard Nixon to meet with Fidel. They met alone in Nixon's Senate office at the Capitol. Nixon was armed with a file full of evidence that he told Fidel documented the Communist ties and sympathies of many of those around him. Fidel made it clear that he was not interested and wanted to talk instead about the tremendous economic and social problems facing Latin America. Somewhat naively, he shared with Nixon all of his plans for social reform in Cuba. Nixon expressed concern about the adverse effect on public opinion of the continuing executions, a matter to which Fidel did pay heed, saying later that night to Ernesto Betancourt that he felt the executions should be stopped. They were, after he returned to Cuba, but he continued to be criticized by U.S. reporters who seemed to think that the executions were still going on. After the meeting, Nixon sent a memo to the State Department warning that Fidel posed a significant threat to the interests of the United States, and that he was either under Communist influence or very naive about the Communists. He recommended that the administration begin arming an exile force to overthrow him. It is very likely that Fidel caught a drift of Nixon's thoughts during their conversation, giving new validity in his mind to the traditional Cuban fear of a United States invasion. In a 1977 interview with Barbara Walters, Fidel said, "Sincerely, I never liked Richard Nixon. From the first moment I could see he was a false man. He always hated our country."

Before leaving Cuba, Fidel had talked about discussing, among other things, U.S. aid for the industrialization of Cuba. Plans for possible aid projects had been drawn up, and Finance Minister Rufo López Fresquet and National Bank President Felipe Pazos were on the trip. The State Department made it clear to these men that U.S. assistance was a possibility. Felipe Pazos says, "In the conversation with the State Department I had the feeling they were almost forcing us to receive loans." However, they never pursued the matter further because Fidel decided that aid from

175

the United States was not going to be part of his plan for Cuba. He came to the conclusion that it would be humiliating and would place him in exactly the same position as all the other subservient Latin American leaders who came to Washington.

Although the trip appeared to be a great public relations success, that is all it was. It in fact served to harden enmity on both sides. Fidel had bent over backward to be moderate and accommodating. It has been reported that Raúl called him from Havana to say that people in Cuba thought he had sold out. He wanted to be acclaimed for the extraordinary historical accomplishment of bringing about the revolution and overthrowing one of the most despicable tyrants in the hemisphere. Instead, most Americans had little interest in what sort of government existed in Cuba or how much rural Cubans suffered, as long as "Communists" were not involved. Fidel, on the other hand, owed a great deal to the Communists, who, although they had differed with him on tactics until close to the end of the war, had, at least in terms of their rhetoric, always shared his ideological commitment to eliminate the human suffering in Cuba. There can be little doubt that he returned to Cuba with his sympathy for the Communists significantly enhanced, and his hopes for any realistic understanding on the part of the American people sharply diminished.

It is also important to note that although large and enthusiastic crowds greeted Fidel wherever he went, this did not accurately reflect public opinion as a whole. The crowds came in part because he was a curiosity and a celebrity of global proportions, and also because he was usually in sections of the United States where his views were most acceptable. Elsewhere, especially in the South, his visit generated hostility and fear. Southern whites, terrified by the recent demands of blacks for social and political equality that threatened to overturn their traditional way of life, saw in Fidel their worst nightmare. Here was a revolutionary who had actually used armed violence successfully to overthrow an oppressive regime. What influence might his example, if unchecked, have on the vociferous young blacks agitating for the right to vote and for other social changes across the United States? In addition to a reflexive xenophobia, middle America found his beard and long hair, at that time associated with radicalism and nonconformity, enough to generate a high degree of fear-driven hatred. After studying U.S news coverage of the revolution during the first year, Zeitlin and Scheer concluded that it was overwhelmingly negative with regard to Fidel.

Had Eisenhower met with Fidel, the course of history might have been quite different. Fatherly, and without Nixon's abrasive qualities, Eisenhower would have likely listened to Fidel and not berated him. The symbolic significance alone of an Oval Office meeting would have signaled the potential for a new chapter in U.S.-Cuban relations. Instead, Fidel was gratuitously snubbed. Perhaps it was already too late; perhaps the imperative of Cuban history plus Fidel's bitter feelings expressed in his letter in the mountains to Celia precluded any rapprochement. But for Fidel, to whom pride was everything, the difference between his reception in Washington and four years later in Moscow could not have been greater.

Fidel and his entourage went on to Canada, where he received a more sympathetic official reception. It would subsequently be one of the factors that influenced his favorable attitude toward that country and, particularly, his handling of Canadian-owned property in Cuba.

Instead of returning directly to Cuba, Fidel accepted an invitation to go on to Buenos Aires, where he would address an economic conference of twenty-one Latin American countries meeting as a committee of the OAS. En route he rendezvoused in Houston with Raúl, who, it is alleged, remained concerned that Fidel was losing his revolutionary commitment. Raúl was also miffed that by extending his trip Fidel was deliberately avoiding being in Havana on May Day, when he might have felt obliged to make a greater public commitment to the international Socialist cause.

In his speech in Buenos Aires, Fidel proposed the creation of a Latin American Common Market (it ultimately became a reality, but excluding Cuba, in 1967), and that the United States launch a ten-year, $30 billion economic aid program for Latin America. The United States representative rejected the latter plan as ridiculous. Three years later, President Kennedy would unveil essentially the same proposal as the Alliance for Progress. Ernesto Betancourt, who accompanied Fidel to the conference but who shortly thereafter went into exile in the United States, was responsible for coining the term "Alliance for Progress" and provided it to Kennedy's staff.

While in Argentina, Fidel also met with his father's brother, Gonzalo, who had emigrated there at about the same time his father went to Cuba.

After brief stops in Montevideo and Rio de Janeiro, where he was accepted without reservation as a conquering hero, he returned on May 7 to Havana. He had a friendly meeting with Bonsal, who still felt, in light of what U.S. officials (as opposed to Fidel) viewed as a successful visit to the United States, that conciliation remained possible.

Fidel's return to Havana represented an important watershed. From that point on, it was clear that he had come to grips in his own mind with the fact that he was going to have to run the country. He was now ready to make the emotional commitment to do so.

From the beginning of his political career, Fidel had viewed agrarian reform as central to the social change required in Cuba. He had set up a committee under the chairmanship of the Communist Antonio Núñez

Jiménez, the distinguished geographer who had joined Che Guevara shortly before the battle of Santa Clara. The plan the committee proposed was not very radical. Indeed, the entire approach to the Cuban economy at that point, as well as Fidel's proposals for Latin America that he laid out in Buenos Aires, came almost verbatim from the recommendations of the United Nations Commission on Latin America. The Commission was headed by the Argentinian economist Raúl Prebisch, who remains today one of the most widely acclaimed authorities on Third World development.

The Cuban agrarian reform law was in many respects similar to those already enacted in Mexico and certain other Latin American countries. Differing somewhat from the plan promulgated in the Sierra Maestra in November 1958, it set a limit of 1,000 acres on the size of landholdings, but allowed an exception for sugar and rice plantations where the yield was more than 50 percent above the national average, in which case the maximum was 3,333 acres. Foreign companies could hold even larger amounts if the government deemed it in the national interest, but foreigners were forbidden to acquire new landholdings. The law did not affect the ownership of sugar mills, the largest of which were in foreign hands. Land over the allowable limits was expropriated and made into cooperatives or distributed to sharecroppers in parcels of sixty-seven acres. There was an appreciation at this stage that sugar production would be seriously compromised if the land was broken up into impractically small units comparable in size to those in Poland and Bulgaria.

The law was signed at a special ceremony in the Sierra Maestra on May 17. The Institute of Agrarian Reform (INRA) was set up to administer the program under the direction of Dr. Núñez Jiménez. Fidel took the title of president of the organizaton. Because the agricultural reform program was so close to his heart, and because he had relatively little faith in or understanding of the operations of the government structure he had inherited, Fidel loaded onto the new agency, in addition to land redistribution, responsibility for virtually every aspect of rural life including health, education, housing, and even road building. It was as though he was creating his own new government to replace the old, but all within the new agency that was his personal creation.

Having made the decision to run the government, Fidel approached it with the same single-mindedness that he had applied to the revolutionary struggle. It became his entire life, twenty-four hours a day. His perspective on government was also shaped by his personality and his experience as a revolutionary leader. He felt strongly that to succeed someone had to be in charge, *completely* in charge. He had immense confidence in his own abilities, even in areas where he had very little knowledge or experience. He suffered fools poorly, and he was increasingly intolerant of those who did not understand or did not share his vision of the new Cuba he wished to create. If he had any doubts about his right to take complete control of the country, he had only to talk to the ordinary Cubans, which he did regularly. Among them he exerted a greater personal hold than any other leader in this hemisphere has ever had over his people. They virtually demanded that he be in charge and make all the decisions.

Fidel understood the skill with which leaders such as Franklin Roosevelt and Benito Mussolini had used radio as a means of mass communication, and had learned firsthand from Eddy Chibás how the same methods could be effectively applied in Cuba. He was, however, the first world leader to appreciate the full potential of television in this regard. During the summer of 1959, he made repeated speeches aimed not so much at the live audience, although it was often massive, but at television viewers all over the country. Through this medium he was able to maintain a sense of rapport with the people, even when serious errors were being made. A related skill that Fidel was developing was what he has referred to as the "dialogue with the people." In making speeches, he would interact with the audience, asking questions and making provocative statements. He acquired immense skill in reading the mood and feelings of the country from the reactions of the mass audiences.

During this period, Fidel continued to talk about maintaining the revolution in a manner that was entirely democratic, and he denied regularly that he was involved with the Communists. The latter statement was true as far as the Cuban Communist Party was concerned. Many party members continued to have serious reservations about Fidel and were in increasing public conflict with the anti-Communist elements of the M-26-7. The people whose advice he listened to most at this stage, however, were Che and Raúl, both of whom were eclectic Marxists even though they had no formal ties to anyone other than Fidel. During his trip to the United States, Fidel had used the term "humanist revolution," and that still probably best described the state of his ideology at that point. At the end of 1959, however, he did begin having regular meetings with representatives of the Communist Party at his house in Cojímar.

He continued to be asked, mainly by foreign journalists, about the holding of elections. Early on he had talked about waiting until the opposition was sufficiently organized to permit meaningful elections, but by May he was saying that they should be deferred until the agrarian reform was complete and everyone could read and write. He clearly had made the decision that elections were not on his agenda. Had he held them he would have won overwhelmingly, and it would have brought him additional credibility in the international arena. However, he increasingly saw them as a time-consuming distraction that would only provide a vehicle for his growing number of critics to exploit.

During his trip to the United States, Fidel had met at an embassy

179

reception a young, attractive Argentinian psychiatrist. Dr. Lidia Vexel-Robertson was a fellow in child psychiatry at Mount Sinai Hospital in New York. She aggressively pursued Fidel and followed him back to Havana. How much encouragement, if any, Fidel gave her is uncertain. Over the next several months, by her account, an intense but proper romance in the Hispanic tradition ensued. Fidel, however, was still involved with Marie Lorenz, who had in fact accompanied him to New York. Fidel implied to the young psychiatrist that Marie was the girlfriend of his bodyguard, Jesús Yañes Pelletier, which she did later become. When the entourage returned to Havana, Marie claims that she was placed under virtual house arrest in the Habana Libre and was even confined for a week on the Isle of Pines. Frank Sturgis, head of Air Force security and later of Watergate fame, befriended her and convinced her to steal documents and provide him with other information from Fidel's suite.

Dr. Vexel-Robertson organized with Fidel's encouragement a psychiatric congress to help bolster the international image of the regime. At the time, she says that there was increasing speculation that she and Fidel would marry. The demise of their plans came about, according to her, because of aggressive intervention by Celia Sánchez. While Celia seemed to see little harm in his dalliance with women like Marie Lorenz, she may have decided to draw the line at any serious romance that might lead to Fidel remarrying and another woman usurping her role as Fidel's guardian and constant companion. Alternatively, she may have seen the psychiatrist not as a threat, but merely as a nuisance with whom Fidel should not be bothered. According to Dr. Vexel-Robertson, Celia made implied threats to her and told Fidel that if he continued the relationship she would take drastic measures. Celia and Fidel have never given their sides of the story. Eventually, Dr. Vexel-Robertson, learning about Fidel's relationship with Marie Lorenz, became involved with and ended up marrying another of the *barbudos*, Davis Bales, with whom she subsequently returned to the United States.

Fidel was daily facing greater opposition and criticism from wealthy landowners, U.S. business interests, and those with ambition who had supported the revolution and now wanted a share of the power. His decision to run the government in the only way he knew how, by taking total control, led critics within Cuba to accuse him of being intoxicated with power. The U.S. government, not surprisingly, delivered a formal protest over the land reform program and the methods of compensation. In 1964, Fidel would tell Herbert Matthews, "The agrarian reform and the reaction to it in the United States and by Americans made me realize there was no chance to reach an accommodation with the United States." His reaction to the criticism was to stand his ground stubbornly. He would

180

not, he said, change one iota of the agrarian reform law. He began to attack publicly critics as traitors and enemies of the revolution. The more he was criticized, the harder became his own position. It was a reflection of his instinctual leadership talents and his understanding of the Cuban people, because although his intransigence served to antagonize his enemies, his supporters—the bulk of the Cuban people—saw his stance as a reaffirmation of his personal strength and unwavering commitment.

During a speech on June 13, in which Fidel was defending the agrarian reform law, three bombs exploded in the city, and others went off later. It triggered fears of the repeated waves of violence that had characterized Cuban politics in the past and clearly prompted Fidel to begin a series of preemptive moves. The Constitution of 1940 was amended to allow the death penalty for "counterrevolutionary activities," and selective arrests were made of conservative opposition leaders. At the end of June, the commander of the air force, Pedro Díaz Lanz, defected with his family in a small boat to Miami. In mid-July, he testified before the Senate Internal Security Subcommittee where, warming to the eager expectations of his audience, he gave lurid and exaggerated accounts of the situation in Cuba. That this particular subcommittee, which had no authority over foreign affairs, should have seen fit to hear the testimony of a defector from a country with which the United States still had diplomatic relations, reflects the minimal regard that official Washington had for the sovereignty of Cuba.

When Díaz Lanz left, Frank Sturgis, his subordinate as head of air force security, went with him. He in turn arranged to smuggle Marie Lorenz out of the country. According to an interview she gave to New York *Daily News* reporter Paul Meskil, Marie returned to Havana several months later disguised as a tourist. She waited until Fidel was in Ciénega de Zapata, then, donning the rebel uniform Fidel had given her and using the key she had retained, she entered his suite and stole all the papers and maps she could stuff inside and into the pockets of her jacket. She returned to Miami and gave the material to Frank Sturgis, who by then was working with the CIA–sponsored exile groups.

While Díaz Lanz was inflaming public opinion in Washington, Fidel was systematically removing from the Cabinet the more liberal members and those who represented the older generation, replacing them with individuals who were generally much less experienced but either loyal to him or, as former participants in the armed struggle, loyal to the more radical objectives of the revolution.

President Urrutia was becoming a more difficult problem. He was now quite out of step with the young revolutionary generation that had moved into most of the major positions in the government. Never a very skilled politician, he had taken it upon himself to try clumsily to drive a wedge between Fidel and the Communists, thinking that he would strengthen his own position by having the backing of the anti-Communists. The Communists responded with a bitter attack, accusing him of undermining the solidarity of the revolution. Eager to oust Urrutia, Fidel had skillfully held back, allowing the older president to press his anti-Communist campaign. Finally, on the morning of July 17, the country awoke to find that Fidel had resigned. That night Fidel went on television to attack Urrutia for everything from his supposedly extravagant lifestyle to his vilification of the Communists. The average Cuban had little fear of communism; he not only associated fervent anti-communism with the United States, but considered it a crude rationale for the interference in the affairs of other nations. Fidel was able to imply that Urrutia's anti-communism showed he had links to hostile groups in the United States and was trying to pave the way for the reassertion of foreign domination in Cuba, a course that struck at the heart and soul of what the revolution was all about.

Fidel's resignation was a ploy to get public opinion behind him, knowing full well that Urrutia had little or no public support. If he made it a choice between himself and Urrutia, the public would overwhelmingly insist that Urrutia be the man to go. Urrutia was a decent but weak man who seemed oblivious to the fact that he no longer fitted in. Fidel's attack on him, however, was gratuitously vicious and unfair. There was, for instance, not the slightest indication that he was trying to encourage foreign intervention. It was one of the first public indications of Fidel's capacity for extreme ruthlessness. He could almost certainly have convinced Urrutia to resign in a private conversation, but he chose to do it in this public and theatrical manner. It might be argued that it showed his political immaturity. In fact, it served three useful purposes: it demonstrated his absolute power; it sent a warning to anyone else thinking of opposing his ideas; and it helped to ingratiate him with the Communists. Psychologically, he also seemed to need to show himself that he had the complete backing of and control over the Cuban people.

Urrutia had little choice but to resign, something he had tried to do on four previous occasions when he could have done so under a much better light, but had been talked out of it. Within a few hours, Osvaldo Dorticós, the minister of revolutionary laws, was sworn in as the new president. Although a successful lawyer from an upper-middle-class background and former commodore of the Cienfuegos Yacht Club, he had been for a brief time a member of the Communist party and secretary to its president. More important, he was a competent, bright, and hard-working individual who had been an active member of the 26 of July Movement and was very much a part of the revolutionary generation of 1953.

For a week, Fidel's role remained nebulous, but he announced that he would submit his political future to the will of the people at a mass rally on July 26, the sixth anniversary of the Moncada attack. Thousands of peasants flocked to Havana, some transported by INRA, others coming of their own accord. A public holiday was declared and amid an atmosphere of national celebration, the gigantic rally in the Plaza Civica was opened by President Dorticós, who announced that in response to overwhelming public demand, Fidel had agreed to resume his role as prime minister. After many minutes of joyous cheering, Fidel began to address the crowd. He spoke for four hours to an enthralled audience with which he had a communion that only he was capable of achieving.

Fidel's magnetic hold over the Cuban people is never better shown than when he addresses a mass audience. He does not make a political speech in the traditional sense, but holds an emotional dialogue with the audience. Behind the gesticulating polemical marathons that the outside world perceives is a completely different level of communication, one that has a strong emotional, if not spiritual, quality to it. Che Guevara described it as "The dialogue of two tuning forks whose vibrations summon forth vibrations in each other. Fidel and the mass begin to vibrate in a dialogue of growing intensity, which reaches its culminating point in the abrupt ending crowned by our victorious battle cry, '*Patria o muerte*' " (fatherland or death).

Most charismatic leaders learn early that political power can derive from the ability to deliver a truly rousing speech. They find that people are quite willing to surrender their individuality to their demagogic leadership. This is particularly true in times of low national self-esteem, when people have a hunger for someone to restore their self-respect and make them feel good about their countries and themselves.

Chapter Nine

IN the fall of 1959, Fidel faced a number of interlocking concerns. He wanted to keep agrarian reform and other social changes developing as rapidly as possible because he believed that the viability of the revolution and its credibility with the Cuban people was tied to maintaining constant forward movement. This in turn fueled the growing criticism from special interest groups. His need to deal with this opposition became progressively more urgent as it began to coalesce into groups that sought clearly to block the progress of the revolution or even to instigate Fidel's overthrow. The pursuit of the agrarian reform measures, as well as his efforts to quell the opposition, aroused further hostility from the United States. That hostility was inflamed every time he made a patriotic speech emphasizing Cuba's new independence and castigating United States imperialism. At the same time, it made him an ever greater hero with the Cuban people, his ultimate political base. In addition, he had not relinquished his internationalist vision and, if anything, his trips to South America and the United States convinced him even more that the time was right for him to play a hemispheric rather than just a national role. Throughout Latin America, there was a growing sense of nationalism that invariably implied antipathy toward the United States. The success of his revolution in overthrowing a U.S.-backed oligarchy had unleashed a wave of similar aspirations throughout the hemisphere. At the same time, the United States was increasingly preoccupied with the Soviet Union and less concerned, as it had been up until World War II, with imposing its will on Latin America. Fidel had grandiose aspirations about being the spiritual leader of a unified nationalistic movement across the hemisphere. It was a concept that Martí had envisioned, of which Fidel was very much aware.

Fidel had no real political organization at this stage. After the failure of the general strike in April 1958, he successfully removed any autonomous power from the lowland leadership of the M-26-7, and as a viable political organization he had allowed it to wither. In the final days of

Batista, despite its weakness compared to the rebel army, it had become a bandwagon onto which people of every political stripe had scrambled. They shared as a common interest a desire to overthrow the dictatorship, but the degree of their loyalty to Fidel varied widely, as did their views about the shape of the new Cuba. They considered Fidel their leader, but among those closest to him, essentially the veterans of the Sierra Maestra, the feelings toward the 26 of July Movement were still colored by the schism between those who had fought the struggle in the mountains and those who had fought it in the cities. There was no real trust and the organization was too much of an ideological grab bag to be of use to him.

It was at this stage that Fidel began increasingly to use the existing Communist Party structure. The pressure to bring order out of chaos in the country was considerable, and the one organization that could achieve that goal was the PSP. As he said later to Herbert Matthews, "The Cuban Communist party . . . had men who were truly revolutionary, loyal, honest and trained. I needed them." In her 1964 interview with *Life* magazine, Juanita Castro says that when she criticized her brother for his involvement with the Communists, he replied, "Look Juanita, we must use these people, we must be politicians. One must have a left hand." Perhaps he got some perverse pleasure, knowing the hostility of the United States to the Communists, in turning to them for help. He still held the reservations about the party that he had had since his student days—that it was too rigid ideologically and that its close association with the Soviet Union conflicted with the independent nationalism for Cuba that was his goal. However, its tight organizational structure increasingly appealed to his psychological affinity for discipline. Now, holding power, he could involve himself with the party on his own terms. Che returned at the end of August from an extensive trip to Africa, Asia, and Europe very enamored with what he had seen in Yugoslavia. The Yugoslavian model of socialism, Che declared, with its success in industrializing an agrarian society and its independent socialism that kept Russia at arm's length, offered the perfect example for Cuba to follow.

The underlying motivation driving Fidel's actions at this point, when his mind was bubbling over with dramatic ideas about the new Cuba he wanted to create, was not so much ideological, or even an attempt to consolidate his personal power. It was rather his frustration with the squabbling factionalism and general disorganization that made it almost impossible to implement the programs he was planning. Always supremely self-confident that he had the answers to Cuba's problems, he was desperately impatient to get on with the job. In a speech on July 5, which was reported under the heading, "Why the Government Cannot Be Shared," he said, "All revolutionary sectors must support the Revolution. To take part in the government, however, is another matter. We need to keep control in our hands or the Revolution will fall apart." It was an accurate assessment of the current state of affairs, and it is a view that has persisted ever since.

Fidel's inexperience, however, led him in his zeal to keep the spirit of the revolution alive, to make decisions which, although immensely popular in the short term, would prove economically disastrous later on. Unlike the victors in most civil wars, he did not inherit a shattered economy. The Cuban economy at the start of 1959 was strong and vibrant. Sugar prices were low but stable, and with the start of the sugar harvest unemployment was at a minimum. Foreign investment in the country was substantial, with an estimated U.S. investment in 1958 of $1.2 billion. Stores were filled with consumer goods, and tourists, particularly attracted by the widespread gambling and prostitution, maintained a constant flow of foreign exchange into the country. The revolutionary war against Batista had done relatively little to hurt the economy.

In order to enable the revolution to demonstrate quickly some concrete benefit in peoples' lives, in March 1959, Fidel had ordered rents for those who paid less than $100 per month cut in half. The government took over the telephone company and cut its rates. Most labor contracts were re-negotiated in the first few months of the year, and the properties owned by Batista and the members of his government were confiscated by the state. The purchasing power of the population was suddenly dramatically increased, and a sudden artificial sense of prosperity was created. The people went on a buying spree so that retail business seemed to be flourishing. There was a sense of economic well-being without any recognition that the economy as a whole was living on borrowed time. Productivity had not increased at all; in fact, it was already going down. This artificial state would continue for nearly two years, as the country's reserves were drained and foreign investment fled. Then suddenly the nation would find itself on the verge of bankruptcy. Perhaps it would have been better in the long run if Fidel had been confronted with these inevitable economic realities and had been forced to take some tough measures when he first came to power.

Historically, relations with the United States hinged above all else around the issue of sugar. Now a decision by the United States to increase the 1959 quota for Cuban sugar above the existing level of 3 million tons at 5.4¢ a pound would have given a significant boost to the Cuban economy and would have been a vote of confidence for the new regime. In a most unorthodox diplomatic move, on June 4, Fidel sent a personal cable to the secretary of agriculture in Washington offering to export 8 million tons at 4¢ a pound. He set a deadline of June 15 for acceptance of the offer. Fidel had visions of a dramatic increase in sugar production, but based on past crop levels Cuba could not have honored this offer and met its other international obligations. The Agriculture Department not only thought the offer unrealistic, they felt that the agrarian reform program would cut production even further. They responded bureaucratically before the deadline, declining the offer, telling Fidel that the United States could not absorb such a large amount of sugar. Making no allowance for his youth and inexperience in diplomatic protocol, officials in Washington interpreted this unconventional offer as evidence that they were dealing with at best an incompetent and at worst an impulsive, dangerous eccentric. Fidel, on the other hand, failing to appreciate that a government the size of the United States could not possibly respond in eleven days with the appropriate political sophistication to the kind of freewheeling impromptu offer he made, took it as further evidence of U.S. hostility toward Cuba. It was one more little step taken by each side on the slippery slide toward the ultimate disruption of relations.

In August 1959, the United States launched a hemispheric strategy to mobilize the governments of Latin America against Fidel. At a meeting of the foreign ministers of the OAS in Santiago, Chile, the United States representatives sought unsuccessfully to mobilize support for a resolution condemning Cuba's role in the hemisphere. Organized pressure had not yet been brought to bear by the United States on the individual governments, and most Latin American leaders were concerned about criticizing Fidel when he enjoyed such widespread admiration among their own people. On September 5, 1959, Fidel met with Ambassador Bonsal as he was about to depart for consultations in Washington. It was a relaxed and cordial meeting, during which Fidel urged that the United States not pay too much attention to "the propaganda excesses of young people working in an atmosphere of revolutionary enthusiasm." It was sound advice that the United States might well have followed, but it was also a luxury that is not afforded anyone actually in power no matter how great his youth or inexperience.

In April 1959, while Fidel had been in Washington, a group of eighty-four Cubans and Panamanians set sail for Panama. They were rapidly captured and their plans to "liberate" that country crushed. It was not a formal venture of the Cuban government, but nothing had been done to stop it and the group's plans were known to the revolutionary leaders. Raúl's visit to Houston, where he intercepted Fidel on his way to Buenos Aires, may have been in part to report on the failure of the mission.

At the beginning of June 1959, two groups were preparing to launch an invasion against the dictatorial regime of Luis Somoza in Nicaragua.

Two planeloads of Nicaraguan exiles based in Costa Rica invaded the country, preempting another group that was training in Cuba and planning an invasion by sea. When the Costa Rican group was crushed the Cuban-based force abandoned its plans. Havana denied any involvement, which was probably true.

Following the rebel triumph in January 1959, revolutionary groups from all over Latin America had flocked to Cuba and had begun using it as a base from which to plan invasions against real or perceived despots in their homelands. Some had credible plans and connections with the revolutionary leaders in Cuba, but many were dreamers and incompetents. There was a high level of tolerance for all such groups on the part of the Cuban government, but this did not mean official involvement. Indeed, the level of disorganization in the government at this time was such that the most the average revolutionary plotters could expect was some general encouragement or advice from the Sierra Maestra veterans and, if they were lucky, a limited amount of old weapons.

The invasion of the Dominican Republic in the middle of June was another matter. Ever since the days of the aborted Cayo Confites expedition, Fidel had nurtured the dream of one day overthrowing Trujillo. He had made it clear to several people while still in the mountains that his preference was not to run the government of Cuba, but to devote himself full-time to planning and leading such an invasion. Even with the inevitable recognition that his place was at the helm of the Cuban government, he had not abandoned his interest in the venture. Trujillo had given political asylum to Batista and members of his regime, lending further legitimacy in Fidel's mind to a plan to overthow him. A force of two hundred Dominicans and ten Cubans was assembled under the command of Delio Gómez Ochoa, a seasoned veteran of the Sierra Maestra. Unable to participate himself, Fidel also ordered Camilo Cienfuegos not to participate, on the grounds that he was too valuable in Cuba.

The force landed in two waves on the north coast of the Dominican Republic. Those who were not immediately killed were soon captured, and the expedition was wiped out before it could even begin to mobilize any indigenous support.

Concerned about possible retaliatory attacks, and in general increasingly concerned about protecting Cuba as relations deteriorated with the United States, Fidel began to cast around in the international market for a place to buy arms. On October 17, 1959, the Cuban ambassador in Washington suggested that if they could not obtain arms from the United States or Western Europe they might turn to the Eastern bloc. Che, on his extended trip overseas, had made tentative inquiries, including holding discussions with representatives of the Czechoslovakian government while he was in Cairo. Subsequently, Czechoslovakia would be the first East European power to supply Cuba with weapons. In the meantime, a limited supply was obtained from Belgium.

One of the clear messages that Che brought back from his trip was that while Cuba could win friends and build a web of influence among Third World nations, they could do little to help her economically. They were, like Cuba, exporters primarily of raw materials; they were equally dependent on the industrialized nations for manufactured goods. Che returned with not a single trade agreement of any consequence.

It was only a matter of time before Fidel would have to consider turning to the Soviet Union. Apart from economic considerations, the powerful symbolic element in involving Cuba with the Soviets had immense appeal to Fidel. Because of United States antipathy toward the Soviet Union, there was no greater way for any nation in the Western hemisphere to make a statement about its freedom from United States domination than to deal with the Soviets on a friendly basis. If there was a single central theme that now epitomized the soul of the revolution, it was that of Cuban nationalism and the sense that the nation for the first time in its history was a truly independent sovereign state.

On October 16, 1959, Camilo Cienfuegos was interviewed at the Havana Riviera Hotel by Alexander Alexayev, a correspondent for the Soviet news agency Tass. Alexayev was actually a KGB official using a journalistic cover. He asked Cienfuegos if he could arrange an interview for him with Fidel. A few days later, a meeting was arranged at the offices of INRA. In addition to Fidel and Alexayev, Dr. Antonio Núñcz Jiménez, the director of INRA, was present. According to Núñez, Alexayev arrived neatly dressed in a suit and tie and clearly felt uncomfortable when he saw the informality with which his hosts were dressed. He brought with him a package wrapped in the pages of a Soviet magazine, which he immediately presented to Fidel. Inside was a bottle of vodka, a pot of caviar, and an album of pictures of Moscow. Fidel received the gifts with great interest and appreciation and listened while Alexayev expressed in warm terms the admiration of the Soviet people for the Cuban Revolution. Fidel talked of his desire for trade relations with the Soviet Union, and when Alexayev asked him about diplomatic relations, Fidel said, "Ah, now I see why you have come with such formality," referring to Alexayev's dress. "What is fundamental now," he continued, "is not diplomatic relations. What is most important is that the Cuban and Russian people be friends." Alexayev suggested that a Soviet trade exhibition currently in New York and with several other stops scheduled in Latin America be brought to Havana, and that Vice Premier Anastas Mikoyan might come for the official opening.

They ate some of the caviar and drank the vodka. The rapport established between Fidel and Alexayev was particularly good. As they grew close personally the friendship exerted its own magnetic effect on the relationship between their two countries.

Fidel's decision to establish relations with the Soviets added urgency to his need to deal with dissident elements in the country. The opposition was becoming not only more organized, but more dangerous. On October 11, a U.S.-based plane dropped three bombs on a sugar mill in Pinar del Río. The need to stop the drift toward communism was both the central theme around which the opposition in Cuba was building its organization and the basis on which the growing exile community was seeking clandestine support from the CIA in the United States. Fidel knew that the steps he planned to take in the next few months would only lend further credence to that argument.

One of the main centers of opposition lay in Camagüey Province, the conservative cattle ranching region where objection to the agrarian reform program had been most vociferous. It was also where criticism of the Communist influence was the most public. For nine months, Raúl had been pursuing a strategy, developed with Che, of indoctrinating the members of the rebel army with Communist ideology and moving loyal supporters who shared their ideological views into key commands. There had been growing objections from anti-Communists, including loyal supporters of Fidel who, they assumed, in light of his public disavowals of communism, must not be aware of what his brother was up to.

On October 15, 1959, Raúl was appointed minister of the armed forces. At about the same time, Hubert Matos, military commander of Camagüey and a loyal veteran of the Sierra Maestra, decided to resign in protest, a step that he hoped would force Fidel to become aware of the growing Communist control of the military. Instead he was denounced as a traitor to the revolution, ostensibly on the basis of his sympathy with those who had opposed the agrarian reform in the province. Fidel arrived in the city of Camagüey and ordered the arrest of Matos and twenty other officers who had resigned with him. The events also provided an excuse to arrest or oust from their jobs many in the province considered to be opponents of the government. While Fidel returned to Havana, he left Camilo Cienfuegos in Camagüey to take over Matos's job.

Although Fidel must have been aware of what his brother and Che had been doing with the rebel army, his own more moderate public position had established them and their supporters in the military as a powerful force outflanking him on the left. Some members of the Cabinet who subsequently left Cuba go so far as to suggest that Raúl was willing to move against his brother if the latter ultimately proved too moderate.

Raúl was always more hard-line than Fidel, but there is nothing to suggest that he was anything but loyal. Nevertheless, Fidel's move against Matos, while erroneously construed as a move against the right-wing opposition, was equally important for the message it sent to those on the left. By defending his brother, and in effect condoning his indoctrination program in the military, he was drawing this far-left faction of the revolution under his own leadership umbrella and eliminating any potential for the emergence of an independent ideological faction. The consolidation was made complete by appointing his brother minister of the armed forces and bringing him into the Cabinet. While serious judicial questions were raised by the seizure of Matos, it was a deft political move that at once crushed the right and co-opted the left.

In the final analysis, however, Fidel's move against Matos reflected his refusal to accept anyone who challenged the direction in which he was leading the revolution, especially someone who enjoyed considerable respect and had a growing independent power base. Fidel's act was dictatorial and authoritarian. It had serious consequences, shaking to the core the confidence that even some of his most loyal supporters had in him.

As was his custom whenever tumultuous events shook the nation, on October 26, Fidel spoke before more than half a million people assembled before the Presidential Palace. Speaking of the Matos affair and subtly linking it to the episodic raids by marauding aircraft, he poured forth heartfelt conviction, gently coaxing forth again the seemingly limitless trust of the ordinary Cuban in his leadership.

But the nation was suddenly shaken by a new development. Camilo Cienfuegos, after departing from Camagüey in a small plane headed for Havana, had disappeared. Next to Fidel and Che, the swashbuckling commandante who habitually wore his cowboy hat was the most loved of the rebel leaders. His loyalty to Fidel was total and he harbored no independent ideology. Some felt that since arriving in Havana he had made up for lost time in the Sierra Maestra by overindulging in soft living, but it only added to his romantic image. His presumed death triggered wide speculation of foul play that persisted, especially in the exile community, for many years. Nothing conclusive has emerged since to suggest it was anything other than an unfortunate accident.

Fidel was clearly shaken by the news of the disappearance, brought to him by Raúl in a Cabinet meeting. The country as a whole reacted to the loss as not just the death of one man, but as a symbolic setback to the revolutionary cause. The death and the exile-sponsored air raids added to the sense of embattlement that was beginning to grip the revolution. But this incipient sense of crisis had the effect of further strengthening Fidel's role, as people turned more to him for leadership.

This was not the case with the remaining liberal leadership. With the arrest of Matos, they saw the writing on the wall, and violent arguments erupted at several Cabinet meetings. Felipe Pazos, the director of the National Bank, had privately confided in President Dorticós his concerns about the Matos affair and expressed his desire to resign. In the Cabinet his views were shared by Faustino Pérez, López Fresquet, and Manuel Ray, all of whom identified with Matos in his effort to sound the alarm about the growth of Communist power and influence. Fidel sought to cajole and reassure them that he had done only what was truly necessary. His personality was so dominant and his public support still so solid that no one dared aggressively confront Fidel, fearing they would suffer the same fate as Matos. Yet over the next six weeks, until Matos went to trial on December 11, the continuing argument around the issues in the case became the grounds on which each of these men and several others resigned from the government. Only Faustino Pérez, who had been on the *Granma* and who shared a special mutual loyalty with Fidel despite their differences, would remain in Cuba and subsequently reemerge in a position of power.

Those who disagreed with Fidel, whether they were the old-line Communists, the liberals in the government, or the conservative reactionaries and large landholders, saw their differences in ideological terms and assumed they could shift Fidel's position by intellectual persuasion. What was really happening, however, was that Fidel now had a clear vision of where he wanted to go. He was consolidating power by making allegiance to himself and his aspirations a prerequisite for political survival. What had started as a split based on differing ideological perspectives had become a question of whether or not every other Cuban leader was willing to subject himself to Fidel's dominance. For Fidel it was *his* revolution, and he could not accept the notion of sharing it with anyone. Even his older brother, Ramón, was in open conflict with the regime at this point, but he says in retrospect, "Many of us had ideas of our own at the time, but they were wrong."

In contrast with those who were abandoning the regime was Raúl Roa, who was appointed foreign minister. Roa, a short man with a mustache, was a distinguished intellectual and radical who had been a liberal activist in the 1930s and a professor during Fidel's student years. Although he had refused to meet with Fidel in Mexico, disparaging him as a gangster, he put aside that earlier skepticism as Fidel's victory became imminent. He now emerged as a loyal and dedicated supporter. Unlike some of the younger, less experienced spokesmen for the revolution, he enjoyed a high level of respect in the international community.

In 1956, Roa had published a scathing attack on the Soviet Union for its suppression of the Hungarian uprising. This made him a source of constant irritation to the Soviets. Despite their good relationship with Cuba and his position as foreign minister, it would, astonishingly, not be until 1971 that Roa was invited to the Soviet Union. It was a reflection of his competence, but even more of Fidel's appreciation of his personal loyalty, that he should have been kept in the position for close to twenty years (1959–1976) under these circumstances.

An opposite dynamic was occurring in the Ministry of Finance, which was becoming a center of dissent and growing disillusionment in the government. Under the leadership of Rufo López Fresquet and Felipe Pazos, there had been assembled a group of bright, energetic economic advisers. Most were young, very well trained, and had been early, vehement opponents of Batista. They envisioned in Cuba after the revolution a democratic pluralistic society; that was what they had risked their lives for in the struggle. Because of their professional training and the self-confidence it gave them, they were not as overawed by Fidel as some of his less-educated followers, and were willing to argue with him, particularly on economic issues. Early on they accepted without question Fidel's overall leadership and saw their job as being to manage the economy as well as possible within the framework of the political decisions he was making. However, it became increasingly difficult for them to do their job when decisions with major economic implications were made without their being involved.

In an effort to resolve this problem, Fidel was persuaded to meet every Thursday afternoon, beginning in June, with this group of economic advisers. This led to some improvement in the coordination of rational economic planning, but Fidel's inexperience in this area and his exuberant, impulsive style of decision making caused enormous frustrations for the professionals.

In the final analysis, the disillusionment that set in was the result of more than just managerial differences. It was increasingly caused by differing economic philosophies and the perception by this group that Fidel was assuming an authoritarian role. Ernesto Betancourt describes a meeting at which the need to oust President Urrutia was being discussed. One of the participants cautioned Fidel that such a move could open the door for U.S. intervention, a fear that was very real at the time. Without a pause, Fidel responded, "Well, I couldn't care less, because if that were to happen, if they were to send the marines, they would have to kill three or four hundred thousand people and I would get a bigger monument than José Martí." For Betancourt it was a decisive moment. "Immediately I said to myself, 'We are here for the size of the monument. This is really what this man is praying for. He is not praying for solving any problem. . . . He is just interested in his image in history.' " He recalls that "it was my stepping down from the train right there."

From July onward, Felipe Pazos had in his desk the resignations of Betancourt and several others. They agreed that if it became necessary to leave they would do so, in the words of Betancourt, "in a harmonious way" so as not to leave some of the team behind to pay the price for those who went into exile. It was a losing battle and they all knew it. It was also like the final months of a finished marriage in which the pretense of normalcy is maintained while each side tries to work out plans for a new and different future. The last of the Thursday afternoon meetings with Fidel occurred on October 15, 1959. In retrospect, it is clear Fidel was already working on a completely different track with little expectation that there would be a role for these liberal economists.

The final break came with the Matos affair and the resignation of Pazos, who barely escaped arrest himself because of his public sympathy for Matos. Fidel appointed Che Guevara to replace Pazos as director of the National Bank, a move that led most of the senior officials with technical expertise to leave over the subsequent weeks. It also signaled a very negative message to the international community. It was not just that someone with a recognized Marxist bent should take over such a sensitive position; the departure of so many widely recognized professionals was seen outside Cuba as a credible vote of no confidence in where the revolution was headed.

The trial of Hubert Matos began on December 11, 1959. It was as much a political event as a judicial proceeding. The thrust of the prosecution's argument was that Matos had sought to obstruct the implementation of the agrarian reform program in Camagüey, and had been in contact with those elsewhere in the country who shared similar views. He was also demonstrably anti-Communist, as evidenced by his own statements and his efforts to have non-Communists appointed officials in the province. Much of the evidence related not to the specific charges, but to a broader effort to discredit him and his counsel on a personal basis. Both Fidel and Raúl testified at the trial, and at one point Fidel entered into a heated and some felt undecorous argument with Matos and his attorney. Finally, Matos was convicted and sentenced to twenty years in prison. Those charged with him recieved lesser sentences. Matos served his term and then left Cuba. He currently lives in Venezuela.

An effort was made to enhance the legitimacy of the Matos conviction by trying at the same time a number of individuals whose subversive and counterrevolutionary activities were beyond question. One of these was Rafael del Pino, who had been with Fidel in Bogotá and had betrayed him in Mexico.

The impact of the trial both inside and outside Cuba was stunning but misleading. Up to this point liberals had wanted to believe the best about Fidel. When he said he was not a Communist, they took his statements at face value. When Communists seemed to be creeping into positions of power, they rationalized that it was happening without Fidel's knowledge. When he acted in an authoritarian way, they convinced themselves that it was necessary to protect the revolution. The outcome of the trial meant that they could no longer rationalize. Not only did many of them agree with and identify with Matos, but it was as though he was on trial as a symbolic representative of a whole segment of the Cuban population. His conviction, in a way that was contemptuous of the traditional judicial process, carried the inescapable implication that there was no role for them in the new Cuba unless they were willing to buy unquestioningly the program Fidel was laying out. Fidel's popularity with the general public had not diminished one iota. It was increasingly apparent that he did not need the liberal bourgeoisie, who anyway constituted at most 10 percent of the population and were more concerned with democratic procedures and their own share of the power than the grand vision of the revolution he was offering the country. In the eyes of the masses, the revolution had already led to the redistribution of some land, a reduction in the cost of essential services, the elimination of corruption, and the promise for the first time of education, health care, and steady employment. What did they care about the rights of one wealthy counterrevolutionary? If Fidel, whom they trusted, felt Matos was guilty and should be in prison, that was good enough for them.

The end of 1959 was a time of decision for many middle- and upper-class Cubans. The decision whether to abandon careers and pack up and leave for an uncertain future in the United States, or stay and make an accommodation with a government with which they had serious differences, was a dilemma faced by hundreds, perhaps thousands, of families. Those who could afford to leave, even if they had been avid supporters of the 26 of July Movement, were generally people who had been beneficiaries of the old order. They were physicians, engineers, managers, and technicians who never wanted a *real* revolution. They had envisioned a purge of the old order under Batista that would reduce corruption and nepotism, reduce the power of the military, and produce a modest degree of independence from the United States that would palliate Cuba's strong nationalistic urge. They had envisioned a democratic form of government, but a government where power would have continued to be passed around among members of the same privileged class and, at least in the short term, would have done very little to alleviate the appalling conditions in which two-thirds of the population lived.

In 1959, most progressive Cubans who had supported the 26 of July Movement believed, or wanted to believe, that in the final analysis Fidel shared their views. After all, he was, they thought, one of them from the same privileged background. But he did not. His commitment was to a complete upheaval of the social system as he had first outlined in "History Will Absolve Me." He envisioned a system in which meeting the basic needs of the rural poor was at the top of the list of national priorities instead of at the bottom. To make that a reality required reshaping the entire economic and political system and assaulting virtually every existing bastion of power. The public dialogue centered on the extent to which identified Communists had gained influence and power, how much Fidel was voraciously grabbing personal power, why elections had not been scheduled, and how the judicial system had been abused. But what these people really had to contend with was that the old order in Cuba had come to an end and they could not remake it. Everything was going to be done the way Fidel wanted it. Either they could stay and accept that Fidel was committed to a true revolution, accommodating their thinking and ambitions to that reality, or they could leave and make a new life for themselves, maintaining their view of how things should have been in Cuba and believing one day that they would return. Fidel's brother Ramón chose the former course. One of the many who would ultimately take the latter course was Fidel's sister Juanita, who left Cuba in 1964 and became a harsh critic of her brother. To stay meant essentially to place one's trust completely in Fidel as he led the country into dangerous and uncharted waters.

For many educated, professional Cubans, it was not too great a cultural dislocation. Most had either been educated in the United States or had spent a great deal of time there. Their professional and business identification was as much American as Cuban, and so the transition was relatively painless.

Fidel knew he was forcing these people to make a decision. If they stayed and continued to be in disagreement with the fundamental goals of the revolution, they would constitute a growing liability. With an increasingly aggressive exile community in Miami and a worsening relationship with the United States, it was better to know who was loyal and who was not. If they had reservations now about the revolution, there was little reason to think they would feel any differently in the future.

If there was one miscalculation Fidel may have made it was in misjudging the extent to which such a rapid exodus of so many trained individuals would have on the running of Cuba's basic institutions. The departure of thousands of doctors severely hurt the ability in the short term to provide health care for all, a major commitment of the regime.

Several key industries were crippled by the loss of middle management. The revolution's ability to deliver on its promises was slowed because there were too few technicians left to carry out the decisions of the revolutionary leaders.

Fidel also recognized that the alienation of many former supporters of the regime would pose an increasing threat to its survival. His reaction was to close ranks and increase the vigilance against any opposition. At the end of November, the right of habeas corpus was suspended, and on December 16, 1959, at a convention of sugar workers, Fidel warned that a tremendous campaign against the revolution had been mounted. "We shall have to defend the revolution with arms in 1960. . . . We shall fight to the last man," he said. He called on ordinary men and women to become soldiers in the revolution, and warned them to denounce to the police anyone speaking against the revolution. He had successfully created in the minds of Cubans the sense that the revolution was an entity that they owned and must defend at all costs against those who wished to take it away from them. Anyone who criticized the revolution in any way was immediately suspect as someone who would seek to destroy it. In one year, Fidel had moved from being reluctant to take on the responsibility for governing to an egotistical obsession for total control even if it meant trampling on citizens' civil rights. Had Batista done some of these same things, Fidel would have been outraged. Because he believed that his ultimate objectives were good, he was blind to any parallels between his actions and those of the previous regime.

Backing the call for vigilance by the public was a growing intelligence operation created by the regime. The G-2 was headed by Ramiro Valdés, a veteran of both Moncada and the *Granma*. He made it an institution of great efficiency and the source of fear for members of the old ruling class, even if they had been politically passive, as well as supporters of the revolution who were still promoting ideas at variance with those of the regime. By the end of 1959, enemies of the revolution were being arrested in significant numbers across Cuba with little guarantee of a fair trial. Despite being a lawyer, Fidel has never seen the law as anything other than a tool for achieving political ends.

Elements of the press led by the conservative Catholic paper, *Diario de la Marina*, had become critical of the revolution. In January 1960, through the Communist-controlled printers and journalists unions the government began demanding that these papers include after each news story a "clarification." There was great anger that these *coletillas*, or "little tails," had to be printed; it clearly signaled the end of an independent press. Several publications that refused to do so were closed over the next few months.

197

The Matos trial and the events surrounding it ended any hope for a reconciliation with the United States, and even Ambassador Bonsal, who had worked so hard to achieve some rapprochement, was ready to cease his efforts. In early January, INRA seized seventy thousand acres of U.S.-owned property for which the owners were to receive twenty-year bonds with $4\frac{1}{4}$ percent interest. By midyear, no bonds had yet been issued, and U.S. protests about expropriation, while relatively low key, were met by regular rebuff in Havana.

During the last three months of 1959, following Fidel's meeting with Alexayev, discussions were proceeding concerning the proposed visit of Anastas Mikoyan and the content of a trade package to be signed while he was in Cuba. The expectation that the Soviet Union would help Fidel establish an economy independent of traditional United States domination gave him new maneuvering room. Now, without fear of committing economic suicide, he would indulge in the bravado that was so much a part of his personality in his dealings with the United States government. At the same time, every defiance of the United States was a way of sending a message to the Soviets that they were making a wise investment in supporting him and encouraging them to increase the size of their largesse.

Some of Fidel's domestic moves at this time can also be attributed in part to the emerging relationship with the Soviets. Although he had received a message through Alexayev that Khrushchev recognized him as the legitimate leader of the revolution, the Soviets could be expected to feel a natural allegiance to the Cuban Communist Party and their leader, Blas Roca, who had maintained loyal ties to Moscow for twenty-five years. Fidel did not want the Soviets trying to make their aid contingent on his acquiescing to some politically unacceptable accommodation with the old-line Communists. He was moving, therefore, to consolidate his power and show the Soviet leaders that he was completely in charge. At the same time, he moved to end the warring that had been going on between the Communist Party and other factions of the revolution. He aligned himself with the party on a number of key issues, most visibly their move to gain control over the labor unions. This left the party leadership with little to complain to Moscow about as far as the way he had treated them.

Fidel was like a man with a foot on each side of a widening chasm. He could not afford to terminate his relationship with the United States before he was assured of sufficient support from the Soviet Union. But relations with the U.S. were deteriorating very fast. His efforts, therefore, to hasten the pace of the revolution in the months prior to Mikoyan's visit were also attributable, at least in part, to a desire to present the Soviet leader with the picture of a county moving rapidly toward what Fidel hoped he would regard as an acceptable Socialist state. The more secure Fidel felt with regard to Soviet military and economic help, the more he would be free to vent his anger at and assert his independence from the U.S. The Soviet Union, contrary to what many in the United States assumed, was cautious and leery about Fidel, uncertain about any involvement in Latin America that went beyond their traditional low-key support of indigenous Communist parties. Fidel knew that to pursue the roles he envisioned for Cuba and for himself in the world, he would have to lure the Soviets into an unprecedented relationship with a Third World nation.

Mikoyan's visit in February 1960 was a great success. He received a red-carpet welcome, he toured the country praising the agrarian reform program, and he signed a major trade agreement. The Soviets agreed to lend Cuba $100 million for twelve years at 2½ percent interest and to purchase 425,000 tons of sugar that year and a million tons a year during each of the next four years. Cuba would also sell citrus, animal hides, and other minor commodities to the Soviets. In return, Russia would supply oil, fertilizer, steel, iron, and various other essential commodities, as well as provide technicians to help build new factories and replace the expertise of those who had fled to the United States. The Cubans raised the question of arms, but no mention of it was made in the official statements.

In what in retrospect seems a curiously naive hope that the private sector could still work out an accommodation with Fidel, the Cuban Association of Industrialists gave a banquet for Mikoyan.

By showing that he could go elsewhere for economic support, Fidel had made a fundamental symbolic statement about Cuba's new independence from the United States, a move unprecedented for a nation in the Western hemisphere. This step was immensely popular with the average Cuban, who saw it as a beginning of the fulfillment of the dream of true independence that had inspired José Martí. At a practical level, it also meant that Fidel now had the financial security to permit him to escalate the attenuation of Cuba's dependence on the United States without undue concern about the economic consequences.

Fidel involved himself totally with the revolution. Having overcome his reluctance to run the government, he was now doing so with a vengeance. But he governed in the same style that he used when planning the revolution and leading the fight in the mountains. It would still be, according to Núñez Jiménez, several years before Fidel could comfortably sit at a desk and behave as a traditional administrator. He was always on the move, traveling from one end of the country to the other, involving himself directly in the detailed implementation of projects, and making decisions on the spur of the moment as problems arose. He and the revolution were one. Wherever he went, he was accessible to people at every level, and always managed to communicate a sense of shared struggle whether it was against imperialism or the problems of inefficiency and incompetence that were plaguing the revolution.

He worked immensely hard, with few other real interests in his life. Unlike other leaders, who see power as an opportunity for personal aggrandizement or a luxurious lifestyle, Fidel's existence continued to be marked by austerity. He often participated in baseball games, but even that was in part a political exercise. As had been his pattern since he was in Mexico, he rarely slept in the same place two nights in a row, rotating instead among the twenty-second floor of the Habana Libre, the small duplex apartment in Vedado where Celia Sánchez lived with her sister, and a house he had received as a present from a wealthy admirer in the suburb of Cojímar. Celia had filled the apartment with furniture brought from her parents' home, including transporting a large elegant double bed. Fidel kept a rowing machine, dumbbells, and other weight-lifting equipment there and worked out regularly. Fidel's need to sleep in different places was a legitimate security measure and was affected by the fact that he frequently worked all night. However, it also gave him a degree of freedom from everyone around him, including Celia. He had no time for frivolity and he rarely drank except for an occasional cognac or when social protocol demanded. He once described alcoholism as "a vice worse than all others combined." Among his few indulgences, if it can be considered such, was his persistent passion for double corona Montecristo cigars.

In most respects, Fidel had a very conservative moral outlook. Life, he believed, was always to be taken seriously. He emphasized hard work, family values, integrity, and self-discipline. Alcohol, drugs, gambling, and prostitution he regarded as major evils.

Rarely was Celia not with him. In her view, Fidel was a national treasure and she was his guardian. She would point to the death of Martí at a crucial moment in the independence struggle, which might have doomed its success. As she saw it, her destiny in the history of Cuba was to insure that nothing happened to deprive this revolution of its leader. As Fidel intensified his grip on Cuba, so Celia intensified her grip on Fidel. As with Dr. Vexel-Robertson, she made sure that no one else was going to become the number-one woman in Fidel's life. She continued to serve as manager, wife, secretary, confidant, adviser, and protector rolled into one. She has been described as having a passion for paperwork, not in a bureaucratic sense, but as someone superbly organized. It was only through her diligent efforts and follow-through that many of Fidel's ideas became reality. She controlled all access to Fidel, yet by most reports, although from time to time she changed her telephone number, she remained available to an astonishing number of people. She also had a reputation for deep compassion. One old-line Communist said of her, "If I believed in Christianity I would say that she came as close to sainthood as anyone on earth." She was always ready to listen to someone with problems or find a bed in Havana for a stranded peasant they had known in the Sierra Maestra. At the same time, like the "gatekeepers" around any powerful person, she had her detractors, who felt she was overly possessive of Fidel. However, no one, not even Celia, could dictate to Fidel and make him do anything he did not want to do.

Notwithstanding his relationship with Celia, Fidel had become a sex symbol of astonishing proportions, even to ordinary Cuban women. When a newspaper photo showing him skin diving revealed that he had skinny legs it was a minor sensation, but it only temporarily dented the image.

During this period, Fidel was widely rumored to have had one other romantic entanglement. He invited the widow of former Colombian presidential candidate Jorge Gaitán, assassinated during Fidel's trip to Colombia in 1948, to come to Havana with her daughter as his guest. It was widely whispered that during the several weeks that the two women were in Cuba, Fidel had an affair with the daughter, Gloria.

The men friends with whom he relaxed were not those who served directly under him in the government. His two closest friends over the years were Pepin Naranjo, the mayor of Havana, and René Vallejo, an American-trained surgeon who was his personal physician. They would spend hours together playing dominoes. As with all his endeavors, it was a game he always played to win.

Fidel later acquired a white wooden ranch house with many bedrooms and a porticoed veranda on the Isle of Pines. He would go there to relax, to fish, and to go skin diving. He also, from time to time, went trout fishing in different parts of the country.

Relations with the United States continued in a fitful decline. Fidel made several gratuitous personal attacks on Bonsal, and the U.S. Senate passed a bill authorizing President Eisenhower to cut the Cuban sugar quota, a move interpreted in Havana as "an act of aggression." Exile attacks from bases in Florida increased and valid claims by the United States government that they were exceedingly hard to stop were ridiculed in Cuba.

On March 4, 1960, a French merchant vessel, the *Coubre*, bringing seventy-six tons of Belgian rifles and grenades, blew up in Havana harbor, killing seventy-five people and injuring two hundred others. It was reminiscent of the explosion of the *Maine* sixty years earlier, and Fidel lost no time in drawing the parallel and in denouncing the tragedy as an act of sabotage in which the United States was implicated. Although suspicions existed at the time, there has never been any hard evidence produced proving that it was not an accident. It is believed in Cuba today that an explosive device was placed on board in Belgium by Cuban exiles with CIA support. In any case, it provided an opportunity for Fidel to give one of his classic speeches rallying the people of Cuba behind the revolution and against the threat of outside intervention. The destruction of the *Coubre* has often been referred to as the event that ended any possibility of a reconciliation between the United States and Cuba. But there is little reason to think it was anything other than another milestone on a preordained path which, at least from Fidel's standpoint, he had long since decided to take. In a heated speech following this event, Fidel first used the phrase "*Patria o muerte.*"

On March 18, 1960, Yugoslavia signed a trade agreement with Cuba, and on April 1, Poland did the same. The Chinese were also taking a special interest in Cuba. The character of the Cuban revolution was far closer to the Chinese than the Soviet experience, and while the Sino-Soviet split was still at an incipient stage, the Chinese were eager to build ideological alliances wherever they could. On April 22, a delegation headed by the secretary-general of the Chinese trade unions arrived in Havana, and among other developments an agreement was reached to start a new Chinese-language newspaper for Cuba's not inconsiderable Chinese population.

In a belated gesture, the United States government launched an active initiative to try to control the illegal activities of the exile groups, and even offered Cuba, through informal channels, the possibility of planes and radar to help them intercept exile aircraft. There was an implication that the initiative might lead to a new round of talks to resolve differences. But for both sides it was a charade; each was now committed to a course of enhanced confrontation. On March 17, 1960, President Eisenhower acceded to the long-standing pressure from the Joint Chiefs of Staff and Vice President Nixon, and accepted a recommendation from the CIA that they be authorized to begin training and arming a Cuban exile force.

By coincidence, the same day, Rufo López Fresquet decided to resign. He was worn down by his repeated inability to exert any meaningful influence over the management of the Cuban economy and the evidence that he had become ideologically isolated in the government. The final straw was Fidel's rejection of the informal offer by the United States to reestablish a dialogue in which Lopez had been an intermediary.

On May 7, 1960, Cuba formally reestablished relations with the Soviet Union. As ambassador to Moscow, Fidel made an interesting choice, Faure Chomon. As a leader of the Directorio, Chomon had not only not been an intimate of Fidel, he had been part of a group that rejected his strategy for overthrowing Batista. He had been anti-Communist, but after the success of the revolution had embraced communism with the particular fervor of a new convert. His loyalty to Fidel was now total, but he was not considered a high-level figure in the government. By the appointment, Fidel suggested that he was sending someone he personally trusted whose ideology Moscow could not complain about, but whose stature in the revolution was such that he would not seem to be overstating the importance he attached to the new relationship with the Soviets. Most significantly, he did not send one of the old Cuban Communists with whom the Soviets would certainly have felt most comfortable.

Chapter Ten

As a student in 1949, Fidel read *For Whom the Bell Tolls* and proposed to a friend that they go to see Ernest Hemingway at his Cuban retreat, "Finca Vigia." They never made it, but Fidel continued to be a Hemingway fan, reading all of his books and saying of him, "He has always been my favorite writer." They had much in common. Both were physically oriented men of action for whom machismo was a virtue, not to mention their beards and passion for guns and Cuban cigars. That which Fidel admired in Hemingway says much about his own values. He described him as "an adventurer in the genuine sense of the word—something which in itself is beautiful because it speaks of a man who does not conform to the world, and who assumes the duty to change it. A genuine adventurer has to break with conventions and launch himself into adventure, quickly learning if he does not know it already. He will not remain unharmed: mutation is inevitable and is part of the risk which one has to accept from the start." Fidel saw a lesson for Cuba in Hemingway's books. "We also have been vulnerable and exposed to destruction for decades. . . . Hemingway was right; a man can be destroyed, but never beaten. For us that was the message of his books."

Hemingway remained in Cuba after 1959 as a supporter of the revolution. On May 15, 1960, Fidel and Ernest Hemingway met for the first and only time. Escaping for two days from the swirl of events that were engulfing Cuba, Fidel competed in the Ernest Hemingway Annual Fishing Contest, winning the overall individual prize. It was presented to him by Hemingway.

That same month, Fidel appointed Che director of the National Bank. Trade agreements were signed with the Soviets marking an important milestone on the road to making Cuba a full Socialist state. There were no longer opponents at any significant level in the government, and those in the private sector who did disagree with Fidel were either preparing to leave the country or joining secret underground movements plotting his overthrow. Che had a clear picture of the type of economic structure he felt needed to be created in Cuba. He was also a careful and methodical planner and administrator. Unfortunately, he was involved in innumerable unrelated activities, particularly in the international arena, and the pace of nationalization that he and Fidel insisted on produced a management nightmare that would have defeated even the most experienced team of administrators.

The pace of events began to quicken significantly. On May 23, 1960, the regime notified three of the major international oil companies with refineries in Cuba—Texaco, Royal Dutch, and Standard Oil—that they would be required henceforth to refine six thousand barrels of Soviet crude oil a day. After hurried consultations with the U.S. State Department, they refused on the spurious grounds that it would be damaging to Venezuela, the current source of Cuba's oil. Left to themselves, they would probably have reluctantly agreed to the Cuban demand, but Washington, seeing what it thought was an opportunity to put a crippling economic squeeze on Cuba, encouraged the companies to refuse. The State Department knew that the Soviet Union did not have the tankers to ship sufficient oil to meet Cuba's needs if the refineries were seized, and believed that pressure could be put on the independent tanker owners not to lease their vessels for the purpose. At the end of June, Fidel signed an order requiring the oil companies to refine Soviet oil or be expropriated. Within days they were taken over by the government. The independent tanker owners proved much more interested in earning a handsome profit than collaborating in any scheme to suffocate the Cuban economy.

On July 6, President Eisenhower reduced the Cuban sugar quota by seven hundred thousand tons. On July 9, in a move that was patently in preparation for a complete nationalization of all U.S.-owned property, six hundred companies were required by the Cuban government to submit sworn statements showing their operating records and inventories. Two U.S. diplomats were expelled as counterrevolutionaries.

Then, Khrushchev announced that the Soviet Union would be willing to purchase the seven hundred thousand tons of sugar that the United States had refused. He also warned that the Soviet Union would stand with Cuba in the event of United States aggression. He spoke of Moscow's ability to flatten the United States with rockets, but qualified the statement by adding that he was speaking "figuratively." It was a statement similar to one he had made in private a month earlier to Núñez Jiménez. In Cuba, however, his pledge was taken literally. Che in particular seized on the statement to say in a speech the following day, "Cuba is a glorious island in the middle of the Caribbean protected by the rockets of the mightiest power in history." Fidel, hospitalized briefly with pleurisy and an intestinal infection, made a televised statement from his bed assuring the Cuban people that the Soviet commitment to defend them with rockets was in fact a literal commitment of rocket power. This was hardly the reaction Khrushchev had wanted, and he learned the lesson that the Cubans had a tendency to take every statement at face value, not concerning themselves too much with the nuances of diplomatic language.

In late August 1960, the OAS met in San José, Costa Rica. Secretary of State Christian Herter sought to get a resolution passed that would condemn Cuba by name as a threat to the hemisphere. Instead, the cautious foreign ministers of the Americas approved, with only Cuba voting against, a resolution that condemned intervention in the region, "even when conditional, from an extra-continental power," and declared totalitarian states to be inconsistent with the traditional system of the hemisphere. Washington was disappointed that they had failed to get Cuba labeled by name, but in Havana, Fidel expressed outrage at the "Declaration of San José."

On September 2, 1960, a crowd of at least a half million people gathered for what Fidel described as a "Plenary Assembly of the Cuban People." The people of Cuba, he declared, had done nothing more than break their chains. They in no way deserved the condemnation of the "Declaration of San José." Throwing down the gauntlet before the United States, he announced that Cuba would establish diplomatic relations with China and would accept the Soviet Union's offer of missiles to repel a United States invasion (implying again that it was a literal offer). It was another in what was becoming a long string of virtuoso performances. Some felt it was the best speech he had ever given. He presented to the crowd his proposals, together with a call to the other nations of Latin America to join Cuba in throwing off their ties to the United States, as the "First Declaration of Havana." There was a deafening roar of approval. The event exemplified Fidel's concept of "direct democracy"; for him it meant having a referendum on every major issue. However, his instinctual awareness of what would appeal to the Cuban sense of nationalism or fairness, and his ability to use his speaking skills to win them over to almost any course of action, meant that he could always be secure in the knowledge that the majority of the people were behind him.

On September 18, 1960, Fidel departed for New York and the United Nations General Assembly. In the less than two years since coming to power, his name had become a household word around the globe. Whether revered or hated he was as widely known as any leader in the world. Such had been his ability to project Cuba onto the world scene that despite his nation's tiny size, he was arriving at the U.N. with a stature that already put him on a par with the long-established leaders of the Third World: Tito, Nasser, Nehru, and Nkrumah, all of whom he would be meeting for the first time. He would also meet with Nikita Khrushchev.

Celia had arrived earlier to rent a house and make other arrangements, but it turned out there was no way the location of the house could be kept secret from the press, nor could its security be guaranteed. Arrangements were then made for the entourage to stay at the Shelburne Hotel, but the hotel insisted on payment in advance. Fidel went into a fury and announced that his delegation would camp on the grounds of the United Nations. Then, in a moment of great inspiration he decided instead to move to the Hotel Theresa at 125th Street and Seventh Avenue in Harlem. It was a dramatic gesture to show his egalitarianism, but also an act of showmanship that guaranteed him center stage throughout his stay. The United States government, beset with racial problems across the South, was at a loss how to respond to this blatant gesture and so kept a discreetly low profile.

Nikita Khrushchev came to New York with a sense of anticipation of his meeting with Fidel. His comments to colleagues on the *Baltica*, in which he sailed to New York, suggest that he was quite preoccupied with the unique potential Cuba presented the Soviet Union within its never-ending chess game with the United States. In his dealings with the Soviet Union, Fidel was lucky in several respects. It was only in the late 1950s that the Soviet Union had become self-sufficient in oil and then a net exporter. Had the attack on Moncada succeeded and had he come to power six years earlier, there would have been no way for the Soviet Union to keep the Cuban economy afloat, and he would not have been able to embark on his independent course from the United States. In addition, Khrushchev was a maverick among Soviet leaders, willing to take the kind of gamble with Cuba that probably no leader before or since would have been willing to risk. There would, moreover, emerge a mutually rewarding personal relationship between the two men that would tie together the destiny of their two nations in a way that more objective geopolitical considerations could never have done.

The Soviet leadership had early been skeptical of Fidel and his revolution. Marxist theory made no provision for the creation of a Socialist state that was not the product of the organization of the masses through the work of the Communist Party. In addition, Fidel, since coming to power, had repeatedly said he was not a Communist, and only a year earlier, at the United Nations, Raúl Roa had adamantly aligned Cuba not with the United States or the Soviet Union, but with the emerging Third World bloc. "Cuba refuses to choose between capitalism, under which people starve to death, and communism, which solves economic problems but suppresses liberties that are so dear to mankind," Roa said in his address to the General Assembly. Of course, what had given the Soviets greatest pause was that they had always accepted Latin America as so

207

completely within the United States sphere of influence that their prospects there seemed negligible. At a time when Khrushchev was working hard to improve relations with the United States, he could easily jeopardize those efforts by meddling in America's own backyard.

Who knew if Fidel's revolution would survive? If the United States decided to invade, as seemed increasingly possible, Fidel could not hope to win militarily in the long run, and Soviet prestige would be seriously damaged if they had too visibly embraced him. They were also reluctant to assume too great a financial burden. But most of all, they did not want to accept a military obligation six thousand miles from home that held the potential for a major confrontation with the United States. While Fidel was trying at breakneck speed to turn Cuba into a Socialist state, in part to convince the Soviets of his ideological affinity with them, they were hoping that he would instead follow the type of model adopted by Nasser in Egypt. The Soviet Union wanted the friendship of Third World nations, wanted them to provide whatever natural resources they had, and to side with the Soviets in disputes with the Capitalist world. In return, they were willing to provide a certain amount of technical and financial aid. The Soviets wanted countries like Egypt to be "on the road to socialism," but not to become full-fledged Socialist states, which Marxism anyway told them was impossible at this stage of underdevelopment. Besides, if they acknowledged a Third World country as truly a Communist state, the Soviets felt they would have to accept it as a full member of the Socialist club and bring it entirely under their own economic and defense umbrella. Their acceptance only of Socialist states contiguous with their borders added to the overall security of the Soviet Union, their primary foreign policy concern. Involvement with Third World countries, unless precisely calculated, offered the potential for obligation, liability, and risk.

It was a world view that did not take into account the unusual character of Nikita Khrushchev. Khrushchev, by far the most unconventional and flamboyant leader the Soviets have produced, came from a peasant background. He was action oriented, with great cunning and an instinct for the use of power. Ideological and administrative concerns took a back seat to his fascination with the manipulation of global forces on the world stage. Reflecting the sense of national inferiority that seems always to have afflicted Russians in their dealings with the West, he was obsessed with the notion that the world should accept the Soviet Union as the second great power on a par with the United States. He saw his trip to America in 1959, the first by a Soviet leader, as an acknowledgment of that equality. Yet he was constantly looking for ways to outmaneuver or gain advantage over the United States, and in that context he saw Cuba as offering an extraordinary opportunity, one that more conventional Soviet leaders might have been too cautious to touch.

Fidel and Khrushchev first met in the General Assembly chamber, when Khrushchev, in an unprecedented gesture for the leader of a great power, walked over to where the Cuban delegation was seated to shake the hand of the Cuban prime minister, thirty years his junior. Later, despite contrary advice from others in the Soviet delegation and the U.S. Secret Service, Khrushchev drove to the dilapidated Hotel Theresa to meet with Fidel, rather than asking him to come to the Soviet Mission. If Fidel could show he was a man of the people by staying in such a place, he too was a man of the people and was not above going there. Later, Fidel did make a return visit to Khrushchev at the Soviet Mission.

The rapport between the two men was instantaneous despite the wide differences in their ages and cultural backgrounds. Both had a strong sense of identification with the rural populations of their countries, both were men of impulse and action, both had an irreverence for traditional diplomacy and protocol, and both recognized in each other the qualities of enormous self-confidence and powerful leadership that had allowed them to acquire their respective positions. Khrushchev was perhaps the first political leader Fidel had met whom he could not immediately outwit or outmaneuver and for whom he had profound respect. Khrushchev saw in the younger man a protégé of great potential, and already began to look on the relationship as that of father and son. Fidel told Khrushchev that he wanted close ties with the Soviet Union, and then, referring to the CIA attempts to train and arm exile groups in the U.S., he asked Khrushchev to provide him with military aid to defend Cuba.

Khrushchev was delighted with the meeting. He had come to the conclusion, he later told his colleagues, that contrary to the fears of skeptics, Fidel would be a good Communist. Then he added, "Castro is like a young horse that hasn't been broken. He needs some training, but he's very spirited—so we will have to be careful." It was by coincidence an interesting choice of simile. In Cuba, Fidel was known by friend and foe alike as "the horse."

Following Khrushchev's example, both Nasser and Nehru made the trip uptown to the Theresa to see Fidel. Fidel had a little memento made of alligator skin, which he presented to Nasser, adding apologetically that he was embarrassed to give him something made of alligator when there must be alligators all over Egypt. Nasser replied that they had only two and they were both in the zoo. Later, commenting privately on his positive reaction to Fidel, he expressed his amusement that he should think Egypt still beset with wild crocodiles.

Fidel's speech to the General Assembly was more remarkable for its length—four and a half hours, a record for that body—than for its content. He repeated many of his previous criticisms of the United States, making, like Roa, a particular appeal for support from the Third World. The speech did not get a great deal of public attention, but this was the memorable year when Khrushchev took off his shoe and beat it on the table during the speech of a delegate with whom he disagreed. It was one of the rare occasions when Fidel was upstaged.

Fidel returned to Havana on September 28, 1960, in a Soviet airliner, borrowed when his own plane was seized by the U.S. courts against outstanding Cuban debts. Unlike his previous visit to the United States, this trip did little to improve the average citizen's image of Fidel. No longer did the press use the honorific title "doctor" generally applied to lawyers in Latin America. Instead, he was treated as a dangerous eccentric who posed a serious threat not only to the security of the United States, but to the moral welfare of her citizens. That he should smoke cigars in a confident, assertive way seemed an arrogant gesture, inconsistent with the generally more humble deportment customary of Latin American leaders visiting the United States. Middle-class America was more than ever fixated on his beard, which for them symbolized radical, subversive thinking. In their eyes, it showed contempt for every value that they held dear and that they had defined for themselves as American. The irrational hatred bred a plethora of jokes and vicious jibes, including the question whether if Fidel was overthrown his beard should be shaved off before he was hanged.

In other respects the trip was a major success. Fidel had established a firm relationship with Khrushchev that provided the base for the economic survival of Cuba. There was also the promise of Soviet military aid. Fidel had also been accepted as a world figure of significant stature, especially by the leaders of the developing nations.

Meanwhile, plans by the United States government to overthrow Fidel were proceeding slowly but relentlessly. The plot against him had begun on January 18, 1960, at a meeting in the office of Colonel J. C. King, the chief of the CIA's Western Hemisphere Division. One of the dozen men present at the meeting was the CIA station chief from Caracas who had witnessed Fidel's mesmerizing effect on the Venezuelan population during his triumphant visit there a year earlier. He had sent King a memo warning that a Latin leader with this degree of charismatic appeal posed a serious potential problem for the United States.

In the meeting that day at CIA headquarters, it was proposed that a force of thirty Cuban exiles, at that point most likely former Batista supporters, be trained in Panama to provide the nucleus for a counterrevolutionary movement in Cuba. The majority of those present had been key players in orchestrating the 1954 overthrow of President Arbenz in Guatemala. The success of that operation had led to a special meeting with President Eisenhower at the White House, where he expressed his appreciation for the efficiency, professionalism, and swiftness with which they had accomplished their mission. The gain had been substantial, the cost low, and the awareness of the public minimal. The happy "Guatemala model" remained foremost in everyone's mind.

The senior CIA official to whom King reported was Richard Bissell, deputy director for plans. Bissell was to adopt the entire Cuban project with an evangelical fervor, sustaining it against those—including President Kennedy—who doubted its wisdom, by overwhelming them with his wealth of knowledge and intellectual acumen. His deep emotional investment, even obsession, with the overthrow of Fidel may well have derived from the fact that they were remarkably similar men. Both were of commanding physical stature (six foot three), boundless energy, formidable strength of character, unusual intellectual ability, and natural leaders with a limitless capacity for self-discipline and faith in their own beliefs and values. For Bissell, Fidel represented a truly worthy adversary for his own well-developed talents.

Under Bissell's skillful guidance, a four-point plan of action had worked its way past CIA director Allen Dulles through the National Security Council, arriving on the President's desk on March 17. The plan, which Eisenhower approved, called for: (1) the creation of a "responsible and unified" government in exile; (2) "a powerful propaganda offensive"; (3) "a covert intelligence and action organization" in Cuba responsive to the exile opposition; and (4) "a paramilitary force outside Cuba for future guerrilla action." On August 13, Eisenhower approved a $13 million budget for the project.

What was not included in the paper that went to the President was any mention of Bissell's counterpart strategy—a plan to assassinate Fidel.

From the beginning, a recurrent obstacle to Bissell's overall strategy was the recalcitrant behavior of the different exile factions. The only thing they had in common was their antipathy to Fidel. It reflected considerable naiveté to think that that alone would be enough to overcome the deep divisions among them that grew out of the previous thirty years of Cuban politics. The problem was compounded by the curious choice of individuals selected to serve as the CIA's liaison with the group. German-born Gerry Droller (also known as Frank Bender), spoke no Spanish and knew next to nothing about Latin America. He spoke English with such a thick accent that even his Cuban interpreter had difficulty understanding him. His colleague, Howard Hunt, later of Watergate fame, spoke Spanish but lived in a fantasy world of unnecessarily exaggerated and artificial intrigue.

211

A colleague said of Hunt, "His judgment is consistent—always wrong."

Eventually, in May 1960, the Democratic Revolutionary Front was formed and was provided with an office and staff at CIA expense. In July, Manuel Artime, former Prío associates Tony Varona and Aureliano Sánchez Arango, and José Miró Cardona as representatives of the Front were taken to the Democratic National Convention in Los Angeles to meet the party nominee, John F. Kennedy.

A fifty-kilowatt transmitter was set up on Great Swann Island off the Honduran coast, and it started broadcasting propaganda to Cuba from a studio in Miami.

Training of exile recruits was begun at military installations around Miami and on a large, isolated coffee plantation in Guatemala. The entire operation was coordinated out of the same two-story barracks of the largely abandoned Opa-locka Air Force Base used for the 1954 Guatemala project.

The sounds of military orders in Spanish, gunfire, and the loose tongues of the recruits drew the attention of the *Miami Herald*, which was able to piece together during August and early September a detailed and accurate picture of the supposedly secret project. It was, however, an era when the press was a good deal more pliant than it is today, and Allen Dulles was able to get the story killed.

On October 30, 1960, however, Clemente Marroquín Rojas, a Guatemalan journalist, published in the newspaper *La Hora* a story disclosing that a military base costing more than $1 million had been constructed by the CIA near Retalhuleu to train an invasion force of Cuban exiles. It was a month before the report appeared in the United States media—in *The Nation*—and three months before a story ran in *The New York Times*.

Bissell's assassination initiative was following its own bizarre course. Originally, efforts of the CIA's Technical Services Division were focused on ways to undermine Fidel's remarkable appeal with the Cuban people. Plans, unbelievable in retrospect, were made to spray a television studio where he was to appear with a hallucinogenic drug, and to impregnate a cigar he would be tricked into smoking with a similar substance. There was even a scheme to dust his shoes, when he sent them to be cleaned, with thallium, which when inhaled was supposed to cause his beard to start falling out. Later, a box of cigars was impregnated with botulism toxin. All of these farfetched ideas were abandoned at an embryonic stage.

The euphemism "eliminate" was widely used in CIA discussions in order to leave vague, for those who wished to see it that way, whether actual killing or merely some manner of incapacitation was proposed. For Colonel Sheffield Edwards, director of the Office of Security, however, there

212

was no question about the ultimate objective. He assigned James O'Connell, a former FBI agent, the job of recruiting Mafia contacts who would carry out the assassination. The mob, it was reasoned, would be highly motivated to see Fidel overthrown so that they could restore their highly lucrative gambling and prostitution operations in Cuba. Furthermore, they had maintained their contacts with members of the Cuban underworld still remaining in Havana, whom it was hoped they could persuade to carry out the actual assassination. This, it was argued, would distance the event still further from an agency of the United States government. As a middleman to deal with the Mafia, O'Connell hired Robert Maheu, a Washingon "consultant" and operator who had done occasional jobs for the CIA in the past, but who was increasingly involved with his primary client, Howard Hughes.

Maheu set up a meeting in early September with Johnny Rosselli, a senior mob figure, and offered him $150,000 plus expenses for the successful assassination job. Rosselli accepted, but he insisted on meeting with someone from the CIA to verify that this was indeed a "national security" venture for the United States government. On September 14, Maheu and Rosselli had lunch with O'Connell at the Plaza Hotel in New York, by coincidence only a few days before Fidel was to arrive in the city for the meeting at the United Nations.

Reassured that he was involved in a legitimate government operation, and sensing the potential for an unprecedented quid pro quo to protect mob activities from government interference in the future, Rosselli recruited into the venture Sam "Momo" Giancana, the Mafia chief in Chicago, and Santos Trafficante, the former underworld king in Havana.

Although unaware of the CIA-Mafia plot against him, Fidel had inevitably given some thought, as do all national leaders in a volatile political climate, to the overall threat of an assassination attempt. He correctly assumed that a paid assassin, eager to escape with his own life to enjoy the fruits of his deed, would be unwilling to take any undue risks to kill him. The ideological fanatic, on the other hand, he could probably not do anything to guard against anyway. His staff, especially Celia, took all reasonable precautions to protect him, but he shrugged off the threat. Like many potential targets of assassination, he did not intend to let this concern interfere with his constant mingling with the ordinary citizens. In fact, that was a situation in which he was probably particularly safe from the kind of danger Rosselli and his people posed.

The CIA envisioned that Rosselli would organize a Chicago-style killing, perhaps with blazing machine gun fire from speeding automobiles. But, as Fidel surmised, they could find no one willing to take such a risk, and resorted instead to trying to persuade various individuals who had occasional contact with Fidel to slip lethal poison, provided by the CIA, into his food and drink. Weeks went by as one dubious scheme after another fell on its face.

Later, Fidel would complain to Senator George McGovern that there had been twenty CIA-sponsored attempts on his life. Former CIA director William Colby says he was aware of only five in which the CIA was directly involved.

In the United States presidential race, Cuba had suddenly become the central issue, with polls showing the American people far more hostile toward Fidel than toward Khrushchev. John Kennedy, eager to refute the charge that he was "soft on communism," and unaware of the plans already underway, issued a statement on October 19 calling for aid to be given to Cuban exiles to launch a counterrevolutionary movement to overthrow Fidel. In the subsequent presidential debate, Vice President Nixon, frustrated by the fact that he could not reveal his knowledge about the administration's initiative, labeled Kennedy's suggestion "the most shockingly reckless proposal ever made . . . by a presidential candidate."

With both the Cuban and U.S. governments now aware that an invasion seemed inevitable, there was little motivation to seek real solutions on the diplomatic front, and relations continued to unravel. On October 13, 1960, Eisenhower placed a ban on exports to Cuba with the exception of medicine and some foodstuffs. The following day, INRA took over 382 private businesses, including most banks. Two Canadian banks were exempted, a result in part of the cordial reception Fidel had received on his 1959 trip to Canada and of Canada's more moderate reaction to Cuba's revolution. On October 25, an additional 166 U.S.-owned companies were seized, including Coca-Cola and Sears Roebuck.

Fidel, however, had another problem, which had been growing steadily over the previous several weeks. Various opposition groups had taken up arms in the Escambray mountains and had created the nucleus of a potentially serious guerrilla movement. Numbering more than a thousand at their peak, the leaders included several former Directorio and 26 of July figures. The presence of this guerrilla movement gave encouragement to underground forces in Havana, especially those led by former minister Manuel Ray, who saw the potential for orchestrating against Fidel the same strategy that had toppled Batista. If the CIA ever had a realistic hope of overthrowing Fidel it might have been through support of this movement. But the CIA had little understanding of it and was already too preoccupied with its exile invasion force and its own network of counterrevolutionaries to consider any alternatives.

The uprising in the Escambray proved to be a prolonged problem that would flare up repeatedly between 1960 and 1965. Fidel ordered fifty thousand militia fighters mobilized from the cities. They attempted to quarantine the rebels, cutting them off from food supplies and contact with the local population. The efforts at suppression were relatively successful, but as new recruits disillusioned with the regime fled to the mountains, the replenished forces regrouped and launched new attacks.

In the final days of 1960, Fidel's greatest need was to obtain arms and make preparations to repel what now seemed an inevitable invasion, occurring perhaps even before Eisenhower left office. The people's militia, which had been formally launched several months earlier, was being urgently trained, but they needed time and weapons. The creation of the militia was particularly important because despite the indoctrination program launched by Raúl and Che, Fidel could not fully trust the military.

Every effort was made to use the evidence of the impending invasion to persuade the Soviets to increase the quantity and speed the delivery time of their arms supplies. Che, on another worldwide tour, was in Moscow on November 7, 1960, standing with Khrushchev atop Lenin's tomb during the parade celebrating the anniversary of the Bolshevik Revolution. He vehemently pressed Cuba's cause.

It was not until November 17 that Kennedy, as president-elect, received a full briefing from Allen Dulles on the invasion plans. Kennedy had misgivings right from that moment, but he was somewhat compromised because the plan was almost exactly what he had proposed in the overheated rhetoric of the campaign.

Ambassador Bonsal had returned to Washington for consultations on October 29, 1960, and would not return. On December 16, the United States ended the Cuban sugar quota in the American market. Diplomatic messages and protests flowed between Havana and Washington with great frequency during the next few weeks, but they were merely flutterings in the wind marking the end of the relationship.

The end came on January 2, 1961, when Fidel again addressed a massive crowd celebrating the second anniversary of the triumph of the revolution. A pouring rain did not deter the hundreds of thousands who came to hear him speak. A deafening roar went up as he told them that within forty-eight hours the United States Embassy must reduce its staff to eleven, a number equal to the size of the Cuban delegation in Washington. At that time there were, according to Fidel, more than three hundred in the Embassy, of whom he said 80 percent were spies. "If they want to leave we won't stop them," he shouted to the cheering crowd. Warning that he believed Eisenhower would launch an invasion prior to going out of office, Fidel also called for a general mobilization. The sense of urgency that he conveyed was clearly intended primarily as a message to the Soviets to increase their moral and material support. The Soviet Mission to the

United Nations responded by warning that they, too, believed that the departing administration was continuing to prepare for direct aggression against Cuba. Dozens of "counterrevolutionaries" were arrested, and citizens lined up all over Cuba to give blood for the coming conflict. In an interview in 1964, Fidel would concede, "We share some of the responsiblity for the breakdown in relations with the United States."

The day after Fidel's speech in the rain, the United States severed diplomatic relations with Cuba. However, in his inaugural speech, Kennedy made several statements that seemed to Havana to offer some potential for conciliation. Fidel had been delighted with the defeat of Nixon, for whom he felt only contempt. Despite Kennedy's campaign rhetoric, Fidel saw in the new President a young man not unlike himself who seemed to be open, idealistic, charismatic, and perhaps able to recognize that the world was changing and the United States' role needed to change with it. In addition, Che, when he returned on January 6, carried back a message from Khrushchev that he was planning a major initiative with the new President in the hope of dramatically improving U.S.-Soviet relations. He asked that Havana not do anything to damage that plan. For a brief period there was the hope in both Moscow and Havana that if they cooled the rhetoric Kennedy might junk the Eisenhower invasion plan. So on January 20, 1960, Fidel told forty thousand members of the armed militia that the moment of tension had passed and the country should go back to work. Three days later, Che made a speech in which he said, "There is almost no reason to say *patria o muerte* because the great threat which hung over our *patria* is gone."

It soon became apparent, however, that Kennedy had not abandoned the now well-advanced project, assessing correctly that Khrushchev was not inclined, at this stage, to let Cuba's fate interfere with his larger agenda to improve relations with the United States. Kennedy's advisers were split on the issue, with Arthur Schlesinger fearing that the invasion would create an unnecesarily harsh image for the young President at the beginning of his administration. America's European allies were distinctly cold to the idea, as were the governments of Brazil, Mexico, and Argentina. Senator William Fulbright, chairman of the Senate Foreign Relations Committee, gave Kennedy a lengthy memo advising against the venture. In the final analaysis, whatever his reservations, Kennedy believed himself to be trapped by his campaign rhetoric and felt his credibility could not stand a 180-degree change in his position.

Bissell and his colleagues at the CIA were aggressively pressing their cause, taking advantage of their Ivy League connections to many in the new administration. Bissell's immense self-confidence and encyclopedic knowledge had a steamroller effect on the more experienced but less articulate and politically less well-connected military types who had serious misgivings about the operation. The plan now called for a preemptive air strike to wipe out Fidel's fledgling air force on the ground, the landing of an invasion force of exiled Cubans to secure a stretch of territory in the area known as the Bay of Pigs, and the arrival of the members of the Cuban Revolutionary Council to establish a "liberation government." Finally, there would be a spontaneous uprising of the Cuban people catalyzed by the CIA's underground network of counterrevolutionaries, resulting in Fidel's overthrow. Should the invasion force get into difficulties, the plan called for them to escape to the Escambray mountains, where the CIA would continue to support them as a guerrilla movement.

A vital element in Bissell's overall strategy was the involvement of the United States Air Force to provide air cover for the invasion force. It was this aspect, however, which gave Kennedy greatest pause. Apprehensive about world opinion, he was determined to create the impression that this was entirely a Cuban exile operation, and he wanted no visible involvement by the U.S. military. He therefore reserved the right to defer a final decision on the air cover until the final twenty-four hours before the invasion was scheduled to be launched.

The plan, however, had a fundamental flaw, more important than whether or not air cover was to be provided. Its basic premises were permeated with a profound lack of appreciation of Cuban history, nationalism, and politics, culminating in the extraordinary misperception that the Cuban people would be ready to rise up against Fidel in the event of an invasion by a U.S.-backed military force. Repeated United States interventions in Cuba, beginning at the time of the struggle for independence from Spain, had left a legacy in the minds of most Cubans that made any resistance seem like a holy war, without regard to whether the attack was solely by the United States military or by a U.S.-backed contingent of disgruntled exiles. Even under mediocre leadership, the Cuban people would have risen in nationalistic outrage against such an invading force. With charismatic leadership of the caliber that Fidel provided, as well as the many benefits in health, social services, and land reform that had already been achieved, any reasonable analyst should have predicted that only the most fanatical defense of the nation could be anticipated.

That no Cuban had been involved at any stage in the overall development of the invasion plan, or at any significant level in formulating the military strategy, never struck the group at Langley as a significant problem. Yet in microcosm it reflected the fundamental pathology that had characterized U.S.-Cuban relations for the last one hundred years.

Fidel knew that nothing could so unite the Cuban nation behind him as the threat of a United States–backed attack. Fidel also had not shaken the guerrilla experience, and he remained in his heart a military man. At one level he genuinely looked forward to an armed struggle in which his talents as a military leader would be tested in defending his revolution against the traditional forces of evil that were trying to destroy it. If he won, he would have achieved a feat of astonishing historical significance, holding at bay the world's greatest military power. He and Cuba would enjoy worldwide acclaim. If he lost, perhaps even giving his life, and from comments he made at the time he appears to have considered this possibility, he would still be the nation's greatest hero, his life having paralleled that of José Martí and having died in a heroic way in the defense of the liberty of his homeland.

Although he may have had private thoughts about defeat, Fidel exuded such confidence that he seemed convinced that he could handle any invasion force. His greatest concern continued to be whether sufficient Soviet arms shipments would arrive before the attack, and whether there would be time enough for the Cubans to learn how to use the equipment properly. A handful of Soviet and Czech technicians were training Cubans to use the newly arrived artillery pieces, but the process was going slowly. To speed things up, Fidel proposed that those who had been taught in the daytime should at night teach others what they had just learned. Within a short period, several hundred militiamen acquired proficiency with the big guns, a development that would prove crucial when the invasion came.

Fifty Cuban air force officers were undergoing training in Czechoslovakia. Both Washington and Havana knew that the attack would have to occur before these pilots returned to Cuba and their planes were delivered from the Soviet Union, or the whole battle would be an entirely different proposition.

To try to blunt a growing perception in the region that the United States was regressing to its historic reliance on "gun-boat diplomacy," Kennedy announced on March 17 the unveiling of his Alliance for Progress for Latin America. In the same speech he made a strong attack on Fidel, warning that his revolution would be spread throughout the hemisphere unless the United States helped to deal with the problems of underdevelopment and poverty. The speech was no small irony, as the Alliance for Progress was essentially the proposal Fidel had made two years earlier, which the United States had at the time rejected out of hand.

The Cuban Revolutionary Council continued to be beset by internal squabbles. The CIA representatives, generally more comfortable with the former Batista supporters than with those who had only recently broken with Fidel, found, as with the invasion force itself, that collaboration with such individuals was quite unacceptable to the majority of exile leaders. The ability of the group to offer decisive leadership either individually or

218

collectively was no greater in Miami than it had been when they were in opposition in Havana. Their potential effectiveness was further irrevocably compromised by their exclusion from the planning for the invasion for which they were to serve as the window dressing. The one potentially strong leader, Manuel Ray, Fidel's competent and popular former minister of public works, who had left Havana in November, was opposed by the CIA as too leftist. Gerry Droller said of Ray, "I'll have nothing to do with that goddamned communist." Eventually, when Kennedy insisted that the base of support of the council be broadened, Ray was included. The committee, after repeatedly coming close to disintegration, finally elected José Miró Cardona as its chairman, but he was as ineffectual in that job as he had been as prime minister of Cuba.

Kennedy continued to play down the United States' role in the invasion. At a news conference on April 12, 1961, he said, "There will not be, under any conditions, an intervention in Cuba by the United States armed forces or American civilians." The Revolutionary Council, the members of Brigade 2506 training in Guatemala, and members of the U.S. military and the CIA advising the force assumed that the statement was merely for public consumption and remained convinced that American sea and air power would be backing them throughout the invasion.

On April 14, 1961, the 1,400 members of Brigade 2506, with an arsenal of weapons including tanks and artillery, embarked by sea from Puerto Cabezas in Nicaragua. They were seen off by Nicaraguan dictator Luis Somoza, who admonished them to bring back some hairs from Fidel's beard. Later in the day, Kennedy called Bissell and authorized him to go ahead with the planned air strikes, but to minimize the image of the elephant stamping on the gnat, it was not to be on the scale originally planned. Instead of sixteen B-26s hitting Fidel's air force, only six would be used.

Chapter Eleven

FIDEL spent the night of April 14 at "Point One," the national military headquarters in a two-story villa on Forty-seventh Street in Miramar. He had had little sleep for several days. Everyone on Fidel's staff knew the attack was imminent, and they had been up most of the night because of reports from Oriente Province suggesting that the invasion might be about to take place there. At 6 A.M. on Saturday morning, April 15, two B-26s with Cuban air force markings flew overhead at low altitude.

"What are these planes?" Fidel asked his staff. No one knew, but moments later they began bombing nearby Ciudad Libertad airport at the old Campo Colombia. Soon, reports were coming in of similar attacks on the airfields at San Antonio and Santiago de Cuba. A number of planes were destroyed, an ammunition dump was blown up, and in all about sixty casualties were sustained. This mini–Pearl Harbor was not, however, the knockout blow that was intended. Anticipating such an attack, Fidel had dispersed his planes and used several that were in need of repair and unserviceable as decoys. It also became apparent that he had slightly more planes than the U.S. intelligence sources had credited him with.

One plane that took off from Nicaragua with the others did not engage in the raid, but flew instead to Miami with an engine deliberately feathered by pistol shots. When it landed, the pilot claimed that he was a member of Fidel's air force who had defected after bombing his own airfield. However, he refused to give his real name, and his wife, living in Miami, recognized him on television and tried to reach him by phone. Knowledgeable journalists noticed that his B-26 had a metal nose cone while those in the Cuban air force were made of Plexiglas. His story became even more of a shambles when Miró Cordona, speaking on behalf of the Revolutionary Council in New York, talked of the defection in a way that betrayed the fact that he had prior knowledge of the plan.

Meanwhile, at the United Nations, Raúl Roa blasted the United States for its aggression against his country. U.S. Ambassador Adlai Stevenson, who had been kept completely in the dark by the White House and the CIA, responded, vehemently defending the government's line that the atttack had been mounted by defectors from Fidel's own air force, believing it to be the truth. It was not until Sunday afternoon that he was told that he had been misled and realized that he had been shamelesssly set up by his own government to lie flagrantly to the world. For a man with an exceptional reputation for integrity, it was a devasting blow. Subsequently, the Cuban government showed that the bullets that were fired by the planes had been manufactured in the United States, and produced auxiliary fuel tanks that had been jettisoned, not something a pilot would do immediately after taking off.

With the invasion force still far out at sea, a hiatus followed, during which Fidel ordered the rounding up of all suspected counterrevolutionaries and anyone else even remotely suspected of antigovernment sentiments. Some reports suggest that as many as one hundred thousand individuals may had been detained, including all of the Catholic bishops and many journalists, among them several from North America. The threat of attack had given Fidel the legitimate justification for eliminating all remaining opposition in the country. No one could object to his taking such steps in the name of national security in a time of true crisis. The dragnet did catch most of the 2,500 alleged CIA operatives and collaborators in the country, but the agency had already largely abandoned them as a consequential element in its overall invasion strategy. Despite the past expenditure of considerable time and money and a high level of enthusiasm and dedication on the part of these agents, there was little or no effort to keep them informed or to integrate their activities into the larger plan. This was true even though a popular uprising by the Cuban people had always been a central feature in the arguments put forth for the invasion's success.

On Sunday morning, Fidel spoke at the funeral of seven airmen killed in the attack at Ciudad Libertad. In addressing the crowd of more than ten thousand, he had a tailor-made opportunity to rally the people of Cuba one last time before the forthcoming ordeal. Emotions were running high, and his speech sympathetically reflected the mixture of anger and grief felt by almost every Cuban. It was not hard to turn those emotions into passionate hostility toward the United States. He praised the Soviet Union for its many accomplishments, including the recent launching of cosmonaut Yuri Gagarin to become the first human in space. He was cautious, however, about detailing the extent to which the Soviet Union would actually support Cuba in the coming crisis, nor did he refer to their past implied commitment to defend Cuba. In part he could not afford to jeopardize his credibility by raising expectations about direct Soviet in-

221

tervention only to find that they had let him down. A more important consideration, perhaps, was his confidence that he could handle anything short of an all-out invasion by U.S. troops, and his desire then to achieve credit for the victory without having to share it with the Soviets.

It was the end of the speech that grabbed the attention of the world. In appealing to the populace to defend the revolution, he addressed his remarks to the poor people of Cuba, those of "humble means." "What bothers the United States most is we have made a socialist revolution right under their noses," he asserted. "Workers and peasants, comrades, this is a socialist and democratic revolution of the poor, by the poor, and for the poor." The next day, *Revolución* would carry a banner headline, "Long Live Our Socialist Revolution." The timing of this first public announcement that his revolution was Socialist seemed strange to many. Even Khrushchev later commented, "We had trouble understanding the timing of this statement in regard to the 'Socialist revolution.'" Some have argued that it was a way of appealing for Soviet support through Socialist solidarity. Carlos Rafael Rodríguez, on the other hand, says, "Fidel wanted the people to know what they were fighting for."

Early the following morning, in New York, public relations man Lem Jones issued "Bulletin No.1," ostensibly a statement by Miró Cardona on behalf of the Cuban Revolutionary Council, but in reality drafted by Howard Hunt. The communiqué announced the launching of the invasion and a suppposed uprising by the Cuban people. In fact, the Cuban Revolutionary Council, whose members still believed the attack would not occur until April 27, had been spirited out of New York the night before and taken to the deserted military base at Opa-locka, where they were confined under armed guard. They were stunned and furious when they heard Lem Jones's release in their name over the radio, but their captors refused them contact with the outside world.

The invasion force of approximately fourteen hundred, led by Pepe San Ramon, a professional soldier trained in the U.S. who had been a member of Batista's army, was composed mainly of men from the moneyed families of Cuba. As one observer noted, the financial interests of the brigade included 371,930 hectares of land, 7 factories, 9,666 estates, 10 sugar refineries, 3 banks, 5 mines, and 12 nightclubs. Some members of the force were from more modest backgrounds, and about fifty were black. There were several participants who had been active during the Batista era and were known to have been responsible together for the deaths of several dozen people. This group had been assigned the task, should the invasion succeed, of liquidating the political opposition.

Shortly before dawn on April 17, they landed on two beaches, Playa Girón and Playa Larga, in the narrow Cochinos Bay (the Bay of Pigs),

222

110 miles southeast of Havana. The site had been chosen because it was a sparsely populated stretch of territory with an existing landing strip, and it was isolated from the rest of the island by a treacherous swamp crossed, prior to the revolution, only by two narrow-gauge railways and tricky pathways known only to the local inhabitants. The impoverished charcoal makers who lived in the area were considered incapable of mounting any resistance and, lacking telephones, were unlikely to be able to sound the alarm before an inconspicuous landing was complete and the beach area secured to receive the provisional government in the form of the Cuban Revolutionary Council.

What Bissell and his people did not know was that the area around the Bay of Pigs was one of Fidel's favorite haunts. He knew it like the back of his hand. He came there regularly to fish for trout in the nearby Laguna del Tesoro. He stayed in a little bungalow on what became known as "Fidel's Key." The ruggedness of the area appealed to what he described as his "guerrilla mentality," and the extreme poverty of the people aroused in him sympathetic concern. Soon after the revolution, he decided that he would make the area a model of development for the rest of the country. Three hard-top roads were built across the swamp, and a resort facility was begun with forty-four octagonal bungalows on stilts, each with television and air conditioning. Fidel had been there the previous November to inspect the progress, especially of unit No. 33, where he intended to stay on future visits. Health programs had been started for the local people, including the building of a hospital. One hundred and eighty concrete houses were under construction. A local militia had also been organized. More recently, the region had become a prime target for the adult literacy campaign and two hundred young "alphabetizers" had flooded into the community. Perhaps nowhere in Cuba was the local population more committed to the revolution and to Fidel than in the area around Girón.

Fidel was awakened at Celia's apartment by a telephone call at 1:15 A.M. The militia units at the beaches had warned by microwave transmission that the invasion was taking place shortly before they withdrew. Fidel, understanding that time was of the essence in preventing the invaders from establishing the secure beachhead they needed, took immediate command. Indeed, his character is such that he would have found it impossible to do otherwise under the circumstances. He had his strategy clearly in mind. On the one hand, he needed to slow and frustrate the landing of the supply ships, so that as he brought pressure to bear on the beachhead it would inevitably collapse. On the other hand, he wanted to get his few remaining planes into the air as quickly as possible to prevent them from being destroyed on the ground by what he felt would be an inevitable wave of enemy air attacks.

223

Fidel telephoned José Ramón Fernández, the chief of militia training, and ordered him to take the militia officer candidates from their school at Matanzas to the front. Then, he called the school to put them on alert. Next, he called Captain Enrique Carreras, the pilot of a Sea Fury, one of nine surviving planes. He personally ordered Carreras to fly attack missions against the ships from which the invaders were disembarking. Constantly pacing up and down when he was not on the telephone, Fidel still could not be sure that the Girón landing was the main assault rather than a diversionary ploy. However, as soon as he heard that paratroopers were landing in the area, he was convinced, and ordered his main force units into action. A battalion of the rebel army under the command of Osmani Cienfuegos, brother of Camilo, was already based at the Central Australia sugar mill on the edge of the swamp. With minimal regard for his own safety, he left in a plane for the front, arriving around 3:15 P.M. He set up his headquarters in the administration building of the old sugar mill.

For the other side, things were not going well. The debacle associated with the inept effort to construe the original air attack as the work of Fidel's own pilots had seriously embarrassed the U.S. government. The result was that at the last minute President Kennedy decided to cancel the additional raids that had been planned to coincide with the landing itself. Many argue in retrospect that it was this decision that doomed the mission, but such a conclusion remains open to serious question. The presence of air cover would almost certainly have guaranteed the establishment of a secure beachhead. The council could then have been landed and been officially recognized by the United States as the legitimate government. However, there would still have been no public uprising, and unless Kennedy had been willing to commit U.S. troops—an unlikely prospect—the invaders would have eventually been destroyed in a slow war of attrition.

The first men ashore was a group of five specially trained frogmen led by Grayston Lynch, a retired Special Forces colonel working under contract to the CIA. He was apparently oblivious to Kennedy's public assurances that no American citizen would be involved in any attack on Cuba. On their way to the beach, they struck a coral reef that the aerial photo analysts back at Langley had interpreted as seaweed. As the day went on, this reef became an insufferable obstacle to the quick landing of the men and equipment that was so vital to the success of the mission.

Fidel's decision to use this minimal air force against the ships was paying off. The *Houston* was hit by a rocket and started to sink, still laden with ammunition and fuel. Thirty men drowned as they scrambled to escape the ensuing fire. The *Río Escondido*, containing the bulk of the ammunition, fuel, and medical supplies, was hit by a rocket from a Sea Fury.

It exploded in a massive ball of fire. And inland, many of the paratroopers had missed their drop zone, landing in the swamp and losing much of their equipment and supplies. The remaining supply ships fled out of the range of aircraft, leaving the brigade abandoned and vulnerable on the beaches.

The element of surprise that had always been seen as an essential prerequisite for success had been lost within minutes of the first men hitting the beach.

After twenty-four hours, Fidel had the brigade surrounded by twenty thousand men armed with artillery and tanks. In addition to the regular army units, the Matanzas militia, under the command of his old friend from the university, Flavio Bravo, were slowly closing the noose on the invaders. Fidel still waited apprehensively, wondering what the next move of the United States might be. At the same time, in Washington, Kennedy was informed as he attended a gala White House ball of the plight of the invasion force. Again he refused to authorize a major U.S. air strike, allowing only that six unmarked jets from the carrier *Essex* be used to provide cover for an attack by the brigade's own slow B-26s flying in from Nicaragua. Fidel says that U.S. jets flying "at a great height" attacked one of his columns, inflicting severe casualties. Given the frustration among the military that Kennedy's decision caused, Fidel's statement is quite plausible, although there is no independent corroboration.

The end was now just a matter of time. Although the brigade had superior fire power and was inflicting significant casualties on Fidel's men, they were not being resupplied and their morale ebbed as their ammunition dwindled. It was only uncertainty about the size of the invasion force and some command confusion among Fidel's forces that briefly slowed the counterattack. For forty-eight hours, the remnants of the brigade were battered with artillery as the steadily advancing tanks and infantry squeezed them into a tighter and tighter perimeter. Finally, between 4 and 5 P.M. on April 19, Pepe San Ramon ordered the heavy equipment destroyed, and the remnants of his force to break into small groups and escape however they could. Kennedy had authorized the U.S. Navy to move in and rescue any survivors they might find. But it was too late, and seeing that they would come under heavy artillery fire from Fidel's forces, the ships turned and fled, in so doing perhaps avoiding a major international confrontation.

Estimates vary of the number of casualties in the conflict. The brigade lost eighty men in combat and another thirty or forty in the disembarkation. Official Cuban government figures originally put the government's losses at eighty-seven, although all indications are that the numbers were considerably higher. Some estimates run as high as sixteen hundred killed

225

in combat or from their wounds and another two thousand wounded. Four Americans died.

There was, however, no doubt about who the victors were. Cuba's stature in the world soared to new heights, and Fidel's role as the adored and revered leader among ordinary Cuban people received a renewed boost. His popularity was greater than ever. In his own mind he had done what generations of Cubans had only fantasized about: he had taken on the United States and won. He had broken through an important threshold established by the independence movement at the turn of the century. Those revolutionaries had carried the struggle for liberty only as far as the United States would allow. Then the U.S. had intervened to limit the aspirations for complete independence and to impose their control over the Cubans. The U.S. had tried to do it again, and this time had failed. Fidel had led his people in a catharsis of their fears of the American giant, vindicating the Cuban patriots' hundred years of struggle. The sense of national pride could never have been higher, or the gratitude and reverence for Fidel greater. The spirit of the victory would be nurtured and kept alive so that in later years, whenever a sense of disillusionment with the regime arose, the fires of nationalism could be quickly restoked by reinvoking the memory of the "Victory of Girón."

The prisoners were rounded up in small groups until eventually 1,180 had been captured, including Pepe San Ramon and most of the other leaders of the brigade. They were transported to Havana, where they were generally treated well, except for the three former Batista assassins who were tried and executed, not for their role in the invasion, but for their earlier crimes.

On Thursday, April 20, Fidel appeared on television for four hours. Bars were empty and streets deserted as virtually every Cuban was glued to a television set. He was in his educating mode, providing a detailed history lesson of what had happened in the last week. Illustrating as he went with maps, diagrams, and captured documents, he sought to set indelibly in the minds of his audience the significance of what had occurred. At the same time, he relished the incompetence of the CIA and the "imperialist planners." The imperalist, he said, thinks only in terms of analyzing the inanimate, the weapons, the geography, the tanks, and the planes. The revolutionary, on the other hand, thinks about people, their motivation, their social composition, and their struggle for freedom. In many respects he had put his finger on the shortcomings of the planners in Washington.

In an event that was certainly unique in the annals of war, Fidel arranged for groups of prisoners to appear on television in marathon interrogation sessions with panels of journalists on four successive nights, beginning on Friday, April 21. The session produced a lively give and take, with the

226

prisoners able to vent openly their reasons for participating in the invasion. What emerged was the strange mosiac of backgrounds represented by the members of the brigade and a wide diversity in their motivations for participating. They reflected a mixed bag of idealism and opportunism, as well as some who seemed hardly to know why they were there at all.

On April 26, Fidel assembled one thousand prisoners in a stadium and took them on personally for five hours, with all of Cuba watching on television. Moving among them with microphone in hand like a talk-show host, he tirelessly debated issues of ideology, politics, history, and racial discrimination. Fidel conceded a few points, but overall he was more than a match for the captives. More important, he had shown himself, with his unpredictable and unconventional style, to have been magnanimous and beneficent to his enemies at a time when most other leaders would have been punitive and vindictive.

As he pointed out to one man, "Be honest, surely you realize that you are the first prisoner in history who has the privilege of arguing in front of the whole population of Cuba, and the entire world with the head of a government you came to overthrow." It was this flare for the unusual and original that consistently made it impossible for the international community to ignore Fidel, and forced even his enemies to concede that he was a remarkable leader.

Ultimately, all the brigade members would be returned to the United States in exchange for $53 million worth of food and medicine.

A week later, on May 1, May Day, Cuba jubilantly celebrated its formal status as a self-declared "Socialist state." There would be no elections every four years as prescribed in the 1940 Constitution, Fidel announced, because the revolution was a direct expression of the people, which made the document an anachronism. Now the people voted every day by their support of the revolution.

Fidel's decision to eliminate elections can be seen as motivated by two considerations. First, having achieved with great difficulty total power it was pointless to him, as he saw it, even to go through the motions of sharing it. Second, and perhaps more important, he was extremely eager, because of his desperate need for Soviet economic help, to ingratiate himself as a dedicated Marxist. To have held elections would potentially have called into question the sincerity of his pledge to create a Marxist state. Either way, one cannot escape acknowledging the hypocrisy of his position. He had vehemently attacked Batista for his failure to hold elections and had pursued a revolutionary career only when Batista's coup thwarted his own success at the ballot box. Even at the university, Fidel had championed mass voting of the entire student body as a way of choosing student political leaders.

He also now attacked the Spanish priests for their reactionary influence in Cuba and said that only those who were not counterrevolutionary would be allowed to remain in the country. This move was of particular interest because of the pervasive influence of the church, and especially the role the Spanish priests had played in shaping his own talents and beliefs. He attacked, however, only the institution of the church, not Christianity itself. Ejecting the remnants of Spanish colonial influence was a natural sequel to his armed rejection of the United States. Indeed, most of the Spanish clerics had identified themselves closely with the wealthy and conservative elements in the country. However, the timing of his repudiation of the organized church coincided with his formally embracing the institutions of socialism. It was as though he was meeting an internal need for structure, authority, and an ideology in which to believe by substituting one for the other.

Notwithstanding Fidel's declaration of Cuba as a Socialist state, the Soviets remained circumspect in their May Day message, describing Cuba as a sympathizer but not as a member of the Socialist bloc. The dominant reaction in the Kremlin to Fidel's victory at the Bay of Pigs must have been one of immense relief. Had the outcome been otherwise, they would have been faced with the dilemma of having either to support Fidel directly or admit that all of their talk about defending Cuba had been hollow rhetoric, a situation that would have seriously undercut their credibility in the rest of the developing world. At the same time, the embarrassing setback for the new young American president before the world was a source of unmitigated glee. With Kennedy on the defensive, Khrushchev seemed in an ideal position to press his initiative for a new era of rapprochement with the United States. His greatest desire was to minimize the impact of Cuba on that agenda, and while his government had made a pro forma attack on the United States over the Bay of Pigs invasion, the words were relatively restrained. On April 22, only three days after the end of hostilities, Khrushchev eagerly sought to smooth the waters by saying in a note to Kennedy, "We sincerely wish to reach an agreement with you . . . on disarmament and other problems whose solution would contribute to peaceful coexistence . . . we have no bases in Cuba or any idea of creating them."

Early in June, Khrushchev and Kennedy met in Vienna. With disarmament, Berlin, and other topics dominating the discussions, Cuba was scarcely mentioned. For both sides, it was a problem they would have been happy to see go away. At that stage, the only benefit Cuba could offer Khrushchev was as a pawn in the overall struggle with the United States.

The meeting did, however, have profound consequences in the long run for Cuba. Khrushchev left the encounter having assessed Kennedy as young, inexperienced, and lacking toughness. He was convinced that in an eyeball-to-eyeball confrontation Kennedy would be the first to blink. On the basis of this evaluation of Kennedy, he decided shortly thereafter to install offensive missiles in Cuba, bringing the world as close as it has ever come to global destruction.

During August 1961, a hemispheric economic conference was held at the Uruguayan resort of Punta del Este to develop the guidelines for implementing the Alliance for Progress. Che Guevara led the Cuban delegation in his new role as minister of industry. His posture was remarkably conciliatory. Although Cuba abstained on the vote endorsing the final report of the conference, he pointedly remarked that his country did not want to stand in the way of anything that would improve the quality of life for the two hundred million inhabitants of Latin America. Che's main thrust, however, was a pitch for coexistence. Cuba was willing, he said, to relinquish any aspirations to promote revolution in the region, with the implication that the quid pro quo would be the respect of Cuba's sovereignty as a Socialist state.

The United States failed to respond to the offer, but in a carefully orchestrated minuet a "chance" clandestine meeting was arranged between Che and Richard Goodwin, President Kennedy's closest adviser on Latin American affairs. Che suggested that the U.S. and Cuba negotiate a hijacking agreement, clearly implying that this could be the starting point for broader discussions. Goodwin returned to Washington believing that there was a sincere desire to improve relations. Meanwhile, before returning to Cuba, Che visited two leaders sympathetic to the revolution, President Arturo Frondizi in Argentina and President Jânio Quadros in Brazil. The supposedly secret meetings proved no favor to the hosts. Frondizi was ousted by a military coup seven months later, and Quadros resigned in anger after he was accused of being pro-Communist.

The events associated with the Bay of Pigs invasion had vigorously reshuffled the deck of internal Cuban politics. Fidel had, within a matter of forty-eight hours, been able to eliminate the remaining opposition to his regime. At the same time, he had squarely identified the philosophy of his government as Socialist. Now he no longer had to placate or mollify those who criticized him for being Marxist. Anyone who did not accept the fundamental doctrine he preached was immediately labeled a counterrevolutionary.

But Fidel had a new problem with which to deal. The old-line Communists had always held out the hope that the revolution would take this turn and, biding their time, they had slowly but steadily consolidated their power with the expectation that they would ultimately achieve control following a more traditional Marxist revolutionary pattern. The Organizaciones Revolucionarias Integradas (ORI) had been set up to serve as a united front for all of the revolutionary organizations. But under the skillful maneuvering of party leader Aníbal Escalante, and to a lesser extent Blas Roca, most of the key positions in the organization had been taken over by old-line Communists. The closer the ties to Moscow, the stronger their position seemed to be, but they were always scrupulously careful to accord Fidel the role of ultimate and unquestioned leader.

On December 1, in a televised speech, Fidel announced, "I am a Marxist-Leninist, and shall remain a Marxist-Leninist until the day I die." He explained that he had held these views since his university days but had consciously concealed them so not to jeopardize the success of the revolution. Certainly he had shared many of the idealistic goals of his Communist friends while at the university, but he was certainly not a Communist then in the traditional sense. Making such a declaration now, however, was an effective way of preempting any old-line party member from questioning his right to be the number-one Communist in a Socialist society.

Whether Fidel had all along intended to make the revolution Communist has been a matter of dispute. In 1964, he told Herbert Matthews, "It was a gradual process, a dynamic process, in which the pressure of events forced me to accept Marxism as the answer I was seeking . . . as events developed [after the revolution] I gradually moved into a Marxist-Leninist position, I can not tell you just when."

Sometimes a chance comment says much more than hours of formal statement. As Lee Lockwood was getting up to leave at the end of his exceptional seven hours of interviews with Fidel in 1965, he asked the Cuban leader to autograph a piece of revolutionary money (issued as a fund-raising technique) that he had purchased on the streets of Havana in 1958. As he did so, Fidel commented jokingly, "You better not let anyone in the United States know you contributed to a Communist revolution."

"But I did not know it was going to turn out to be Communist when I bought it," Lockwood replied.

Fidel laughed and handed him the bill. "You know something," he said, "neither did I."

Far more important, though, than the domestic considerations of his irrevocable commitment to socialism was the message that he was clearly trying to send to Moscow. He made a stilted effort in the four-hour speech to set Cuba's revolutionary struggle within a more traditional Marxist framework. But with few similarities between Cuba and the Soviet Union, he was forced to draw on the Chinese example of peasant struggle, a parallel that cannot have been well received in Moscow. He was using a battering ram to try to get through the doors of the Socialist bloc. He remained constantly insecure about the possibility of a new U.S. attack and feared that the Soviets might sacrifice him to their larger agenda with Washington, as they had appeared willing to do during the Bay of Pigs crisis. In addition, Fidel understood as well as anyone in Cuba that the nation's economy was in serious condition and rapidly deteriorating. On July 1, 1962, foodstuffs were rationed for the first time. If he could gain official acceptance into the Socialist bloc, then he would be assured of the military and economic support essential for Cuba's survival. On June 7, the first Soviet technicians arrived in the country, but they were merely a drop in the bucket compared to what was needed.

In late 1961, Fidel had sent Fidelito to school in the Soviet Union, a move that greatly alarmed many of the remaining middle-class parents who feared that their own children might be separated from them and sent away for a Soviet education. Because of his own separation at an early age, Fidel did not seem too concerned about sending his thirteen-year-old son off to a strange country, but he was clearly using Fidelito as a way of building goodwill with the Soviets by showing that he would give them his only son.

The speech was splashed all over the media in the United States, providing smug confirmation to those who had always called Fidel a Communist. But in Moscow, *Pravda*, to Fidel's annoyance, made no mention of his declaration, and the government maintained a stony silence. In January, when the Soviets sent their customary message of congratulations on the anniversary of the revolution, they made no mention of Cuba's socialism, much less Fidel's Marxism-Leninism.

In September 1962, the first summit of nonaligned nations was held in Belgrade. Moscow urged Cuba to participate as a way of trying to push it further into the mold of other developing countries sympathetic to the Soviet Union but not technically Socialist. President Dorticós, rather than Fidel, who did not yet see the potential for involving himself in the organization, headed the Cuban delegation. Cuba was the only country among the twenty-five at the meeting from Latin America, and the respect it was accorded there, on the heels of its humiliation of the United States, was visible testimony to the stature and influence it now enjoyed among the less powerful nations of the world. Following the meeting, President Dorticós went on to Moscow and Peking, receiving in the latter city a warm reception from the Chinese, who were already trying to line up allies in their impending split with the Soviets.

Blas Roca was also in the delegation to Belgrade, and he subsequently went separately to Moscow, where he was welcomed at a meeting by Khrushchev, Aleksey Kosygin, and Mikhail Suslov. Considering that he was no longer secretary-general of the party or a senior figure in the government, the level of his reception was unprecedented. It was clearly based on his long-standing relationship with the Soviets and their feeling that he could give them an honest assessment of what was happening in Cuba, particularly some explanation of Fidel's recent behavior. The role of China in Cuba was a major topic of conversation. At the end of the year, Blas Roca spoke as the official representative of the ORI at the Twenty-Second Congress of the Soviet Communist Party, taking a hard-line pro-Moscow position in the rapidly widening split with Peking.

At an OAS meeting in January 1962, again held in Punta del Este, the United States finally succeeded in getting Cuba expelled from the organization even though most of the larger states—Argentina, Brazil, Mexico, and Chile—abstained.

In February, Fidel disappeared from public view. He was depressed and worn down. Once the euphoria of the Bay of Pigs victory had worn off, he was left with a sea of problems. He had cast off the yoke of the United States, but the possibility of retribution in the form of a new and even more substantial invasion seemed increasingly likely. The Soviet Union, which had given him every encouragement in his break with Washington, was now leaving him dangling in the wind. He had burned most of his bridges in the Western hemisphere and now had been ousted from the OAS. Despite his most urgent entreaties and his public willingness to declare his ideological loyalty to the Socialist world, the Soviets were ignoring him. To make matters worse, the Soviets were increasingly locked in an ideological conflict with the Chinese, in part over the issue of the appropriateness of armed struggle in the Third World. It was an issue over which Fidel would naturally have felt closer to the Chinese, but his priorities were economic and military, areas in which only the Soviets could help him.

In moving old-line Communists into positions of power, he had assured people that they were the only ones who really understood how a Socialist state should operate and that their experience was vital to the country. Now he was finding that he had created a monster as they consolidated a power base that was competing with his own. In addition, despite Fidel's rapport with Khrushchev in New York, Aníbal Escalante and Blas Roca still had the ear of the Kremlin leadership at a time when Moscow was ignoring him.

Domestically, the economy was in a deplorable mess. For the first three years after the revolution, Cubans had lived off the fat in the economy. For a brief time, sugar production had been exceptional and the international price high. Consumption, however, had been maintained at a level far above what could be sustained even without the U.S. embargo. There had been little long-range planning beyond the general commitment to socialism. Cattle had been slaughtered so that those who had never been able to afford meat could enjoy an adequate diet, but little thought was given to how the depleted herds would be replenished. As a symbol of colonial rule, sugar cultivation had been discouraged. Now sugar production had dropped to one of the lowest levels on record, and the production of rice and other foodstuffs was in steady decline. Production was the lowest on the cooperatives. By March 1962, systematic rationing of virtually all consumer goods would be instituted.

The steady flight of the professionals and managers had greatly aggravated the problem. Che had organized the industry of Cuba into fifty large state-owned and state-run businesses, but the lack of trained personnel to operate them meant they were disorganized and failing. Che believed that you ought to be able to convince people to work hard and increase production merely out of their revolutionary zeal and their commitment to the "new society." He believed, as he later wrote, that Cuba could create the "new man," free from the material corruption of traditional Capitalist societies. Others, including the Communists, knew from their own bitter experience that even revolutionaries worked harder for material rewards. In his heart, Fidel wanted to believe that Che was right, but as a hard-nosed pragmatist, he was ultimately forced to accept the view of those who believed in material incentives.

The formal move toward socialism and the rounding up of thousands who had expressed only modest dissent had signaled the beginning of an orgy of initiatives taking the country toward totalitarian orthodoxy. There were campaigns against homosexuals, there were campaigns to rid Cuban art of "counterrevolutionary influences," there were campaigns to induce ideological conformity among writers. The security system under Ramiro Valdés tightened down on the average citizen so that neighbor became suspicious of neighbor, and a pervasive fear began to seep through the society. The Committees for the Defense of the Revolution that existed on every block and would later become important vehicles for ensuring that health and welfare benefits reached all citizens were also instruments of control and intimidation. Innocent individuals would be held without charges for weeks, and when they returned home they found their houses ransacked. Fidel cannot be excused from the ultimate responsibility for these actions. Some of the abuses that occurred were the result of an excess of zeal on the part of officials desperately eager to ingratiate themselves with Fidel. There were several instances in which Fidel intervened to limit extreme abuses. However, he directed the overall drive partly because he seemed to feel that the country's economic woes could be solved by creating a totally disciplined society, and because he seemed determined to show both the Soviets and the Communists in Cuba that he could be more totally Communist than any of them.

There were things of which he could be rightfully proud. The literacy campaign had been an overwhelming success. And while the agrarian reform had moved much more slowly than planned, for many of the poorest people in the countryside, the revolution had meant a significant improvement in their lives.

However discouraged and disillusioned Fidel may have felt, it was hardly the first time he had had to overcome a setback. The only difference was that now he had much more to lose. However, after a brief period of withdrawal, he overcame his despondency and aggressively attacked the problems that confronted him. In response to the OAS's expulsion of Cuba, he issued a document entitled "The Second Declaration of Havana." In it he condemned the United States for the suffering and despair in the hemisphere, and he urged the people of Latin America to rise up against imperialism and launch guerrilla wars based on the Cuban model. It was warmly received by the Chinese, who interpreted it as an endorsement of their position in the doctrinal struggle with the Soviets. In Moscow, it was viewed coldly. But having still received no response to his affirmative appeal in December, when he declared himself a Marxist-Leninist, one can only assume that part of Fidel's motivation for giving this speech was to goad the Soviet leaders into finally paying attention to him by playing up to their enemies.

After more than two weeks' delay, the Soviet Union finally responded, condemning the United States for orchestrating Cuba's expulsion from the OAS but giving only passing mention to "The Second Declaration of Havana." The statement pointedly referred to "the Republic of Cuba" instead of "Socialist Cuba," Fidel's term. It also ignored the central theme of the Declaration by reiterating the Soviet commitment to peaceful coexistence and the principle of noninterference in the affairs of other nations. In a superb display of one-upmanship, Fidel published in *Revolución* a lavish acceptance filled with gratitude toward the Soviet Union for support of the Declaration. In his response, he subtly changed the wording of their statement to fit the interpretation he wished to place on it.

"The Second Declaration of Havana" also separated Fidel's position from that of Moscow loyalists Aníbal Escalante and Blas Roca. The Communist Party of Cuba had been accredited with the Comintern, which until 1943 had been the body in Moscow that coordinated the activities of Communist parties throughout the world. It was also in good standing with the Comintern's successor, the periodic International Conference of the Communist Party. It was a conservative club with rigid rules for admission and a strict adherence to the Marxist view that only the party could lead the working class and the people forward to socialism. Marxism also dictated to them that the party should hold the power while the government implemented its directives. That way, failures could be blamed

234

on the shortcomings of the government, while the party remained above reproach. For them, Fidel was a doctrinal embarrassment. To acknowledge that he had achieved socialism without the party being in the vanguard would be tantamount to repudiating a fundamental tenet of Marxism. Even for Khrushchev, who cared relatively little about ideology, this issue carried some weight, although his primary reason for holding back was to let the power struggle play itself out. He could not afford to get out on a limb backing Fidel and then have him lose out in Cuba to the party regulars, proving that his own ideologues and Marx were right. By March 1962, Fidel had decided the time had come to launch a counteroffensive against the Moscow-oriented old-line Communists and cut them down to size. He was determined to show the Soviets that he was not a transitional leader whom the party would ultimately usurp.

During this period, he chose on several occasions to criticize the inflexibility of Communist theory as practiced by the Soviets, saying on one occasion, "Marxism is not a catechism." He was ready to demonstrate to the Soviets that there was to be only one leader in Cuba with whom they could deal, and it would be his version of Marxism that would be practiced in Cuba. At a celebration on March 13, 1962, commemorating the attack by the Directorio on the Presidential Palace, Fidel paused during his speech to criticize an earlier reading of a statement that had been made by the slain student leader, José Antonio Echevarría. The sentence "We trust that the purity of our aims will attract the favor of God, to allow us to establish the rule of justice in our country" had been deleted. He attacked those who had been responsible for the omission, criticizing their willingness to misrepresent what Echevarría had actually said merely because he had mentioned God. He went on to blast what he referred to as "sectarianism," a term he would use frequently in the coming months as a catchall to describe the rigid doctrinaire Soviet line and those in Cuba who adhered to it.

As a separate issue, but of particular interest with regard to the role of religion in Fidel's life, it is worth noting that it was over the omission of the reference to God that he elected to launch his attack.

Fidel was determined to make it clear who was in charge. On March 27, 1962, he followed up his earlier oblique criticism with a direct attack on Escalante, loading him now with blame for the oppression of the average citizen and quite unfairly also for the failing economy. Fidel used the opportunity to make Escalante the scapegoat for the excesses many Cubans were now complaining about, excesses for which he himself really deserved the blame. Escalante was dispatched immediately to become ambassador in Hungary. Over the next several weeks, Fidel publicly castigated several officials who had been closely associated with Escalante in his reach for power. He was particularly hard on those who had been guilty of criticizing the early Fidelistas. What became clear was that while he was a professed Marxist-Leninist, what counted was loyalty to his interpretation of that doctrine and to him personally. To underscore this, he replaced Dr. Antonio Núñez Jiménez, the Director of INRA, with Dr. Carlos Rafael Rodríguez. Rodríguez remains one of the most underacclaimed figures in the Cuban revolution, and an individual of exceptional talents. He was an old-line Communist, but had from the beginning been the person in the party most sympathetic to Fidel and most willing to accept his leadership. By appointing him, Fidel showed that he was not against the old party regulars as such, but only those who were seeking to build their own power base or who insisted on adhering to the rigid Soviet line.

In another strong political statement, he brought back from Moscow Faure Chomon, the former Directorio leader and avid Communist convert, and made him minister of communications. In so doing, Fidel showed again that what he would reward was a willingness to remain ideologically flexible. He also prized the ability in people who were nominally Communists to remain, in the final analysis, Fidelistas who would be prepared always to follow his lead.

Fidel had now achieved in Cuba what Khrushchev would dearly have liked to do with the rigid party apparatchiks in the Soviet Union, the self-appointed guardians of the immutable Holy Grail of Marxism. The free-wheeling Khrushchev constantly chafed with these ideologues, who ultimately would be his undoing.

The purge in Havana generated an immediate response in Moscow. Khrushchev could now point to his protégé, Fidel, as clearly in charge, and could ignore those who had argued that the Soviet Union's obligation remained with Blas Roca and Escalante. The procedural problems that had been used to exclude Cuba from the Socialist club were suddenly resolved with astonishing ease. *Pravda,* on April 11, 1962, praised Fidel for his move against Escalante, blaming the latter for the conflict. Fidel was described as authentically Marxist-Leninist, as the national hero of the Cuban people, and as "perfectly correct in his criticism of sectarian errors." When the program was published for the coming May Day celebration, Cuba was ranked number twelve, one slot ahead of Yugoslavia, on the symbolically important ranking list of countries to receive fraternal greetings.

Fidel's new acceptability in Moscow was significantly reflected by his ability to get the Soviets to withdraw their ambassador, Sergei Kudryatsev, and replace him with Fidel's friend Alexander Alexayev. This was an astonishing concession; Alexayev was quite outside the normal line of promotion for an ambassadorial position.

The new attention focused by Moscow on Havana was partly due to recognition that Fidel was and would likely remain the decisive winner of any internal political struggles. It was also partly due to apprehension over a possible Cuban drift toward China. But most important, the attention was the result of a major decision by Khrushchev, probably in late March or early April 1962, to use Cuba as a strategic pawn in the struggle with the United States by placing offensive missiles in the country. It was to be as in a chess game, when a player moves a piece to the center of the fray, dramatically forcing his opponent to reassess the ramifications across the board and the entire balance of the game. It also reflected Khrushchev's victory over those in the Kremlin who had argued that Fidel was a maverick who could not be trusted.

Fidel has always been careful not to claim full credit for the decision to install the missiles. Hc has spoken of having had earlier internal discussions with other Cuban leaders about such weapons, and having had the topic raised in earlier conversations with the Soviets; he has also described the deployment as a joint decision. Probably there is truth to all these comments. However, it appears that there was a period of a few weeks between the time Khrushchcv made the decision to proceed with the plan and Fidel being made aware of it and agreeing to it. During that time, Fidel continued to nurture relations with China, including signing a new trade agreement, but then he suddenly shifted his posture toward a strong pro-Soviet tack. This presumably occurred at the point the missile deployment began.

Fidel's primary concern was to protect Cuba and the revolution from U.S. attack. He had long wanted and lobbied the Soviets for short-range missiles capable of striking Miami, in the belief that this would serve as a sufficient deterrent to a U.S. invasion. What Khrushchev was now suggesting was the installation of offensive missiles with a range of up to 2,200 nautical miles, capable of hitting any point in the United States. In addition, his first concern was not the security of Cuba, but to increase dramatically his strategic leverage with Washington in the global context. A specific consideration was to use the missiles, whose presence would be revealed only after they were in place, as a bargaining chip to secure Western withdrawal from Berlin.

Fidel was not entirely happy with the decison. These medium-range rockets would not specifically help the security of Cuba. Indeed, they made it a potential target, albeit a target of far greater global significance than it was before. As they would be Soviet-owned and -operated, their deployment would mean an influx of as many as twenty thousand Soviets, which could pose a variety of problems. However, the deployment of these weapons, linking their own prestige with the fate of Cuba, drew the Soviets into deep water. Inevitably, this helped Cuba's overall security,

237

and also made it a central player in the major foreign policy events of the era, thereby enhancing its prestige and worldwide recognition.

Fidel's public position has been that his acceptance of the plan was an act of gratitude and Socialist solidarity. "Since we are getting a large amount of help from the Socialist camp, we felt we could not refuse. That is why we accepted them. It was not in order to ensure our own defense, but primarily to strengthen socialism on the international scale."

There are indications that work on installing the missiles began as early as late May 1962. At the beginning of July, Raúl went to Moscow, where he negotiated the commitment of a veritable arsenal of other military equipment, including twenty-four batteries of surface-to-air missiles (SAMs), one hundred MIG fighters, ship-to-ship missiles, and Ilyushin 28 bombers.

On August 23, 1962, the new director of the CIA, John McCone, told President Kennedy that he believed the Cubans were about to install offensive weapons. It was, however, still in the category of well-informed speculation without hard evidence. In late August, the presence of SAMs was detected, causing U.S. intelligence analysts to surmise that offensive weapons would be installed for them to protect. Between September 9 and 20, the medium-range ballistic missiles began to arrive, being unloaded and moved to their secret installation sites under cover of darkness.

Speculation in the U.S. press about missiles and rumors about the presence of Soviet troops in Cuba became intense. An atmosphere of legitimate concern, but with a strong overtone of jingoism, welled up across the country. There were widespread demands that Kennedy take tough action including, from some quarters, insistence that he mount an invasion using U.S. troops. Khrushchev added to the problem by taking a new hard and provocative line, including denying that SAMs would be introduced into Cuba when photographic evidence showed that he was patently lying. Kennedy, despite mounting intelligence suggesting that offensive weapons were being installed, remained calm. Although U-2 flights over Cuba had failed to produce hard evidence up to that point, a flight on October 14, 1962, showed excavations that seemed to suggest they were the sites for IRBMs. Over the next six days, additional flights were able to identify between thirty and thirty-five missiles.

After two more days of feverish deliberation in the upper echelons of the Kennedy administration, second-guessing Khrushchev's motivations and weighing the implications of the few options open to him, on October 22, the President went on television to address the nation. Offensive weapons were, he announced, being installed in Cuba, an act that altered the international balance of power. It constituted an aggressive act of the sort that led to World War II, and was unacceptable to the United States. While the United States opposed nuclear war, it would not be intimidated from such a course if it became necessary. He was ordering, he said, "a strict quarantine on all offensive military equipment under shipment to Cuba." The line of quarantine was drawn five hundred miles from the island.

The world held its breath for six hair-raising days as the two superpowers met eyeball to eyeball with the prospect of nuclear war hanging in the balance. United States troops were massed in Florida for a possible invasion. Finally, Khrushchev conceded. Russian ships stopped as they approached the quarantine line, turned, and steamed back toward the Soviet Union. Khrushchev then sent Kennedy a letter offering to remove the missiles in return for a guarantee not to invade Cuba. Kennedy accepted the terms, with the proviso that the withdrawal be verified by U.N. inspection teams.

Throughout these tense days, Fidel continued to excoriate Kennedy and mobilized his country for what he assumed would be a United States invasion. On October 25, a U-2 spy plane was shot down over Cuba. There were reports in *Hoy* (the newspaper of the old-line Communist party) in 1964, and more recently by Carlos Franqui, that Fidel convinced a Soviet SAM crew to show him how to launch a missile and then, without warning, fired the rocket that downed the U.S. plane. All indications are, however, that the story is apocryphal.

Kennedy's original public announcement was addressed directly at Khrushchev and over the head of Fidel, with no acknowledgment of Cuba's role other than that of a passive vehicle for Soviet policy. Kennedy's treatment of Fidel as a nonplayer in the crisis raised anger in Cuba, but was accepted as a predictable insult. When Khrushchev responded to Kennedy in a similar vein, Fidel's anger and hurt were uncontrollable. He heard about the agreement to withdraw the missiles through the Associated Press, without Khrushchev having consulted with him at all. Che, who said he was with Fidel at the time the news was received, described him swearing, kicking the wall, and breaking a mirror in his fury. Another witness says that Fidel referred to Khrushchev variously as that "son of a bitch, bastard, asshole." The Soviets had abandoned him and made a deal with the Americans behind his back.

Fidel's anger was tied very much to a sense of personal hurt and betrayal by Khrushchev. He admired the older man, whom he not only thought he could trust, but through whom he got vicarious pleasure as someone who had both the firepower and guts to stand up to the United States. Not only had the trust been destroyed, but the hero image was gone as Khrushchev seemed to have caved in prematurely, or at least without extracting sufficient concessions. In an informal speech at the University of Havana, Fidel accused Khrushchev of having no *cojones* (balls).

While Fidel acknowledged that the missiles were Soviet property, he argued that the Ilyushin bombers and MIG-23s now belonged to Cuba. It was an argument he could not ultimately sustain. He did, however, adamantly refuse on-site inspections by representatives of the U.N. The Soviets, embarrassed by their inability to comply with this aspect of the agreement they had made with Kennedy, found Fidel intransigent. It was one small way in which he could still assert Cuba's sovereignty.

In an attempt to smooth over the ruffled feelings of the Cubans, Khrushchev sent Anastas Mikoyan to Havana, where he remained for three weeks, not even returning when his wife died in Moscow. He was not well received, and spent much of his time trying to see Fidel, who kept avoiding him.

In the short term, Fidel seemed to be a major loser in the October crisis. In fact, it was a historic turning point through which he had achieved the primary goal of the revolution. Cuba was now truly independent of the United States. De facto recognition had been given to the right of a nation in the Western hemisphere to exist with a government of which Washington did not approve. And there was an assurance, if not absolute because of Fidel's refusal to permit U.N. inspections, that the country would finally, after sixty-five years, be safe from U.S. military intervention.

Chapter Twelve

KHRUSHCHEV'S failure to involve Cuba in the settlement of the missile crisis hit the Cuban people very hard. There was an extremely strong reaction, with Cubans feeling that their sovereignty and dignity, issues on which they were acutely sensitive, had been completely overlooked. To make matters worse, Khrushchev was well liked in Cuba, and there was a sense that he had taken advantage of their good will. Fidel's outspoken reaction was not just his own response; it reflected exactly the outrage his countrymen felt.

Fidel moved quickly and skillfully to counter the impression that he had been ignored by friend and foe alike in determining the destiny of his country. That the weapons were offensive, incontrovertibly part of a worldwide Soviet agenda, and far exceeded the legitimate defensive needs of Cuba opened him also to the criticism that he had merely become a vassal of Russia instead of the United States.

While Moscow and Washington had settled on their own terms for ending the crisis, Fidel prepared independently his own five-point plan for reconciliation. In a letter to U.N. Secretary-General U Thant dated October 28, Fidel asserted that Kennedy's avowal not to invade Cuba meant little unless in addition to lifting the "quarantine" he also agreed to: (1) remove the economic blockade; (2) stop the subversive activities, including the support for the counterrevolutionaries; (3) stop the attacks on Cuba by exile groups in the United States and Puerto Rico; (4) terminate violations of air space and territorial waters by U.S. vessels and aircraft; and (5) withdraw from the Guantánamo Naval Base and return it to Cuba.

The five-point plan was given all the worldwide publicity that Cuba could muster. Its validity was dramatically enhanced when Burmese U Thant, whose sympathies lay far more with the Third World than with the superpowers, arrived in Havana on October 30. The reason for his visit was to negotiate Cuba's acceptance of the United Nations inspection teams. Fidel, by the lavish reception he accorded U Thant and the clever public promotion of their two lengthy discussions, was able to expand and redefine the context of the visit to an astonishing degree. The implication he achieved was that he and the secretary-general were still engaged in negotiating the overall settlement of the crisis along the lines of Fidel's five-point plan. It was a successful face-saving strategy that reasserted Cuban sovereignty and salvaged, to some degree, the sense that Cuba was a full player in the nuclear drama. It was a ploy in which U Thant was a willing accomplice. Yet despite U Thant's cooperation, Fidel forced him to leave without agreeing to permit U.N. inspection teams to come to Cuba. It was Fidel's trump card. He was telling the world and the Soviet Union that they did not own him, and he was determined to play it.

Fidel's anger toward the Soviets was aggravated when in the course of his discussions with U Thant he learned that the U.S., in private communications, had shown far greater concern for Cuban sovereignty than had Khrushchev.

Fidel was, however, walking a difficult line. He wanted to send a clear message to the Soviet leadership and Khrushchev in particular that he was angry and hurt by the way he had been treated. His pride, which was so intimately tied to his sense of Cuba'a independence, had been badly bruised and he was determined to let Khrushchev know that no matter what he had done for him he was not his puppet and would not be taken for granted. At the same time, expressing his feelings publicly in terms that were too strong ran the risk of unleashing widespread anti-Soviet feeling among the Cuban people, something to which they were inclined anyway. It also potentially raised the question of the wisdom of his foreign policy: if the Soviets were so bad and such untrustworthy friends, had not Fidel made a mistake by getting himself and Cuba so deeply involved with them to begin with? So as soon as it was clear that Khrushchev had received the message about the magnitude of his upset, Fidel changed his tone. Speaking primarily to the Cuban people he talked of the tremendous debt that Cuba owed to the Soviet Union for its past help. "We are friends of the Soviet Union," he reminded them.

Khrushchev got the message and was deeply dismayed at Fidel's reaction. That he had been forced to back down by Kennedy over the missiles had significantly hurt his standing within the Soviet leadership; that he had also created a situation where Cuba, supposedly a Soviet ally, was denouncing the country in front of the world was an intolerable embarrassment. However, it was at a personal emotional level that he, like Fidel, seemed most seriously injured by the disagreement. In a unique gesture of conciliation he ordered the Hymn of the Twenty-sixth of July to be played as part of the celebration of the fortieth anniversary of the Bolshevik Revolution on November 7. It was the first time a foreign anthem had ever been played during the parade.

The first senior Cuban official to go to Moscow after the missile crisis was Carlos Rafael Rodríguez, who headed a delegation in early December for what were to become annual visits to negotiate Soviet-Cuban economic collaboration for the succeeding twelve months. Because of delays caused by weather, the delegation reached Moscow twenty hours late, making the last leg of the trip by train from Czechoslovakia in subzero weather. As the train arrived in Moscow, Rodríguez found, despite the cold and delays, a delegation waiting at the station to receive him that included, to his amazement, both Mikoyan and Podgorny.

The Cuban delegation was accorded red-carpet treatment, and at a meeting of the Presidium, Rodríguez was seated in the front row with Khrushchev, Mikoyan, and Brezhnev. As Rodríguez describes it, "Khrushchev explained the recent period and said what had happened with Cuba, which provoked the audience to stand and applaud. I stood up but I did not applaud. That was a scandal. In the diplomatic circle, it caused a tremendous furor." Kudryatsev, the recently removed ambassador to Havana, said in a loud voice that everyone could hear, "Rodríguez is not clapping."

Rodríguez had lengthy private meetings with Khrushchev and Mikoyan. They expressed their surprise at Fidel's reaction and repeated assurances that they had not intended in any way to offend him.

Khrushchev told Rodríguez, "Fidel is a son to me," and repeated it on several occasions.

Rodríguez responded by saying, "That is the mistake. Fidel is not your son. Fidel is the leader of the Cuban revolution, and you have treated the Cuban revolution as a daughter of the Soviet revolution, which it is not, and Fidel as your son, which he is not. You have taken liberties that you can take with a son, but not with a leader."

Khruschchev answered, "You are right." But Rodríguez says, "On several occasions he told me, 'Because of Fidel I cannot sleep.' He was almost crying. He was so worried about Fidel's reaction. . . . He did not know how to recover the relationship."

A reception was held for the Cuban delegation to which, in an unprecedented gesture, the entire Soviet leadership came. It was, says Rodríguez, "a way of showing Cuba that the Soviet Union was with Cuba."

Years later Fidel would say to Rodríguez, "You know something. Every day I think of the October crisis and I can tell you that old man saved the peace of the world."

For the moment, however, Khrushchev's gestures of contrition were not enough for Fidel. He continued, to the delight of the Chinese, to speak out in support of armed struggle as the route to Socialist revolution in the Third World. Latin America was ripe for revolution, he declared.

Fidel was, as usual, adroitly walking a tightrope. The support for armed struggle in the hemisphere served to establish even more strongly his role as *the* revolutionary leader of Latin America. It advanced his commitment to roll back United States domination in the region and it asserted his independence from the Soviets by taking an opposing ideological position on an issue about which they were supremely sensitive. At the same time, he could not in the long run push the Kremlin too far. President Dorticós and Faustino Pérez, returning in December from China, reconfirmed the view that while China's leaders were giving Fidel vigorous public support for his position backing armed revolutionary movements, clearly hoping to win him to their side in the Sino-Soviet dispute, they could not hope to offer the economic backing essential for Cuba's survival that the Soviets could provide. Fidel knew that for a brief period while the Kremlin was still on the defensive over the missile crisis he could get away with some strong public pronouncements showing his independence, but in the long run he had no choice but to toe the Soviet line.

Despite the settlement of the missile crisis, CIA-supported exile groups continued to make hit-and-run attacks on Cuba, blowing up installations, killing militia members, and carrying out other forms of sabotage. The assassination plots against Fidel slowed significantly in March when it was discovered that Mafia leader Sam Giancana's girlfriend, Judith Campbell, was also a friend of President Kennedy. After FBI head J. Edgar Hoover confronted Kennedy with the potentially embarrassing information concerning the more than forty phone conversations Kennedy had had with Campbell since coming to the White House, the relationship was terminated. At the same time, the CIA sought to sever its ties with the Mafia hit men.

Desultory assassination plots against Fidel continued, but with little prospect of success. It was, however, the willingness of Kennedy to allow the U.S. government to continue backing the exile attacks in direct violation of the Neutrality Act that irked Fidel the most. With little real power to hit back directly at the United States, he knew that actual or rhetorical support for anti-U.S. guerrilla groups in Latin America was one of the few ways he could express his displeasure to Washington. It was a sure way to make government leaders aware of Cuba's independence and sovereignty and to show that it was not passively willing to accept attacks on its territory without doing something to even the score. More than anything, it reflected Fidel's insistence that despite Cuba's tiny size he was determined to conduct her affairs as though she were on a par with the superpowers and repudiate completely the traditional expectation that nations of Cuba's size and strength should accept a secondary role in the world, tolerating a double standard for the rights of sovereignty.

In early April. following an attack on a Soviet ship, the *Baku*, in a

Cuban harbor, Kennedy, responding to repeated Cuban and Soviet complaints, ordered a cessation of U.S. government support for attacks by the exiles. It was the only rational course of action to avoid a further confrontation with the Soviet Union, but it was a decision for which he was virulently attacked by Cuban exile leaders and conservative hard liners. And it was a decision that, together with the failure of the Bay of Pigs invasion, may well have cost him his life.

On April 19, 1963, Fidel left for his first trip to the Soviet Union. It was probably the most magnificent reception ever given to a foreign dignitary in Russian history, and it reflected Khrushchev's absolute determination to go all out to win Fidel's forgiveness and renewed personal loyalty. It was an extraordinary spectacle for the leader of a superpower to go to such humiliating lengths to woo the leader of a tiny Caribbean island of eight million people. But it also reflected the unprecedented position that Fidel, still only thirty-six years old, had been able to achieve for Cuba on the world stage in the short time since he come to power.

Fidel made the trip without any old-line Communists in the delegation. He took the Soviet Union by storm in a stupendous personal triumph. After staying overnight in Murmansk, where he visited the icebreaker *Lenin* and attended a reception by the naval leaders of the northern fleet, he flew to Moscow. His plane, escorted by a squadron of fighters, circled over Red Square before landing at Vnukovo airport. There he was met by Khrushchev and all the other senior Soviet officials. They drove to Red Square where a crowd of one hundred thousand waited to participate in a lavish welcoming ceremony. The crowd roared as Khrushchev introduced Fidel in a flattering speech that implied almost an acceptance of parity between the two leaders. That day the entire front page of *Pravda* was devoted to praise of Fidel.

Over the next three weeks, there were a dozen banquets and receptions. Everywhere there were cheering throngs sprinkled with Cuban students who led the Soviets in chanting "Feedell, Feedell." On May 1, Fidel had the place of honor next to Khrushchev atop Lenin's tomb for the May Day parade. Cuban flags were everywhere and the Cuban national anthem was played repeatedly. The two leaders were inseparable. For eight days, Khrushchev abandoned all his other responsibilities to devote himself full time to the entertainment of his guest. Fidel for his part responded with insatiable enthusiasm, repeatedly disconcerting his protocol-conscious hosts with his informality, spontaneously plunging into the crowds to shake hands and taking unplanned nocturnal forays to spend time with Cuban students. Every hydroelectric scheme, every manufacturing plant, every collective farm he approached with fascination and genuine interest. The visit was not only a political and diplomatic triumph, it was also a learning experience of immense importance, in which he was determined to soak up like a sponge everything he saw and heard. During an eleven-day tour he visited Volgograd, Tashkent, Samarkand, Irkustsk, Lake Baikal, and Sverdlovsk.

On May 21, 1963, Fidel was awarded an honorary doctor of laws by Moscow University in recognition of "the distinguished contribution he has made to the application of Marxist-Leninist doctrine in matters involving state and law." It represented an important symbolic step in investing Fidel and his maverick version of communism with the cloak of legitimacy in the Socialist world. He had upended Marxist theory about how socialism was achieved, he had come to Moscow without a single member of the old-line Cuban Communist Party with whom the Soviets had dealt comfortably for the past thirty years, yet he was being honored for his contribution to Marxism-Leninism. Later he would also be honored with the Gold Medal of Hero of the Soviet Union.

Khrushchev had reasons, rooted in his own tenuous grip on power, for honoring Fidel in this way, and indeed for making the entire trip possible. Under sharp criticism from other Politburo members for what they saw as a debacle in Cuba, Khrushchev was determined to rationalize what had happened by showing that his actions were justified in defending and fulfilling obligations to a true Marxist brother. In that case, his actions that led to the missile crisis would be slightly more acceptable. If Fidel continued to be defined by Moscow as an eccentric maverick whose approach to socialism was rejected, then the risk incurred by Khrushchev in Cuba in hazarding both the prestige and the military security of the Soviet Union was indefensible. At the same time, Khrushchev sought to distort history, implying that somehow the Cuban revolution was an event generated by the Soviet Union and therefore a part of, rather than a contradiction to, their Marxist doctrine. He also used every opportunity in his speeches, with Fidel at his side, to envelope Cuba in the Soviet position in the struggle with the Chinese.

Fidel remained in the Soviet Union for forty days, ending his stay with a week of "unofficial visit" at Khrushchev's summer residence near Sochi on the Black Sea. In a joint communiqué issued on May 23, 1963, Cuba was identified formally as a full member of the international Communist community. The document also contained a pledge by the Soviet Union to increase the price they paid for Cuban sugar. That concession presaged an increasing return by the Cuban leadership to reliance on sugar as the central element in the country's economy.

Sugar had been an important topic of conversation between the two leaders, with Khrushchev convincing Fidel that sugar had to be the basis of the Cuban economy whether he liked it or not. When Fidel mentioned that the development of a mechanical cane harvester would revolutionize

246

the industry, Khrushchev grandiosely and impulsively volunteered that Soviet scientists could easily solve such a problem and would provide him with such a machine within two years. After years of research and several abortive prototypes, the project was abandoned. Eventually such a machine would be developed in Cuba based on Australian designs, so that today 70 percent of the sugar crop is harvested mechanically.

Returning to Cuba, Fidel had much to be satisfied with from his trip. He had solidified the Soviet commitment to guarantee the security of Cuba against military attack, he had achieved full-fledged recognition of Cuba as a Communist state, and he had been anointed as the sole legitimate leader of the party. In effect, he had been given a license from the Soviets to shape the party in Cuba in any way he saw fit. He no longer needed to worry about being usurped by the old-line party members. He had reaffirmed the Soviet commitment to shore up the Cuban economy. Also, quite apart from the gushing flattery that had been lavished on him, Fidel had been genuinely impressed by what he saw in the Soviet Union. The vastness of the country with its magnificent scenery and diverse cultures, and the fervent revolutionary spirit that had wrenched the country from the feudal grasp of the czars and turned it into a modern superpower made a deep impression on him. He was also impressed by the bureaucratic organization. Seeing little of its debilitating shortcomings, he was, as someone from a nation chronically beset by organizational disarray, greatly taken by the orderliness that the Soviets seemed to have achieved. The disciplined society held an impelling psychological attraction for him, and the encroachments on the freedom of the individual seemed to Fidel a small price to pay for the ultimate benefits that each person derived. Whatever the failings of the Soviet system, he was convinced that it had a great deal to offer him in solving Cuba's problems. Contrasted with his 1959 visit to the United States, when he was snubbed by Eisenhower, there was little doubt that the Soviet people and especially Khrushchev acted like true friends.

In a four-hour television appearance using a "Meet the Press" format with journalists asking toothless, uncritical questions, he set about sharing the marvels of his trip with the Cuban people. He performed in his best fatherly teaching mode. He needed, in particular, to rehabilitate the image of the Soviets in the eyes of the Cuban population. The Soviets who had come to Cuba had not much impressed the average citizen, long attuned to the efficiency of Western-style know-how and technology. In addition, Fidel's blasting of them during the time of the missile crisis had taken deeper root than he had expected. Now he wanted to convince people that the Soviets were the only friends Cuba had and that their commitment was reliable and sincere.

The overriding issue for Fidel, a headache that never went away, was the economy. Sugar cultivation, so long the hated symbol of imperialism in Cuba, was a natural target for the revolution. The early idealism had envisioned a society with a diverse economy, including a strong industrial base, and sugar cultivation relegated to a minor role. Fidel increasingly regretted the early rash, destructive decisions that had been made with regard to maintaining the strength of the sugar industry. The reality was that a small island with few natural resources and limited technical competence could not become in five years a self-sufficient industrial state. In addition, the U.S. embargo had severely limited the economic options. No matter how much he wanted to change it, Fidel was forced to the inevitable conclusion that the basis of the Cuban economy had to remain sugar. This was a reality that Khrushchev had repeatedly attempted to drive home to him.

He needed now to explain this reversal of policy to the Cuban people and convince them that after the international excitement of the last six months attention to the economy with hard work, discipline, and improved production must be their priority. His impulsive and often disorganized approach to his own job was no example for others, and his admonition to the people was equally a statement to himself. He promoted the Soviet system as a model, not only because the Kremlin had urged it on him as a way of showing solidarity with the Soviet bloc, but because at this point he sincerely believed that it offered the best hope for solving Cuba's many problems.

Fidel concluded his report with a eulogy of his mentor, Nikita Khrushchev. The personal affection, admiration, and esteem in which he held the older man was stressed heavily in his comments. It was not merely a statement of appreciation for the magnificent hospitality he had received, but rather a sincere statement of his intimate feelings about their relationship, expressed in a manner that was unique for any national leader. More than ever Fidel now saw the relationship between the two nations as embodied in his relationship with the chairman.

Fidel moved to tidy up the loose ends that remained irritants in his "national socialist corporation." The freewheeling days of political pluralism, where consolidation of power was a prime consideration, had long since passed. Now he wanted to eliminate all those activities that seemed to detract from a 100 percent national commitment to achieving the Socialist goal he had set for Cuba. Having been admitted to the Socialist club he had promised Khrushchev in return that he would make Cuba a model of Socialist success for the Third World. As in every other endeavor, he was determined to excel and he was not willing to have undisciplined people who did not share his views compromise that effort. So much of what was still going on in Cuba he now saw as either counterproductive to his goals or merely an irrelevant dissipation of talent and effort.

The journalistic and intellectual communities, expressing themselves within a general context of support for a Socialist Cuba, still offered interpretations of events that differed from the official line. Individual journalists showing a degree of creativity continued to express their personal views about happenings in Cuba. *Revolución*, the newspaper of the revolution edited by Carlos Franqui, frequently carried stories that irked Fidel, and it continued to have periodic rifts with *Hoy*, the only other remaining newspaper. Sometime after his return from the Soviet Union, and impressed by *Pravda*, Fidel ordered the abolition of both newspapers and the creation in their place of a single new daily, *Granma*, under the direction of Jorge Enrique Menéndez, an old and loyal friend. Franqui was ousted and ultimately left Cuba to become a severe critic of the regime. Menéndez says that for more than fifteen years he talked by phone with Celia Sánchez virtually every day, suggesting the degree of direct personal interest and control that Fidel exerted over the publication. Menéndez and his editors understood precisely that the role of *Granma* was to promote the interests of the revolution, not provide a forum for differing points of view. This they did by strict adherence to Marxist ideology and constant close monitoring of Fidel's thinking.

Over the years, *Granma* has become in some respects a creditable publication, which despite its ideological bias offers its readers a wide range of information on world affairs. The acceptance of Marxist ideology has produced a way of looking at censorship that is hard for those used to a free press to comprehend. There is still respect for journalistic excellence. One editor says, "I admire very much American journalists because they are very audacious, because they conduct very thorough research, they want the truth, they double check opinions, they are not passive, they are active, and they are honest." But it is argued that such aggressive journalism is required only in corrupt Capitalist societies. It would be disloyal in Cuba, they rationalize, to criticize the revolution. In recent years the press has had greater freedom to criticize the shortcomings of government programs, but this criticism is itself orchestrated from inside the government. What always has been and remains forbidden is any criticism of Fidel or his policies.

The regimentation of Cuban society and the abrogation of personal freedoms was mixed with visible evidence of an almost aristocratic sense of noblesse oblige on Fidel's part. He implied that he and only he knew what was best for the people; he had their best interests at heart and they should trust him. In a way he was turning Cuba into a giant Jesuit school in which he was the principal. His intense desire to see Cuba succeed in international sporting events, and the creation of a sports program in which he invested heavily, was geared to raising national self-esteem and enhancing Cuba's global prestige but at the same time was like an effort

249

to raise the school spirit. In this, like other areas in which he invested intense personal interest, he has achieved impressive success, making Cuba, despite its tiny population, a major force in international sport.

Discipline was mixed with benevolence and his own selfless dedication to the revolution. His rejection of a luxurious lifestyle and his constant travels throughout the country served to maintain people's personal faith in him. Fidel had earlier said that Marxism was not a catechism, but in many respects he wanted people to believe that that was exactly what his version of Marxism was. "Hard work and faith in the revolution," which he now preached to the people of Cuba, was not very different from the message the Jesuits had instilled in him at Belen. The values that he sought to impose on the society, including a deep sense of morality, reflected far more his own view of how people ought to behave than a rigid adherence to Socialist ideology.

On July 26, 1963, the tenth anniversary of the attack on the Moncada barracks, Fidel gave a major speech in the Plaza de la Revolución. His mother attended as an honored guest. Eleven days later she died at the home of Fidel's younger sister, Juanita, in the Havana suburb of Miramar. Fidel and Raúl attended the wake with an entourage, and the manner of their participation was roundly criticized later in Juanita's 1964 interview with *Life* magazine. She particularly resented their arrival surrounded by intelligence agents rather than in the more humble role she thought would be more appropriate on the death of their mother.

The death of Fidel's mother was the last time Fidel's private life was mentioned in the Cuban press. A curtain descended around him that concealed, even from relatively senior officials, any information about how he spent his nonworking hours, what his relationship was with other members of his family, or the nature of his personal friendships either male or female. Fidelito, when he returned from school in the Soviet Union, was for a time enrolled in school under an assumed name. In 1965, Mirta and her husband moved to Madrid. According to members of her family, she reached an agreement with Fidel whereby she could come and go from Cuba to see Fidelito provided she agreed not to talk to reporters or anyone else about their relationship, life in Cuba, or the revolution.

Fidel's decision to conceal his private life was in part copied from the Soviet leaders who frequently endeavor to hide from the public even such basic biographical information as their marital status. After years in the public spotlight, and the subject of constant, often outlandish rumors among his fellow Cubans, who have a special national proclivity for being rumormongers, Fidel seemed to crave some relief and privacy. More than ever, he was devoting himself to the work of the revolution and leading close to a monastic life. It was also true that concealing from the Cuban people anything about his personal life enhanced the impression that he worked on the revolution twenty-four hours a day.

Prior to his trip to the Soviet Union, Fidel had made conciliatory overtures toward the United States. Despite the continuing hit-and-run attacks by various exile groups, he was now quite secure against a direct U.S. government invasion, and the time was ripe for some rapprochement. Given his own continuing effort to improve relations with the United States, Khrushchev had no reason to object to such a move. Fidel, having achieved a maximum level of commitment from the Kremlin, was eager to temper the perception of absolute dependence on the Soviets. Improved relations with the United States, especially if they led to the lifting of the trade embargo, would not only expand his maneuvering room in the Soviet orbit, but could give a much needed boost to Cuba's sagging economy.

Most important, he viewed the move in a broad historic and nationalistic context. Cuba, in his view, could have an honest relationship with the United States only if the old imperialist relationship was eradicted. Having moved through his involvement with the Soviets to an opposite ideological and geopolitical extreme, it was as though the old history had been purged and he was now ready to re-create for Cuba a relationship with the United States that could be based on mutual respect.

William Attwood, a member of the United States delegation to the United Nations who was close to the Kennedy inner circle, received information directly and indirectly from the Cuban delegation suggesting that Fidel was interested in some kind of accommodation. Robert Kennedy, McGeorge Bundy, and others around the President encouraged Attwood to pursue the dialogue with Ambassador Carlos Lechuga and Dr. René Vallejo, Fidel's close friend and personal physician, with the aim of arranging a site of a meeting between the two sides (probably somewhere in Mexico), and the establishment of an agenda.

At the same time, Jean Daniel, a writer for *L'Express* of Paris, interviewed Kennedy. The President, aware of the ongoing discussion Attwood was having, and that Daniel was leaving shortly for Havana, gave the reporter a cryptic message with the clear expectation that he should pass it on to Fidel. He told Daniel that the United States should accept a measure of guilt for its past exploitation of Cuba and especially for its support of the Batista regime. In addition, America would have to pay for its past sins and take responsibility for making amends. Kennedy's implication was clear: America could accept some modus vivendi with the Cuban regime, and would be willing to make some concessions. Kennedy asked Daniel to come to see him when he returned from Cuba.

Daniel sat down with Fidel on the night of November 19 and related his discussion with Kennedy. Fidel, stroking his beard, listened with rapt attention, getting Daniel to repeat parts of the discourse several times as he sought to divine exactly the intent of what Kennedy was trying to communicate to him. Fidel told Daniel, "I believe Kennedy is sincere." He expressed warmth toward Kennedy, and an appreciation that he was the first American President to begin to grasp the complexities of Latin America. He also left little doubt that he, too, was eager to pursue a meaningful dialogue. Kennedy was someone he felt he could understand and deal with honestly. "If you see him again, you can tell him I'm willing to declare Goldwater my friend if that will guarantee Kennedy's reelection," he told Daniel. It was a comment similar to that he would make to this author several years later with regard to Carter's reelection race against Reagan.

All the evidence suggests that a historic reconciliation would have occurred had another tragic event not invervened. While Daniel was actually meeting with Fidel, a phone call from President Dorticós brought the news that Kennedy had been assassinated. The White House immediately put the discussions on ice, and there they remained.

Before and immediately following the assassination, there were what now seem like clumsy attempts to associate Lee Harvey Oswald with the Cuban regime. Several days before Kennedy's death, Oswald had ostentatiously distributed "Fair Play for Cuba" literature on the streets of New Orleans, and made an unsuccessful effort to obtain a visa to visit Cuba from the embassy in Mexico City. When he was refused, he apparently created an uproar so that several people vividly remembered him. Over the years, and particularly as a result of the House Select Committee on Assassinations investigations in 1977, the evidence has mounted that Oswald had strong ties to the Cuban exile community, their associates in the world of organized crime, and various conservative groups. The bitterness toward Kennedy among these people for the failure of the Bay of Pigs invasion, and his failure to oust Fidel in any other way, was intense enough to make assassination talk common. It was a solution right out of Cuban politics of the 1940s and 1950s from which much of the leadership of the exile community had come. There were clearly those who felt that if Lee Harvey Oswald could be tied in the public mind to Fidel's regime, a full-scale U.S. invasion of the island might result to satisfy the national outrage at Kennedy's death. So many years have now passed and so many of the principals have died, several in suspicious circumstances, that even though the evidence strongly suggests a conspiracy linked to U.S.-Cuban policy it will probably never be conclusively demonstrated.

In a 1977 interview with Barbara Walters, Fidel said, "I am convinced Lee Harvey Oswald was no friend of Cuba."

Nineteen sixty-four was a year of consolidation. The death of Kennedy left an air of uncertainty over U.S.-Cuban relations. There was neither the prospect of significantly improved relations nor the likelihood of invasion. President Johnson was more concerned about his domestic agenda and the growing war in Vietnam than he was with this chronic irritant in the hemisphere. The State Department, however, armed with Fidel's absolute commitment to communism and the Soviet bloc, worked painstakingly with the OAS and individual Latin American governments to isolate Cuba further from any economic or political access in the region. It was a process greatly facilitated by recent right-wing military coups in Argentina, Brazil, Bolivia, and Peru.

Fidel dedicated himself to further Sovietizing Cuba and trying to make the floundering machinery of government work. Economic salvation in the form of unprecedented prices for sugar on the world market lightened what might have been disastrous consequences wrought on the nation by a combination of mismanagement and the U.S. embargo. Nevertheless, particularly for urban Cubans, it was a time of growing austerity and the absence of any luxury items. The growing power of the secret police, and the Committees for the Defense of the Revolution on each block, intruded increasingly into people's lives, sowing fear and distrust throughout much of the society. Dissent was suppressed. Some who criticized the regime and had resources were still able to flee the country; others ended up serving prison terms. At the same time, corruption, so long the bane of Cuban society, and freelance violence were eliminated from the political landscape.

The missile crisis and his spectacular reception in the Soviet Union had shown Fidel that through the adroit use of his singular political talents he could—despite leading such a small country with a near bankrupt economy and modest military potential—wield great power over the major nations of the world and take his place among a handful of leaders shaping the global destiny. He had acquired an enviable position of freedom of action. He no longer needed to pay much attention to the United States, which had exhausted all courses of action through which they might have exerted control over him. The Soviet Union had completely embraced him despite his unconventional political beliefs, and after the orgy of adulation they had just given him they could hardly condemn him, no matter what he did. The Soviets were primarily concerned about keeping him in their corner in the growing conflict with the Chinese. Aware of Fidel's stubborn resistance to anyone trying to pressure him, they assessed their prospects as being better through tolerance and wooing than by economic blackmail.

Fidel had recognized long before most of the leaders of the developed nations that a new and potent political force was emerging in the world, the so-called nonaligned movement. Made up mostly of Third World nations, many of which were only just emerging from colonial status, it was a movement whose aspirations and experiences Fidel could readily identify with and of which he was a natural leader. He had far more in common with Algeria's Ben Bella and the other leaders of emerging nations than he did with the leaders of the industrialized world. The nonaligned movement offered Fidel an independent constituency that he could represent in the world, separating himself from total reliance on the patronage of the Soviet Union. In time, Fidel would use his powerful influence in the Third World as a bargaining chip to get more out of the Soviets for Cuba's domestic needs. While Fidel's growing independent influence in these countries did not sit well in Moscow, it did have the effect of blocking the growth of Chinese expansionism, and therefore was not all bad from their standpoint.

Fidel now made a fundamental decision to do exactly what the United States had long accused him of doing—actively foment revolution. With the exception of his unofficial and haphazard involvement with the amateurish revolutionary groups when he first came to power, he had in fact done little more than give verbal encouragement to existing insurgency forces. Indeed, much of his effort during this period had been directed toward establishing close relations with the more progressive nonrevolutionary leaders of Latin America. Now, however, with the overthrow of several of those leaders, and frozen out of the region politically and economically, he had nothing to lose by adopting an aggressive attitude toward support of armed revolution.

Unduly enamored of their own success in Cuba, Fidel and Che, who served as the primary liaison with the revolutionary groups, remained committed to the concept of the *foco* (focus)—a small, highly trained, and dedicated guerrilla unit. Operating from a rural stronghold, this unit would mobilize a growing wave of grass-roots supporters, ultimately generating an overwhelming armed insurrection. It was a flawed strategy based on a romantic distortion of what had really happened in Cuba. Fidel, Che, and others who had been in the Sierra Maestra still thought of themselves as swashbuckling military heroes who with a tiny force had defeated an entire army. They were still unwilling to recognize the crucial role of the urban middle-class revolutionaries in destroying the credibility and morale of the Batista regime. Moreover, they did not acknowledge the internal collapse of the army and the fact that their success depended largely on the unique social and political history of Cuba and the political circumstances that existed there in the 1950s. Perhaps it was attributable also to a certain kind of modesty on Fidel's part; he seemed not to appreciate fully how unique his own role had been and that what he had done could not be duplicated without a similar kind of leadership.

There is a tendency to view this phase in Fidel's career solely in terms of his support for revolution in Latin America. From his standpoint, the decision at this stage was to initiate a global involvement for Cuba, and what he and Che launched in Africa in 1964 was, in the long run, far more consequential than what they did in this hemisphere.

Although Fidel had Moscow's approval, he still faced opposition from the old-line Communist parties throughout Latin America who adhered to the same philosophy as the PSP had in Cuba. They believed that socialism was achieved not through armed struggle, but by organizing the masses and through political action, including strikes, and the elective process. With armed groups promoting the Fidelista model in several Latin countries, this put Fidel in the position of supporting factions in direct opposition to the official Communist Party in those countries. In an attempt to mediate this embarrassing conflict, the Soviets sponsored a conference of the Communist parties of Latin America in Havana in December 1964. At that meeting, an important compromise was reached. The official Communist parties and the groups committed to armed struggle agreed, at least in principle, to assist and support one another's strategy. This was followed by a period of a year or so when the Communist parties in Guatemala, Colombia, and Venezuela gave active support to their indigenous guerrilla movements.

The nature of the struggle in Africa was quite different. There were no established oligarchies, no old-line Communist parties, and the struggle was primarily among the many tribal groups and against the remnants of European colonialism rather than against U.S.-backed vested economic interests. The Cuban presence in Africa had begun early, and had been entered into without any prior consultation with the Soviet Union. It was based on two factors. The first was Fidel's sense of solidarity with the African heritage of one-third of the Cuban population. Some would argue that this was merely Fidel's attempt to rationalize in Cuba a decision to insert his own political power and influence into a relative vacuum that he saw on the continent. But it was consistent with his efforts to build a sense of self-esteem and pride among even the most humble Cubans. Second, Africa was the one part of the world where there were several leaders already in power whose careers and political philosophies closely paralleled his own. Leaders like Ben Bella, Nkrumah, Nyerere, Sékou Touré, Kenyatta, and others were avowed populists with deep commitments to improving the quality of life of their people. They also had personal experience or immediate understanding of armed struggle, imprisonment, and colonial oppression.

Putting political considerations aside, Fidel's support of revolutionary causes outside Cuba can be seen as tied to his psychological needs. Fidel's

255

vision of the importance of his role in world history could not possibly be fulfilled by restricting himself to the traditional concerns of the leader of a small country of eight million people. Fidel clearly felt constrained and overqualified as merely the leader of Cuba. There were never any limits to the scope of the vision he had for his global work. Support of revolutionary movements in the Third World offered in the early years the best and perhaps the only avenue for expanding his influence on a worldwide basis. In later years, as his stature has grown, his support of revolutionary movements has diminished and he has promoted a more statesmanly role for himself, building alliances with government leaders already in power.

In 1959, the struggling Algerian National Liberation Movement had given Fidel its Medal of Honor, and in 1960, Fidel had sent arms and medical supplies to aid Ben Bella. This was the primary reason that Ben Bella visited Cuba on the eve of the missile crisis, flying directly from Washington to Havana. There he stated unequivocably, "Just as Cuba gave unstinting support to Algeria, so Algeria supports and will support Cuba." During this visit, Fidel asked for fifty medical students to volunteer for service in Algeria. There was an immediate enthusiastic response, initiating a program through which thousands of Cuban physicians and technical experts would eventually be sent to twenty-five other Third World countries.

In 1961, Cuba established a guerrilla training base in northern Ghana, and the following year opened a second base in Algeria, which by then had won its independence from France. In October 1963, when a border war broke out between Algeria and Morocco, Fidel sent four hundred troops with tanks and artillery to support his Algerian friend. While Fidel's action was quite consistent with Soviet policy toward Algeria, there is every reason to believe he took the action on his own initiative and not at the Kremlin's instigation.

In December 1964, following the Havana Conference of Communist Parties, Che set off on a three-month trip through Africa. On the surface it seemed like yet another of his good will tours aimed at promoting Cuban political influence and economic links. But the real intent of his mission was to lay the groundwork for a new guerrilla initiative that he planned to return to lead himself.

When Che joined Fidel in Mexico City in 1955, the commitment he made was to remain with the revolutionary forces until the point of victory. When he led the victorious army from Las Villas into Havana in January 1959, that obligation had been technically discharged. During the months in the mountains, however, the emotional bond that had already developed between the two men had grown far stronger. As one of the few members of the rebel band with an education comparable to his own, it was natural that Fidel should appreciate Che's company. However, Che had an astute mind, a more distinctly crystallized political philosophy than Fidel's, and considerable world experience resulting from his travels though South and Central America. There was not only affection between the two men; Fidel respected Che's views and was influenced by his opinions. He also trusted his judgment, his loyalty, and his military skills more than those of any other member of the group with the possible exception of his brother Raúl.

In the months immediately following the revolution, Che remained a loyal aide who was willing to take on some of the tougher tasks, such as the investigation, trial, and execution of those responsible for atrocities under Batista. He was a competent manager, at least compared with the other revolutionaries, and he was willing and able to shoulder major responsibilities in trying to make the new revolutionary government a success. Perhaps most important, during the first two years, when the jockeying for power was still intense, he was a valued adviser who adeptly assisted Fidel in consolidating his position. Although an ardent critic of the old-line Communists, he was publicly perceived as the most identifiable Marxist among the revolutionary leaders, and as such reinforced the contrasting view of Fidel as a moderate.

Pictures of Che, bearded and wearing a black beret with a red star, adorned the walls of more would-be revolutionaries around the world than any other figure, including Fidel. Wiry and slight of build, he had a drawn appearance from the chronic asthma that afflicted him. His interest in revolution as a romantic ideal for its own sake was stronger than that of any of the other *barbudos*. He was highly literate, and his writings on revolutionary war are classics of their type. Fidel from the start put him in charge of all of the government's contacts with other revolutionary movements. Che had married the Peruvian Communist Hilda Gadea in Mexico, but during the later months of the war in Cuba he had met and eventually married an M–26–7 organizer, Aleida March. In the final year of his life, he had an affair with the mysterious Argentinian-born East German, Haydee Tamara Bunke Bider (the last being her mother's name), known as Tania. Unknown to the Cubans, she was an agent for the East German Ministry of State Security, and simultaneously worked for the KGB. There is every suspicion that part of her job was to keep tabs on Che for the Soviets, who had no love for the freewheeling professional revolutionary. She accompanied him to Bolivia, where they both died.

In a way, Che was Fidel's alter ego. Fidel could not indulge his fond desire to be a career revolutionary, personally leading the struggle for social justice in one country after another. Che, however, unburdened by the ultimate responsibility for the survival of the Cuban revolution, *could* play that role.

Although Fidel was not shy about using provocative rhetoric, in the early years he tended to let Che make the most extreme statements, freeing himself to back off from the position later if the reaction was too strong.

The nature of their relationship began to change as Fidel's position became stronger and as his attachments to the Soviet Union intensified. There was no longer a role for Che in helping to consolidate Fidel's power, as he had done so effectively against the moderates, all now in exile. In addition, his efforts with the economy had been close to disastrous. In a situation of the blind leading the blind, Fidel had been strongly swayed by Che's confident advice and had allowed him greater and greater authority over the management of the nationalization process. For someone without formal training in economics, Che was knowledgeable, and many of his instincts were correct, but he could not overcome his lack of experience. His errors, particularly his efforts to socialize the economy with unrealistic speed, were compounded by his constant trips overseas, distractions with other matters, and the absence of enough competent managers to carry out his directives efficiently.

It was, however, Che's inability to adapt to the hardening political environment created by Fidel that caused him the greatest difficulty. Che did not grasp, as Fidel did, that responsibility goes with power, and he became increasingly a loose cannon on the Cuban ship of state. Che likened himself, as did his mother, to Don Quixote—a fair description. For Fidel, winning was everything; for Che, the struggle was a goal in itself. Che, a revolutionary romantic purist, believed that being morally right was ultimately more important than achieving victory. He believed in the basic goodness of people, and his concept of the "new man" selflessly committed to society and the Socialist cause was a utopian idea that he never relinquished.

Particularly in the early days of the revolution, Che would say what he believed because he thought he was right without considering the consequences for himself or others. After a brief trip to Yugoslavia, he praised the country as a model that Cuba should follow, a comment that predictably earned him the lasting resentment of the Soviet Union. Subsequently, as Fidel sought diligently to lure the Soviets into supporting him unconditionally, Che continued to criticize them for their failure to live up to Marxist ideals and particularly for their lukewarm support of revolution. Fidel always looked for ways to assert his independence from Moscow, but in the final analysis he was a pragmatist. Che invariably conveyed a position of moral superiority, and they resented it. He also actively encouraged the Chinese to increase their presence in Cuba and helped them to promote their ideology. Philosophically, he felt closer to the Chinese than to the Soviets, but he was slow to recognize how little they had to offer in Cuba's struggle with the United States for survival.

It is hard to imagine that the Soviets did not communicate to Fidel their discomfort with Che. At a personal level the relationship was one of mutual admiration and affection. Yet when Che emerged as a folk hero and a symbol of revolutionary idealism for young people around the world, it inevitably created tensions in Cuba. His book *Guerrilla Warfare: A Method* further promoted his international image as a great military strategist, an image that Cubans felt should more deservingly have been accorded to Fidel. There could be only one maximum leader, and it was Fidel.

More and more, Che was unable to find a role in Cuba that satisfied his needs. Some feel that he was pushed out, particularly after he was critical of Fidel both in private comments and, in the eyes of some, in the Uruguayan periodical *Marcha*. Although it is vehemently denied in Cuba today, the fact that he was Argentinian by birth and displayed a certain aloofness in style considered characteristic of his nationality, influenced feelings toward him and made him a permanent outsider. He had been given Cuban citizenship and had cultivated a Cuban accent, but his mother in a letter to him shortly before she died, knowing that the doors had closed in Cuba, said, "Yes, you will always be a foreigner. That seems to be your eternal destiny."

Recognizing that there was no real place for him in Cuba anymore, Che turned to the only option open to him. He would close the Cuban chapter in his life and invoke his original agreement with Fidel— he would move on now that the revolution was won. The decision was reached only after many hours of discussion with Fidel, who remained loyal and willing to give full backing to Che in his new venture. This encouragement was partly due to their personal bond, but if Che was successful in leading revolutions elsewhere it would be in Fidel's interest.

Throughout his time in Cuba, Che had maintained close ties to his friends in Argentina and never tired of hearing about the latest political developments there. He sought on several occasions to encourage the launching of guerrilla movements in his homeland. The most consequential was led by his friend, journalist Jorge Ricardo Massetti, who in late 1963 set up a guerrilla base on the Argentinian-Bolivian border. His group included several Cuban revolutionary veterans.

Poor understanding of the limited revolutionary potential in Argentina and faulty operations that allowed the Argentinian police to infiltrate the guerrilla movement resulted in its annihilation and Massetti's death. Massetti had labeled himself "Commandante Segundo," suggesting that there was, although absent, a "Commandante Uno"—Che. Che's ultimate ambition was to return to Argentina as a conquering revolutionary hero and to become the national leader, a dream his mother had long held for him. The failure of the Massetti mission in April 1964 convinced Che, for the moment, that the time was not right for him to try to lead a guerrilla movement in Latin America, a decision reinforced by the constraints imposed by the compromise worked out at the Havana Conference of Communist Parties in December 1964.

Instead, he turned his eyes toward Africa. In an interview in the December 26 issue of *Revolution Africaine*, he telegraphed his thinking: "Africa represents one of the most important, if not the most important, fields of battle against all forms of exploitation existing in the world, against imperialism, colonialism, and neocolonialism."

During his preliminary trip to Africa at the beginning of 1965, Che visited Algeria, Ghana, the Congo, Guinea, Mali, Dahomey, Tanzania, and Egypt. In Brazzaville, he met with leaders of the liberation movements from Mozambique, Portuguese Guinea, and Angola, and promised direct Cuban aid for their causes. Almost simultaneously, in Havana Fidel announced that Cuba was willing to send troops abroad to aid liberation movements wherever they were fighting.

On February 12, during a speech in Dar es Salaam, Tanzania, Che said, "I am convinced that it is possible to create a common front of struggle against colonialism, imperialism, and neocolonialism." What he and Fidel were promoting was the idea of solidarity among the peoples of Latin America, Africa, and Asia in a unified battle to promote their own interests against the entrenched powers of the developed world, especially the United States and, in a different way, the Soviet Union.

Later that month in Algiers, speaking to the Afro-Asian Peoples' Solidarity Organization (AAPSO), Che spoke not just of the importance of political liberation, but of economic development as the basis for true independence. It was, he said, the moral obligation of the Soviet Union and the rest of the Socialist bloc to underwrite the cost of this development throughout the Third World, as had been done in Cuba. It was not a welcome message in Moscow.

The President of the People's Republic of the Congo, Alphonse Massamba-Débat, had a strong Socialist orientation with a leaning toward the Chinese, which appealed to Che. Massamba-Débat was backing an effort by rebel forces to overthrow the pro-Western government of Moise Tshombe in the neighboring Republic of the Congo (now Zaïre). He asked Che, and through him Fidel, for Cuban support of the rebels. It was an immediate opportunity to turn words into action, and a few weeks later Che arranged to meet with the rebel leaders in Algeria. He even found time for a secret visit to their clandestine military bases.

On his return to Cuba in March 1965, Che began to disengage himself from the government. He resigned as minister of industries and renounced all of his other posts. He even relinquished his Cuban citizenship. He was attacked by Blas Roca in *Hoy*, and went into seclusion. This was no longer the proud young revolutionary departing on a new adventure, but an aging and defeated man struggling to recapture past glories. British journalist Edwin Tetlow described him at the time. "I had not seen Major Guevara in the flesh for over two years, and I was shocked at his appearance. He had put on at least twenty pounds, and most of his youthful elegance had gone."

Che's disappearance caused considerable interest, especially among the international press corps. Fidel was repeatedly asked about his whereabouts, but he remained evasive, especially after Che returned from Africa, and a note of irritation crept into his responses suggesting that he resented the continuing promotion of Che's celebrity status.

Che returned to Africa in June, under the pseudonym Commandant Tatu, with a force of 125 Cubans, many of whom had been with him in Las Villas. They infiltrated the rebel-held territory across Lake Tanganyika. The Katangese rebels had been receiving Soviet arms and some training from the Algerians. What they needed was leadership, and with it Che was convinced that they could achieve a full-blown revolution. Che's men fought well, but the rebels had little real motivation, their own leaders were corrupt, and Che became increasingly disgusted with them. Late in 1965, when they failed to defend their well-fortified base at Atshoma, Che decided to withdraw. Tshombe was overthrown in a coup by Mobutu Sese Seko, and the rebels negotiated an armistice. Che returned to Cuba, but most of the men under his command remained in Africa to train guerrillas in Angola and in what became Guinea-Bissau in the struggle against Portugal.

Massamba-Débat had not only asked Che to assist the rebels, he had also sought Cuban training and support for his own militia. In 1965, seven hundred Cuban military advisers arrived in the Congo, serving initially as the presidential guard and later setting up and training a popular militia. The following year the number of Cubans was increased to one thousand, which equaled half of the country's entire regular armed forces. This was a full ten years before the presence of Cuban troops in Angola would be erroneously heralded by the Western press as the start of Cuban involvement in Africa.

In the Congo, as everywhere else that he sent his soldiers, Fidel also dispatched cadres of doctors, teachers, and agricultural technicians to assist the local population.

The Cuban force remained in the Congo until 1968, when Massamba-Débat was overthrown. After that a small contingent remained for three years to serve his successor, Marien Ngouabi. In early 1966, President Sékou Touré of Guinea asked Fidel to provide advisers to train a popular militia and serve as a presidential guard. They have remained there since. At the same time, the guerrillas from Agostinho Neto's Popular Movement for the Liberation of Angola (MPLA) began training at Dolisie on the Congo-Cabinda border. It was the beginning of a twenty-year relationship that would lead, in 1975, to the large-scale introduction of Cuban combat forces into the country to defend the government after the MPLA came to power. A small group of advisers was also working with the North Western University–educated Eduardo Mondlane and his Frelimo guerrillas in Mozambique.

Che, in large part because of his personal problems, had provided the impetus for the Cuban involvement in Africa. But Che's disillusionment, plus the overthrow of two of Cuba's closest allies, Ahmed Ben Bella in Algeria and Kwame Nkrumah in Ghana, led Fidel to a major reassessment of the benefits of additional investments in the region. While maintaining the modest level of involvement to which he was committed, he placed what amounted to a moratorium on further troops and resources, a moratorium that would last until the mid-1970s.

Chapter Thirteen

EARLY in 1964, Fidel made a second, brief visit to Moscow. The purpose of the trip was ostensibly to sign a new five-year sugar agreement, but Fidel was particularly anxious to discuss with Khrushchev the impact of Kennedy's assassination on U.S.-Soviet relations, and the potential for the resuscitation of an agreement between Havana and Washington. Khrushchev remained optimistic about improving relations, believing that Johnson would continue Kennedy's policies. Persuaded by his mentor's optimism, Fidel maintained throughout 1964 the hope that the embryonic dialogue started with Kennedy could be revived with the new President, and he remained relatively restrained in his attacks on the United States. At the same time, he was becoming increasingly annoyed with Khrushchev, who he felt was deliberately misrepresenting the Cuban position on Soviet foreign policy as ammunition against the Chinese.

Khrushchev's ouster, however, in October 1964 left Fidel without his primary advocate in Moscow. At the same time, he was freed from the personal obligations and private commitments he had made to that leader. The Soviet Union's economic obligations to Cuba were a matter of record and could not easily be rescinded. The secret political concessions and understandings that had been reached between the two men were not public knowledge and now could be broken with impunity. Fidel and the Cuban venture had always been inherently a personal project of Khrushchev's, and it would be some time before the new leadership in the Kremlin picked up all the threads and reshaped any new Cuban policy. In the meantime, Fidel made the most of the vacuum by asserting to the limit his ability to make foreign policy independent of Moscow.

Perhaps in part because in his own country power was completely invested in one man, Fidel always viewed foreign policy as first and foremost a matter of interpersonal rather than intergovernmental relations. Accordingly, he has always felt deeply obligated to honor the commitments he made to other leaders. He has felt much less strongly about the sanctity of institutional agreements.

Khrushchev's departure signaled the start of Fidel's emergence as a truly global figure pursuing a course as the champion of the impoverished and oppressed throughout the world. As a natural extension of the way he had seen himself in leading the revolution in Cuba, this worldwide role would now become the focus of his career. It reflected the security that he felt Cuba now enjoyed, and at another level his need to be always in the role of David against the Goliaths. The initiatives launched by Che were just one element in that grand strategy.

Although Khrushchev had been out of power for two months by the time of the Havana Conference of the Latin American Communist Parties, the compromise agreement to support armed struggle in six countries was a direct legacy of his policies. However, his successors began almost immediately to back away from this ideological concession. As a practical matter, they saw in 1965 and 1966 place after place where armed struggle had failed to produce the sort of Moscow-oriented Socialist revolution they hoped for. The overthrows of Ben Bella and Nkrumah were stunning setbacks to Soviet influence in the Third World. Moscow retrenched, arguing that Cuba was a unique and isolated example that could not be duplicated elsewhere. Armed struggle only antagonized the United States, undermined the validity of their ideological arguments with the Chinese, and sapped their economy while offering little in return.

The Soviets roundly rejected Che's demand that they underwrite the economic development of the Socialist Third World. In a major policy shift, the post-Khrushchev leadership decided to base Russia's relations with Third World nations not on ideological compatibility, but on their strategic or economic importance to the Soviet Union. Building the economic security of the Soviet Union was given priority over ideological expansionism. They moved to establish or improve diplomatic relations with key right-wing military governments as well as their traditional left-leaning friends. In Latin America, this meant opening negotiations with Colombia, Brazil, Chile, Ecuador, Costa Rica, Bolivia, and Uruguay. In Venezuela, they were in discussions with President Raúl Leoni despite their long-standing ties to his enemies in the Venezuelan Communist Party. The party, in turn, was locked in conflict with the guerrilla movement of Douglas Bravo, backed by Fidel.

Fidel was moving in the opposite direction from Moscow. He felt little obligation or loyalty to the new Kremlin leadership. The defeat of the Socialist-Communist Alliance led by Salvador Allende in the 1964 elections in Chile convinced him that the traditional, peaceful path advocated by the old-line Communist parties would not work. The escalating war in Vietnam, with the bombing of the North by U.S. warplanes in February 1965, and the invasion of the Dominican Republic by twenty-three thousand U.S. troops in April to overturn an election victory unwelcome in Washington (key elements in Fidel's decision to send troops to the Congo), dispelled any hope of an accord with the United States. Moreover, it reaffirmed Fidel's view of Washington's continuing malevolence toward the nationalistic aspirations of developing countries.

However, what peeved him considerably more was the relatively restrained attitude of the Soviet Union toward these developments. When it came to the interests of developing nations, Moscow's policies were clearly closer to those of Washington than those of Havana. Without Khrushchev, and with his faith in the new Soviet leadership soundly shaken, Fidel was determined to show where his true loyalty lay regardless of where his bills got paid.

The Tricontinental Congress, which opened in Havana on January 3, 1966, was a turning point for Fidel, thrusting him into a position of unparalleled leadership in the Third World. It was also a watershed in Cuba's relations with the Soviet Union. As early as 1961, Fidel had argued for the admission of Latin America to the Afro-Asian Peoples' Solidarity Organization (AAPSO), a group created by Egypt, the Soviet Union, and China to promote the influence of the Communist bloc in the Third World. It significantly overlapped the Non-Aligned Movement in its membership, but was generally more ardently anti-Western and anti-imperialist. It had become a battleground in the Sino-Soviet struggle with the continuing exclusion of Latin America being due primarily to disagreement over which of the array of pro-Chinese and pro-Soviet groups should represent the region. In a major coup for Fidel, a compromise was reached. The organization's next meeting would be held in Havana, and he would pick the representatives. The Chinese could hardly dispute his revolutionary credentials, and at the time the agreement was reached, shortly after the Havana conference and compromise of 1964, the Soviets assumed that Fidel would pick only Moscow-leaning groups. In the meantime, he was profoundly disillusioned with the new leadership in Moscow. As he saw it, they had abandoned armed struggle, and were acquiescing passively to the behavior of the United States in the Third World. Thus, he considered the Tricontinental Congress a solid opportunity to take an ideological and moral stand against Moscow that would immeasurably enhance his credibility with the more militant forces of the developing world.

By 1966, Fidel had already been in power longer and had greater experience in the international arena than all but a handful of world leaders. His orchestration of the conference was a scintillating testimony to the adroit political skills that have kept him consistently in the forefront of world leadership.

Ideologically, Fidel's commitment to armed struggle seemed inevitably

265

to place him on the side of the Chinese in the Sino-Soviet dispute. Yet despite all his differences with Moscow, he had always meticulously avoided acknowledging the views he shared with the Chinese. Nor did he give them any public support, the one thing the Kremlin could not have tolerated. Now, on the eve of his most overt split with Soviet ideology, he chose to attack the Chinese for supposedly cutting their rice shipments to Cuba, for distributing propaganda to the military, and for trying to impose their beliefs on the Cuban people. Past efforts by the Chinese to promote their ideology in Cuba had, in fact, been done with the encouragement of the absent Che. Fidel's strong criticism of the Chinese preempted any possibility that his intended criticism of the Soviets at the conference could be interpreted as sympathy for the Chinese.

Fidel manipulated the meeting to his own design, leading it in a direction quite different from what the Soviets had intended. He had selected from Latin America representatives of all of the major groups involved in armed struggle and he used the conference to showcase their causes and those of the revolutionary left around the world. At the same time, he played down and restricted the visibility of the traditional party representatives. This was not difficult—the colorful revolutionary leaders imparted a sense of energy, vigor, and excitement to the meeting that contrasted sharply with the air of the stodgy diplomats and Moscow-oriented party functionaries. In his rousing opening statement, Fidel captured the spirit of the meeting by again announcing that any revolutionary movement anywhere in the world could count on Cuba's help. From that moment on, the conference was his.

The presence of an array of the world's leading revolutionaries together with representatives of the Viet Cong and North Vietnam led superficial observers in the United States to interpret the conference as yet another exercise in anti-Americanism, missing the fact that the most striking aspect of the meeting was its anti-Soviet tone. Prior to the meeting, Fidel's proximity to the Soviet Union had raised serious questions in the minds of many revolutionaries whether he had sold out and abandoned them in favor of Cuba's short-term economic interests. By the end of the conference, Fidel had not only established his credibility beyond any doubt, he had emerged as the unquestioned champion and spokesman of the diverse revolutionary movements. He articulated their position, which was that they expected the Chinese and the Soviets to foot the bill for armed struggle but not try to dictate its course.

The meeting ended with Fidel pushing for the secretariat of the newly established tricontinental organization to be established in Havana. After aggressive lobbying, he succeeded.

During 1966 and 1967, Fidel continued to criticize the Chinese and the

Soviets. His strongest barbs against Moscow were directed at what he felt was inadequate support for the North Vietnamese, with whom he felt a special affinity in their struggle against the United States. The Communist parties of Latin America continued also to be prime targets of his wrath, fueled in part by his annoyance at the failure of the Communist Party in Bolivia to support Che's guerrilla band, now operating in its country. His anger led him increasingly to impugn the legitimacy of these organizations, despite their backing from Moscow.

Matters came to a head in Venezuela early in 1967 when the Venezuelan Communist Party (PCV) officially abandoned its support for armed struggle. Fidel vigorously condemned the party members as defeatists and traitors, and shifted his support exclusively to guerrilla leader Douglas Bravo, whom he endorsed as the true Socialist force in the country, sending arms and money directly to his group fighting in the mountains. When a boat carrying Cuban and Venezuelan revolutionaries was captured, the PCV joined the Caracas government in denouncing Cuban interference in the country.

By turning his allegiance away from the Venezuelan Communist Party while it still had Moscow's backing, Fidel was making his most profound challenge to the Soviets yet. The right to determine who was a *true* Communist had always resided with the Comintern and its successor bodies in Moscow, and as Fidel had found in Cuba, they jealously guarded that right. Fidel now asserted that he would determine who were the *true* Communists in Latin America, and his definition extended only to those who were willing to engage in all-out armed struggle.

Fidel's creation, the Latin American Solidarity Organization (OLAS), an outgrowth of the Tricontential Congress, held its first meeting in Havana in August 1967. With the slogan "The duty of a revolution is to make revolution," its militant intent was clear. Addressing the meeting, Fidel frankly declared that the OLAS, not Moscow, was now the focus for leadership for the Marxist-Leninist movement in Latin America. The conference also passed a resolution condemning "certain socialist countries" for pursuing economic relations with counterrevolutionary governments in Latin America. It was a direct rebuke to the Soviet Union.

Meanwhile, Che, having failed in Africa, had returned to reconsider his options in Latin America. The Tricontinental Congress and the subsequent meeting of OLAS had given the region a new priority on Fidel's agenda. More important, the general abrogation of the 1964 Havana compromise, the schism with Moscow, and Fidel's rededication to the primacy of armed struggle in Latin America made it easy for Che to reconsider leading his own guerrilla movement in the region. Again his first choice was his native Argentina, but Bolivia offered better immediate prospects for a successful revolution. In November 1966, Che and seventeen loyal followers—mostly Cuban friends of the Las Villas campaign, some of whom had also been in Africa—set up a guerrilla *foco* in southeast Bolivia near Nancahuazu. The dream was that success in Bolivia would be the spark to ignite a continentwide revolution.

Che's year-long campaign in Bolivia was a story of faith, hardship, ineptitude, betrayal, heroism and, ultimately, death. Che still believed that the Cuban revolutionary model could be replicated, but he quickly found that the circumstances in Bolivia were dramatically different. The band of mostly foreign fighters was shunned and betrayed by the local peasant population, which was not subjected to the same oppressive treatment as its counterpart had been in Cuba under Batista. The physical terrain was a good deal harsher than the Sierra Maestra, and the constant deprivation and suffering wore the men down. The Communist Party of Bolivia, which could have played a vital role in organizing an urban support base, largely abandoned Che's men. And the Bolivian military, unlike the demoralized forces of Batista, developed a competent antiguerrilla force trained by a U.S. Special Forces team.

Despite Che's extraordinary valor and leadership in holding his beleaguered band together, they were eventually surrounded on October 8, 1967, in the Quebrada del Yurro canyon near the banks of the Río Grande. Che was wounded and captured. After being tortured, he was executed twenty-four hours later. He was thirty-nine years old.

It has been argued that Fidel, happy to have the erratic Che out of his hair and seeing the futility of the guerrilla's efforts in Bolivia, allowed the vital pipeline of supplies and communications to dry up, dooming the force. In fact, the dynamic was probably a good deal more complex. Fidel had a great deal riding on Che's mission, and he was devastated by his death. From their first meeting at the apartment of Maria Antonia González in Mexico City in November 1956, their relationship had been one of deep mutual understanding. Fidel understood Che's restless drive to meet some insatiable inner need and his quixotic urge to take on potentially self-destructive challenges. He was also very aware that Che had become a square peg in a round hole in Cuba. The hopelessness of the Bolivian situation must have been evident to Fidel, if not to Che, long before the latter's death. Che might have made an effort to extricate himself and his men, but it is apparent that he felt he had burned all his bridges behind him. Having nothing to return to, he was determined to play out events to their inevitable conclusion. He had unquestionably made the decision that he would rather die in character as a romantic guerrilla hero fighting for justice against oppression than return to what he saw as relative obscurity in Cuba, sidelined because he no longer had a place in the revolution. If anyone could understand this it would have been Fidel, and a point must have come when he realized that Che's death was inevitable.

Che's failure in Bolivia coincided with severe setbacks for other guerrilla movements in Peru, Guatemala, Venezuela, and Colombia. Despite Fidel's initial contention that Che's death would not in any way affect the commitment to armed struggle, it was a turning point. Afterward, Cuba for all practical purposes abandoned for more than ten years its support of armed revolution in Latin America.

Fidel's confident assertion of an independent foreign policy directly contrary to that of the Soviet leadership left the Soviets at first somewhat flat-footed. They did not react with the furor that they had shown against the Chinese when they had asserted a similar doctrinal independence. This was in part because of the deft way in which Fidel had handled their differences. Unlike the Chinese, he was not seeking a public schism. When the new Soviet leadership finally decided that it had to act to stop Fidel from stealing all its influence in the Third World, it did so timidly lest its actions make him even more of a hero to the revolutionary movements. Moscow rebuked the Cuban position largely through the writings and speeches of Communist surrogates in the parties outside the Soviet Union, especially those in Latin America. The argument that armed struggle was the only strategy for Latin America was condemned as naive and ill-advised, while Fidel's efforts to cast the fundamental global struggle as being between the underdeveloped world and the imperialist nations was castigated as divisive to the "international alliance of revolutionary forces."

Criticism of his ideological deviancy within the Socialist family did little intially to get Fidel to change his views. If anything, it predictably hardened his resolve. In May 1967, he refused to sign the Nuclear Non-Proliferation Treaty cosponsored by the Soviet Union and the United States, arguing that it was a conspiracy by the great powers against the Third World. He was more interested in seizing an issue on which to assert his independence than he was in the substance of the treaty.

In 1967, a new problem arose from an old quarter. Aníbal Escalante, who had returned from three years in quasi-exile as ambassador to Czechoslovakia, began to rebuild a network of opposition to Fidel among Moscow-loyal old-line Communists. They criticized Fidel's domestic policies, but particularly attacked his commitment to armed struggle. It is uncertain whether their activities were instigated by Moscow as a way of reminding Fidel that, however improbable, there were alternatives to his leadership, or whether Escalante, seeing the rift with the Soviets, sought to exploit the situation. Escalante clearly sensed that ultimately the Soviets could not tolerate Fidel's deviancy. When they did clamp down, as inevitably they must, he would have placed himself squarely on the right side of the conflict. During this period, Escalante was in regular contact with the Kremlin leadership, to whom he was passing classified documents and secret material. His loyalty to Moscow was such that it is inconceivable he would have mounted his challenge had he not been given strong encouragement, even if the original initiative was his own. Fidel publicly exposed Escalante and his fellow conspirators in August. Eager to resolve the disloyalty without a major public confrontation, he waited for nearly six months to allow Escalante to back down, which he did not do. Then in January 1968, Escalante and his so-called "microfaction" were arrested and sentenced to prison. Indeed, the imprisonment of Escalante may have been retribution against the Soviets for the more overt pressure they exerted against Fidel during those months.

Escalante was right in one respect—the Soviet Union could not tolerate indefinitely Fidel's lack of ideological discipline. Fidel had taken advantage of the confusion over Cuban policy that existed in the Kremlin during the oscillations of power following Khrushchev's ouster. He made the most of the Soviets' uncertainty about how to control him without jeopardizing their fragile new alliances in the Third World and especially without aggravating the conflict with the Chinese. However, as each month went by Fidel more and more successfully drove a wedge between the Soviet Union and the Socialist-oriented countries of the developing world, gaining greater and greater credibility as the arbiter of what constituted acceptable Marxist-Leninist behavior in those countries. It had become an intolerable situation for Moscow.

Annual discussions on the Soviet-Cuban economic aid program for the following year began in the fall, and culminated in December in a delegation headed by Carlos Rafael Rodríguez going to Moscow to sign the agreements. The negotiations in 1967 were particularly lengthy and difficult, and they continued into the new year. The details of those discussions and the agreements reached have remained secret, but the evidence suggests that the Soviets used this one club they could hold over Fidel's head to exert some significant curtailment in his increasing autonomy. According to one report, to press their point that they held the economic life and death of Cuba in their hands, the Soviets cut the flow of oil, at that time arriving at a rate of one tanker every fifty-four hours, to a trickle. Fidel's pride has always made him highly antagonistic to any attempt to try to dictate to him what Cuba's policies should be, yet the potential for economic strangulation could not be ignored. The failure of armed struggle, and particularly the death of Che during the period of these discussions, made a policy of fomenting revolution one that was likely to become an increasing liability for Fidel. The outcome of these discussions suggests

270

that the Soviets insisted that Fidel's priority should be to make the Cuban economy a model for the developing world if he was to be guaranteed the continuing and expanded economic backing he needed. At the same time, he was to abandon his independent foreign policy.

So major was Fidel's concession and so out of character his capitulation, that one must assume that the pressures brought to bear on him were extreme. He was no longer dealing with the jovial, avuncular Khrushchev, who viewed him and indulged him as a son. Now he was dealing with the traditional dour style of Soviet leadership and particularly with the un-imaginative, bureaucratic Brezhnev. One wonders whether they threatened not only the Cuban economy, but Fidel's very survival as the country's leader to achieve his submission.

Fidel very quickly had an opportunity to demonstrate his new loyalty to Brezhnev and the Soviet Union. On August 20, 1968, he went on Cuban television to announce his support for the Warsaw Pact forces' invasion of Czechoslovakia. In what a year before might have seemed an inconceivable abandonment of his blanket support of the sovereign rights of small nations, Fidel spoke of the "necessity" for the invasion in order to prevent what he described as a counterrevolutionary situation that would only benefit imperialism. It was a salutary experience in several respects. Not only did he feel obliged to defend the role of the Soviet Union, but he also got the message that the new leadership in the Kremlin meant business when it came to dealing with deviancy within the Socialist family. Because of the distances involved, he was not vulnerable to the sort of military intervention that had been used against Czechoslovakia. However, there was no doubt that Brezhnev intended to act on his threats, and was more concerned about Socialist discipline than world opinion.

Although Fidel's hopes for a rapprochement with the Johnson administration had been dashed, the threat of a direct U.S. invasion of Cuba during LBJ's time in office had remained remote. In November 1968, however, with the election of his old nemesis Richard Nixon, who had close ties to the Cuban exile community, the fear of an invasion plan once again became very real. Since coming to power in 1959, Fidel's primary concern has always been the threat of an American invasion. It was the greatest risk to the survival of his regime. Such an attack would come only if he was abandoned by the Soviet Union. Throughout his time in power, Fidel has never lost an opportunity to remind the Soviets of their responsibility for Cuban security. With Nixon in office, he needed desperately to be in good favor in Moscow and be reassured of the Soviet commitment to him and to Cuba.

Hovering over him like a constant, menacing shadow, Cuba's beleaguered economy remained as decisive a factor in Fidel's retrenchment as the external forces. Nearly ten years after the revolution, the Cuban people were still subjected to food rationing, and such rudimentary consumer items as writing paper, shoelaces, and light bulbs were in short supply or nonexistent. The failure of the revolution to provide a reasonable standard of living for the bulk of the population was a matter of deep concern to Fidel, particularly because it was leading to a degree of public disillusionment with the revolution among even his most loyal supporters. Up to this point, he had tended to ignore the problem by focusing his attention elsewhere, especially on international issues, and by looking for convenient scapegoats to blame—the United States for its embargo, the government bureaucracy (which he had helped to create), and the abandonment of the country by the thousands of emigrés with technical and managerial training who had fled to the United States. But at this stage in Cuba's development, the economy was also afflicted with the problem of having so much power vested in one man, whose style was to shift his personal attention and that of the government—indeed, that of the whole country—from one issue to another as he deemed that issue to be a priority. The result was that whatever areas of national concern were not currently of interest to Fidel languished with almost no progress occurring until they again reclaimed his attention.

Now, through his own concern and with the encouragement of the Russians, the economy became the focus of his attention. As is so characteristic of his style, Fidel chose a grandstand play as the central response to his critics. Ever since 1964, when it was accepted that sugar production would have to remain the backbone of the economy in place of rapid industrialization, Fidel had talked about achieving a ten million ton harvest by 1970. Now he enshrined it as a major target for his regime, staking not only his own prestige, but seemingly the entire future of the revolution on its achievement. It was a way of galvanizing the population behind his leadership. Posing this goal as the most important solution to Cuba's problems was also a way of distracting people's attention from the legions of other serious shortcomings in the economy. If achieved, the ten million ton harvest would be a sharp rebuke to Fidel's Soviet critics, who had cast aspersions on his ability to meet his obligations under the Cuban-Soviet economic agreement.

Throughout his career, Fidel's success has come from his willingness to take audacious gambles. However, in this instance the objective evidence so clearly showed the impossibility of achieving the ten million ton target that the strategy has to be seen as a serious miscalculation. Because of the neglect of sugar during the early years of the revolution, production levels in the 1960s had fallen below the figures achieved in the 1950s. The harvest of 1960 produced only 4½ million tons. Nevertheless, Fidel turned the energies of the entire country toward achieving the new goal. Everyone in the country was cutting cane, including Fidel and his Cabinet. Even foreign dignitaries, such as a visiting delegation from North Vietnam and the Soviet defense minister, Marshal Andrei Grechko, spent time working in the fields as a symbolic gesture of support. The citizens of Cuba were flooded for months with propaganda about the campaign as though no other issue mattered. Fidel sought to mobilize the country as he had done at the time of the Bay of Pigs, posing the campaign as though it were a military challenge. "Every worker should act as he would in the face of an enemy attack, should feel like a soldier in a trench with a rifle in his hand."

One of Fidel's most endearing qualities has always been his readiness to engage in physical labor alongside the poorest Cuban. He has spent countless hours in the sugar fields doing the backbreaking work of cutting cane. Many national leaders prefer to remain aloof in their palaces and are rarely willing to mix and play with their people in the informal and egalitarian way that Fidel does. At the same time, there is a certain arrogance when he is dealing with people of pretensions. In the style of leaders of many countries, he is happy to keep even the most distinguished visitors waiting for hours or even days. It is a pattern that started when he was still in the mountains. People made the hazardous trip from Havana, and then were obliged to wait, sometimes for days, in his immediate presence before he deigned to talk with them.

One frequently hears Cubans who are having difficulty with the government say, "If I could only tell Fidel about my problem, he would solve it." There is a great deal of truth to this. One young woman who had known Fidel prior to the revolution encountered him in the early 1960s. He asked what she was doing, and she replied that she had intended to get married but her husband was a political prisoner on the Isle of Pines. Fidel, without inquiring any more about the case, turned to an aide and gave instructions that the man be released. "This is my wedding present to you," he said. Critics argue that such actions reflect not his generosity but his need to be like a Caesar holding in his hands the power of life and death over every citizen. Equally, and perhaps more accurately, it also shows a certain paternalistic quality—he treats all the Cuban people as though they were a part of his own giant family. There is in Fidel something of the grand seigneur. It is a European, Hispanic style in which he sees himself as the good and benevolent ruler who, while secure in his right to permanent power, feels a deep moral obligation for the welfare of his humble subjects. He believes that the deep sincerity of his commitment, which few dispute, should obviate any criticism of his absolute power. At the same time, when he feels that he has let the people down, he shows remarkable public contrition. However, it does not alter his view that ultimately he knows what is best for the Cuban people and they must abide by his discipline.

As the harvest began, Fidel was a man obsessed, fired with an exhilaration that exceeded even his normal prodigious energy level as he galloped around the country urging and exhorting the people to an ever greater effort. Finally, in mid-May, in a nationally televised speech, Fidel was forced to concede that the target would not be met. It was a poignant moment. "If you want me to tell you the truth it is simply that we will not make the ten million tons. I am not going to beat around the bush. I believe that for me and all Cubans this is painful to say." It was for Fidel a deeply emotional moment and he was quick to shoulder the blame for the failure. He was clearly shaken that this was one occasion when, despite his most monumental efforts, he was unable to snatch victory from the jaws of defeat. The crop in the end amounted to between eight and nine million tons.

The effort to achieve the ten million ton harvest produced damaging dislocations in other sectors of the Cuban economy as more than half a million workers abandoned their regular jobs to go into the cane fields. In many respects, this disruption, which wreaked havoc with the entire economy, was far more damaging than the failure to make the target itself. Some analysts have argued that the ten million ton harvest served an important function in forcing Fidel, in the most dramatic way, to come to grips with both the inherent limitations of his small island economy and the difficulties that inattention and mismanagement had added to the problem.

Speaking two months later on the seventeenth anniversary of the Moncada attack, Fidel again accepted blame not only for the failure of the harvest, but also for the mess the entire economy was in. In a continuing posture of contrition he pointed out "the responsibility which all of us, and I, in particular have for these problems. . . . I believe that we cost the people too much in our process of learning." He then offered to resign, which the crowd predictably rejected uniformly.

A new era was opened, in which the sorting out of Cuba's domestic problems was Fidel's priority. The severe shortage of trained personnel caused by the exodus in the years following the revolution was being gradually alleviated as a new generation of physicians, engineers, managers, and technicians was graduated. These young people, many of them from poor backgrounds who would not previously have had access to higher education, had not only the skills but also a fervent dedication to the revolution.

Prior to 1959, the statistical picture of life in rural Cuba was bleak:

Seventy-five percent of rural dwellings were huts made from palm trees.

In rural areas, there was one physician for every two thousand persons. A third of the population had intestinal parasites, and vaccination programs were nonexistent.

Only 4 percent of the Cuban peasants ate meat on a regular basis; 1 percent ate fish; less than 2 percent ate eggs; 11 percent milk; 3 percent bread; none ate green vegetables.

More than 50 percent of rural dwellings had no sanitation, 85 percent had no running water, and 91 percent had no electricity.

Twenty-seven percent of urban children and 61 percent of rural children did not attend school. Among adult peasants, 43 percent were completely illiterate.

Twenty-five percent of the labor force was chronically unemployed.

There was virtually no system of rural roads, keeping much of the peasant population in perpetual isolation.

It was to change this picture of Cuba, a picture he understood so well from his childhood, that Fidel had seen as his primary obligation from the earliest days of the revolutionary movement. He had articulated both the problem and the solution in "History Will Absolve Me." Only his appreciation of the complex intertwining of these problems with the rest of the economy had changed. From the day he came to power, he had started to launch programs that would reverse these statistics. He had begun projects to build houses and roads, to open schools, to provide adequate nutrition, to create jobs, to provide for people in their retirement, and to establish a network of health centers. He had also initiated the massive nationwide literacy campaign.

For nearly thirty years, these programs have remained closest to Fidel's heart, and in the 1970s, with cadres of newly trained and dedicated professionals, they began to have a dramatic impact on the quality of life in rural Cuba. In a conversation that this author had with him in 1979, he was able to quote infant mortality rates for every province in Cuba off the top of his head, to discuss in detail the technical aspects of mass vaccination programs, and to philosophize about the strategies for launching a health promotion program that would involve reducing smoking, increasing exercise, and checking blood pressure levels.

The accomplishments of the Cuban social programs are laudable and impressive. In thirty months, Fidel opened more classrooms than his predecessors had in thirty years. Today every child has access to high-quality basic education in the context of a work-study program where half of the day is spent in the classroom and the other half in some productive activity, such as working in citrus groves or, for younger children, working in flower gardens around the school. Free higher education is universally available, with entrance based entirely on merit.

Cuba's health-care system is the best in the developing world, and in certain respects is superior to that of the United States. With a network of rural health centers and urban "polyclinics," it offers every Cuban immediate access to quality primary health care, which like all services is entirely free. Universal vaccination against childhood diseases, the virtual eradication of traditional scourges such as malaria and tuberculosis, and an intensive focus on factors that influence maternal and child health have impressively reduced infant mortality rates to around fifteen per thousand. This figure is 25 percent better than that for Washington, D.C., and to Fidel's great delight is exceeded in the Socialist world only by East Germany. With strong endorsements from the World Health Organization and other international bodies, Fidel is justifiably proud of what he has done for the Cuban people in this area. Certainly he feels he has redeemed a thirty-year-old pledge he made to the Cuban people for their support of the revolution.

Six hundred miles of rural roads were built in the first six months of the revolution, water and sanitation schemes costing $300 million were launched in the rural areas, and housing for the peasant population was constructed at a rate of over eight hundred per month. Children's nurseries and day-care centers were put up, as well as institutions for the handi-capped and homes for the aged. The old mental hospital in Havana, a monument to inhumanity in the Batista era, was renovated, restaffed, and turned into a model institution equal to any in the world.

The cost of these programs in terms of the rest of the economy during the 1960s had been high, not so much in actual money, although that was considerable, but in terms of the reduced investment in other sectors. Sympathetic critics have argued that in the long run the entire population might have been better off if there had been a greater investment of resources in the economic sector, especially agriculture, rather than in the social sector. But in Fidel's list of priorities, meeting the basic needs of the rural poor took precedence over everything else, and neither he nor anyone around him had the economic expertise to analyze fully the impact of such a decision. Like so many decisions in the early years of the rev-olution, it was what Fidel described as "action by impulse."

Now, after the failure of the ten million ton harvest, he was willing to accept Soviet help to begin systematic planning of the entire Cuban econ-omy under the umbrella of the overall economic needs of the Socialist bloc. In the past, the Soviets and other East European nations had provided Havana with a plethora of technical experts, but they had never been involved at a policy-making level, a function the Cubans had jealously guarded for themselves. Fidel now ceded a part of that authority to the Soviets. There were high-level meetings between senior Cuban officials and the Soviet Central Planning Board. A Cuban-Soviet Commission of Economic, Scientific, and Technical Collaboration was formed to study in depth the Cuban economy and make recommendations for a new joint trade agreement between the two countries. In an interview with the Soviet publication *Ogonek*, Fidel said, "We did not fulfill many pledges and accordingly, very naturally and justifiably a certain scepticism developed concerning our economic plans."

Negotiations to reshape both the Cuban economy and the basis for Soviet-Cuban aid-trade relations continued for nearly two years. During that time, a flock of senior economists shuttled back and forth across the Atlantic. Toward the end of 1971, Soviet Premier Aleksey Kosygin came to Havana for discussions with Fidel and other top members of the government.

In July 1972, Cuba applied for membership in the Council for Mutual Economic Assistance (COMECON). Founded in 1949 by Russia and its East European satellites, its ostensible goal was to develop mutual aid and trade among Socialist countries. In practice it discouraged the diversification of the economies in the individual countries, encouraging each nation instead to specialize in producing only those products for which it was best suited, or which met a need for products that could not be produced elsewhere in the Communist bloc. It has the effect of interlocking the economies of the Socialist world, and secondarily of discouraging any propensity for political independence. Cuba's reasons for joining remain obscure. To receive massive Soviet aid was one thing, but to become involved in the intricate planning process and division of labor with nations with whom it had no common language and potential ideological differences made little sense. It inevitably locked Cuba even more permanently into an agricultural role and especially sugar cultivation. As the Soviets seemed to be calling all of the shots at this point, one has to presume that Cuba's membership in COMECON was primarily their idea. It did enhance the prestige of the organization to have a member outside Eastern Europe, and it was a way of sharing with its Socialist allies the not inconsiderable financial burden Cuba represented. Perhaps COMECON also felt it would be a useful learning experience for senior Cuban planners to be exposed to, and indeed tied to, the ponderous and methodical planning processes of these other nations.

From the Cuban standpoint, one should probably not underestimate Fidel's omnipresent concern for both economic and military security. From his perspective, the relative cost of membership probably did not seem that high, and in return he had a new and broader guarantee for Cuba's economic survival. At the same time, he achieved for Cuba further symbolic acceptance as a full member of the Socialist club. However reluctantly, he had long ago concluded that the dependence on sugar was inevitable whether Cuba was a member of COMECON or not.

A completely new economic agreement was signed between the two countries in December 1972. To give Cuba economic breathing room, the Soviets agreed to suspend the interest charges on Cuba's $4–5 billion debt to them and to defer payments on the principal until 1986 (a further deferment was later secured). At the same time, they would increase the price they paid for sugar to almost twice the existing level, and increase to a lesser degree the amount they paid for all other Cuban exports. There was also a renewed pledge to provide increased technical assistance to expand and improve the output of all of Cuba's basic industries.

The tone of the discussions between Fidel and Moscow during this period was perceptibly shaped by the personality of Leonid Brezhnev. A somber, plodding bureaucrat by background, his primary concern was the efficient management of the Socialist world. He could hardly have been less like Khrushchev, and less like Fidel. Khrushchev's mercurial, seat-of-the-pants style and his love for unconventionality and the grandstand gamble played into the very same characteristics in Fidel, exerting a reciprocal, synergistic effect. Khrushchev inadvertently activated all of Fidel's rebel instincts. Brezhnev, by contrast, was like the iron hand of the Jesuits. He had complete power, set limits, and demanded discipline. He did not want high-risk gambles, only conformity, hard work, and performance. But as was the case when he was at Belen, Fidel found the external structuring reassuring and comfortable rather than suffocating. For his psychological makeup, the provision of a rigid framework by an outside authority seemed to reduce his anxiety level about the Cuban economy, whether or not it truly held the answer to the country's problems.

In the international arena, the election, finally, of Salvador Allende as president of Chile was a stunning triumph for the Socialist world. Fidel's personal ties to Allende were old and strong. He applauded the success in extravagant terms, even though the victory at the polling place was an implicit repudiation of his former position that armed struggle was the only route through which to achieve socialism in Latin America.

In November 1971, Fidel made a widely publicized visit to Chile. By then his ideological differences with Moscow were forgotten by most of the world, if they had ever been aware of them, and Fidel as the champion of revolution was seen by friend and foe alike as somehow deserving a share of the credit for Allende's success. Except in a broad inspirational sense he had had nothing to do with it. To his credit. he was the first to acknowledge this, and his posture in Chile was uncharacteristically humble. He said he had come to learn, not to teach, and was not trying to hold up the Cuban model as a flawless example to follow.

While in Santiago he spoke to an order of nuns working under conditions of great sacrifice to alleviate disease and suffering among the poorest and most oppressed segments of society. "You are the true Marxists," he told them. It was an interesting comment, reflecting the continuing overlap in his mind of Christian and Marxist ideals, and what he clearly believed were, or should be, the central values of Marxism. It is hard to imagine a Russian or East European Communist making such a comment.

Although Allende had risen to power through the electoral process and had repudiated armed struggle, Fidel brought him as a gift a gun inscribed, "*A Salvador, De Su Compañero de Armas. Fidel Castro*" (To Salvador, from your companion in arms). In part it was a standard gesture—it was Fidel's custom to present guns to friendly heads of state. It was also, however, a warning to Allende. Allende's trust in free elections and other democratic institutions would, Fidel feared, be his undoing. Chastened by Che's experience in Guatemala, and his own in power facing constant efforts to overthrow his regime, Fidel warned Allende that the counter-revolutionary forces were too strong, and unless he took a more authoritarian line to protect himself he would not survive.

Twenty months later, as the United States was moving with increasing success to strangle Chile economically and to orchestrate and fund a military-led coup, Fidel sent Allende a handwritten letter. Dated July 29, 1973, the tone of the letter implies Fidel's assessment that Allende's prospects were bleak, and suggests that in a previous communication between them Allende had expressed his intent to fight to the end, ultimately sacrificing his life. "Your decision to defend the process with firmness and with honor even if the price is your own life, and all that the people know you are capable of accomplishing, will bring to your side all the forces able to fight and all the worthy men and women of Chile. Your valor, your serenity, and your audacity in this historic hour of your fatherland, and, above all your leadership, decisive and exercised with heroism, constitute the key to the situation."

On September 11, 1973, Allende was overthrown by a military coup led by General Augusto Pinochet, in which thousands of Chileans were hunted down and put to death without trial. In the final moments, as the military was assaulting the presidential palace, Allende, to avoid capture, killed himself using the gun Fidel had presented to him. For a long time afterward, his supporters, eager to preserve their leader's image and concerned that a deeply Catholic population would react negatively to suicide, insisted that he was killed by his adversaries. The evidence of suicide now seems conclusive.

The reaction of the Soviet Union to the involvement of the United States in Allende's overthrow was muted. Fidel blasted the United States for its role, and labeled Pinochet, whom he had met during his trip in 1971, a sworn and lasting enemy of the Cuban people, a position that he has maintained by regular vilification of the Pinochet regime during the subsequent years. It is interesting that Fidel studiously avoided criticizing the Soviet Union for its mild reaction to Allende's death.

Fidel's fear of Richard Nixon proved to be largely unfounded. The new President and his peripatetic national security adviser, Henry Kissinger, preoccupied with a war in Southeast Asia, détente with the Soviet Union, and later the opening of a new era of rapprochement with China, had little time to worry about Cuba. In a State of the Union speech in which he presented a global review of U.S. foreign policy, Nixon made no mention of Cuba. In many respects it was the most "correct" policy that any President has adopted since 1959. Cuba was treated as a small, economically dependent nation with limited aggressive military capacity, which posed no significant threat to the United States. Above all, Nixon took the position that by ignoring Cuba he was denying Fidel the global stature he would have received if the leader of a superpower had taken him on in the international arena.

The new economic agreements with Moscow were linked to an enhanced commitment by the Kremlin to maintain Cuban security. Additional military hardware, including by 1972 ten MIG-23s, began to arrive, and in 1969, Soviet submarines started to visit the island. With the growing importance of submarines in the nuclear balance of power, the potential in having a base on the western side of the Atlantic was highly attractive to Soviet military planners. In August and September 1970, U.S. aerial reconnaissance missions detected evidence of what appeared to be a permanent submarine base being built at Cienfuegos Bay on Cuba's south coast.

At a press conference on September 25, Henry Kissinger declared that the United States would view the establishment of strategic bases in the hemisphere with the utmost concern. In a private meeting with Soviet Ambassador Anatoly Dobrynin, he bluntly asserted that the submarine base was a violation of Kennedy's 1962 agreement with Moscow and demanded that the installation be closed. The Soviets quietly complied.

What was significant about this episode was that Fidel did not cause a fuss when the Soviets backed down. Presumably they had learned a lesson from the missile crisis, and this time they kept him fully informed about the discussions. Unlike eight years earlier, the security of Cuba was now virtually assured and Fidel had nothing to gain by again publicly embarrassing the Soviets. Brezhnev, unlike Khrushchev, would not for a moment have tolerated a tempestuous outburst by Fidel, who at that moment he was holding over an economic barrel. And Fidel knew it. Perhaps most important, the years had dramatically changed Fidel's demeanor. He was now a mature statesman who no longer felt a need to see international confrontation as a test of virility by which the Cuban people would judge him. Also, eight years earlier when he thought that the chances of a United States invasion and his overthrow were real possibilities, he was determined to grab every opportunity to promote Cuba's visibility and his image as a fearless national hero. Now, with his future and Cuba's relatively secure, he had every reason to avoid crises rather than promote them.

By 1974, preliminary discussions were again underway aimed at the normalization of diplomatic relations with the United States. The successful conclusion of an antihijacking agreement in February 1973 had paved the way for a meaningful dialogue and helped to remove mutual suspicions about the goodwill of the other side. For Henry Kissinger, normalizing relations with Cuba offered the opportunity to add another diplomatic triumph to his list, this one at minimal cost and probably some benefit to the United States. Fidel's antipathy toward Nixon was a modest stumbling block, but following the President's resignation in August 1974, that obstacle was removed. Detailed discussions continued for more than a year, as an attempt was made to resolve differences over compensation for nationalized properties, the trade embargo, Guantánamo, and political prisoners.

A satisfactory conclusion to the discussions seemed likely when in the spring of 1975 Cuba began sending troops to support the fragile regime of Fidel's longtime ally, Agostinho Neto in Angola. Although applauded for his actions throughout most of the developing world, Fidel was condemned in Washington, and the U.S. negotiators threatened to cut off the talks if the troops were not immediately withdrawn. Fidel declined, asserting Cuba's right to make its own foreign policy decisions without interference from Washington. The talks were cut off.

Fidel may have thought this would not be enough to end the talks. More likely he made the judgment that on balance his obligation to Neto, the maintenance of a foothold in Africa, and the widespread support for the intervention he received across the Third World outweighed the benefits of normalizing relations with the United States at that time.

Chapter Fourteen

IT is a curious irony that the more Fidel became securely incorporated under the Soviet umbrella the more he became acceptable to Western nations and their political leaders. The heads of large nations, especially the heads of superpowers, are made distinctly uncomfortable by small countries that act as though they are under nobody's control but their own. They prefer the predictability of having every country squarely in the camp of one or the other of the members of their own club, even if it means forcing the little nation irrevocably into an opposing ideology. For a decade, while Fidel struggled for ideological independence from the Soviet Union, Cuba remained the pariah of the Western hemisphere. The moment he acceded to Moscow's pressures, many unexpected doors began to open.

In February 1970, the distinguished statesman-scholar Eric Williams, then prime minister of Trinidad and Tobago, speaking at an Inter-American Economic and Social Council meeting in Caracas, called for the resumption of diplomatic and trade relations with Havana. His call was seconded by President Rafael Caldera of Venezuela, the host of the conference. Over the next two years there were several unsuccessful but increasingly close votes in the OAS to lift the multilateral economic and political sanctions against Cuba. In December 1972, Barbados, Jamaica, Guyana, and Trinidad and Tobago dramatically rebuffed the OAS and the United States, and independently established diplomatic relations with Cuba. Finally, in the summer of 1975, a majority of the members of the OAS voted to lift all sanctions. Sensing the drift of the sentiment, and eager to make a positive gesture toward Fidel, the United States, at Kissinger's direction, voted with the majority.

Economically, also, Cuba was increasingly viewed as an acceptable and reliable trading partner. By 1974, 45 percent of Cuba's exports were to Western nations, and by the end of the decade Japan alone had 14 percent of Cuba's foreign trade. Cuba had little difficulty obtaining trade credits from Canada and the major West European nations, including Franco's

Spain. In addition, Cuba was favorably regarded in European banking circles, and readily secured hard-currency loans.

In 1974, Chairman Leonid Brezhnev made a visit to Cuba. For him to make such a trip was a profound gesture of recognition and approval for the work Fidel had done over the previous four years to shape the economy along Soviet lines, and for allowing the Soviets to have a finger in virtually every aspect of Cuban economic affairs.

In 1975, Cuba finally held its frequently postponed first Communist Party Congress, by which Cuba formally became a Communist state. The congress made the party the paramount institution in Cuba. Addressing the congress, Fidel said, "The party is everything. The party is the dream of all the revolutionaries in our history. It is the party that makes the ideas, the principles, and the forces of the revolution a reality." Fidel urged his people to think in terms of Che's concept of the Cuban "new man"—to work hard and sacrifice for the revolution, putting personal gain and ambition aside.

The Party Congress was the grand finale for the endeavors Fidel had launched after admitting the failure of the ten million ton harvest. The only surprise was that the event had been so long delayed, when the irrevocable commitment to communism had been made so much earlier.

A new constitution instituted at the time combined the role of prime minister and president. Fidel assumed that position, making him for the first time head of state as well as leader of the government. Dorticós, who had been ill for some time, resigned, but he remained a respected and revered elder statesman.

Fidel's recognition more than ten years earlier of the coming importance of the Third World as a potent political force had led him to build and nurture a string of personal relationships, usually unnoticed in the West, with leaders across the globe. Beginning with the Tricontinental Congress in Havana in 1966, he had steadily emerged as one of the dominant and most influential figures in the movement. Even his detractors gave him grudging credit for his stand against the power of the United States. His enforced capitulation to the Soviets, however, had severely tarnished his reputation as the independent and fearless spokesman for nonalignment. By 1970, Douglas Bravo, on whose behalf Fidel had gone up against the Venezeulan Communist Party in 1967, was attacking Fidel, accusing him of selling out to the Soviets and putting Cuba's selfish economic needs ahead of the international revolutionary cause. By the time of the Non-Aligned Summit in Algiers in 1973, Fidel's reputation had slipped so badly that even Cuba's right to remain a member of the organization was seriously questioned. One of those most critical of Cuba's relationship with the Soviets, and most outspoken in opposing Cuba's continued membership in the Non-Aligned Movement, was Libya's Colonel Muammar el-Qaddafi.

However intimate Fidel's connection with the Soviet Union, it was above all else a relationship of expediency. His heart and his loyalties continued to lie with the Third World and its struggle to overcome the legacies of colonialism, underdevelopment, economic exploitation, and human misery. The criticism to which he was being subjected was a bitter pill to swallow, and he began to redouble his efforts to regain the sympathies of other Third World nations. During 1972, following a trip to Eastern Europe, he continued to Africa, where he met with both government and liberation movement leaders. Within weeks after the Algiers summit, the Yom Kippur War broke out in the Middle East, providing Fidel with a convenient opportunity to demonstrate his solidarity with the Arab world. According to both Cuban and Israeli sources, as many as four thousand Cuban troops were airlifted to Syria and remained there until 1975. A military aid mission with doctors and other technical advisers was sent to South Yemen.

When Agostinho Neto, leader of the Popular Movement for the Liberation of Angola (MPLA), asked Fidel for direct military assistance in the spring of 1975, the request was ideally timed. Cuban advisers had been involved with MPLA forces for ten years, and Fidel had a high regard for Neto, one of the most thoughtful and capable of all the African leaders. In the United States, there was a lack of familiarity with the history of Cuba's involvement in Africa, and an ethnocentric urge to interpret all events in the Third World only in terms of the U.S.-Soviet struggle. Consequently, Cuba was seen as acting in Angola solely as a tool of the Kremlin. The Soviet Union had been providing arms and training for Neto's MPLA forces in the struggle against their Portuguese masters even before Fidel came to power, but at a relatively low level and without any direct involvement of personnel. In addition, unlike the consistent level of help over ten years from Cuba, Soviet support for the MPLA had ebbed and flowed. The original commitment by Fidel to support Neto had been established by Che, not the Soviets. In 1973, Moscow's strongest advocate in Neto's hierarchy, Daniel Chipenda, switched allegiances to the rival National Front for the Liberation of Angola (FNLA). Moscow agreed to start supplying arms to this faction, and cut off virtually all involvement with the MPLA, which they increasingly saw as a losing cause. This put them, for a while, in direct opposition to Fidel, whose support for Neto was unwavering.

The overthrow of the Caetano dictatorship in Portugal in April 1974, and the visible intent of the new leaders of that country to divest themselves of their African colonies touched off an intensified scramble for supremacy between the MPLA, the FNLA, and the third guerrilla faction, the National Union for the Total Independence of Angola (UNITA). Superpower interest was also piqued as the ideological allegiance of an independent Angola seemed up for grabs. The opportunistic efforts by the Soviets, the Chinese, and the United States during 1974 and 1975 to switch allegiances and arm the MPLA, the FNLA, and UNITA according to whom they thought at any moment most likely to win or be potentially susceptible to their influence if they came to power, was in striking contrast to Fidel's consistent loyalty to his friend.

In January 1975, the new regime in Portugal convened a meeting of the leaders of the three guerrilla movements, Agostinho Neto, Jonas Savimbi, and Holden Roberto, at Alvôr, Portugal. Out of that meeting came the Alvôr Agreement, under which all three factions agreed to be part of a coalition government under Portuguese leadership until Lisbon formally withdrew on November 11. China, the Soviet Union, and the United States all endorsed the Alvôr Agreement, but all apparently began immediately to undermine it by increasing military aid to their individual clients in anticipation of the November independence day.

The actions of Henry Kissinger on behalf of the United States seemed the most flagrant, perhaps only because they were the best documented. He arranged for substantial secret funding to the FNLA and UNITA, the recruiting of mercenaries to strengthen the indigenous guerrilla force, and direct CIA involvement to provide logistical support and training through bases in Zaïre. Kissinger, who for six years had viewed the liberation struggles in Africa with disdain, made no secret of the fact that he saw the situation in Angola merely as a test of strength with the Soviets, and he was determined to stop any faction sympathetic to Moscow from coming to power, regardless of the agreement reached at Alvôr.

It is a matter of dispute whether the Soviet Union simultaneously increased its arms supply to the MPLA, or whether it did so only as a response to the massive infusion of U.S. armaments and advisers. What is agreed is that with the new commitment of support, the FNLA broke the truce arranged at Alvôr, and launched a massive offensive against the MPLA aimed at dislodging them from the capital of Luanda. Neto made a plea to Moscow for more arms and military advisers to train his troops in their use. The Soviets supplied the arms, but were adamant in their refusal to commit any personnel. It was at this point that Neto turned to Fidel and asked him to expand dramatically Cuba's ten-year-old military adviser program.

It might be argued that the Soviets encouraged Neto to get help from Fidel, and then instructed him to provide it. Such an explanation, however, flies in the face of the entire history of Fidel's relationship with the Soviets.

His involvement in Africa, as elsewhere in the Third World, was always aimed primarily at promoting Cuban, not Soviet, interests. That there was an overlap in objectives should not obscure the fundamental competitive nature of the relationship. After being reined in by the Soviets in the late 1960s, Fidel had complied with their demands that he address Cuba's domestic economic situation, but he had steadfastly retained the right to make his own foreign policy. At the same time, he was careful not to antagonize gratuitously those who held his economic lifeline. Africa offered the opportunity to inch away from Moscow and demonstrate to the constituency he was courting in the Third World that he would go not against, but well beyond the Soviets in supporting Third World interests.

With the influx of 230 Cuban military advisers in June 1975, the MPLA was able to hold off the FNLA/UNITA offensive. A further 1,500 Cuban advisers would arrive by October. But the battle was being fought as much in the political arena as on the battlefield. Senator John Tunney (D-Cal.) won Senate passage for an amendment preventing the use in Angola of any funds from the Defense Appropriations Bill for fiscal year 1976. As this bill contained the budget for the CIA, it meant that $14 million intended for the support of the FNLA and UNITA were immediately frozen.

Part of this money was to go to South Africa, which was taking an increasingly active role in the conflict. In July, it had established guerrilla training camps for UNITA in Namibia, and had been involved in a series of cross-border raids against the MPLA. A Marxist Angola posed a serious threat to South Africa's continuing control over Namibia. By October 14, with the November 11 independence day nearing and the MPLA's hold on the country still strong, a degree of panic began to set in in Washington and Pretoria. That day, with United States encouragement, one thousand South African combat troops invaded Angola with the intent of capturing the capital and installing an FNLA/UNITA government in time for the Portuguese withdrawal. Over the next three weeks, the number of South African Defense Force troops in Angola increased to between five and ten thousand. Their progress against modest resistance was dramatic, and within a couple of weeks they were operating on a four-hundred-mile front and controlled half of the country. But when they reached the coastal town of Benguela, they encountered heavy fire from Soviet-made Katyusha rockets. They had no weapons with a comparable range, and were pinned down for several weeks while they sought to bring up sufficiently powerful artillery pieces.

It was in response to the South African invasion and urgent requests from Neto that Fidel dispatched his own force of eighteen thousand combat troops to Angola. They began to arrive on November 7. The tide started to turn. Not only had the South Africans met their match militarily,

286

but the Tunney amendment prevented the promised level of support from the CIA. What help they did receive was apparently surreptitiously channeled through Israel. In addition, in early December, the Senate passed an amendment sponsored by Senator Dick Clark (D-Iowa) that cut off all U.S. aid to the guerrillas in Angola and restricted further connivance with South Africa. November 11 had come and gone with the MPLA remaining in control of Luanda.

With Cuban help, the new official government was able to force the South Africans into an ignominious retreat and also turn the tide against an FNLA force operating in the north out of, and with the support of, Zaïre.

The Neto government won quick endorsement from the Organization for African Unity (OAU). The OAU had originally favored a negotiated coalition government as the Alvôr Agreement had proposed, but the hated South Africans' attempt to overthrow the MPLA and their backing of the FNLA and UNITA immediately eliminated any reservations the organization's members may have had about Neto. The United States had done itself no favor with black Africa, which saw little point to the claim that the U.S. was seeking to prevent Soviet expansionism. Instead, the blacks were consumed by their perception of Washington as the conspiring ally of Pretoria.

Apart from Neto, the big winner in Angola was Fidel. A tidal wave of pride swept the Cuban people in the wake of the victory, producing a surge of national esteem unrivaled since the Bay of Pigs invasion. Fidel's prestige had never been higher, despite the sacrifices that many families had made in seeing their sons go off to a distant war.

But it was in the international arena that the biggest payoff came. Largely unappreciated in the United States was the fact that Fidel received almost universal endorsement from the Third World for his actions in Angola. His willingness to commit troops was for many a demonstration of the sincerity of his commitment to the cause of the developing world. Unlike the mere rhetoric of the superpowers, the Soviet Union included, he had committed his own resources and people to the struggle. When the Non-Aligned Movement met in Sri Lanka in the summer of 1976, the contrast with Algiers three years earlier, when Cuba's expulsion was discussed, could not have been greater. Cuba's role in Angola was officially recognized and unanimously endorsed in the proceedings of the meeting. The ultimate accolade came when the meeting invited Havana to host the next Non-Aligned summit in 1979, automatically making Fidel chairman of the organization for a three-year term. The Soviet Union's role in Angola was not mentioned in the official text of the meeting.

The Cuban presence in Angola provided an important base from which

Fidel was able to broaden his influence on the continent. One particularly interesting development that has received little publicity in the Western press but has important long-range implications is a training program established in Cuba for future African leaders. A series of boarding schools has been set up among the citrus groves on the Isle of Youth (formerly the Isle of Pines). Several hundred high-school-age students are brought to these schools from Angola, Mozambique, Ethiopia, Ghana, the liberation movement in Namibia, and the Polisario movement in what was Spanish West Africa, and is now a disputed part of Morocco. The program is quintessential Fidel. The students come for four years and are given an academically rigorous training in an environment of strict discipline. They are taught by teachers from their own countries, and by Cubans who handle mainly science and mathematics. There is a minimum of formal ideological training. In keeping with the Cuban work-study tradition, half of the day is devoted to classroom teaching while the other half is spent working in the citrus groves. Periodically, the students return home for vacation, and at the end of the four years some stay in Cuba for university-level education.

Contrary to the claims of critics that these schools are used for military training or intensive ideological indoctrination, the approach is light-handed and untarnished by any crude political agenda. The rationale appears to be that by giving these students an exceptional education compared to that received by the students who remained at home, the program assures that they will ultimately comprise the leadership of their nations. The goal is less to produce dedicated Marxists than competent future leaders with a sense of deep indebtedness and appreciation toward Cuba.

A Cuban Foreign Ministry representative, when asked whether the ultimate effect of this schooling program would not be to usurp Soviet influence at the highest level of government in these developing nations, smiled and said, "Of course."

Agostinho Neto's problems did not end once he attained power. The opposition guerrilla movements continue to be a serious threat to his government, and his regime has survived only because of the continued presence of Cuban troops for ten years. The troops had been supplemented by thousands of doctors, nurses, agricultural specialists, and teachers. Although the Soviets ultimately threw overwhelming support behind the MPLA, Neto knew that it was more because he was emerging as the most likely winner and because the West had lined up behind the other factions, not out of any loyalty to him personally. Now that he was in power, Fidel and the Cubans had substantially greater influence with Neto than did the leaders in the Kremlin. This did not sit well in Moscow. Besides, it appeared that Neto had taken Fidel's advice on how to avoid some of the mistakes he had made in Cuba. Neto retained for Angola a nonaligned status, refusing Moscow's request for military bases and maintaining a mixed economy with the continued presence of United States oil companies. He was determinedly independent. An added bonus for Fidel was that oil-rich Angola paid him in hard currency for the services of his troops and technicians.

As they would later do again in a similar way in Grenada, the Soviets attempted to establish their influence over Angola by fostering a relationship with one of Neto's top lieutenants, Nito Alves, who was in favor of a more hard-line Marxist policy and substantially closer ties to Moscow. Through flattery and promises of support, they encouraged him to lead a coup against Neto in May 1977. The coup was unsuccessful, but only because Cuban troops fought with the loyal MPLA forces against the Soviet-leaning Alves forces.

Talks initiated by Kissinger aimed at restoring U.S.-Cuban diplomatic relations had been broken off when Cuba sent troops to Angola. It was for Fidel a small and perhaps laughable price to pay for the stunning success of the Angola venture and the worldwide acclaim it won him. According to Cuban sources, however, Cuba was told that if Ford won reelection the talks would be reconvened even while troops remained in Angola.

When the Carter administration came in, talks were restarted with no prior conditions. A new atmosphere of optimism and conciliation prevailed as a boat filled with visiting American jazz musicians sailed to Cuba in a goodwill gesture. A flood of congressmen, including Senator Frank Church (D-Idaho), chairman of the Senate Foreign Relations Committee, visited Cuba and spent time with Fidel. They were charmed and impressed by his intellect and his knowledge of United States history and politics.

During Barbara Walters's 1977 interview with Fidel, in which she asked him his feelings about President Carter, he replied, "I have appreciated in Carter an idealistic man, an idealistic man with his roots in his religious convictions." It would have been an unusual comment for the head of any Western democracy to make, and coming from a Communist leader it was unprecedented. But it reflected Fidel's continuing religious frame of reference.

Fidel's religious background has always been close to the surface. In the period immediately following the revolution, he sought to avoid a direct confrontation with the Roman Catholic Church, but its strong anti-Communist position eventually made conflict inevitable. The hierarchy of the church in Cuba was mostly Spanish and conservative; therefore Fidel was able to focus his attack on the church as an ally of the old privileged

289

elite rather than on religion per se. He expelled virtually all of the Spanish priests. In the sixties, when all Cuban institutions were being made to conform to a Marxist mold, religion was actively disparaged and the celebration of Christmas was abolished. However, diplomatic relations with the Vatican were always maintained, and in 1964, Fidel told Herbert Matthews, "I don't care whether a person is religious or not, or what his religion is." In April 1960, he had attended the marriage of his sister Emma in Havana Cathedral.

Fidel's oratory has always been peppered with religious references, and by the early 1980s he shifted from a relatively neutral position on religion to seeking actively an alliance between his regime and religious leaders. He has particularly sought to align himself with the liberation theology movement in Latin America, and progressive church leaders have been welcome visitors in Havana. In 1985, he met with a delegation of Methodist ministers holding a convention in Havana and a delegation of Catholic bishops from the United States. Christmas is again celebrated in Cuba, and there are few restrictions on religious freedom. He has repeatedly made it clear that the Pope has an open invitation to visit Cuba. In May 1985, Fidel conducted a book-length interview with Brazilian priest Frei Betto. Published under the title *Fidel y La Religión*, it contains lengthy descriptions by Fidel of the profound effect of religion in his life.

Preliminary discussions to restore diplomatic relations were begun between the United States and Cuba, with both sides initially taking mutually unacceptable positions. Fidel argued that although he was eager for improved relations with the United States, Cuba could not negotiate under "unequal conditions," namely, the embargo. The United States took the position that as the embargo had been imposed only after the nationalization without compensation of U.S. property, it could not be lifted without resolution of that issue. Nevertheless, when a State Department delegation went to Havana in April 1977, the possibility of establishing Interest Sections in each other's capital was raised. Clearly the problems of compensation, the embargo, and other issues could not be resolved without adequate communications, and both parties agreed that the establishment of the Interest Sections was a reasonable first step to facilitate that process. Wayne Smith, a State Department participant in that process and subsequently the head of the U.S. Interest Section in Havana, says, "We fully expected it was very temporary. We would set up the 'Interest Section,' we would begin the process of dialogue, and in short order we would move to full diplomatic relations."

The dialogue began with a possible scenario in which simultaneous negotiations might take place on lifting the embargo, with separate talks to be considered on compensation for seized U.S. properties. The entire process, however, became the victim of the traditional power struggle between the secretary of state and the President's national security adviser. The move toward normalizing relations was primarily a State Department initiative backed by Carter but sponsored in the administration primarily by Secretary of State Cyrus Vance. It was never a particularly popular move with National Security Adviser Zbigniew Brzezinski, and on November 17, at a breakfast with reporters, he warned that he had recent reports that Cuba was dramatically increasing its troop strength in Angola and moving military personnel into several other African countries. He warned Cuba against further increasing its military presence on the continent, and stated that its actions jeopardized improvement of U.S.-Cuban diplomatic relations. There was, according to Wayne Smith, no evidence to suggest that the Cubans were increasing their troop strength in Angola. The other African countries Brzezinski cited where alleged Cuban military presence had been discovered were those countries in which Cuba had had advisers since the mid-1960s. Brzezinski was either unaware of the history of the Cuban role in Africa or was merely seeking to take advantage of the ignorance of others on the subject. His announcements were, however, enough to stall the normalization talks and win one more round in the ongoing battle with the State Department.

Bzrezinski and his staff would later rather lamely argue that the purpose of the announcement was to warn Cuba against becoming involved in Ethiopia.

But Ethiopia did not prove to be the unequivocal victory for Fidel that Angola had been. Shortly after the Marxist coup in February 1974, which overthrew the U.S.-backed venerable King Haile Selassie and brought Colonel Mengistu Haile-Mariam to power, Fidel began to establish a collaborative relationship with the new regime. This was an awkward and tense situation, as Fidel and the Soviets also had close ties to Siyad Barrah, the Socialist leader of neighboring Somalia. Ethiopia and Somalia enjoyed a traditional mutual enmity arising from the disputed territorial claims over the Ogaden region that substantially transcended any ideological similarities. In the hope that Cuba and the Soviets could maintain their alliances and influence with both countries, Fidel sponsored a meeting in March 1977 in South Yemen aimed at creating some form of consolidated Socialist state between all three countries (a somewhat naive proposition that failed to take into account the historical animosity between Ethiopia and Somalia). Then, driven by the geopolitical interests of the two superpowers, these two client states exchanged partners. As the Soviets increased their military supplies to Ethiopia, the U.S. withdrew. And as the Soviet presence in Ethiopia increased, Somalia turned increasingly to the West, especially to the U.S., for its defense. At the same time, the Soviet and Cuban presence there dwindled.

It was not an easy or happy situation for Fidel. The choice of Ethiopia

291

over Somalia was not based on a clear ideological distinction or the need to expel an old colonial power or opposition to marauding South Africa. Instead—as was evident to the rest of the Third World—the Cuban presence was primarily at the behest of the Soviets as part of a simple pragmatic power play in the Horn of Africa. In addition, Fidel did not have a particularly close relationship with Mengistu, whose regime was harsh and often brutal. At one point, the Cubans initiated an ill-conceived plot to replace Mengistu with a leader more acceptable to Fidel. The matter was substantially improved when Somalia, emboldened by its new Western allies, invaded Ethiopia in November 1977, seeking to reclaim control of the Ogaden. Fidel then felt he could more plausibly commit seventeen thousand Cuban troops to defend his new Ethiopian allies against the invading Somalis. However, unlike in Angola, Cuban troops in Ethiopia were under the overall command of a Soviet general.

The uncomfortable situation in Ethiopia was aggravated for Fidel by the problem of Eritrea. Largely Muslim, Eritrea had for years been waging a war of independence against the rest of Ethiopia, made up mostly of Coptic Christians. The nations of the Muslim world, out of religious solidarity and ignoring their different shades of political ideology, had been providing support to the Eritrean rebels. Once the Somali invasion had been defeated, the Mengistu regime saw the crushing of the Eritrean rebellion as its priority, an objective with which the Soviets concurred. In addition to their Arab backers, the Eritreans enjoyed wide sympathy in the developing world, and for Fidel to be involved in attempts to suppress them spelled disaster for his image among the very nations with which he had worked so hard to cultivate support. He refused to become directly involved in the Eritrean conflict, keeping his forces on the Somali border, ostensibly to maintain the peace and prevent another invasion. However, by so doing he freed the Ethiopian military to commit all of its forces to the struggle against the Eritreans. In addition, constant rumors, whether true or not, seeped out of Ethiopia to the effect that Cubans had been involved against the Eritreans. The Cuban troops were withdrawn after 1980, but today neither the Cubans nor the Ethiopians have much good to say about each other. The Soviets, however, remain deeply involved in Ethiopia.

Within a matter of months, Fidel had, perhaps without choice, squandered the acclaim he had received across most of the world as a result of Cuba's intervention in Angola. He had gone from being the hero of the Non-Aligned Movement back virtually to where he was in 1973 when there was talk of expelling Cuba from the Movement. Above all else, Cuba's involvement in Ethiopia was seen, in contrast to its role in Angola, as evidence of subservience to the Soviet Union. At the Non-Aligned meeting in Belgrade in July 1978, there was talk of boycotting the summit meeting in Havana scheduled for the following summer, and again there were moves to have Cuba expelled from the organization.

In the Western hemisphere, Fidel was faring better. A new generation of young leaders, especially in the more recently independent microstates of the eastern Caribbean, looked to Fidel as a hero. In March 1979, Maurice Bishop and his New Jewel Movement in Grenada seized power from the corrupt Sir Eric Gairy. Grenada immediately sought close ties with Cuba, and received technicians, doctors, and military advisers. In St. Lucia, George Odlum was openly admiring of the Cuban system. Fidel's most important ally in the region was Michael Manley, the prime minister of Jamaica, who came from a distinguished political family and shared Fidel's global perspective and aspirations to make the Third World a consequential force. There was a personal affinity between the two men that led them to meet frequently.

By far the most important development in the region in 1979 was in July, when after twenty years of struggle the Sandinistas in Nicaragua finally overthrew the hated and corrupt Somoza dynasty. For all of Fidel's past efforts to promote revolution in Latin America, he had played a relatively minor role in this, the one great success of armed struggle in the hemisphere. Cuba provided only two planeloads of light weapons, and had no military personnel actually involved in the civil war. Fidel's participation was largely as a senior adviser to the factionalized guerrilla leadership, negotiating with the feuding groups to get them to form a united opposition front, and after the victory urging a course of moderation with the United States, and caution in too rapidly socializing the economy.

The Sandinista victory, occurring two months before the Non-Aligned summit was held in Havana in September 1979, could not have come at a better time. As chairman of the Non-Aligned Movement and host of the summit, Fidel was in many respects at the zenith of his career. The Sandinista victory by association helped to restore some of the luster to his role that the controversial participation in Ethiopia had taken away. He spoke at the conference as a statesman addressing the hard realities of underdevelopment and debt facing the Third World. Responding to the discord that had wracked the movement because of the perception that he was a tool of the Soviets, he talked of the importance of unity among developing nations and avoided any mention of a natural alignment with the Soviet bloc. Although the conference was not quite the event Fidel might have hoped for in 1976, it was, under the circumstances, highly successful. In particular it allowed Fidel to use his extraordinary charm to build solid personal relationships with other leaders. A notable example was his growing rapport with Indira Gandhi.

The conference of the Non-Aligned Movement marked an important milestone in the changing role Fidel saw for himself in the world. Although he had been moving in the direction for several years, the conference can be considered the start of the "statesman" phase of his career. Increasingly, he was playing the role of mediator in Third World conflicts, rather than protagonist. The decision to move into a different role was probably more a reflection of his age and a desire to maximize his impact in the world in his remaining years, than a consideration of the political interests of Cuba. Since the Non-Aligned summit, he seems to have mellowed and to be looking to build a record for posterity no longer as a revolutionary but as a conciliator. How he will be remembered seems to be of increasing importance to him.

A month later, Fidel was in New York to address the U.N. General Assembly in his role as chairman of the Non-Aligned Movement. In a speech that was stunningly free of the polemics he had used in earlier orations before this body, he spoke of the unnecessary human suffering in the world, of injustice, of ignorance, of the lack of health care, and of malnutrition and hunger. In tone and substance his speech was strikingly similar to the message delivered a few days later by the Pope.

At a time when Fidel was poised to capitalize on his cherished term as the global spokesman for the oppressed of the world, he suffered several severe setbacks, none of which was of his own making. Most devastating was the Soviet decision in December 1979 to invade Afghanistan. To have endorsed the invasion would have destroyed his credibility in the developing world; to condemn the Soviets would have been economic suicide. When the motion to condemn came up at the United Nations, Cuba abstained, which for much of the developing world was tantamount to knuckling under to the Soviets. The Kremlin had inflicted on Fidel close to a mortal wound as far as his credibility in the developing world was concerned. Interestingly, Robert Pastor, of the National Security Council, who together with Peter Tarnoff, executive secretary of the State Department, met with Fidel shortly after the invasion, says he was amazed how little detail the Soviets had provided Fidel about their actions in Afghanistan. He and Tarnoff were put in the unusual position of providing Fidel with basic information from U.S. sources that he could not obtain elsewhere.

One fallout from the Afghanistan invasion was that Cuba was defeated in its bid for a a seat on the U.N. Security Council. It was a seat that should rightfully have been theirs unchallenged, as chairman of the Non-Aligned Movement.

On January 11, 1980, Celia Sánchez, a heavy cigarette smoker, died of lung cancer. The effect on Fidel and on the whole country was profound. Deeply depressed, Fidel became for several months withdrawn and subdued. One observer seeing him at official functions said that "he was just not himself." Although he eventually recovered, the enormous importance of their relationship was open for everyone to see. Seeing him several months later at a ceremony where he was dedicating a factory in her honor, one participant stated, "He was so emotionally affected that I did not think he could finish his speech without breaking down."

The impact of Celia's death pointed up just how centralized the power in Cuba was, and to what a significant degree Fidel is involved in every aspect of the government. With his usual indefatigable energy seriously slowed for the first time since he came to power, diplomats noted a perceptible slowing of the wheels of government. Not only were there delays in decisions normally handled with dispatch, and the usual steady stream of visitors reduced to a trickle, but some of the decisions themselves appeared to reflect that Fidel's judgment was impaired. More than any other event, Celia's death showed how much Cuba is Fidel. It is a personal fiefdom shaped to his personal philosophy and his wishes. Rarely if ever have a country and a people been so totally under the domination of the personality of one man.

Some feel the impact of Celia's death was reflected in his seemingly erratic handling of the Mariel boat lift during the summer of 1980. A large crowd of Cubans entered and camped out on the grounds of the unguarded Peruvian Embassy, seeking political asylum. Fidel, to remove the embarrassment of having these people visible in the center of Havana, offered to let them and others who wished to do so leave for the United States from the port of Mariel. A flotilla of small boats transported more than a hundred thousand Cubans out of the country. Apparently Fidel was quite shaken not only that so many should want to leave, but that they were not from the professional classes. These were working people, the bedrock of the revolution. In a fit of pique, he ordered that several thousand mental patients and prisoners be added to the emigré crowd. It was a way of thumbing his nose at the United States for being such a lure to his people.

As word spread that the doors to the United States were open, many thousands more decided to leave the country. Reception facilities in Florida were overwhelmed, and with complaints from state authorities to the administration in Washington becoming intense, the need to terminate the flow became acute. Fidel, however, seemed to feel he was exacting some perverse justice from the United States. Eventually, following strong protests from the State Department on the matter, Fidel met with Congressman Mickey LeLand (D-Texas) and Carlos Rafael Rodríguez, and was convinced to shut off the flow of refugees. It was not his finest hour.

Later in 1980, the Carter administration would get itself stuck in a fix of its own making. Senator Frank Church (D-Idaho), chairman of the Senate Foreign Relations Committee, was in a tight race for reelection. He needed an issue to show his hard-line stance to refute his liberal image. He made public information from the CIA that indicated the presence of a Soviet combat batallion in Cuba. Caught off guard and eager not to seem to have been napping, the administration quickly announced that the presence of the Soviet unit was unacceptable and insisted to the Soviet and Cuban governments that it be removed. On more sober analysis it emerged that the unit had been there for more than ten years and that no new introduction of forces had occurred. The demand for its departure was allowed to die a quiet death.

Although there was some indication from Secretary of State Vance that the normalization process with Cuba might be restarted once the Iranian crisis was resolved, the issue remained moot until the end of the Carter administration.

The arrival of the Reagan administration in January 1981 heralded a return to a hard-line position against Cuba. From the start, Reagan officials made it clear that they intended to adopt a policy of hostility and confrontation toward Cuba, Nicaragua, and Grenada. A White Paper purporting to show direct Cuban involvement in El Salvador proved to be largely fabricated, and Secretary of State Alexander Haig was eventually forced to concede that several of the allegations could not be substantiated.

A similar situation existed when President Reagan stated inaccurately that a much needed civilian airport being built in Grenada, in part by U.S. and British companies, was being constructed for military purposes. Fidel had seen U.S. administrations come and go. He adopted a highly restrained posture, with the apparent intention of waiting out the Reagan administration. He did, however, comment, "Now I have a competitor as a communicator—Reagan."

In 1981, the Reagan administration launched military exercises on a small island off Puerto Rico in a thinly veiled dress rehearsal for an invasion of Grenada. Cuba's involvement with Grenada was not unlike the Soviet Union's relationship with Cuba. Grenada was not of strategic consequence to Cuba; in fact it was a financial and technical drain. Although it served an important propaganda role, demonstrating Cuba's growing influence in the Caribbean, it was also a serious potential liability.

Fidel's relations with Maurice Bishop were close. Bishop's mother said that her son viewed Fidel like a father, reflecting among other things that Fidel had become very much a part of the older generation of revolutionaries. When Fidel had spoken at the United Nations at the end of 1979, Bishop had rushed to the podium to embrace him in a display reminiscent of Fidel's first meeting with Khrushchev in the same auditorium. When Bishop had run out of funds to complete his ambitious airport project he had turned to Fidel for help. Fidel, short of hard currency, had instead sent four hundred Cuban construction workers to help finish the job.

Fidel's close relationship with Bishop, and his espousal to him of his philosophy of independent national assertion under the Socialist umbrella, again caused serious problems for Moscow, exactly as had his relationship with Neto and Angola. In 1982, the Soviet Union established an embassy in Grenada headed by a senior diplomat with a staff of twenty. While working superficially in close collaboration with the Cubans, they assiduously cultivated their own channels of influence in the Grenadian government. Their strongest supporter was Minister of Finance Bernard Coard, an outspoken, doctrinaire Marxist and a Moscow loyalist. An intelligent man, Coard had always aspired to the leadership of the New Jewel Movement, but he lacked the charisma of Bishop and therefore had been content up to that point to let Bishop be the front man. Again, similar to their strategy in Angola with Neto, the Soviets encouraged Coard to oust Bishop and seize power. Their objective, however, was to remove Grenada from Fidel's dominant influence and bring it squarely under their own.

Their strategy proved to be a disaster. After grabbing power from the popular Bishop and placing him under house arrest, Coard found that he could not control public opinion, which rallied in support of Bishop. Soldiers loyal to Coard killed Bishop and several of his supporters in a melee of gunfire, an act some believe to have been instigated by the Soviets. Coard went into hiding, leaving the country in something approaching anarchy. The Reagan administration seized this long-awaited and heaven-sent opportunity to invade the island, using the dubious pretext that they were going to evacuate American citizens at the St. George's University Medical School. They proceeded to take military control of the whole country.

A small contingent of Cuban military advisers and the lightly armed construction workers put up token resistance. They were quickly overcome, with a significant number of fatalities. With the invasion imminent, Fidel had ordered the Cubans to resist to the last man, a gesture which, while consistent with the Cuban tradition of heroism and martyrdom, did not seem well conceived either militarily or politically. After the event, Fidel called a news conference at midnight to condemn the United States for its role. But there was an element of resignation in his protest, perhaps a sign of his frustration with the Soviets, which he could not publicly disclose.

Since the Grenada invasion, relations between the United States and

Cuba have continued at a low ebb. The Reagan administration has sought to keep to a minimum contacts between the countries and especially to limit the flow of hard currency to Cuba as a result of Americans traveling there. Radio Martí, a government-funded station to broadcast propaganda to Cuba, has started operations over Cuban protests, but it is of minimal consequence offering little different from the existing Voice of America broadcasts. There is also little likelihood that its appeal to the average Cuban will ever compete with that of Miami's commercial stations.

In the months surrounding the Grenada invasion, Fidel seemed to be moving more slowly and, in a most unusual departure, on several occasions read speeches from prepared texts. There was considerable speculation about his health and it was suggested that he might be suffering from some serious illness. That view is still held by some knowledgeable individuals in the exile community, although there is no hard evidence. Fidel has shown no sign of illness in the last three years, although his recently announced decision to give up smoking cigars and drinking coffee may be for his health rather than, as he has stated, to set an example for the Cuban people. He may have suffered a mild heart attack and have chronic hypertension. It is also possible that the episode in 1983 was a bout of depression.

In 1985 and 1986, two issues held Fidel's visible attention. He aggressively championed the cause of developing nations with substantial international debts, urging them not to pay their creditors, and he actively promoted an enhanced relationship between the Cuban government and the progressive elements in the Roman Catholic Church. Neither issue is tied directly to political ideology and his strategy is clearly to move himself back toward the mainstream of Latin American politics by identifying himself with issues that cut across the political spectrum. He also shows growing concern about the internal operation of the Cuban government. The era of leadership by his peers who were with him at Moncada or on the *Granma* is coming to an end and a new generation of leadership is coming to power. Many of those moving into positions of influence were born, or at least received their education, since the revolution. Fidel takes immense pride in these products of his revolution, who are for the most part bright, well-trained, and well-traveled technocrats.

Yet he is faced with serious concerns. The bureaucracy he has created is slow and inefficient. At the Third Communist Party Congress in February 1986, he minced no words in criticizing the shortcomings of his managers. In an effort to streamline the government, he has moved aside such old friends as Sergio del Valle, the minister of health, Guillermo Garcia, Minister of Transportation and one of his earliest supporters in the Sierra Maestra, and most significantly, Ramiro Valdés, the head of state security, in part because he opposed Fidel's more liberal move on religion. Fidel also has the problem of how to keep his revolution alive. With a growing percentage of the population having no memory of Batista, the benefits that Fidel has brought Cuba are increasingly taken for granted by the younger generation. They are more interested in consumer goods and far less willing than their parents to make sacrifices. Satisfying their demands may be the greatest challenge Fidel faces during the remainder of his years in power.

Especially since the death of Celia Sánchez, Fidel has led a relatively solitary life without any close emotional attachments. To some it would seem a lonely existence. However, he entertains frequent visitors from outside Cuba, perhaps finding it easier to establish friendships with them because by holding such absolute power in Cuba he has made it virtually impossible for any Cuban to have a purely personal relationship with him. He probably has more regular personal contacts with the leaders of more nations than any government head in the world today. His visitors include not just government officials but a startling range of intellectuals, U.S. business leaders, religious figures, and media luminaries. He is particularly close to the Nobel prize-winning novelist Gabriel García Márquez of Colombia. His mind is as fertile as ever and he exhibits a hunger for intellectual stimulation that can be adequately satisfied only by visitors from outside his own society. He also exhibits remarkable mental flexibility in his ability to adapt his strategies to the changing world political climate. Very few who meet him are not seduced by his personal charm, even those who violently disagree with him on ideological grounds. He has a special quality, shared by few politicians, of giving his undivided attention to anyone speaking to him, no matter how lowly he is or how insignificant his comments. He also has the capacity to pick the brains of his visitors in a way that is flattering to them and at the same time of immense value to him.

Fidel still works extremely hard and the revolution remains the one consuming interest in his life. Ever since he was in the mountains he has done most of his work at night. He frequently schedules meetings for ten or eleven in the evening that continue until daybreak. His capacity for talking is legendary, and he has often given interviews that went on for five or six hours, giving the interviewer in that time the opportunity to ask only a handful of questions. It is a style that among other things allows him to control the interchange and limit the in-depth pursuit of issues he prefers not to discuss.

Those who know him well frequently speak of what they see as a love/hate relationship with the United States. He is attracted and fascinated by some aspects of American society, especially its vitality and its technological genius, and at the same time repelled by other features. In many respects his views are identical to those his hero, José Martí, wrote about a hundred years ago.

Fidel is evasive about his personal life and it continues to be clouded in secrecy, even though there does not seem to be much to hide. He does take visitors, including U.S. congressmen, skin diving and fishing, which remain his major forms of recreation. But as has been the case throughout his life, he is a self-sufficient individual who long ago learned to survive without any real family life. He occasionally spends time with Ramón and Raúl, but he is not particularly close to them.

Fidelito, quiet and scholarly, after graduating in 1972 from Moscow's Tomorrasov University with a degree in nuclear physics, has gradually risen to become the executive director of the Cuban Atomic Energy Commission. He is married and has two children. Although Fidel's relationship with his son is carefully hidden from public view, he takes a great interest in his grandchildren. While many Cubans are unaware that Fidel has grandchildren, enough do so that a large number of girls have been named Alena in recent years after his granddaughter. For Fidel, his primary family remains the Cuban people and *his* revolution, which is still the main source of his emotional gratification.

The most closely guarded secret of all is Fidel's succession. There is no indication who might succeed him. He seems acutely aware that his eventual departure will leave a vacuum of gargantuan proportions and his intensive efforts to build the strength of the party and the government apparatus are a way of trying to reduce that impact. In the past, it has always been clear that in the event of a sudden catastrophe Raúl would take over the leadership, but if, as expected, Fidel stays in power throughout his lifetime, Raúl, by then, would be reaching retirement age. That Fidel seems disinclined to give any indication of whom he favors to succeed him suggests that he expects to remain in power for many years to come.

Looking back on Fidel's life and career as he approaches his sixtieth (or fifty-ninth) birthday, one sees a man who in some respects has changed dramatically over the years, but who in other ways is still driven by the same forces that motivated him thirty years ago. His illegitimacy and his overwhelming need for recognition and acceptance have long since subsided as primary factors affecting his psyche. However, age has brought out even more clearly the elements in his parents with which he most strongly identified—his mother's deeply religious values and his father's aggressive, dominant style. It has been argued that Fidel's father had an insatiable appetite to acquire all of the land around their home in Birán, and Fidel, inheriting the same urge, has acquired all of the land in Cuba. It is hard to separate Fidel's personal psychological needs from the inevitable historical imperative that drove him into conflict with the United States, but for those who argue that history might have taken a different course had the United States acted differently toward the revolution, I argue that the die was cast historically and psychologically before Fidel came to power. He himself had foreseen an inescapable need to break the bond with the United States as an inevitable part of his destiny.

He could not have done it without the patronage of the Soviet Union. He was not Marxist when he came to power, and only he knows in what ideology he truly believes today. He did aggressively embrace Marxism–Leninism for several pragmatic reasons. He had to have the trust and confidence of the Soviet Union to get the military and economic support he required to survive. He needed to usurp the old-line Communists in Cuba who sought to shunt him aside, and there was no better way of doing that than by making himself the most dedicated Communist in the country. Some say that the primary attraction of communism was that it was an ideology that would allow him to justify assuming total power and keeping it for the rest of his life without being accused of being just another Latin American dictator driven solely by a desire for power and personal aggrandizement. Without doubt, adopting communism provided him the most potent symbol with which to assert his independence from the United States.

Fidel's egotism has never allowed him to accept that he may have merely exchanged the subservience to one superpower, the United States, for subservience to another, the Soviet Union. Some theorists argue that little nations must inevitably be the pawns of superpowers and, given that, he made the decision that it was better to be the pawn of a nation six thousand miles away than one ninety miles away. If that is the case, he has shown no evidence of it. To Western eyes it may seem like splitting hairs, but Cubans see Fidel as having taken every opportunity to assert his nation's sovereignty and independence from the Soviet Union. Certainly there is little doubt that Fidel has been in varying degrees a constant headache to the leadership in Moscow.

The greatest force to sweep the globe in the last forty years has been the success of the anticolonial movements that have remade the maps of entire continents and increased the membership of the United Nations from 35 in 1946 to 160 today. It was not, as perceived by many American politicians, the result of the sinister hand of the Soviet Union. Rather it was the inevitable turn of the tide against the European domination throughout the nineteenth century of the world's trade patterns. Perhaps because his background and education were strongly influenced by both a European and a colonial heritage, Fidel early understood the significance and potential of this trend. Since his university days, he has seen for himself a destiny that lays beyond merely the island of Cuba. His experience in playing off the United States against the Soviet Union had shown him that he could, if audacious enough, operate in the same league as the superpowers. By adopting a leadership role at the forefront of the anticolonial movement, first as a sponsor of revolution and then ultimately as the chairman of the Non-Aligned Movement, he acquired a constituency comparable to the superpowers'. This constituency has allowed him to operate as an influential world leader who is listened to with great respect.

His increasingly restrained oratory and his statesmanlike role have gained him growing acceptance in the Third World across the full ideological spectrum. In a little over a month in late 1985, he played host for state visits by presidents Kenneth Kaunda of Zambia, Julius Nyerere of Tanzania, José Dos Santos of Angola, Junius Jaywardene of Sri Lanka, and prime ministers Robert Mugabe of Zimbabwe and Rajiv Gandhi of India. He has made Havana an obligatory stopping point for all but the most reactionary leaders of the developing world.

Within Cuba, Fidel's domination of every aspect of the government and the society remains total. His personal need for absolute control seems to have changed little over the years. He remains committed to a disciplined society in which he is still determined to remake the Cuban national character, creating work-oriented, socially concerned individuals. It is still the Jesuit school in which he is the principal. He wants to increase people's standard of living, the availability of material goods, and to import the latest technology. But the economic realities, despite rapid dramatic growth in the gross national product, severely limit what Cuba can buy on the world market.

No matter how it is rationalized, Fidel's greatest problem is his economic dependence on the Soviet Union. Without the estimated $4 billion a year they provide, the economy of Cuba would sink. It is especially the supply of oil that has him hobbled. Small amounts of oil have been found in Cuba, and the first of four projected nuclear power stations will soon come on line. By 1990, they expect that 25 percent of their electrical power needs will be met from this source. However, Fidel still cannot escape Martí's warning that, "Without economic independence there can be no political independence."

His dependence on the Soviet Union is also his greatest liability in his cherished role as a leader of the Third World. Despite his efforts to minimize the appearance of Soviet domination, including, in 1985, declining to attend Konstantin Chernenko's funeral, his gestures are too often seen as more symbolic than substantive. At the very point when his credibility in the Third World was at its highest, the Soviets undercut him by invading Afghanistan and involving him in Ethiopia. No matter how much personal respect Third World leaders have for him, they know that in the final analysis on major issues he cannot oppose the Soviet Union.

After years of severe austerity, the Cuban people are now enjoying a rise in their standard of living. High-quality health care, excellent education, and equal opportunity have allowed people from very humble backgrounds to become professionals and hold influential jobs in all phases of Cuban society. Basic necessities in the way of food staples, clothing, simple electric appliances, and such things as children's toys are provided to every citizen on a rationed but highly subsidized basis so that every Cuban has his or her basic needs met at a minimum cost. In addition, in the last four years the government has instituted a "parallel economy," through which at unsubsidized and therefore substantially higher prices Cubans can spend their money on a wide range of luxury items, from running shoes to video cassette recorders. The streets are sprinkled with new cars, mainly Fiats manufactured under license in the Soviet Union. The biggest problem, however, is that the desire for consumer items is enormous, and in general people have an excess of money with not enough to spend it on. Also, while the standard of living for the poorest people has improved immeasurably since 1959, even greater improvements have occurred in several other countries in the region during the same period.

A recent campaign has been launched to repaint and spruce up the decaying and peeling buildings of once-elegant Havana, long neglected in favor of projects for the rural population. A restoration program in old Havana is renovating with museum-quality precision the centuries'-old Spanish mansions, shops, and restaurants to their original condition.

Cuba remains a country under the tightest control. While there is great equality of opportunity, the access to power is carefully controlled. There is only one woman member of the Politbureau, and despite a strong public commitment to eradicate racism, there are few blacks in the upper echelons of the party or the government. A remarkably high percentage of the Central Committee members are military officers, an insidious intrusion into civilian affairs, suggesting that Fidel has not forgotten that the military invariably holds the ultimate power. It is perhaps significant that Fidel's first title is commander in chief.

Committees for the Defense of the Revolution continue to keep a watchful eye on every block. Any suspicious behavior, whether it is unexplained affluence, criticism of the revolution, or an inclination to antisocial activities, is liable to be reported, drawing the scrutiny of authorities. It exerts a chilling effect on any form of deviancy, on the one hand virtually eliminating crime but at the same time suffocating free expression. Cubans today seem to be far more open in their willingness to criticize their government's failings, the role of the Soviet Union in Cuba, and the restless demand for consumer goods than they were five years ago. There are no longer campaigns against homosexuals, intellectuals, churchgoers, or others labeled as counterrevolutionaries. Instead of polemics, Cubans today tend to appeal to outsiders for sympathy and understanding of their efforts to build socialism, being only too willing to admit their shortcomings. Yet the press, radio, and television remain tightly controlled. There are no labor unions or any organization that is allowed to provide people with a view different from that of the government. Above all, there is no criticism of Fidel.

In the past, there were substantial numbers of political prisoners, as many as twenty thousand at one point. The numbers have been reduced dramatically in recent years; some two thousand were released in a deal with the United States, and others have completed their sentences. Nevertheless, many of those who are still incarcerated have been there since the early years of the revolution, and have probably served longer terms than political prisoners anywhere else in the world. Cuba has refused to allow any human rights monitoring group, such as Amnesty International or Americas Watch, to visit and investigate the state of political prisoners in the country. Ironically, as a result of the emptying of Cuban jails during the 1980 Mariel boatlift, more than 1,500 Cubans have remained without trial and without being charged with any crimes in the Federal Penitentiary in Atlanta for nearly six years. They may well exceed in number the political prisoners who remain in Cuban jails.

Cuba is certainly not the utopia that Fidel thought he could create. On many counts he must be given a failing grade as far as life in Cuba today is concerned. Part of the problem may well be attributed to the preoccupation he has had with affairs outside Cuba. Why should a little country like Cuba be trying to play a major role on the world scene? Fidel, however, is like de Gaulle when he said, "I am France." There is a fusion in Fidel's mind between his own ego and the national identity. What he sees as good for himself he inevitably sees as good for Cuba. He knows that most Cubans are willing to accept this view. His need to thrust himself on the world stage with an impact outrageously disproportionate to Cuba's tiny size is an acceptable overcompensation for the generations of humiliation and denigration of the national spirit that Cubans feel they suffered at the hands of other nations. There is no resentment in Cuba over Fidel's international role, only pride and a sense of vindication.

At the same time, there can be little doubt that Fidel's consuming desire to achieve the greatest historical stature for himself has led him to neglect people's desperate desire for a higher standard of living. His need for total control and to be completely authoritarian in his rule has often blinded him to the circumstances in which many Cubans have to live. Had he been able to follow a democratic course, the quality of life might be very different in Cuba today.

Most Cubans would probably be willing to trade some of the international prestige Fidel has brought to them for even a modest improvement in their standard of living.

Fidel has outlasted seven U.S. Presidents and five Soviet leaders. He has been in power longer than any world figure except King Hussein of Jordan, and he could well be Cuba's leader for another twenty years. From his earliest years, he was obsessed with the goal of becoming an enduring historic figure who would be acknowledged as one of the most important and influential leaders of the twentieth century. In that objective he has certainly succeeded, but it is the very psychological characteristics that have driven him to need dictatorial power over his fellow countrymen for nearly thirty years and elbow his way onto the world stage that may ultimately be seen as the flaws that prevented him from achieving the worldwide acceptance that he so deeply desired.

Chapter Notes

The primary sources of information for this book were interviews conducted by the author in Havana, Miami, New York, and Washington. Those interviewed had for the most part been intimately involved with the life of Fidel Castro, some briefly, others throughout his entire career. Some have remained loyal to him, others have become bitter enemies. For their own reasons several of those interviewed requested anonymity. The material used includes information obtained in a lengthy discussion the author had with Fidel Castro in 1979. In addition, a special effort was made to take advantage of his personal statements about himself and his life in the many interviews he has given over the years, as well as the frequent autobiographical comments he has made in his speeches.

The author has also drawn on the voluminous number of books, documents, newspaper stories, and scholarly studies that have appeared over a span of more than thirty years.

Prologue

There are many excellent histories of Cuba in English, including Irene Wright's *Early History of Cuba*, Charles Chapman's *A History of the Cuban Republic*, Leland Jenks's *Our Cuban Colony*, and Hugh Thomas's encyclopedic *Cuba: The Pursuit of Freedom*. Teresa Casuso provides an excellent compact review in *Cuba and Castro*. In Spanish, the four-volume *Historia de Cuba en Sus Relaciones Con Los Estados Unidos y España*, by the distinguished Cuban historian Herminio Portell Vilá, is definitive.

John Kirk's *José Martí* offers a comprehensive picture of Martí's life and works, particularly his early attraction to and later disillusionment with the United States. Teresa Casuso in *Cuba and Castro* refers to Martí's perception of the "dark side" of the American political character.

An article in *Philadelphia Manufacturer*, March 16, 1889, entitled "Do We Want Cuba?" suggested that the country would have to be completely Americanized before it could be considered for statehood.

A document in the form of a memo was prepared in the office of the assistant secretary for war and sent to General Nelson A. Miles, army chief of staff. It is now in the National Archives. It contained instructions and guidelines to govern the United States military intervention in Cuba.

General Leonard Wood, as military governor of Cuba, wrote on several occasions to President Roosevelt. The letter quoted is in Hermann Hagedorn's *That Human Being: Leonard Wood*.

The United States and Cuba: Business and Diplomacy, 1917–1960, edited by Robert Smith contains a useful perspective on the symbiotic relationship that developed between the two countries during those years.

Luis Aguilar, in *Cuba 1933—Prologue to Revolution*, offers a detailed insight into the period around the fall of Machado, and analyzes the social and political forces set in motion at that time that would have a direct bearing on the emergence of Fidel Castro as national leader and successful revolutionary.

Chapter 1

Accounts of Fidel Castro's childhood have appeared in several places, including Jules Dubois's *Fidel Castro*, Herbert Matthews's *Castro: A Political Biography*, Lionel Martin's *The Young Fidel*, Hugh Thomas's *Cuba: The Pursuit of Freedom*, Frei Betto's *Fidel y La Religión*, and several of the books by Luis Conte Agüero. Much of the information is conflicting and in some instances clearly wrong. Family embarrassment over divorce, illegitimacy, and the original relationship of Fidel's mother to the Castro household, as well as a later inclination to romanticize and interpret events in the most desirable political light, has led family members and others who knew Fidel as a child to present a less than candid picture of his early years. At the same time, his enemies have often sought to present his family and his childhood in the worst possible context, creating distortions at the other extreme. Perhaps because of the conflict with his father, or because his childhood was often an unhappy time, Castro has spoken relatively little about this period of his life. By far the most comprehensive account he has given appears in Carlos Franqui's *Diary of the Cuban Revolution*.

In preparing this volume, the author attempted to pick his way with discretion through a prickly array of anecdotal material. A major source of information was Fidel's older brother Ramón (interviewed in Havana, March 25–26, 1985) whose account, allowing for the blood relationship and the fifty years that have elapsed, seemed to be substantially accurate. Every effort was made to document key material with other sources.

Although Hugh Thomas's *Cuba: The Pursuit of Freedom* contains several apparent factual errors concerning Fidel's childhood, it offers an exceptional picture of life in Oriente Province in the early years of this century.

Juanita Castro, Fidel's younger sister, now in exile in Miami, gave an interview to *Life* magazine, August 28, 1964. She provided in that article several of the anecdotes of their childhood, although her account reflects the antipathy she now feels toward her brother.

The charge by a vice president of the United Fruit Company that Angel Castro was charged with theft is cited by Hugh Thomas.

Lee Lockwood conducted a lengthy series of interviews with Castro in 1965 in which Fidel was explicitly critical of his father.

Castro's letter from prison, in which he refers to his classmates when he first went to school, is cited by Lionel Martin in *The Young Fidel*.

The description of Castro's early school years in Santiago de Cuba, including the several quotes from Castro, is drawn substantially from Carlos Franqui's *Diary of the Cuban Revolution*.

The year of Castro's birth remains a matter of dispute. The official position of the Cuban government has changed over the years. Earlier it was given as 1927, today it is said to be 1926. In 1976, world leaders, including Leonid Brezhnev, sent him congratulations on his fiftieth birthday. To avoid causing embarrassment to his well-wishers, Castro seems to have formally accepted the earlier date. In his recent interview with Frei Betto he not only said the year of his birth was 1926, but went on to talk about how twenty-six has been a lucky number throughout his life. The account of his brother, Ramón, however, has a particular ring of truth to it, in part because it runs counter to the official position.

The threat by the young Castro to burn down his parents' house was related to Herbert Matthews and was repeated by his sister Juanita in her interview with *Life* magazine.

The story concerning the radio dramatization has various versions, although there seems to be little disagreement about the essential facts. Hugh Thomas is one of several authors who have also mentioned that at about the same time Fidel's older half-brother Pedro Emilio, an aspiring Auténtico politician, broke with their father and in a radio program denounced him for a variety of misdeeds including the fathering of illegitimate children. In the mists of time these events have become confused in people's minds.

In Hugh Thomas's *Cuba: The Pursuit of Freedom*, the incident with the bicycle is erroneously placed during Fidel's university years.

Information concerning Castro's years at Belen was provided by Carlos Rafael Rodríguez, vice president of Cuba, interviewed in Havana, March 25, 1985, and Alice Martínez in an interview in Washington, D.C., June 18, 1985.

Fidel's relationship with Father de Castro is described in Jaime Suchlicki's *Cuba: From Columbus to Castro*.

The author was provided with some useful observations on Castro's childhood by Cuban psychiatrist Reuben Rumbaut, now living in Houston, Texas. Dr. Rumbaut, a distinguished poet and one-time leader of the Movimiento Nacional Revolucionaria, published in the sixties a psychological profile of Fidel Castro in the now defunct Miami publication *Cuba Nueva*.

Chapter 2

Accounts of Fidel's years at the University of Havana are provided in Suchlicki's *University Students and Revolution in Cuba*, Lionel Martin's *The Young Fidel*, Thomas's *Cuba: The Pursuit of Freedom*, and Rolando Bonachea and Nelson Valdés's *Revolutionary Struggle*. A general background on the higher education system in Cuba is covered in *The Universities of Cuba, Haiti, and the Dominican Republic* by Harriet Bunn and Ellen Gut.

The anecdote concerning the car was related by Juanita Castro in her 1964 interview with *Life* magazine. It has also been recounted by Cuban artist Renee Méndez Capote.

Castro described his decision to study law in an interview published in *Revolución*, April 10, 1961. He subsequently referred to his regret about not being made to study something else in another interview in *Revolución*, March 14, 1964.

The description of Castro at the café, Las Delicias de Medina, as well as other observations on his university years, was made by a fellow student now practicing medicine in the United States. Interviewed by the author on October 4, 1984, he asked to remain anonymous.

Alfredo Guevara's comments about Castro were made to Lionel Martin and quoted in *The Young Fidel*.

Information on Castro's early venture into student politics was provided by Rolando Amador, a fellow student now practicing law in Miami. He was interviewed there by the author on October 16, 1985.

Castro's comments on his conflicts with the gangs and his moment of decision on the beach were made in an interview with Gloria Gaitán de Valencia and published in Colombia in *America Libre*, May 22–28, 1961.

There seems to be little doubt that Castro was for a while a member of the UIR. One former fellow student is adamant that he was a formal member, and was both an admirer and friend of its leader, Emilio Tro. For years after he left the university he carried the reputation of being a "gangster" because of this association. There is no evidence, however, that he benefited financially or was involved in the corrupt practices of the organization.

309

The power and excitement of the group were what appear to have attracted him. The statement made by José Diegues, cited by Bonachea and Valdés, that Fidel merely used the organization for his own political ends is probably very accurate. In later years, however, the association became a serious embarrassment, and sympathetic biographers, such as Lionel Martin, have implied that Fidel had no formal association with the UIR.

In an interview conducted in Havana, March 13, 1985, Dr. Antonio Núñez Jiménez provided the author with detailed information concerning Castro's relationship with the 30 of September Movement and his successful emergence as a dynamic student leader.

Castro described his near assassination at the university stadium in an interview, "Fidel Castro Visitó la Universidad," *Diario de la Marina* (Havana) January 14, 1959.

Information on Castro's swim across the Bay of Nipe was provided to the author by Horacio Ornez, Jr., whose father accompanied Castro.

In November 1977, on the tenth anniversary of the incident with the bell of Demajagua, a detailed account appeared in *Granma*.

Fidel provided to Carlos Franqui a detailed description of his time in Bogotá, which appears in *Diary of the Cuban Revolution*. A well-researched account was published by Mario Mencia in *Bohemia* (Havana), April 1978. U.S. Ambassador to the United Nations William Pawley later claimed that he had heard a voice on the radio say, "This is Fidel Castro from Cuba. This is a Communist revolution." The Colombian chief of police, Alberto Niño, is quoted by Hugh Thomas as claiming that Castro and del Pino were Communist agents sent to foment riots and that Castro killed thirty-two people including priests and nuns. Thomas also quotes a source saying that Castro carried a passbook identifying him as "Grade I Agent of the Third Front of the USSR in South America." A thorough investigation of the riots, conducted by Sir Norman Smith, chief of Scotland Yard, and submitted as a report to the Colombian government, gives no credence to any of these charges. An account given by Jules Dubois, who was in Bogotá at the time, in *Fidel Castro* also generally supports Fidel's version of the events.

Chapter 3

Revolutionary Struggle by Bonachea and Valdés provides an account of Fidel's final years at the university and his initial emergence on the national political scene. Hugh Thomas in *Cuba: The Pursuit of Freedom* covers much of the same ground but with an excellent analysis of the Cuban political context at the time. Lionel Martin in *The Young Fidel* provides some interesting detail, but focuses specifically on trying to show the early evidence of Fidel's later attraction to Marxism-Leninism. *El Grito del Moncada* by Mario Mencia offers meticulous documentation of Fidel's activities following the Batista coup.

Information on the period covered by this chapter was provided to the author in interviews with Rolando Amador (Miami, October 15, 1985), Carlos Rafael Rodríguez (Havana, March 25, 1985), Melba Hernández (Havana, March 19, 1985), Dr. Antonio Núñez Jiménez (Havana, March 13, 1985), Rafael Díaz Balart, Jr., (Washington, D.C., September 4, 1984), Marta Rojas (Havana, March 15, 1985), Raúl Martínez Arará (Miami, September 8, 1984), Orlando Castro (Miami, September 7, 1984), Max Lesnick (Miami, September 7, 1984), Faustino Pérez (March 23, 1984), Justo Carrillo (September 9, 1984), and four sources who wished to remain anonymous.

Castro described his honeymoon visit to New York and his thoughts about enrolling at Columbia in a 1977 interview with Barbara Walters shown on ABC television.

The author examined records of Castro's attendance at the University of Havana, including a full academic transcript, a copy of his thesis, and the report of a disciplinary hearing relating to a fight. The latter is an interesting reflection of the impotence of the university administration, which felt safe in disciplining an individual student for a fistfight, while powerless to deal with the armed violence, including murder, inflicted on the university community by the gangs.

Castro's early minimal relations with the Cuban Communist Party were described to the author by Rolando Amador and Carlos Rafael Rodríguez.

Details of Castro's congressional race were provided to the author by Marta Rojas. It is also well described by Lionel Martin.

It is perhaps simplistic to interpret Castro's vehement antipathy toward Batista (and earlier toward Grau and Prío) as a displacement of his hostility toward his father. However, such an explanation has appeal as at least a partial explanation.

Castro gave the personal account of his thinking that led to the strategy against Batista in his 1965 interview with Lee Lockwood (*Castro's Cuba: Cuba's Fidel*).

"Son Los Mismos" ("They Are the Same"), published by the Santa Maria group, was named to suggest that one corrupt politician was the same as another, hence that some radical change was needed.

Haydée described the early days when Fidel joined their group in her book *Moncada*.

Castro's brother-in-law, Rafael Díaz Balart, had taken him, prior to the March 10 coup, to meet with Batista at his home. It was a cordial but cool session. Castro agreed to the meeting only to keep his options open for the remote possibility that Batista might win the presidential election. According to one source Castro offered to support Batista if he were promised the position of mayor of Havana, a quite unrealistic offer, but not inconsistent with Fidel's audacity. After March 10, 1952, Fidel's relationship with his friend Díaz Balart deteriorated and it was with some reluctance that he went to see him immediately before the Moncada attack.

Chapter 4

Every book dealing with the life of Fidel Castro or his rise to power includes, of necessity, some account of the attack on the Moncada barracks. Probably the most comprehensive is Robert Merle's *Moncada: Premier Combat de Fidel Castro*. In English, Robert Taber's *M-26-7: Biography of a Revolution* offers a vivid and detailed account, as do the biographies of Castro by Herbert Matthews and Jules Dubois. Similar information is included in Ernst Halperin's *Fidel Castro's Road to Power*. By far the most comprehensive account of this entire period with the richest detail, including that of the attack itself, appears in Mario Mencia's *El Grito del Moncada*. However, it does reflect the official view of the Cuban government.

Information on this period, including first-hand accounts of the attacks at Moncada and Bayamo, was provided to the author in interviews with Melba Hernández (Havana, March 19, 1985), Orlando Castro (Miami, September 7 and 8, 1984), Raúl Martínez Arará (Miami, September 8, 1984), Jesús Montané, (Havana, March 22, 1985), and Marta Rojas (Havana, March 15, 1985).

The dialogue in this chapter, including the statements by Fidel Castro, was reconstructed from information provided in the interviews conducted by the author and from the accounts of Haydée Santamaría in *Moncada*.

Fidel obtained a supply of army uniforms from a sergeant in Batista's army, Florentino Fernández, whom he had converted to his cause.

The account of Juan Almeida's reaction to finding his gun was only a .22 is cited by Hugh Thomas in *Cuba: The Pursuit of Freedom*.

Most accounts identify Raúl as leader of the group that captured the Palace of Justice. Lester Rodríguez, the actual leader, escaped, and in order not to divulge his name to the police Fidel identified his brother as the leader.

The encounter of the car containing Fidel with the "cossack patrol" is the reason most widely cited for the sounding of the alarm. In Mario Mencia's *El Grito del Moncada* a slightly different version is given in which an off-duty sergeant walking out of a side street sees the men with guns in the backed-up stationary cars and alerts the guards at the gate and the soldiers in the jeep.

Marta Rojas has recently completed extensive research on the period between the failure of the Moncada attack and Fidel's capture, interviewing all those still alive who had contact with the fleeing rebels as well as those who were involved in pursuing them. Some of this material appears in her book, *La Generacion del Centenario en el Juicio del Moncada*. She also shared unpublished material with the author.

Rolando Amador (Miami, October 15, 1985) described to the author his efforts with Mirta to obtain the intercession of the Catholic Church on Fidel's behalf.

Chapter 5

The period immediately following Fidel's capture, his trial, and the trial of his fellow conspirators have been intensively researched by Marta Rojas, who was herself a participant in the events of those three months. Her accounts are widely cited by those who have written about this period and she served as a primary source for the author. Additional information was provided by Melba Hernández (Havana, March 19, 1985). A detailed first-person account by Haydée Santamaría of the first days of her imprisonment appears in *From the Palm Tree*, edited by Jane McManus.

The account by a cellmate, Gerardo Poll Cabrera, of Fidel reciting to him "History Will Absolve Me" appeared in *Granma*, October 15, 1983.

Although fragmented descriptions of Castro's time in prison appear in most books concerning his rise to power, the most comprehensive account is Mario Mencia's *Time Was on Our Side*. He wrote letters prolifically to Luis Conte Agüero, his girlfriend Naty Revuelta, Melba Hernández, and others. Many of these letters from which the quotations are taken have been preserved and appear in *Revolutionary Struggle* by Rolando Bonachea and Nelson Valdés, *Time Was on Our Side*, and *Cartes del Presidio* by Conte Agüero. They are a particularly valuable source in that they detail not only the effect of prison life on Castro, but also his prodigious efforts at self-education and the manner in which his political thinking and sophistication evolved during this period.

Max Lesnick (Miami, September 7, 1984) provided information on Fidel's relationship with Mirta at this time.

Information on the period following Fidel's release from prison was provided to the author by Orlando Castro (Miami, September 7, 1984), Raúl Martínez Arará (Miami, September 8, 1984), Melba Hernández (Havana, March 19, 1985), Faustino Pérez (Havana, March 23, 1985), and Justo Carrillo (Miami, September 9, 1984). Lionel Martin, *The Young Fidel*, and Rolando Bonachea and Nelson Valdés, *Revolutionary Struggle*, also provide detailed accounts of these three months from different perspectives. Mario Mencia published a detailed fourteen-part series on Fidel's activities during these three months, which appeared weekly in *Bohemia* between May 17 and August 16, 1985. It is, however, a sanitized version.

Fidel made his comment about Naty Revuelta "missing the train" to Justo Carrillo.

Chapter 6

The time Fidel spent in exile in Mexico is the most poorly documented period of his life. The most detailed accounts, such as Ramón Barquín's *Las Luchas Guerrilleras en*

312

Cuba, are in Spanish. Teresa Casuso's *Cuba and Castro* and Miguel G.-Calzadilla's *The Fidel Castro I Knew* provide interesting personal accounts of part of his time there.

The author is indebted to Orlando de Cárdenas for providing extensive detailed information on his relationship with Fidel Castro and the M-26-7 in Mexico (Miami, September 9 and 11, 1984, and May 15, 1985). Other material was obtained in interviews with Justo Carrillo (Miami, September 9, 1984), Faustino Pérez (Havana, March 23, 1985), and Melba Hernández (Havana, March 19, 1985).

Biographical material on Che Guevara and descriptions of his first meeting with Fidel are drawn from Daniel James, *Che Guevara: A Biography*, Ricardo Rojo, *My Friend Che*, and *Ernesto: A Memoir of Che Guevara* by his first wife, Hilda Gadea. There are those, including Argentinian physicians, who argue that Che either never went to medical school or at least never graduated. The quote from Dolores Moyano Martín is cited by Daniel James.

Rolando Bonachea and Nelson Valdés, *Revolutionary Struggle*, give a detailed account of Fidel's fund-raising trip to the United States and the support structure for the M-26-7 that was set up.

Signed receipts for the books purchased by Fidel are in the possession of Orlando de Cárdenas.

In 1985, Gutiérrez Barios was the head of the Traffic Police in Mexico City.

There is considerable disagreement about the extent to which Fidel's followers opposed his decision to launch the invasion of Cuba before the end of 1956. De Cárdenas asserts that there was a near revolt led by Melba Hernández against Fidel's autocratic decision-making. Today all those in Cuba, including Melba Hernández, who were involved at this stage with him in Mexico minimize any suggestion of dissension. De Cárdenas's version is probably nearer to the truth.

Some authors give October 28, 1956 as the date of Angel Castro's death. Fidel, however, recently told Frei Betto that it was October 21.

Chapter 7

A detailed account of the voyage of the *Granma* is given in *De Tuxpan a La Plata* by Thelma B. Pubillones, et al. General descriptions of the war in the Sierra Maestra are provided in many places, including Hugh Thomas's *Cuba: The Pursuit of Freedom*, Lionel Martin's *The Young Fidel*, Rolando Bonachea and Nelson Valdés's *Revolutionary Struggle*, Ernesto Guevara's *Episodes of the Revolutionary War*, and Herbert Matthews's *Fidel Castro: A Political Biography*. An interesting firsthand account of an American who fought with the rebels is provided by Neill Macauley in *A Rebel in Cuba: American Memoir*.

Personal accounts were provided to the author by Faustino Pérez (Havana, March 23, 1985), Melba Hernández (Havana, March 19, 1985), Justo Carrillo (Miami, September 9, 1984), Jesús Montané (Havana, March 22, and October 14–26, 1985), and two other sources who requested anonymity.

Carlos Franqui's *The Twelve* is a romanticized version of the landing and trek into the mountains.

The execution of the traitor Eutimio Guerra occurred the same day that Fidel met with Herbert Matthews. The meeting occurred in the early hours of the morning and the execution took place that following evening. The two events were entirely coincidental. In response to the question, "Who killed Guerra?" those who know will say only, "The Twenty-six of July Movement executed Guerra."

In *Fidel Castro: Psiquiatría y Política*, Luis Conte Agüero asserts that Castro has always suffered from periods of severe depression. An above average energy level and a hyperactive

313

state much of the time, as Castro evidences, are often associated with a labile affect and periodic mood swings. The reclusive periods in the mountains and similar episodes after he came to power add credence to Conte Agüero's view.

Information on the relationship between Castro and Celia Sánchez was provided to the author in interviews with her cousin Alice Martínez (Washington, D.C., June 18, 1985) and Dr. Antonio Núñez Jiménez (Havana, March 13, 1985).

The letter of Frank País to Fidel was published in *Verde Olivo* (Havana), August 1, 1965.

Carlos Franqui's letter to Frank País sent in January 1958 was published in *Diary of the Cuban Revolution*.

Fidel's article that he gave to Andrew St. George appeared in *Coronet* magazine, July 1960.

Fidel's letter to Celia Sánchez, June 5, 1958, was first published in the *Granma Weekly Review* (Havana), August 27, 1967. It was first published in English by Rolando Bonachea and Nelson Valdés in *Revolutionary Struggle*. Facsimiles of the letter are today available in stores in Havana as souvenir items.

Fidel's comment to Justo Carrillo about the Communists is quoted by Hugh Thomas in *Cuba: The Pursuit of Freedom*.

The anecdote concerning the intercepted letter between Raúl and Che is mentioned by Enrique Meneses in *Fidel Castro*.

Carlos Rafael Rodríguez, in an interview with the author on March 25, 1985, described his experiences with Castro during the final weeks of the campaign.

Chapter 8

Among the best of the several accounts of the months immediately following the victory of the rebel forces are Edwin Tetlow's *Eye on Cuba*, Antonio Núñez Jiménez's *En Marcha Con Fidel*, and Robert Taber's *M-26-7: Biography of a Revolution*. Hugh Thomas's encyclopedic *Cuba: The Pursuit of Freedom* offers an exhaustive analysis of the political, social, and cultural implications of the rebel victory.

Information on this period was provided to the author by Carlos Rafael Rodríguez (Havana, March 25, 1985), Dr. Antonio Núñez Jiménez (Havana, March 23, 1985), Jorge Mendoza (Havana, March 18, 1985), Ernesto Betancourt (Washington, D.C., November 28, 1984), Orlando Castro (Miami, September 8, 1984), Bernardo Benes (Miami, September 6, 1984), Alice Martínez (Washington, D.C., June 18, 1985), and Dr. Lidia Bales (née Vexel–Robertson) (telephone interview, February 8, 1986).

The story concerning Buck Cannell was told to the author by Jeffrey Blyth.

Fidel's comments about his ignorance of government operations and his attempt to stay away from day-to-day involvement appeared in *Revolución*, October 4, 1961. He made a similar statement to Radio Television Française in April 1961.

The statement of the Presbyterian minister is quoted by Rafael Cepeda, "Fidel Castro y el Reino de Dios," *Bohemia* (Havana), July 17, 1960. The second quote equating Fidel's ideas with those of Jesus Christ is from Lloyd Free's *Attitudes of the Cuban People Towards the Castro Regime*. The survey material is from *Cubans in Exile* by Richard Fagen et al.

Fidel's statement about only executing murderers is quoted by Jules Dubois in *Fidel Castro*.

Alice Martínez described to the author Castro's personal instructions for the types of people he wanted visible in the audience when he spoke about the executions. Fidel's statement about missing the mountains is quoted in Enrique Meneses's *Fidel Castro*.

Information on Castro's visit to Washington was provided by Ernesto Betancourt, who accompanied him.

Marie Lorenz gave her story to Paul Meskil, "CIA's Mata Hari Stole Castro's Secrets," New York *Daily News*, April 10, 1975, and "In Havana, Rooms under the Pool," New York *Daily News*, June 20, 1975. She claims to have been present at meetings between Lee Harvey Oswald, Frank Sturgis, and other members of the Cuban exile community.

Fidel's comments about the agrarian reform to Herbert Matthews appear in "Return to Cuba," *Hispanic American Report* (Stanford: Stanford University Press, 1964).

The chaos that afflicted the government during this period is graphically described in Rufo López Fresquet's *My Fourteen Months with Castro* and Mario Llerena's *The Unsuspected Revolution—Myths and Realities*.

Chapter 9

Hugh Thomas, *Cuba: The Pursuit of Freedom*, Maurice Halperin, *The Rise and Decline of Fidel Castro*, and Rufo López Fresquet, *My Fourteen Months with Castro* provide detailed accounts of this period.

Interviews concerning the period covered in this chapter were conducted by the author with Ernesto Betancourt (Washington, D.C., November 28, 1985), Dr. Antonio Núñez Jiménez (Havana, March 26, 1985), Enrique Jorge Mendoza (Havana, March 18, 1985), Ramón Sánchez Parode (Washington, D.C., November 1, 1984), Carlos Quijano (Washington, D.C., June 22, 1984), Faustino Pérez (Havana, March 23, 1985), and Br. Bernardo Benes (Miami, September 6, 1985).

Castro's comments about using the Communist Party were made to Herbert Matthews, *Castro: A Political Biography*.

The account of the first contact between Castro and the Soviets appears in *En Marcha Con Fidel* by Antonio Núñez Jiménez, who recounted it to the author.

There have been accusations blaming Raúl and his wife Vilma Espin for the death of Cienfuegos. But there were many people who might have been happy to have this popular and charismatic figure out of the way. Nevertheless, his body was never found and no evidence has emerged to confirm the allegations of foul play.

Chapter 10

The relationship between Fidel and Ernest Hemingway is described in *Hemingway in Cuba* by Norberto Fuentes. Castro's statements about Hemingway were reported by Geoffrey Matthews in an article in *South* magazine, February 1985.

Antonio Núñez Jiménez says that he was one of the drafters of the "First Declaration of Havana," but when he looked at it Fidel insisted on making it more radical.

Accounts of Khrushchev's reaction to Fidel are provided in Arcady Shevchenko's *Breaking with Moscow*.

In *My Fourteen Months with Castro*, Rufo López Fresquet gives a graphic description of the disarray and increasing breakdown of the government that occurred in the period immediately prior to his own departure.

The description of Fidel's gift to Nasser was given to the author by Mahmoud Riad, Egyptian foreign minister at the time.

Fidel's statement about deserving some of the blame for the breakdown in relations with the U.S. was made in an interview in *Revolución*, July 19, 1964.

The secret planning at the CIA that would ultimately lead to the Bay of Pigs invasion is meticulously documented in Peter Wyden's *Bay of Pigs*. The details of the assassination plans against Castro were first revealed by Senator Frank Church, chairman, Select Committee to Study Government Operations with Respect to Intelligence Activities, Alleged Assassination Plots Involving Foreign Leaders, Senate Report No. 94-465, November 20, 1975 (Washington, D.C.: U.S. Government Printing Office, 1975). A more colorful account focusing specifically on the CIA's enlistment of the Mafia in the anti-Castro movement and the assassination efforts appears in *The Fish Is Red* by Warren Hinckle and William Turner.

The existence of a Cuban exile training site in Guatemala was revealed in the following sequence: *La Hora* (Guatemala City), October 30, 1960; *The Nation*, editorial, November 19, 1960; *The New York Times*, "U.S. Helps Train an Anti-Castro Force at Secret Guatemalan Air-Ground Base," January 10, 1961. After this last story broke the entire invasion plan began to emerge.

The statement by William Colby, former director of the CIA, was made to the author on May 24, 1985.

Castro believes that he came nearest to being killed by a man working in the kitchen at the Havana Hilton. Castro would frequently go into the kitchen to get himself ice cream, and the assassin was to put poison in it. He lost his nerve at the last minute and turned himself in.

Chapter 11

In *Bay of Pigs*, Peter Wyden provides a superb comprehensive account of the invasion effort from its inception in the U.S. government to the final military defeat. Haynes Johnson's *The Bay of Pigs* is an equally thorough book, but unlike Wyden, the author was dependent on exile sources. A purely Cuban view is provided by Fidel Castro in *Playa Girón: Victory of the People*.

Additional information on this period was provided by Carlos Rafael Rodríguez (Havana, March 25, 1985), Antonio Núñez Jiménez (Havana, March 16, 1985), and Ramón Sánchez Parode (Washington, D.C., November 1, 1984).

The statement by Khrushchev appears in his memoirs, *Khrushchev Remembers*.

The composition of the exile brigade is cited by K. S. Karol in *Guerrillas in Power*.

The events that led to the "secret" meeting between Che Guevara and Richard Goodwin are detailed in Daniel James's *Che Guevara: A Biography*.

Castro's statement that "Marxism is not a catechism" suggests the continuing strong pervasive influence of Catholicism as one of his frames of reference.

The struggle with the old-line Communists is well described by Maurice Halperin in *The Rise and Decline of Fidel Castro*.

There are many excellent accounts of the Cuban missile crisis. Robert Kennedy's *Thirteen Days: A Memoir of the Cuban Missile Crisis* offers a unique inside view of the highest level of decision-making on the U.S. side. *Khrushchev Remembers* offers a Soviet perspective. Also see *The Cuban Crisis of 1962*, edited by David Larsen, and Arthur Schlesinger's *One Thousand Days*. Carlos Franqui's *Family Portrait with Fidel* suggests that Castro personally fired the missile that shot down the U-2 spy plane. In the same book he provides an interesting picture of domestic events occurring in Cuba during this period.

Castro's statement concerning Socialist solidarity in accepting the missiles appears in Maurice Halperin's *Rise and Decline of Fidel Castro*.

The degree of anger in Cuba toward the Soviet Union over its handling of the missile crisis remains intense more than twenty years later. It says a great deal about how sensitive the issue of sovereignty is to the Cuban people and why Castro has always been so successful in capitalizing on these feelings, which have often been erroneously interpreted in the United States as simply anti-Americanism.

Chapter 12

The extraordinary visit of Fidel Castro to the Soviet Union is vividly described in Maurice Halperin's *The Rise and Decline of Fidel Castro*.

Information concerning this period, including Fidel's trip to the Soviet Union and his relationship with Khrushchev, was provided to the author by Carlos Rafael Rodríguez (Havana, March 25, 1985).

The continuing hit-and-run attacks against Cuba by the exile community with CIA support is detailed in *The Fish Is Red* by Warren Hinckle and William Turner.

The steps taken by Fidel to tighten his control on Cuba following his return from the Soviet Union, and especially his handling of the press, were discussed with the author by Marta Rojas (Havana, March 15, 1985) and Enrique Jorge Menéndez (Havana, March 17, 1985).

A great deal has been written about the Cuban economy under the Castro regime. René Dumont's *Socialism and Development* and Leo Huberman and Paul Sweezey's *Cuba: Anatomy of a Revolution* provide sympathetic perspectives. Hugh Thomas's *Cuba: The Pursuit of Freedom* and Dudley Seers's *Cuba: The Economic and Social Revolution* provide more objective perspectives.

The intriguing story of the near rapprochement between Castro and Kennedy is described by William Attwood in *The Reds and the Blacks: A Personal Adventure*. Daniel gave an account of his role in two articles in *The New Republic*, December 7 and 14, 1963.

The role of Lee Harvey Oswald as a tool of anti-Castro groups is persuasively argued in Warren Hinckle and William Turner's *The Fish Is Red*. Also see *Report of the House Select Committee on Assassinations* (Washington, D.C.: Government Printing Office, 1977). Castro made his comments to Barbara Walters in an interview on ABC television in 1977.

The relationship of Cuba to the Third World and Castro's ambitious involvement in Africa and Latin America during the mid-sixties and early seventies is traced in Carla Anne Robbins's superb book, *The Cuban Threat*.

Daniel James's *Che Guevara: A Biography* chronicles the steady decline of Che's role in Cuba and his increasing involvement in new revolutionary ventures in the Third World.

Chapter 13

Castro's emergence as a dominant figure in Third World politics is detailed in *The Cuban Threat* by Carla Anne Robbins, *The Rise and Decline of Fidel Castro* by Maurice Halperin, *Castro, the Kremlin, and Communism in Latin America* by Bruce Jackson, *Castro's Cuba: Soviet Partner or Non-Aligned* by Wayne Smith, *Revolutionary Cuba in the World Arena* by Martin Weinstein, and *Cuba in the World* by Cole Blasier and Carmelo Mesa-Lago.

Additional material was provided to the author in interviews with Wayne Smith (Washington, D.C., September 20, 1984 and June 25, 1985) and Carlos Rafael Rodríguez (Havana, March 25, 1985).

Che's final venture in Bolivia is described by Daniel James in *Che Guevara: A Biography*, which argues strongly that Che had become an unwanted burden to Castro and was deliberately abandoned in his final months. After his death, however, Che became, and has remained in Cuba, next to Castro the most revered of the revolution's heroes.

The prerevolution statistics on the human condition in Cuba are cited by Eric Williams in *From Columbus to Castro*.

Fidel's statement admitting Cuba's economic failures appeared in an interview with the Soviet magazine *Ogonek*, May 1970.

317

Cuba's involvement with COMECON is detailed by Edward A. Hewett in *Revolutionary Cuba in the World Arena*, edited by Martin Weinstein.

Information concerning Castro's visit to Chile was provided to the author by Andres Allamand Zavala (Washington, D.C., May 25, 1985) and by letter. He also provided the author with a copy of the July 29, 1973 letter from Castro to Allende. Although there were reports cited by Hinckle and Turner of efforts to assassinate Castro during that trip using a gun inside a movie camera, the author has been unable to confirm the report from Chilean sources.

The preliminary discussions aimed at normalizing relations between the U.S. and Cuba during the Ford administration were conducted on a highly informal basis with some meetings occurring in such places as a coffee shop at LaGuardia Airport.

Chapter 14

Detailed analyses of the Cuban involvement in Angola and Ethiopia have been provided by Nelson Valdés, "Revolutionary Solidarity in Angola," in Cole Blasier and Carmelo Mesa-Lago's *Cuba in the World*, and "Cuba's Involvement in the Horn of Africa: The Ethiopian-Somali War and the Eritrean Conflict," in J. Belkin and C. Mesa-Lago's *Cuba in Africa*. Carla Anne Robbins in *The Cuban Threat* sets this period in a broader context.

The sending of Cuban troops to Syria in 1973 was confirmed to the author by Dr. Antonio Núñez Jiménez (Havana, March 21,1985). The exact size and nature of the units involved are uncertain. According to the *Jerusalem Post*, February 2, 1976, Defense Minister Shimon Peres told the Israeli Knesset that the Cubans had sent a tank brigade that was stationed on the Golan Heights for about a year and a half. Another report describes the force as an infantry brigade with mechanized elements. For a more detailed discussion see "The Arab-Israeli Conflict" by Yoram Shapira, in *Cuba in the World*, edited by Cole Blasier and Carmelo Mesa-Lago.

Observations on the schools for students from Third World countries are based on a visit made to these facilities by the author in May 1981.

Fidel's comments to Herbert Matthews on religion are quoted in "Return to Cuba," *Hispanic American Report* (Stanford: Stanford University Press, 1964).

Some of the information on Cuba's role in Grenada and Ethiopia was obtained in discussions the author had with a range of people during visits to those two countries.

The discussions during the Carter administration aimed at normalizing relations were described to the author by Wayne Smith (Washington, D.C., June 25, 1985).

Bibliography

Aguilar, Luis E. *Cuba 1933—Prologue to Revolution*. Ithaca: Cornell University Press, 1972.

Attwood, William. *The Reds and the Blacks: A Personal Adventure*. New York, Harper & Row, 1967.

Barquín, Ramón, *Las Luchas Guerrilleras en Cuba*. 2 vols. Madrid: Playor, 1975.

Belkin, J., and C. Mesa-Lago, eds. *Cuba in Africa*. Pittsburgh: University of Pittsburgh Press, 1982.

Betto, Frei. *Fidel y La Religión*. Havana: Officina de Publicaciones del Consejo de Estado, 1985.

Blasier, Cole, and Carmelo Mesa-Lago, eds. *Cuba in the World*. Pittsburgh: University of Pittsburgh Press, 1979.

Bonachea, Rolando, and Nelson Valdés. *Che: Selected Works of Ernesto Guevara*. Cambridge, Mass.: M.I.T. Press, 1969.

Bonachea, Rolando, and Nelson Valdés. *Revolutionary Struggle: The Selected Works of Fidel Castro*. Vol. 1. Cambridge, Mass.: M.I.T. Press, 1971.

Bonsal, Philip W. *Cuba, Castro and the United States*. Pittsburgh: University of Pittsburgh Press, 1971.

Bunn, Harriet, and Ellen Gut. *The Universities of Cuba, Haiti, and the Dominican Republic*. Washington, D.C.: Pan American Union, 1946.

Castro, Fidel. *Playa Girón: A Victory of the People*. Havana: Editorial en Marcha, 1961.

Casuso, Teresa. *Cuba and Castro*. New York: Random House, 1961.

Chapman, Charles E. *A History of the Cuban Republic*. New York: Macmillan, 1927.

Conte Agüero, Luis. *Cartes del Presidio*. Havana: Editorial Lex, 1959.

——. *Fidel Castro: Psiquiatría y Política*. Mexico: Editorial Jus, 1968.

——. *Fidel Castro: Vida y Obra*. Havana: Editorial Lex, 1959.

——. *Los Dos Rostros de Fidel Castro*. Mexico: Editorial Jus, 1960.

Dominguez, Jorge. *Cuba: Order and Revolution*. Cambridge, Mass.: Belknap Press of Harvard University Press, 1978.

Draper, Theodore. *Castroism: Theory and Practice*. New York: Praeger, 1965.

——. *Castro's Revolution: Myths and Realities*. New York: Praeger, 1962.

Dubois, Jules. *Fidel Castro: Rebel—Liberator or Dictator?* New York: Bobbs-Merrill, 1959.

Dumont, René. *Socialism and Development*. New York: Grove Press, 1970.

Fagen, Richard R., Richard A. Brody, and Thomas J. O'Leary. *Cubans in Exile*. Stanford: Stanford University Press, 1968.

Fitzgibbon, Russell H. *Cuba and the United States, 1900–1935*.

Franqui, Carlos. *Diary of the Cuban Revolution*. New York: Viking Press, 1976.

——. *Family Portrait with Fidel*. New York: Random House, 1984.

————. *The Twelve*. Secaucus, N.J.: Lyle Stuart, 1968.

Free, Lloyd A. *Attitudes of the Cuban People Towards the Castro Regime*. Princeton: Princeton University Press, 1960.

Fuentes, Norberto. *Hemingway in Cuba*. Secaucus, N.J.: Lyle Stuart, 1984.

G.-Calzadilla, Miguel A. *The Fidel Castro I Knew*. New York: Vantage Press, 1971.

Gadea, Hilda. *Ernesto: A Memoir of Che Guevara*. New York: Doubleday, 1972.

Gerassi, John. *Fidel Castro: A Biography*. New York: Doubleday, 1959.

Goldenberg, Boris. *The Cuban Revolution and Latin America*. New York: Praeger, 1965.

González, Edward. *Cuba under Castro: The Limits of Charisma*. Boston: Houghton Mifflin, 1974.

Guevara, Ernesto. *Episodes of the Revolutionary War*. New York: International Publishers, 1969.

————. *Man and Socialism in Cuba*. Havana: Book Institute, 1967.

Guggenheim, Harry F. *The United States and Cuba*. New York: Macmillan, 1934.

Hagedorn, Hermann. *That Human Being: Leonard Wood*. New York: Harcourt Brace and Howe, 1920.

————. *The Works of Theodore Roosevelt*. New York: Scribners, 1923.

Halperin, Ernst. *Castro and Latin American Communism*. Cambridge, Mass.: M.I.T. Press, 1963.

————. *Fidel Castro's Road to Power*. Cambridge, Mass.: M.I.T. Press, 1970.

————. *The Ideology of Castroism and its Impact on the Communist Parties of Latin America*. Cambridge, Mass.: M.I.T. Press, 1961.

Halperin, Maurice. *The Rise and Decline of Fidel Castro*. Berkeley: University of California Press, 1973.

————. *The Taming of Fidel Castro*. Berkeley: University of California Press, 1981.

Hilsman, Roger. *To Move a Nation*. Garden City, N.Y.: Doubleday, 1967.

Hinckle, Warren, and William Turner. *The Fish Is Red*. New York: Harper & Row, 1981.

Horowitz, Irving Louis, ed. *Cuban Communism*. New York: Aldine Press, 1970.

Huberman, Leo, and Paul M. Sweezey. *Cuba: Anatomy of a Revolution*. New York: Monthly Review Press, 1960.

Jackson, D. Bruce. *Castro, the Kremlin, and Communism in Latin America*. Baltimore: Johns Hopkins Press, 1969.

James, Daniel. *Che Guevara: A Biography*. New York: Stein & Day, 1969.

————. *The Complete Bolivian Diaries of Che Guevara and Other Captured Documents*. New York: Stein & Day, 1968.

Jenks, Leland. *Our Cuban Colony*. New York: Vanguard Press, 1928.

Johnson, Haynes. *The Bay of Pigs*. New York: Norton, 1964.

Karol, K. S. *Guerrillas in Power*. New York: Hill & Wang, 1970.

Kennedy, Robert F. *Thirteen Days: A Memoir of the Cuban Missile Crisis*. New York: Norton, 1969.

Kenner, Martin, and James Petras, eds. *Fidel Castro Speaks*. New York: Grove Press, 1969.

Khrushchev, Nikita. *Khrushchev Remembers*. Boston: Little, Brown, 1970.

Kirk, John M. *José Martí: Mentor of the Cuban Nation*. Tampa: University of South Florida Press, 1982.

Kirkpatrick, Lyman B., Jr. *The Real CIA*. New York: Macmillan, 1968.

Langley, Lester D. *The Cuban Policy of the United States*. New York: John Wiley, 1968.

Larsen, David L., ed. *The Cuban Crisis of 1962*. Boston: Houghton Mifflin, 1963.

Lazo, María. *Dagger in the Heart: American Policy Failures in Cuba*. New York: Funk and Wagnalls, 1968.

320

LeoGrande, William. *Cuba's Policy in Africa, 1959–1980*. Berkeley: University of California Press, 1980.

Llerena, Mario. *The Unsuspected Revolution—Myths and Realities*. Ithaca: Cornell University Press, 1978.

Lockwood, Lee. *Castro's Cuba: Cuba's Fidel*. New York: Macmillan, 1967.

López Fresquet, Rufo. *My Fourteen Months with Castro*. Cleveland: World Publishing Co., 1966.

Macauley, Neill. *A Rebel in Cuba: An American Memoir*. Chicago: Quadrangle, 1970.

MacGaffey, Wyatt, and Clifford R. Barnett. *Twentieth-Century Cuba: The Background of the Castro Revolution*. New York: Doubleday, 1965.

Martin, Lionel. *The Young Fidel*. Secaucus, N.J.: Lyle Stuart, 1983.

Matthews, Herbert L. *Castro: A Political Biography*. London: Penguin, 1969.

——. *The Cuban Story*. New York: George Braziller, 1961.

McManus, Jane, ed. *From the Palm Tree: Voices of the Cuban Revolution*. Secaucus, N.J.: Lyle Stuart, 1973.

Mencia, Mario. *El Grito del Moncada*. Havana: Editora Política, 1985.

——. *Time Was on Our Side*. Havana: Editora Política, 1982.

Meneses, Enrique. *Fidel Castro*. London: Faber & Faber, 1966.

Merle, Robert. *Moncada: Premier Combat de Fidel Castro*. Paris: Robert Laffont, 1965.

Moran Arce, Lucas. *La Revolución Cubana: Una Version Rebelde*. Ponce, Puerto Rico: Imprenta Universitaria, 1980.

North, Joseph. *Cuba: Hope of a Hemisphere*. New York: International Publishers, 1961.

Núñez Jiménez, Antonio. *En Marcha Con Fidel*. Havana: Editorial Letras Cubanas, 1982.

Pflaum, Irving. *Tragic Island: How Communism Came to Cuba*. Englewood Cliffs, N.J.: Prentice-Hall, 1961.

Plank, John, ed. *Cuba and the United States: Long Range Perspectives*. Washington, D.C.: Brookings Institution, 1967.

Portell Vilá, Herminio. *Historia de Cuba en Sus Relaciones Con Los Estados Unidos y España*. 4 vols. Havana: Editorial Jesús Montero, 1930.

Pubillones, Thelma B. et al. *De Tuxpan a La Plata*. Havana: Editorial Orbe.

Robbins, Carla Anne. *The Cuban Threat*. New York: McGraw-Hill, 1983.

Roca, Blas. *The Cuban Revolution*. New York: New Century Publications, 1961.

Rojas, Marta. *La Generacion del Centenario en el Juicio del Moncada*. Havana: Editorial de Ciencias Sociales, 1979.

Rojo, Ricardo. *My Friend Che*. New York: Dial Press, 1968.

Santamaría, Haydée. *Moncada*. Secaucus, N.J.: Lyle Stuart, 1980.

Schlesinger, Arthur M., Jr. *A Thousand Days*. Boston: Houghton Mifflin, 1965.

Seers, Dudley, ed. *Cuba: The Economic and Social Revolution*. Chapel Hill: University of North Carolina Press, 1964.

Shevchenko, Arkady. *Breaking with Moscow*. New York: Alfred A. Knopf, 1985.

Smith, Robert F., ed. *Background to Revolution: The Development of Modern Cuba*. New York: Alfred A. Knopf, 1966.

——. *The United States and Cuba: Business and Diplomacy, 1917–1960*. New York: Bookman Associates, 1961.

Smith, Wayne. *Castro's Cuba: Soviet Partner or Non-Aligned*. Washington, D.C.: Woodrow Wilson Center, 1984.

Sorensen, Theodore C. *Kennedy*. New York: Harper & Row, 1965.

Suárez, Andrés. *Cuba: Castroism and Communism, 1959–1966*. Cambridge, Mass.: M.I.T. Press, 1967.

Suchlicki, Jaime. *Cuba, Castro and the Revolution*. Miami: University of Miami Press, 1972.

———. *Cuba: From Columbus to Castro*. Miami: University of Miami Press, 1972.

———. *University Students and Revolution in Cuba, 1920–1968*. Miami: University of Miami Press, 1968.

Taber, Michael, ed. *Our Power is That of the Working People*. Fidel Castro's speeches. 2 vols. New York: Pathfinder Press, 1983.

Taber, Robert. *M-26-7: Biography of a Revolution*. Secaucus, N.J.: Lyle Stuart, 1961.

Tetlow, Edwin. *Eye on Cuba*. New York: Harcourt Brace and World, 1964.

Thomas, Hugh. *Cuba: The Pursuit of Freedom*. New York: Harper & Row, 1971.

Weinstein, Martin, ed. *Revolutionary Cuba in the World Arena*. Philadelphia: Institute for the Study of Human Issues, 1979.

Weyl, Nathaniel. *Red Star over Cuba*. New York: Hilman McFadden, 1961.

Wilkerson, Loree A. *Fidel Castro's Political Programs: From Reformism to Marxism-Leninism*. Gainesville: University of Florida Press, 1965.

Williams, Eric. *From Columbus to Castro*. New York: Random House, 1970.

Wright, Irene A. *The Early History of Cuba, 1492–1586*. New York: The MacMillan Co., 1916.

Wyden, Peter. *Bay of Pigs*. New York: Simon & Schuster, 1979.

Yamamoto, Makiko. *Women of Flames*. Tokyo: Yimuri Press, 1969.

Zeitlin, Maurice, and Robert Scheer. *Cuba: Tragedy in our Hemisphere*. New York: Grove Press, 1963.

Index

Betto, Frei, 290
Bider, Haydee Tamara Bunke (Tania), 257
Bishop, Maurice, 293, 296–97
Bissell, Richard, 211–12, 216–17
Boat lift (1980), 295
Bogotá: Castro in (1948), 46–52, 309
Bohemia (periodical), 108, 122–23, 125, 126, 132, 167
Bolivia, 267–69
Bonsal, Philip, 174, 177, 187, 198, 201, 215
Bosch, Juan, 32–33
Bravo, Douglas, 264, 267, 283
Bravo, Flavio, 73, 129, 225
Brazil, 170
Brezhnev, Leonid, 271, 278, 281, 283
Brigade 2506, 219, 222–26
Brzezinski, Zbigniew, 291
Buehlman, Victor, 144

Caldera, Rafael, 282
Calle, La (newspaper), 108–9
Calzadilla, Mark, 120–21
Camagüey Province: as center of opposition, 190
Campbell, Judith, 244
Canada: and Cuba, 177, 214
Cannell, Buck, 163
Cantillo, Gen. Eulogio, 158–59, 160
Carreras, Capt. Enrique, 224
Carrillo, Justo, 72, 123, 124, 127, 142
Carter, Jimmy
  Castro and, 289
  Cuba and, 289, 291
Casals Fernández, Maj. Rafael, 61
Castro, Angel, 14–18
  death of, 131
  Fidel and, 17–18, 31, 62, 69, 131, 300
Castro, Fidel (Fidel Alejandro Castro Ruiz)
  alcohol and, 120, 200
  assassination plots against, 212–14, 244
  as athlete, 19, 25, 28
  austerity of, 200, 250, 299
  authority figures and, 17, 67
  birth of, 14, 21–22, 307
  books read by, 95–96, 107, 121
  charisma and charm of, 69, 107, 119, 137, 183, 293, 299
  depression of, 102, 144, 232, 294–95, 298, 312–13
  discipline and, 18, 29, 119–20, 162, 233, 247, 250
  education of, 20–46, 55–57, 309–10
  exile in Mexico (1955–56), 106, 109–33
  father and. *See* Castro, Angel.
  financial situation of, 18, 58, 110, 116, 119
  friends of, 201
  in government. *See* Government of Cuba (post-revolutionary): Castro's role in.
  health of, 25, 45, 166, 205, 298
  illegitimacy of, 17, 25–26, 89, 110, 300
  injustices and suffering and, 19, 20, 22, 99, 155
  international stature and influence of (1957), 141–42; (1960), 206, 210; (1961), 226; (1963), 245; (1964), 253, 264; (1966), 265; (1970s), 283, 287, 292–94; (1980s), 301–2, 304–5; in Latin America, 170, 184, 244, 266–67, 269; in Third World, 264, 265, 283, 287, 292–94, 302–3
  interviews with, 299; with Alexayev, 189–90; with Hoffman and Taber, 143–44; with Lockwood, 230; with Matthews, 140–42, 180, 185, 290; with Sullivan (Ed), 163; with Walters (B.), 175, 252, 289
  Khrushchev and. *See* Khrushchev, N. S.
  law and, 31, 57–58, 197
  loyalty to: at Bay of Pigs invasion, 223; in Mexico, 120; at Moncada, 77; in post-revolutionary era, 185, 192; in prison, 95; in revolutionary movement, 105, 106; at university, 33
  moral attitudes and convictions of, 17–18, 23, 47, 200
  oratorical style and skills of, 40, 42–43, 92, 179, 302
  overthrow of, attempted by U.S., 210–14, 216–19, 244–45
  physical appearance and characteristics of, 17, 32, 125; beard, 138; capacity to forgo sleep, 57, 80, 166, 200; cigar-smoking, 200; energy and endurance, 19, 57
  political ideology of, 33, 95–97, 147–48
  political interests of: as candidate for House of Representatives (1952), 60–64; in school days, 25; at university, 32–57
  popularity of: (1954), 101, 103; (1955), 105, 122; (1959), 162–63, 165–66, 171, 182, 184, 192, 195; (1960), 212; (1961), 226; (1975), 287; invasion plans by U.S. and, 217; in Soviet Union, 245; in U.S., 168, 174, 176, 210
  presidency of Cuba and, 153
  in prison: (1953–55), 93–105; (Mexico, 1956), 124–25
  psychological influences and themes of (early), 17–30
  recreation of, 19, 201, 300
  religious influences and beliefs of, 18, 21, 23, 29–30, 235, 289–90, 300
  secrecy of, 70, 71, 77, 81, 105
  self-image of, 20, 76, 164–65, 166
  sense of destiny of, 14, 27, 65–66, 67, 111, 138, 155, 166, 256, 301–2, 305
  as sex symbol, 201
  speeches of. *See* Speeches by Castro.
  as teacher, 94, 226, 247

324

travels of: to Africa (1972), 284; to Chile (1971), 278–79; to Soviet Union, 245–47, 263; to U.S., 55, 117–18, 174–77, 206–7, 209–10, 294
women and, 54–55, 73, 102, 110, 120, 125–26, 128, 130–31, 173–74, 180, 200–201
work and, 17, 250, 273, 299
writings. *See* Writings of Castro.
Castro, Fidelito
as adult, 300
birth of, 55
Fidel and, 102, 103, 110, 126–27, 163, 173, 300
schooling of, 231, 250
Castro, Juanita, 196
on Castro, 18, 185, 250
Castro, Lidia, 16, 46, 97, 102
Castro, Lina Ruz González, 16–17, 18–19, 31
death of (1963), 250
Castro, Manolo, 35–36, 41, 44
death of, 45
Castro, Mirta Díaz Balart
marriage to Castro (1948), 55
Moncada aftermath and, 86, 97
moves to Madrid, 250
relationship with Castro, 73, 102–3, 131, 173
Castro, Orlando, 106–7
Castro, Ramón
after revolution, 196
on family, 17, 18–19
on father, 15, 16
Fidel and, 300
on Fidel, 19, 192
Castro, Raúl
exile in Mexico, 109
on Fidel in school, 24
influence of, on Fidel, 179, 191, 257, 300
Marxism of, 73, 179, 190
in Moncada attack, 73, 82, 83
in mountain phase of revolution, 137, 145, 148, 154
Casuso, Teresa ("Tete"), 125–26, 127, 131, 132, 162
Catholic Church. *See* Roman Catholic Church.
Central Intelligence Agency. *See* CIA.
Céspedes, Carlos Manuel de, 4
Chao, Rafael, 137
Chibás, Eduardo, 39–40
Castro and, 53, 54, 58, 59–60, 76, 89, 123
Communists and, 57
death of, 59–60, 62
Gaitán and, 48
as presidential candidate, 53–54
Chibás, Raúl, 142, 149–50
Chile, 170, 264, 278–80
China
Castro and, 265–66

Cuba and, 202, 206
Guevara and, 258–59
in relation to Soviets, 231–32, 234, 237, 244, 253, 263, 265, 266
Chomon, Faure, 156, 202–3, 236
Church, Frank, 289, 296
CIA
Cuban exiles and, 190, 211; arming and training of, 202, 212
efforts of, to overthrow Castro, 210–14, 216–19, 244–45
See also Bay of Pigs invasion.
Cienfuegos, Camilo, 137, 145, 156, 158, 160, 162, 188, 189, 190
disappearance of, 191, 314
Coard, Bernard, 297
Colegio Dolores, Santiago de Cuba, 24–26
Colombia, 170, 255. *See also* Bogotá.
COMECON (Council for Mutual Economic Assistance), 277
Committees for the Defense of the Revolution, 233, 253, 303
Common Market for Latin America, proposed by Castro (1959), 177
Communist parties of Latin America, 255, 266
Castro and, 267
conference of (Havana, 1964), 255, 264
Communist Party of Cuba
Batista and, 91
Castro and, 64, 73, 129, 156–58; after revolution, 166, 179, 185, 195, 230, 269–70, 301; U.S. concerns about, 175, 176; in university years, 56–57, 230
Congo. *See* Zaïre.
Constitution of Cuba (1940)
amended (1959), 181
Castro declares it anachronism (1961), 227
restoration of called for, 108
Consumer goods
availability of, 9, 186, 253, 272, 299, 303
rationing of, 233
Conte Agüero, Luis, 18, 75–76, 97, 98, 104
Corruption in government
intractability of, 51
protests against, 39, 42, 43, 58–59
Coubre (merchant vessel), 201–2
Creoles, 2–3
Crowd, power of, 42, 52, 54
Cuba
Castro's expedition to, from Mexico (1956), 132–35
economy of. *See* Economy of Cuba.
foreign relations of. *See* Foreign relations (Cuban); Soviet Union and Cuba; Third World Nations and Cuba; U.S. and Cuba

Fuentes, Justo, 54
Fulbright, William, 216

Gadea, Hilda, 116, 257
Gaitán, Gloria, 201
Gaitán, Jorge Eliécer, 47–48, 51
Gandhi, Indira, 293
García, Gen. Calixto, 4, 8
García, Guillermo, 136, 137, 139, 298
García Bárcena, Rafael, 71–72, 110
García Marquez, Gabriel, 299
Garvey, Michael L., 144
Ghana, 256
Giancana, Sam ("Momo"), 213, 244
Goodwin, Richard, 229
Government of Cuba (post-revolutionary)
  (1980s), 298–99
  Castro's role in, 163, 164–65, 177, 183; becomes
    prime minister, 173, 183, 283; style of govern-
    ing, 178–79, 199–200; total control by, 171,
    178–79, 182, 186, 191, 192, 193–94, 195, 196,
    272, 273–74, 295, 301, 302, 304
  Communists and, 172, 182, 229–30
  democratic form urged, 172, 193, 195
  executions and retribution by, 167–68, 175
  opposition to, 171, 172, 180–81, 184, 190, 192–
    93, 197, 204, 214–15, 221, 233, 249, 253, 269–
    70, 295, 303–4
  repressive measures of, 197, 221, 233, 249,
    253
  uncertainty and vagueness in, 163, 171
  weapons acquired by, 189, 199, 215, 218, 231,
    237, 277; missiles, 206, 229, 237–41, 315
Granma (motor boat), 132–35
Granma (newspaper), 249
Grau San Martín, Ramón, 35, 38, 41, 103, 104
  Castro on, 40, 42, 43, 44
Grenada, 293, 296
G-2 (intelligence agency), 197
Guatemala, 116, 165, 255
Guerra, Eutimio, 140, 312
Guerrilla movements
  anti-Castro, 214–15
  in Cuban revolutionary movement, 137–58
  in Latin America, 255, 264, 269
  training of, in Mexico, 114, 119, 121
Guevara, Alfredo, 32, 40, 46, 47
Guevara, Che (Ernesto Guevara Lynch)
  Castro and, 115, 121, 256–58, 268–69; access to
    Castro, 164, 179, 257
  on Castro, 183, 239
  death of (1967), 268
  early life of, 115–17
  Guerrilla Warfare, 259

in post-revolutionary era, 172, 190, 256–62, 267–
  69; as director of National Bank, 194, 204–5;
  international role, 185, 215, 229, 256, 260–62;
  as minister of industry, 229, 233
in revolutionary movement, 137, 145, 150, 156,
  158, 160, 162
women and, 116, 257
Guitart, Renato, 75, 77, 80, 81–82, 83
Guiteras, Antonio, 76, 89
Gutiérrez, Alfonso ("Fofo"), 113

Hart, Armando, 110, 114, 142
Havana
  provinces and, 13
  restoration of (1980s), 303
Havana Conference of the Latin American Com-
  munist Parties (1964), 255, 264
Health care, 276
  Castro's interest in, 25
  exodus of professionals and, 196–97
Hemingway, Ernest, 204
Hernández, Melba, 68
  Moncada attack and, 73, 76, 78, 79, 80, 83, 87;
    trials and imprisonment of leaders and, 90, 92,
    98
  26 of July Movement and, 106, 113, 129
Herter, Christian, 206
"History Will Absolve Me" (Castro), 93, 98–102,
  147, 148, 149, 196, 275
Hoffman, Wendell, 143
Hunt, Howard, 211–12, 222

Illiteracy, 149
  campaigns to eradicate, 223, 234, 275
Independence movement, Cuban (19th century), 3–
  5. *See also* Martí, J.
  charismatic leaders and, 10–11, 12
  as model for Castro, 155
INRA (Institute of Agrarian Reforms)
  creation of (1959), 178
  expropriation of property by, 198, 214
Intelligence operations
  Cuban, 197, 233
  U.S. *See* CIA.
Inter-American Conference (9th, Bogotá, 1948),
  46, 48
Isle of Pines
  prison on, 10; Castro *et al.* in (1953–55), 93–105
  ranch house on, 201
  schools for African leaders on, 288

Jamaica, 293
Jesuits, influence of on Castro, 24–30, 95, 120, 249,
  278, 302

327

aftermath of, 84–89
planning for, 71, 77
preparations for, 77–78
public response to, 88, 101
reprisals for, 87–88, 100, 108
trials and imprisonment of leaders of, 90–105
"Moncada Manifesto, The," 76
Montané, Jesús, 68, 77, 81, 85, 107
Mozambique, 262
MSR (Movimiento Socialista Revolucionaria), 35, 36
M-26-7. See 26 July Movement.
Muñoz, Marie, 70, 75, 78, 80, 83, 84

Naranjo, Pepin, 201
Nasser, Gamal Abdal, 208, 209
Nationalism, Cuban
(18th century), 3
charismatic leadership and, 10–11, 12
frustration of, 11
Nationalization of foreign property, 178, 198, 205, 214
Castro on, 148
Neto, Agostino, 262, 281, 284, 285, 288–89
"New man" (Socialist), 233, 283
Nicaragua, 187–88, 293
Nixon, Richard
Castro and, 175, 281; Castro's fear of, 271, 280; plots to overthrow Castro, 214
Cuba and, 271, 280
visits Cuba (1955), 104
Nkrumah, Kwame, 255, 262, 264
Non-Aligned Movement, 253–54
AAPSO and, 265
Castro and, 254, 287, 292
summit meetings of: (1962, Belgrade), 231; (1973, Algiers), 283; (1976, Sri Lanka), 287; (1978, Belgrade), 292–93; (1979, Havana), 287, 293–94
Nuclear Non-Proliferation Treaty (1967), 269
Nuñez Jiménez, Antonio, 164–65, 177–78, 189, 236

OAS. See Organization of American States.
O'Connell, James, 213
Odlum, George, 293
Oil, Soviet
Cuban supply of, 171, 207, 270, 302
to be refined in Cuba, 205
OLAS (Latin American Solidarity Organization), 267
Opposition to Castro and revolutionary government, 171, 172, 180–81, 184, 190, 192–93, 204, 214–15, 221, 233, 253, 269–70, 295, 303–4
by press, 197, 249

Organization of American States
Castro and, 170, 177
creation of, 46
Cuba and, 187, 206, 232, 253, 282
ORI (Organizaciones Revolucionarias Integradas), 229–30
Oriente Province, 13–14
as base for revolutionary movement, 71
Castro's youth in, 14–26
Ortodoxo Party, 39–40. See also ARO.
Batista and, 66, 67, 108, 123
Castro and, 62, 105, 109, 113, 123
Chibas's death and, 60
Communists and, 63–64
National Congress (Havana, 1955), 113–14
Oswald, Lee Harvey, 252
Ovares, Enrique, 47

País, Frank, 110, 128–29, 146–47
death of (1957), 150
leads uprising in Santiago (1956), 134–35
Palma, Tomás Estruda, 9
Panama, 187
Partido Socialista Popular. See Communist Party of Cuba.
Pastor, Robert, 294
"Patria o muerte," 202
Patriotism, Cuban. See Nationalism, Cuban.
Pazos, Felipe, 142, 149–50, 151–52
in post-revolutionary era, 175, 192, 193, 194
Peasants in Cuba
Castro identifies with, 18
living conditions of, 13
politicians and, 13–14
revolutionary movement and, 139, 144
Pedrero Pact (1958), 158
People's Socialist Party. See Communist Party of Cuba.
Pérez, Crescencio, 136, 139
Pérez, Faustino, 110, 114, 127, 136, 137, 140, 142, 151, 153, 154, 192, 244
Pérez Serantes, Enrique, archbishop of Santiago, 21, 86, 161
Perón, Juan Domingo, 46
Pinochet, Gen. Augusto, 279, 280
Pino Izquierdo, Odilia and Oneida, 113
Platt Amendment (1901), 8–9
rescinded, 10
Poland, 202
Political parties, Cuban
dissolution of: by Batista, 66–67; by Castro, 171
Presidio Modelo, Isle of Pines: Castro et al. in, 93–105

329

26 of July Movement (*cont.*)
  popular support for, 124
  takeover of Cuba by, 160–64
  trek to the mountains, 137
  urban component of, 142, 146–47, 154, 184–85,
    254
  weapons for, 118, 119

UIR (Unión Insurrecional Revolucionaria),
    35
  Castro and, 37, 39, 45, 62, 63, 118,
    308–9
Unions, 44–45, 198
United Fruit Company, 15, 16, 19–20
United Nations. General Assembly: Castro's
  speeches to, 209–10, 294
U.S.
  Castro in, 55, 117–18, 174–77, 206–7, 209–10,
    294
  Castro's attitude toward, 117, 155, 157, 167, 170,
    180, 265, 299–300
  Guevara's attitude toward, 117, 155
U.S. and Cuba. *See also* Bay of Pigs invasion.
  American efforts to overthrow Castro and gov-
    ernment, 210–14, 216–19, 244–45.
  American invasion and intervention: (1898), 7–8;
    (1912), 9; Castro's response to, 217–18; Platt
    Amendment and, 8; planned (1960s), 210–12,
    214, 215, 216–19; security from, 240, 251, 271;
    threat and fear of, 9, 154–55, 157, 167, 175,
    208, 214, 231, 237, 240, 271
  annexation proposed (18th century), 3
  Cuban dependence/independence, 5, 7, 8, 11, 53,
    170, 189, 199, 226, 240, 301
  cultural values, disparate, 11
  deterioration of relations, 187, 196, 198–99, 201–
    2, 214, 296, 297–98
  early phase, 5–7
  economic relations: early, 6, 10, 11; embargo,
    154, 241, 253, 290; post-revolutionary, 170–71,
    175–76, 186–87, 214, 251; sugar trade, 9, 186–
    87, 205, 215
  relations severed (1961), 215–16; conciliation of,
    216, 251–52; normalization of, 281, 289, 290–
    91, 296
  in Roosevelt administration, 10
  war of 1898, 7–8
U.S. and Soviet Union: Cuba as factor in relation-
    ship, 205–6, 207–8, 228, 237

University of Havana
  (18th century), 3
  Castro at (1945–50), 31–46, 55–57, 309–10
  Castro and (post-1950), 106
  gangs and violence at, 34, 35, 36, 54, 63
  revolutionary movement and, 122
Urrutia Lleó, Manuel, 153, 160, 161, 164, 171, 173,
    181–82, 193
USSR. *See* Soviet Union.
U Thant, 241–42

Valdés, Ramiro, 81, 124, 197, 233, 298
Vallejo, René, 201, 251
Vance, Cyrus, 291, 296
Vasconcelos, Ramón, 58, 61, 109
Venezuela, 169, 170, 255, 264, 267
Vexel-Robertson, Lidia, 180

Walters, Barbara: interview with Castro (1977),
    175, 252, 289
War of 1898, 7–8
Weapons for Cuba, 188–89, 199, 215, 218, 231,
    237, 277
  missiles, 206, 229, 237–38; crisis over (1962),
    238–41, 315
Wood, Gen. Leonard, 8–9, 12
Writings of Castro
  Fidel y La Religión (1985), 290
  "First Declaration of Havana" (1960), 206
  "History Will Absolve Me," 93, 98–102, 147,
    148, 149, 196, 275
  "Manifesto No. One to the People of Cuba"
    (1955), 113
  "Manifesto No. 2 to the People of Cuba" (1955),
    117–18
  "Message to the Congress of Ortodoxos Mili-
    tants, A" (1955), 113
  "Moncada Manifesto" (1953), 76
  Revolucion no: Zarpazo! (1952), 65
  "Second Declaration of Havana" (1962), 234
  Sierra Maestra manifesto (1957), 149–50

Yañes Pelletier, Capt. Jesús, 92, 164
Youth
  Batista and, 114
  Castro's appeal to, 101, 109
Yugoslavia, 185, 202, 258

Zaïre (Congo), 260, 261–62
Zeitlin, Maurice, 171, 176